Exchange 2010 SP1

A Practical Approach

By Jaap Wesselius

Copyright Jaap Wesselius 2011

ISBN 978-1-906434-66-3

The right of Jaap Wesselius to be identified as the author of this work has been asserted by him in accordance with the Copyright, Designs and Patents Act 1988.

All rights reserved. No part of this publication may be reproduced, stored or introduced into a retrieval system, or transmitted, in any form, or by any means (electronic, mechanical, photocopying, recording or otherwise) without the prior written consent of the publisher. Any person who does any unauthorized act in relation to this publication may be liable to criminal prosecution and civil claims for damages.

This book is sold subject to the condition that it shall not, by way of trade or otherwise, be lent, re-sold, hired out, or otherwise circulated without the publisher's prior consent in any form other than which it is published and without a similar condition including this condition being imposed on the subsequent publisher.

Technical Review by Michael B Smith

Cover Image by Paul Vlaar

Edited by Chris Massey

Typeset & Designed by Matthew Tye & Gower Associates

Copy Edited by Gower Associates

Table of Contents

Introduction 13

Chapter 1: Introduction to Exchange Server 2010 15

1.1 Getting started 15
1.2 What's been removed from Exchange Server 2010? 16
1.3 What's new in Exchange Server 2010? 17
    1.3.1 Outlook Web App 18
    1.3.2 High Availability 19
    1.3.3 Exchange Core Store functionality 19
    1.3.4 Microsoft Online Services 20
    1.3.5 New administration functionality 21
    1.3.6 Exchange Control Panel 22
    1.3.7 Active Directory Rights Management 23
    1.3.8 Transport and routing 23
    1.3.9 Permissions 24
    1.3.10 Messaging policy and compliance 24
    1.3.11 Mailbox archive 25
    1.3.12 Unified Messaging 25
1.4 What's new in Service Pack 1 25
    1.4.1 Revised Outlook Web App (OWA) interface 26
    1.4.2 Mailbox archive revisited 26
    1.4.3 Import and Export Mailbox 27
    1.4.4 Management changes in Service Pack 1 27
1.5 Exchange Server 2010 SP1 and Active Directory 29
    1.5.1 Active Directory partitions 29
    1.5.2 Delegation of control 30
    1.5.3 Active Directory sites 32
1.6 Exchange Server coexistence 33
1.7 Exchange Server 2010 SP1 Server Roles 34
    1.7.1 Mailbox Server Role 35
    1.7.2 Client Access Server Role 38

		1.7.3	Hub Transport Server Role 40
		1.7.4	Edge Server Role 42
		1.7.5	Unified Messaging Server Role 44
	1.8	Summary	 46

Chapter 2: Installing Exchange Server 2010 SP1 47

	2.1	Exchange Pre-Deployment Analyzer 48
	2.2	Installing Exchange Server 2010 SP1 prerequisites 49
	2.3	Performing a typical Exchange Server 2010 install 57
	2.4	Unattended setup 64
		2.4.1 PrepareSchema 64
		2.4.2 PrepareAD 65
		2.4.3 PrepareDomain 67
		2.4.4 Install Server Roles 69
	2.5	Check the Exchange installation 71
	2.6	Installing dedicated Server Roles 74
	2.7	Installing the Edge Transport Server 75
		2.7.1 Installing Active Directory Lightweight Directory Services 79
		2.7.2 Installing the Edge Transport Server Role 79
		2.7.3 Configuring Edge Transport Synchronization 81
	2.8	Post-setup configuration 83
		2.8.1 Exchange Server 2010 SP1 license key 84
		2.8.2 Accepted Domains 84
		2.8.3 Email Address Policies 86
		2.8.4 Configure a Send Connector to the Internet 88
		2.8.5 Add a Certificate to the Client Access Server Role 89
		2.8.6 Configure the Client Access Server Role 93
	2.9	Upgrading Exchange Server 2010 97
	2.9	Summary 100

Chapter 3: Exchange Server 2010 SP1 Coexistence 101

	3.1	Coexistence with Exchange Server 2003 103
		3.1.1 64-bit support 104
		3.1.2 Administrative Groups are no longer used for delegation of control 105

		3.1.3	Routing Groups are no longer used for routing messages.................... 106
		3.1.4	Link State is no longer used for updating the routing table.............. 107
		3.1.5	Recipient Update Service versus Email Address Policies 108
3.2	Installing into an existing Exchange Server 2003 environment........................ 109
		3.2.1	Exchange Server 2010 SP1 Order of Installation................................ 111
		3.2.2	Installing Exchange Server 2010 SP1 113
		3.2.3	Finishing the installation... 126
		3.2.4	SMTP Infrastructure 134
		3.2.5	Final Exchange 2003 coexistence notes 136
3.3	Coexistence with Exchange Server 2007.. 137
		3.3.1	64-Bit in Exchange Server 2007 138
3.4	Installing into an existing Exchange Server 2007 environment........................ 139
		3.4.1	Exchange Server 2010 SP1 order of installation 140
		3.4.2	Installing Exchange Server 2010 SP1 141
		3.4.3	SMTP Infrastructure 152
		3.4.4	Moving Mailboxes to Exchange Server 2010 SP1........................... 153
3.5	Summary 154

Chapter 4: Managing Exchange Server 2010 SP1...................... 155

4.1	The Exchange Management Shell... 156
	4.1.1 Exchange Management Shell help... 159
	4.1.2 Pipelining 159
	4.1.3 Bulk user creation in the Exchange Management Shell...................... 161
	4.1.4 Remote PowerShell... 163
	4.1.5 Reporting with the Exchange Management Shell............................ 167
4.2	The Exchange Management Console 174
	4.2.1 PowerShell and the EMC.. 176
	4.2.2 Evolution of the Exchange Management Console........................... 178
4.3	The Exchange Control Panel (ECP) 180
4.4	Role Based Access Control (RBAC)... 184
	4.4.1 RBAC architecture.. 187
4.5	Archiving and Compliancy 192

	4.5.1	Exchange 2010 Archiving	193
	4.5.2	Messaging Records Management	196
	4.5.3	Discovery search functionality	206
	4.5.4	Litigation Hold	213
4.6	Summary		214

Chapter 5: High Availability in Exchange Server 2010 SP1 215

5.1	High Availability		215
5.2	Exchange Server Database Technologies		216
	5.2.1	Extensible Storage Engine	219
	5.2.2	Log files	220
	5.2.3	Checkpoint file	221
	5.2.4	The Mailbox Database	222
5.3	High Availability in Exchange Server		223
	5.3.1	Exchange database replication	225
	5.3.2	Database Availability Group and Continuous Replication	227
	5.3.3	DAG architecture	228
	5.3.4	Configuring a Database Availability Group	234
	5.3.5	Managing database copies	241
	5.3.6	Lagged copies in a DAG	244
	5.3.7	Online Move-Mailbox	250
	5.3.8	Import and export Mailbox	252
	5.3.9	Backup and restore	254
5.4	High Availability on Other Server Roles		265
	5.4.1	Hub Transport Servers	265
	5.4.2	Client Access Servers	267
5.5	Summary		270

Chapter 6: Unified Messaging 273

6.1	Unified Messaging Server Role Architecture		274
	6.1.1	Voicemail preview	276
	6.1.2	Play on Phone functionality	277
	6.1.3	Outlook Voice Access	278
6.2	Unified Messaging Server Role Terminology		279

6.3 Installing the UM Server Role..280
    6.3.1   Installing additional language packs..285
6.4 Configuring the UM Server Role..286
    6.4.1   UM Dial Plans..286
    6.4.2   UM IP Gateway..288
    6.4.3   UM Mailbox Policy..289
    6.4.4   UM Auto Attendant...290
    6.4.5   Configuring the actual UM Server..290
6.5 UM Enabling Mailboxes..292
6.6 Summary..294

Chapter 7: Exchange Server 2010 Security 295

7.1 Server Security..296
    7.1.1   Server hardening..296
    7.1.2   Baseline Security Analyzer...298
    7.1.3   Patching your Exchange Servers..301
    7.1.4   Certificates or Public Key infrastructure.................................305
7.2 Network Security..315
    7.2.1   Firewall..315
    7.2.2   Reverse Proxy by using TMG..316
7.3 Anti-Spam Solutions...321
    7.3.1   Connection filtering...324
    7.3.2   Sender filtering..325
    7.3.3   Recipient filtering..326
    7.3.4   Sender ID filtering...326
    7.3.5   Content filtering..328
    7.3.6   Sender Reputation...331
    7.3.7   Attachment filtering..333
    7.3.8   Anti-spam on the Hub Transport Server.................................336
7.4 Conclusion..337

Summary..339

About the author

Jaap Wesselius is an independent consultant focusing on Unified Communications solutions; primarily Exchange Server solutions, with a touch of Unified Messaging, Office Communications Server 2007 or Lync Server 2010 to keep things fresh. Together with a few other independent consultants, he spends most of his time working on Exchange Server solutions. In fact, he's being doing that ever since Exchange Server 4.0 came out, long, long ago in 1995.

After working in Microsoft for eight years, Jaap decided in 2006 that the time had come to leave Redmond and start his own business. This was also the period when he got a chance to commit more of his time to the Exchange community in The Netherlands, resulting in an Exchange Server MVP award in 2007 which he's held on to ever since. Jaap is also a regular contributor at the Dutch Unified Communications User Group (HTTP://WWW.UCUG.NL), and a regular author for Simple-Talk (HTTP://WWW.SIMPLE-TALK.COM). Besides Exchange Server, Jaap really likes to work with Hyper-V and, as a result, he also founded the Dutch Hyper-V (HTTP://WWW.HYPER-V.NU) community in early 2008.

When time permits (and it never permits enough), Jaap savors life with his wife and three sons, and also enjoys doing some serious hiking and cycling when he gets the chance. It's an ongoing dream of his to hike or cycle across Europe, but this will probably always stay a dream for as long as he spends his time writing.

About the Technical Reviewer

Michael B. Smith is an Exchange MVP who owns and operates a consulting firm that specializes in Exchange Server and Active Directory. He has had over 25 years of experience in the IT field, and focuses on providing solutions that support customers' goals for operational excellence. Michael is also a well-known writer for such publications as *WindowsITPro* and *Exchange Messaging & Outlook*, to name just two. He also recently completed his second book, *Monitoring Exchange Server 2007 with Operations Manager*, and was technical editor for two other books, recently published with O'Reilly Media: *Active Directory, Fourth Edition* and *Active Directory Cookbook, Third Edition*. Michael is active in a number of online Exchange communities, and you can read his blog at HTTP://THEESSENTIALEXCHANGE.COM/BLOGS/MICHAEL.

Acknowledgements

This is the second edition of my first book and, to start with, I wasn't actually planning to write one at all. I tried to write a book on Exchange Server Disaster Recovery in the past, but Exchange Server changes so significantly with each Service Pack that I ended up rewriting quite a lot of my material every six months. After realizing this was a never-ending story, I made a tactical decision to quit while I was ahead…

…until early 2009, when Michael Francis asked me if I'd ever considered writing a book. He persuaded me to try again, and I'm really thankful to him. Also, to Michael B. Smith as my Technical Reviewer, Steven van Houttum as a local Dutch peer, everybody from the Red Gate team, and the people from the Exchange Server MVP Group – you were all very helpful. Thank you all.

I guess my wife and sons suffered the most when I was behind my laptop, writing again, and trying to figure out what was going wrong *this time*. The legacy of beta software, I'm afraid. And when things got really annoying, I went out hiking or cycling to clear my mind. Oh boy, isn't it lovely to write a book? :-)

And to anybody else, especially in my local community (who really don't know anything about Exchange Server, but know a lot about potatoes, onions, cows and stuff), this is my book. And I have to be honest, it's not about "love at first sight" as I've said for such a long time. Maybe one day I'll write a novel, but right now I stick to technical books. I hope you like it, and I'd love to know what you think of it. Feel free to send me a note at: mybook@jaapwesselius.nl.

Cheers,

Jaap Wesselius

Introduction

Being a trainer, I always wonder why official curriculums are so theoretical and lack so many real-world scenarios, which would surely be the most useful thing to learn about. In my articles for Simple-Talk, I always try to write about real-world scenarios and that's also the case for this book, hence the name, *A Practical Guide*.

Of course, you need some theory as well; without knowing anything about Active Directory you'll never understand what Exchange Server 2010 is doing and why things are the way they are. However, I've tried to write all the chapters in this book from an administrator's perspective, covering what steps you have to take at each stage, and why. It's nothing like an Exchange Server 2010 resource kit, it's a more practical approach, and I hope you'll agree that it earns its title. Inside, you'll find seven chapters, covering the topics below.

- **Chapter 1** is an overview chapter; what's new in Exchange Server 2010 and what has deprecated with respect to Exchange Server 2007. Also, there's some information regarding Active Directory, the three containers in Active Directory and some information regarding Active Directory sites.

- **Chapter 2** is an installation chapter, dealing with a fresh installation of Exchange Server 2010 SP1 (or an upgrade from Exchange Server 2010) and the subsequent basic configuration to get it up and running.

- **Chapter 3** is the coexistence chapter, and I deal with probably the most common scenarios: installing Exchange Server 2010 SP1 in an existing Exchange Server 2003 or Exchange Server 2007 environment.

- **Chapter 4** is about managing the Exchange environment using the Exchange Management Console, the Exchange Management Shell and the Exchange Control Panel. A really cool set of features in Exchange Server 2010 are the remote options in PowerShell Version 2, so be sure to read about those.

- **Chapter 5** is the High Availability chapter. It deals with the new continuous replication when using Database Availability Groups, the best Exchange Server High Availability solution ever made.

- **Chapter 6** is a detailed look at Unified Messaging (UM), covering everything from architecture and terminology to installing and configuring a fresh UM Server Role and enabling Unified Messaging on your users' mailboxes.

- **Chapter 7** is where we take a look at security. I'll cover instructions on how to secure your server, secure your network, and implement anti-spam solutions, all of which is achieved through Exchange Server 2010 SP1 and related technologies.

I realize that I did not cover all aspects of Exchange Server 2010 in just seven chapters, nor could I have done so. Just for a start, think about compliance, or integration with Office Communication Server (OCS) R2 for presence information and Instant Messaging. These are significant topics in their own right! There are a lot of areas I just can't cover here (even though I want to), and a lot more depth I could go into but, because I wanted to make this a light, quick-start book and not an Exchange Server 2010 "Bible," I've had to be very focused. I hope you find that focus to be useful, and this guide to be practical.

Chapter 1: Introduction to Exchange Server 2010

First things first – let's cover some basic background: Exchange Server 2010 is an email and calendaring application that runs on Windows Server 2008 and Windows Server 2008 R2 and, like its predecessor, Exchange Server 2007, can also integrate with your phone system. It is the seventh major version of the product and, while not revolutionary, it does include some important changes and lots of small improvements over Exchange Server 2007.

The scalability of Exchange Server 2010 has improved, especially when compared to the complex storage requirements of Exchange Server 2007. The user experience has also improved in Outlook Web App, and a lot of complex issues have seen solved, or the complexity has been removed, to make the administrator's life much easier.

In this chapter, I will give a brief overview of what's changed in Exchange Server 2010, what the new features are, what features have been removed, and how it makes your life as an Exchange administrator easier. I will also give an overview of what's new in Service Pack 1 of Exchange Server 2010, compared to the RTM (Release To Manufacturing) version.

1.1 Getting started

Exchange Server 2010 is available in two versions.

- **Standard Edition**, which is limited to hosting 5 databases.
- **Enterprise Edition**, which can host up to 100 databases. However, the available binaries are identical for both versions; it's the license key that establishes the

difference in functionality. Exchange Server 2010 is also only available in an x64 version; there is absolutely no 32-bit version available, not even for testing purposes. Bear in mind that, as x64-only software, there's no Itanium version of Exchange Server 2010.

Exchange Server 2010 also comes with two Client Access License (CAL) versions.

- **Standard CAL** – this license provides access to email, calendaring, Outlook Web App and ActiveSync for Mobile Devices.
- **Enterprise CAL** – this is an additive license, and provides Unified Messaging and compliance functionality, as well as Forefront Security for Exchange Server and Forefront Online Protection for Exchange for anti-spam and antivirus functionality.

This is not a complete list; for more information about licensing, check the Microsoft website at www.microsoft.com/exchange/2010/en/us/Licensing.aspx.

1.2 What's been removed from Exchange Server 2010?

As always, as new features come, old features go. There are inevitably a few that have found themselves on the deprecated list this time around, and so will not be continued in Exchange Server 2010 and beyond. Since this is a much shorter list than the new features, we'll start here.

- There are some major changes in Exchange Server clustering: in Exchange Server 2007 you had **LCR** (Local Continuous Replication), **CCR** (Cluster Continuous Replication) and **SCR** (Stand-by Continuous Replication) – three different versions of replication, all with their own management interfaces. All three are no longer available in Exchange Server 2010.

- **Single Copy Clusters**, the traditional Exchange Cluster has been removed in Exchange Server 2010. It is no longer possible to create an Exchange Cluster using "shared storage."
  Some might think that fail-over clustering itself has been removed from Exchange Server 2010, but that's not the case. The fail-over clustering bits are still used in Exchange Server 2010, but it is managed in a different way, due to the complexity and vulnerability to error present in previous versions of Exchange.

- **Storage Groups** are no longer available in Exchange Server 2010. The concepts of a database, log files and a checkpoint file are still there, but now it is just called a database. It's like CCR in Exchange Server 2007, where you could only have one database per Storage Group.

- Due to major reengineering in the Exchange Server 2010 databases, the **Single Instance Storage** (SIS) is no longer available. This means that when you send a 1 MB message to 100 recipients, the database will potentially grow by 100 MB. This will surely have an impact on the storage requirements in terms of space, but the performance improvements on the database are really great. I'll get back on that later in this chapter.

- WebDAV has been removed from Exchange Server 2010. Does this have a major impact? Well, yes, but it depends; if you use an older version of Entourage for Apple Macintosh, for example, which is using WebDAV.

1.3 What's new in Exchange Server 2010?

Exchange Server 2010 contains a host of improvements and a lot of new features, as well as minor changes and improvements. Over the coming sections, I'll provide an overview of the most significant updates and additions, and point you to the relevant chapters for full coverage of individual features where necessary.

Chapter 1: Introduction to Exchange Server 2010

1.3.1 Outlook Web App

The most visible improvement for users is Outlook Web App (previously known as Outlook Web Access). One of the design goals for the Outlook Web App was a seamless cross-browser experience, so users running a browser like Safari, even on an Apple MacBook, should have exactly the same user experience as users running Internet Explorer.

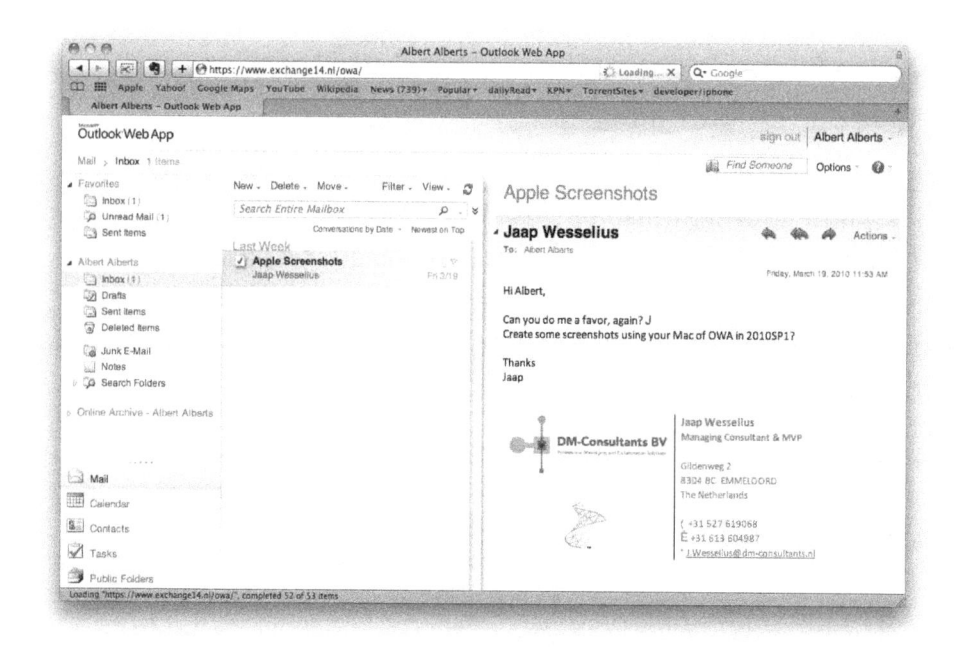

Figure 1.1: Outlook Web App running on an Apple MacBook using a Safari browser. The Online Archive is visible on the left-hand side of the screen.

Outlook Web App offers a very rich client experience and it comes closer to the fully-fledged Outlook client than ever before. To reinforce that experience, a lot of new features have been introduced. To name a few: Favorites, Search Folders, attaching messages to messages, integration with Office Communicator, a new Conversation View (which works very well!), integration with SMS (text) messages, and the possibility to create Outlook Web Access policies which give the Exchange organization administrator the ability to fine-tune the user experience. The Web App is a feature which you will find mentioned throughout the book.

1.3.2 High Availability

The Exchange Server 2007 Cluster Continuous Replication (CCR) and Stand-by Continuous Replication (SCR) features are now combined into one new feature called **database availability**.

Database copies exist, just as in an Exchange Server 2007 CCR environment and are created in a "Database Availability Group," but it is now possible to create multiple copies of a particular Mailbox Database. The Mailbox Database fail-over is not on a server level as in Exchange Server 2007, but on a database level, which gives the Exchange administrator much more fine control and granularity when it comes to creating a highly available Exchange organization. The servers in such a Database Availability Group can be at the same location, or other locations to create an offsite solution. There's also no longer any need to install the Microsoft Cluster Service (MSCS) before setting up the Database Availability Group, as all cluster operations are now managed by Exchange. *Chapter 5* of this book deals exclusively with all the new High Availability features of Exchange Server 2010.

1.3.3 Exchange Core Store functionality

Compared to Exchange Server 2003, Exchange Server 2007 dramatically decreased the I/O on the disk subsystem (sometimes by 70%). This was achieved by increasing the Exchange database page size from 4 KB to 8 KB and by using the x64 operating system. The memory scalability of the x64 platform makes it possible to use servers with huge amounts of memory, giving them the opportunity to cache information in memory instead of reading and writing everything to the disk.

One of the design goals of Exchange Server 2010 was to use a single SATA disk for the Mailbox Database *and* its log files. Another goal was to allow multi-GB mailboxes without any negative performance impact on the server. To make this possible, the database schema in Exchange Server 2010 has now been flattened, making the database structure used by the Exchange Server much less complex than it was in Exchange Server 2007 and earlier. As a result, the I/O requirements of an Exchange Server 2010 server can be up to 70% less than for the same configuration in Exchange Server 2007.

As a result of the flattened database schema, Microsoft has removed Single Instance Storage (SIS) from Exchange Server 2010, but the improvements in performance are much more significant, and more than adequate compensation for the (comparatively minor) loss of SIS. I'll touch on some of these points in *Chapters 2* and *3*.

1.3.4 Microsoft Online Services

Microsoft is gradually moving into "the Cloud." Besides an Exchange Server 2010 implementation on premise, it is now also possible to host mailboxes in a datacenter; you can host your mailboxes with your own ISP, or with Microsoft Online Services.

Exchange Server 2010 can be 100% on premise, 100% hosted, or it can be a mixed environment, with some percentage of your mailboxes hosted and the rest on premise. This is, of course, fully transparent to end-users, but it has its effects on the administration. Instead of managing a single on-site environment, you'll have to manage the hosted organization as well. This is can all be handled through Exchange Server 2010's Exchange Management Console, where you can connect to multiple forests containing an Exchange organization.

1.3.5 New administration functionality

As a consequence of the major changes made to the High Availability features of Exchange Server 2010, the Exchange Management Console has also changed rather significantly.

Due to the new replication functionality, the Mailbox object is no longer tied to the Exchange Server object, but is now part of the Exchange Server 2010 organization. Also, since the concept of Storage Groups is no longer relevant, their administration has been removed from both the Exchange Management Console and the Exchange Management Shell. PowerShell cmdlets like `New-StorageGroup`, `Get-StorageGroup`, and so on, have also all been removed, although the options of these cmdlets have been moved into other cmdlets, like database-related cmdlets.

Speaking of which, Exchange Server 2010 also runs on top of **PowerShell Version 2**. This version not only has a command-line interface (CLI), but also an Integrated Scripting Environment (ISE). This enables you to easily create scripts and use variables, and you now have an output window where you can quickly view the results of your PowerShell command or script.

In addition to PowerShell V2, Exchange Server 2010 also uses **Windows Remote Management** (WinRM) Version 2. This gives you the option to remotely manage an Exchange Server 2010 server without the need to install the Exchange Management Tools on your workstation, and even via the Internet!

One last small but interesting new feature is "**Send Mail**," allowing you to send mail directly from the Exchange Management Console – ideal for testing purposes. *Chapter 4 is all about managing Exchange Server 2010, so that's where you'll find more information in this vein.*

Chapter 1: Introduction to Exchange Server 2010

1.3.6 Exchange Control Panel

It is now possible to perform some basic Exchange management tasks using the options page in Outlook Web Access; not only on the user's own properties, but also at an organizational level. With this method, it is possible to create users, mailboxes, distribution groups, mail-enabled contact, management email addresses, etc. The Exchange Control Panel (ECP) is a big topic in *Chapter 4*.

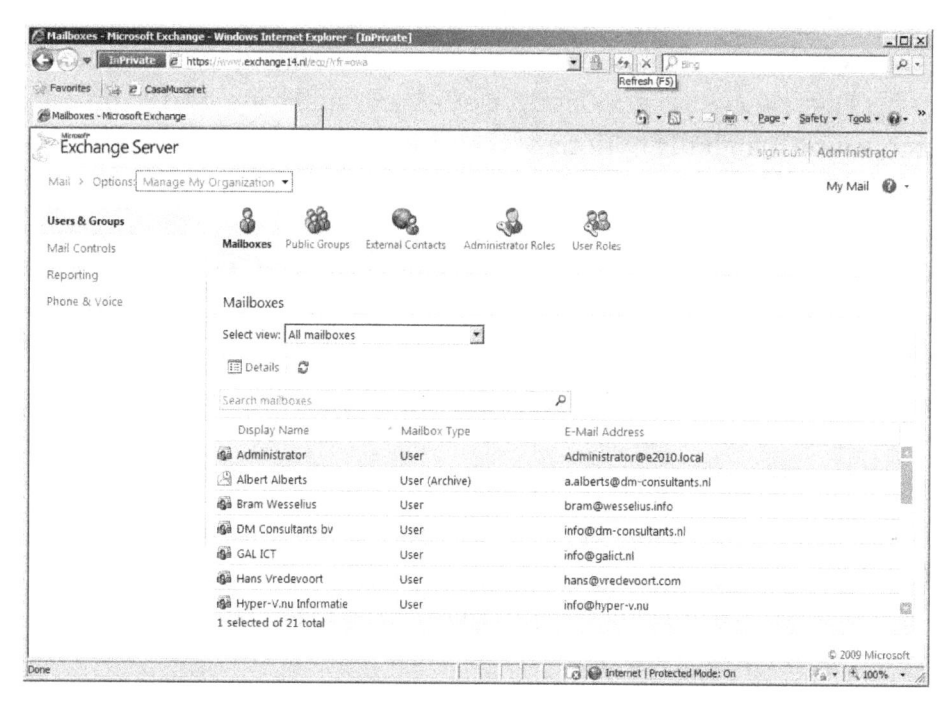

Figure 1.2: The Exchange Control Panel for basic management functions.

1.3.7 Active Directory Rights Management

Active Directory Rights Management Service (AD RMS) lets you control what users can do with email and other documents that are sent to them. It is possible, for example, for classified messages to disable the "Forward" option to prevent messages being leaked outside the organization. With Exchange Server 2010, new features have been added to the Rights Management Services, such as:

- **integration with Transport Rules** – a template for using Rights Management Server (RMS) to protect messages over the Internet
- **RMS protection for voicemail messages** coming from the Unified Messaging Server Role.

Active Directory is discussed throughout this chapter and this book, as the Exchange Server 2010 is tight one-on-one with Active Directory.

1.3.8 Transport and routing

With Exchange Server 2010 it is possible to implement **cross-premises message routing**. When using a mixed hosting environment, Exchange Server 2010 can route messages from the datacenter to the on-premise environment with full transparency.

Exchange Server 2010 also offers (at last) **enhanced disclaimers**, making it possible to add HTML content to disclaimers to add images, hyperlinks, etc. It is even possible to use Active Directory attributes (from the user's private property set) to create a personal disclaimer.

To create a highly available and reliable routing model, the Hub Transport Servers in Exchange Server 2010 now contain **Shadow Redundancy**. A message is normally stored in a database on the Hub Transport Server and, in Exchange Server 2007, the message is deleted as soon as it is sent to the next hop. In Exchange Server 2010, the message is *only* deleted after the next hop reports a successful delivery of the message. If this is not reported, the Hub Transport Server will try to resend the message.

For more High Availability messaging support, the messages stay in the Transport Dumpster on a Hub Transport Server, and are only deleted if they are successfully replicated to all database copies. The database on the Hub Transport Server has also been improved on an ESE (Extensible Storage Engine) level, resulting in a higher message throughput on the transport level.

1.3.9 Permissions

Previous versions of Exchange Server relied on delegation of control via multiple Administrative Groups (specifically, Exchange Server 2000 and Exchange Server 2003) or via Group Membership. Exchange Server 2010 now contains a **Role Based Access Control** (RBAC) model to implement a powerful and flexible management model. I'll cover this in much more detail in *Chapter 4*. There's also the option (in a new deployment) to implement a strict, split permissions model. This can be interesting in large Active Directory and Exchange Server 2010 deployments with separate Active Directory and Exchange Management departments.

1.3.10 Messaging policy and compliance

As part of a general compliance regulation, Microsoft introduced the concept of Managed Folders in Exchange Server 2007, offering the possibility to create some sort of compliancy feature. This has been enhanced with new interfaces in Exchange Server 2010, such as the option of tagging messages, cross-mailbox searches and new Transport Rules and actions.

1.3.11 Mailbox archive

Exchange Server 2010 now contains a personal archive; this is a secondary mailbox connected to a user's primary mailbox. Since Microsoft made a considerable number of changes regarding the Mailbox Archive in Service Pack 1, I'll cover this more in Section 1.4.2, although you can find more detailed information in *Chapters 4* and *5*.

1.3.12 Unified Messaging

The Exchange Server 2010 Unified Messaging Server Role integrates a telephone system, like a PABX, with the Exchange Server messaging environment. This makes it possible to offer Outlook Voice Access, enabling you to interact with the system using your voice, listen to voicemail messages, or have messages read to you. Exchange Server 2010 offers some new functionality including **Voicemail preview**, **Messaging Waiting Indicator**, **integration with text (SMS) messages**, additional **language support**. Unified Messaging is, unfortunately, a little outside the scope of this book, so you won't find me going into too much detail later on regarding these topics.

1.4 What's new in Service Pack 1

Microsoft has integrated a number of hot-fixes in Exchange Server 2010 Service Pack 1 and, at the same time, added significant improvements. There are some small changes, like the Prerequisite Software installation in the setup program, but there are also major changes like the support for the personal archive in separate databases on separate servers.

There are changes in the Core Store functionality, improvements in the various management options in Exchange Server 2010 SP1, and some performance improvements, especially in the user experience. For a complete overview of all topics that are

Chapter 1: Introduction to Exchange Server 2010

new in Exchange Server 2010 Service Pack 1, take a look at the *What's new in Exchange 2010 SP1* article on the Microsoft website (WWW.TINYURL.COM/NEWINEX2010), but there are a couple of interesting topics I'd like to discuss here.

1.4.1 Revised Outlook Web App (OWA) interface

One of the most important aspects of a new version of an application or a Service Pack is how it impacts the user and, from a user perspective, there are a few changes in Service Pack 1. Back from Exchange Server 2003 are the Themes; it is once again possible to customize the look of your own OWA interface! OWA now also uses some Silverlight technology under the hood; when you add an attachment to a message in OWA you see a regular Windows interface, but this is basically a Silverlight application. This also works more smoothly than the original interface and it is easier to work with when adding (large) attachments. There are also some improvements in terms of the way the personal Exchange Control Panel (using Options in OWA) is presented to the user.

1.4.2 Mailbox archive revisited

Exchange Server 2010 RTM supported a personal archive. The main issue with this original feature was that it was a secondary mailbox and so it was required to be located in the same Mailbox Database as the primary mailbox. Although this solution can be viable when using a JBOD (Just a Bunch of Disks) solution for the Exchange Server Mailbox Server Role, almost all customers wanted a solution where the personal archive could be stored in a separate database and, when possible, on a separate server. Microsoft has built this support into Service Pack 1, so it's now possible to create a dedicated "archive server" where all personal archives are stored.

Even more, it will also be possible to have the primary mailbox on-premises and the personal archive in the Cloud, although it is unknown yet how this will be built into the product.

1.4.3 Import and Export Mailbox

The Import and Export Mailbox functionality in Exchange Server 2010 RTM had some sharp edges, to say the least. To function correctly on an Exchange Management Server, you had to install the Mailbox Server Role (luckily, mounting a Mailbox Database was not needed) and Office 2010 x64 needed to be installed. This has improved in SP1, and Outlook 2010 is no longer a prerequisite for the Import Mailbox functionality. The Import and Export Mailbox features now use the same technology as the online Move Mailbox feature. This is certainly a great improvement, with the option to directly import into the personal archive, and it will be covered more in *Chapter 5*.

1.4.4 Management changes in Service Pack 1

Microsoft made quite a few changes in the management area in Service Pack 1. For example, in Exchange Server 2010 RTM it was only possible to create Retention Policies using the Exchange Management Shell. This is now available in the Exchange Management Console. There's also now additional functionality available in the Exchange Control Panel (ECP), such as configuring Transport Rules or configuring Journaling Rules.

1.4.4.1 Core Store changes

In Service Pack 1, Microsoft made some changes to the Core Store functionality compared to Exchange Server 2010 RTM. For example, in hard disk technology in general, the size of SATA disks grows faster than the number of IOPS (I/Os per second) of the particular disk. The performance of the store, especially for larger databases, has been improved to deal with even larger disks.

Also, when moving mailboxes from one Mailbox Database to another, it is no longer necessary to restart Outlook after the mailbox move, meaning that the dialog in Figure 1.3 will no longer be shown after moving mailboxes.

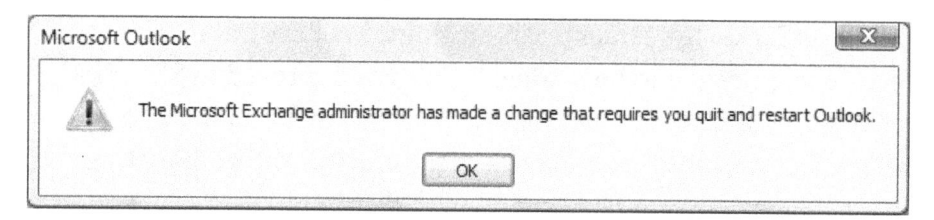

Figure 1.3: It is no longer necessary to restart Outlook after moving mailboxes.

This works only when moving mailboxes from one Exchange 2010 SP1 Mailbox Database to another Exchange 2010 SP1 Mailbox Database. A restart of Outlook is still required when moving mailboxes between different versions of Exchange Server (including Exchange Server 2010 RTM).

1.4.4.2 Retention policies

In Exchange Server 2010 RTM it was possible to create Retention Policies to move messages to the Archive, to delete messages, to move messages to the Deleted Items or to tag messages as "past beyond retention," although this could only be achieved using the Exchange Management Shell. This has improved in Service Pack 1 and is now also available in the Exchange Management Console. At the same time, the management of Managed Folders has been moved from the Exchange Management Console to the Exchange Management Shell, which is a pity for those working with Managed Folders.

1.5 Exchange Server 2010 SP1 and Active Directory

As far as Active Directory is concerned, its minimum level needs to be on a Windows Server 2003 level, both for the domain functionality level and for the forest functionality level. This might be confusing, since Exchange Server 2010 only runs on Windows Server 2008 or Windows Server 2008 R2, but that's just the actual server which Exchange Server 2010 SP1 is running on!

The Schema Master in the forest needs to be Windows Server 2003 SP2 server (Standard or Enterprise Edition) or higher. Likewise, in each Active Directory site where Exchange Server 2010 SP1 will be installed, there must be at least one Standard or Enterprise Windows Server 2003 SP2 (or higher) server configured as a Global Catalog Server.

From a performance standpoint, as with Exchange Server 2007, the ratio of 4:1 for Exchange Server processors to Global Catalog Server processors still applies to Exchange Server 2010. Using an x64 version of Windows Server for Active Directory will naturally also increase the system performance.

Note

It is possible to install Exchange Server 2010 SP1 on an Active Directory Domain Controller. However, for performance and security reasons it is recommended not to do this, and instead to install Exchange Server 2010 on a member server in a domain.

1.5.1 Active Directory partitions

A Windows Server Active Directory consists of one forest, one or more domains, and one or more sites. Exchange Server 2010 SP1 is bound to a forest, and therefore one Exchange Server 2010 SP1 organization is contained within one Active Directory forest. The actual information in an Active Directory forest is stored in the three locations, also called partitions, shown below.

- **Schema partition** – this contains a "blueprint" of all objects and properties in Active Directory; it's a database of classes and attributes. When an object, like a user, is created, it is instantiated from the user blueprint in Active Directory.

- **Configuration partition** – this contains information that's used throughout the forest. Regardless of the number of domains that are configured in Active Directory, all Domain Controllers use the same configuration partition in that particular Active Directory forest. As such, it is replicated throughout the Active Directory forest, and all changes to the configuration partition have to be replicated to all Domain Controllers. All Exchange Server 2010 SP1 configuration information is stored in the configuration partition. Please note that recipient information is *not* stored in the configuration partition.

- **Domain partition** – this contains information regarding the domains installed in Active Directory. Every domain has its own domain partition, so if there are 60 domains installed there will be 60 different domain partitions. Recipient information, including Mailbox information, is stored in the domain partition.

1.5.2 Delegation of control

In Exchange Server 2003, the concept of "Administrative Groups" was used to delegate control between different groups of administrators. A default "First Administrative Group" was created during installation, and subsequent Administrative Groups could be created to install more Exchange 2003 servers and delegate control of these servers to other groups. The Administrative Groups were stored in the Configuration Partition so all domains and thus all Domain Controllers and Exchange Servers could see them.

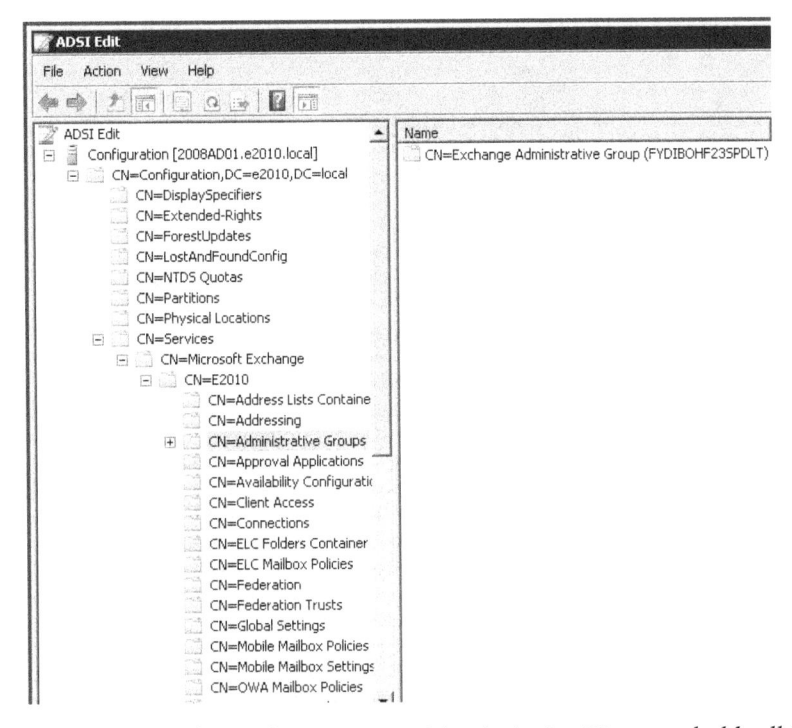

Figure 1.4: The configuration partition in Active Directory holds all information regarding Exchange Server 2010 in an Administrative Group.

Exchange Server 2007 used Active Directory Security Groups for delegation of control, and only one Administrative Group is created during installation of Exchange Server 2007, called Exchange Administrative Group (FYDIBOHF23SPDLT[1]). All servers in the organization are installed in this Administrative Group. Permissions are assigned to Security Groups and Exchange administrators are members of these Security Groups.

Exchange Server 2010 SP1 uses the same Administrative Group, but delegation of control is not done using Active Directory Security Groups, as Microsoft has introduced the concept of Role Based Access Control or RBAC. RBAC is covered in more detail in *Chapter 4*.

---
1 Just shift all letters in the word FYDIBOHF23SPDLT to the left and you get EXCHANGE12ROCKS.

Chapter 1: Introduction to Exchange Server 2010

1.5.3 Active Directory sites

Exchange Server 2010 uses Active Directory sites for routing messages. But what is an Active Directory site?

When a network is separated into multiple physical locations, connected with "slow" links and separated into multiple IP subnets then, in terms of Active Directory, we're talking about sites. Say, for example, there's a main office located in Amsterdam, with an IP subnet of 10.10.0.0/16. There's a Branch Office located in London, and this location has an IP subnet of 10.11.0.0/16. Both locations have their own Active Directory Domain Controller, handling authentication for clients in their own subnet. Active Directory site links are created to control replication traffic between sites. Clients in each site use DNS to find services like Domain Controllers in their own site, thus preventing using services over the WAN link.

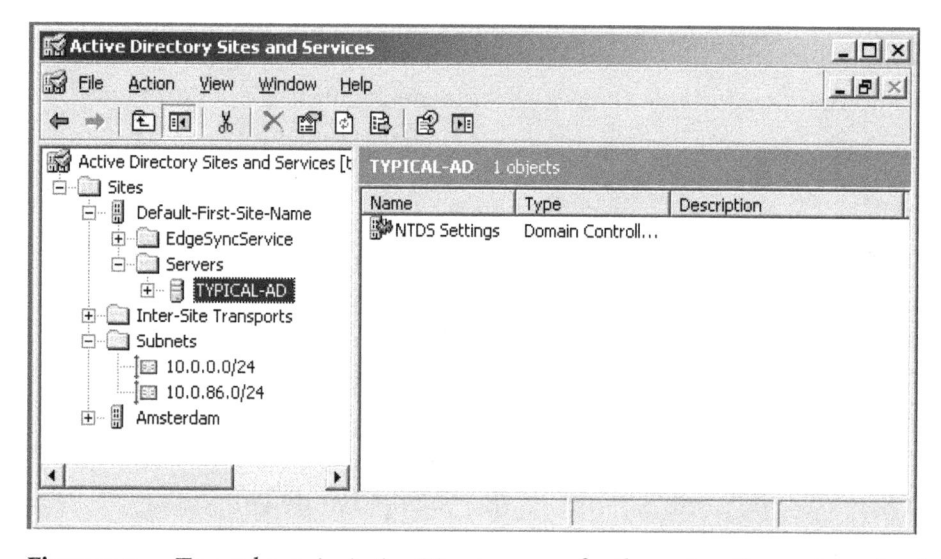

Figure 1.5: Two subnets in Active Directory, one for the main office and one for the Amsterdam datacenter.

Exchange Server 2010 SP1 uses Active Directory sites for routing messages between sites. Using our current example, if there is an Exchange Server 2010 SP1 Hub Transport Server in Amsterdam and an Exchange Server 2010 SP1 Hub Transport Server in London, then the IP Site Links in Active Directory are used to route messages from Amsterdam to London. This concept was first introduced in Exchange Server 2007, and nothing has changed in Exchange Server 2010 SP1.

Exchange Server 2003 used the concept of Routing Groups, where Active Directory already used Active Directory sites; Active Directory sites and Exchange Server Routing Groups are not compatible with each other. To have Exchange Server 2003 and Exchange Server 2010 SP1 work together in one Exchange organization, some special connectors have to be created – the so-called Interop Routing Group Connector.

1.6 Exchange Server coexistence

It is very likely that large organizations will gradually move from an earlier version of Exchange Server to Exchange Server 2010 SP1, and Exchange Server 2010 SP1 can coexist, in the same forest, with (both) Exchange Server 2007 SP2 and Exchange Server 2003 SP2. It is also possible to move from a mixed Exchange Server 2003 SP2 and Exchange Server 2007 SP2 environment to Exchange Server 2010 SP1, as I'll discuss in *Chapter 3*.

Please note that it is not possible to have a coexistence scenario where Exchange Server 2000 and Exchange Server 2010 SP1 are installed in the same Exchange organization. This is enforced in the setup of Exchange Server 2010 SP1. If the setup detects an Exchange Server 2000 installation, the setup application is halted and an error is raised.

Integrating Exchange Server 2010 SP1 into an existing Exchange Server 2003 SP2 or Exchange Server 2007 SP2 environment is called a "transition" scenario. A "migration" scenario is where a new Active Directory forest is created where Exchange Server 2010 SP1 is installed. This new Active Directory forest is running in parallel to the "old" Active Directory with a previous version of Exchange Server. Special care has to be taken in this scenario, especially when both organizations coexist for any significant amount of time. Directories have to be synchronized during the coexistence phase, and the free/busy information will need to be constantly synchronized as well, since you'll still want to offer this service to users during the coexistence period.

This is a typical scenario when third-party tools (like Quest's Migration Manager) are involved.

1.7 Exchange Server 2010 SP1 Server Roles

Up until Exchange Server 2003, all roles were installed on one server and administrators were merely unable to select which features were available. I have to admit, it was possible to disable certain functionalities, or use some registry keys to cause changes in behavior and performance, but everything was *always* installed, on every server. It was possible to designate an Exchange 2000 or Exchange 2003 server as a so-called "Front-End Server," but this server was just like an ordinary Exchange server acting as a protocol proxy. It still had a Mailbox Database and a Public Folder database installed by default.

Exchange Server 2007 introduced the concept of "Server Roles" and this concept is continued by Exchange Server 2010 SP1. The following Server Roles, each with a specific function, are available in Exchange Server 2010 SP1:

- Mailbox Server (MB) Role.
- Client Access Server (CAS) Role.
- Hub Transport Server (HT) Role.
- Unified Messaging Server (UM) Role.
- Edge Transport Server (Edge) Role.

These Server Roles can be installed on dedicated hardware, where each machine has its own role, but they can also be combined. A typical server installation, for example in the setup program, combines the Mailbox, Client Access and Hub Transport Server Roles. The Management Tools are always installed during installation, irrespective of which Server Role is installed.

By contrast, the Edge Transport Server Role cannot be combined with any other role. In fact, the Edge Transport Server Role cannot even be part of the (internal) domain, since it is designed to be installed in the network's Demilitarized Zone (DMZ).

There are multiple reasons for separating Exchange Server into multiple Server Roles:

- **enhanced scalability** – since one server can be dedicated for one Server Role, the scalability benefits are huge; this specific server can be configured and optimized for one particular role, resulting in a high-performance server
- **improved security** – one dedicated server can be hardened for security using the Security Configuration Wizard (SCW); since only one Server Role is used on a particular server, all other functions and ports are disabled, resulting in a more secure system
- **simplified deployment and administration** – a dedicated server is easier to configure, easier to secure and easier to administer.

I will explain each Server Role in detail, in the following sections.

1.7.1 Mailbox Server Role

The Mailbox Server Role is the heart of your Exchange Server 2010 SP1 environment. This is where the Mailbox Database and Public Folder Database are installed. The sole purpose of the Mailbox Server Role is to host Mailboxes and Public Folders – nothing more. In previous versions of Exchange Server, including Exchange Server 2007, Outlook clients

Chapter 1: Introduction to Exchange Server 2010

using MAPI still connected directly to the Mailbox Server Role, but with Exchange Server 2010 this is no longer the case. MAPI clients now connect to a service called RPC Client Access, running on the Client Access Server. Unfortunately, this is only true for accessing mailboxes in Exchange Server 2010. When an Outlook client using MAPI needs to contact Public Folders, the client still connects to the Mailbox Server directly, bypassing the RPC Client Access Service.

The Mailbox Server Role does not route any messages, it only stores messages in mailboxes. For routing messages, the Hub Transport Server Role is needed. This latter role is responsible for routing all messages, even between mailboxes that are on the same server, and even between mailboxes that are in the same Mailbox Database.

For accessing mailboxes, a Client Access Server is also always needed; it is not possible to access any mailbox without a Client Access Server.

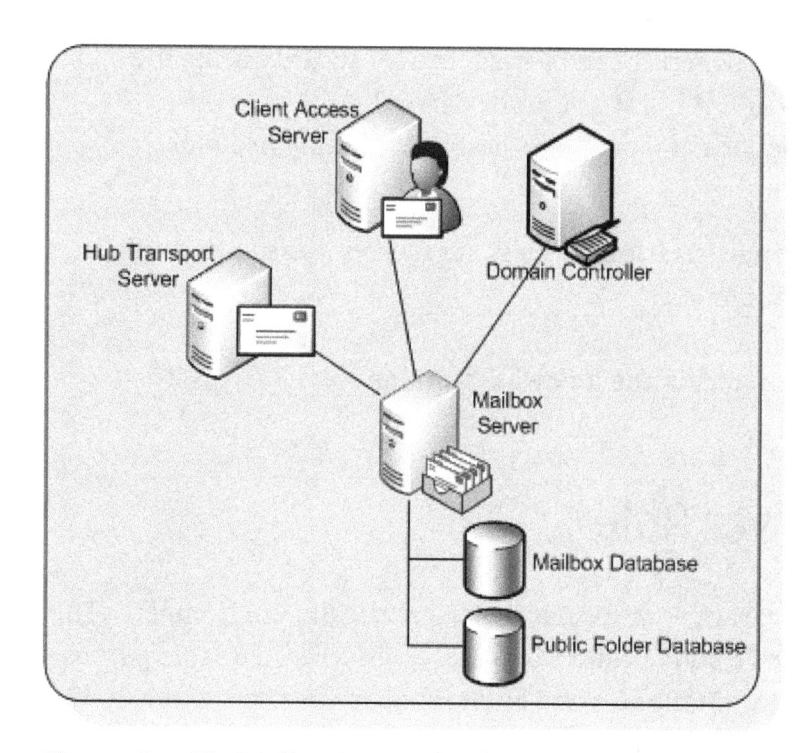

Figure 1.6: The Mailbox Server Role is hosting Mailboxes and Public Folders.

Chapter 1: Introduction to Exchange Server 2010

Note that Internet Information Server is needed on a Mailbox Server Role in order to implement the Role Based Access Control (RBAC) model covered in *Chapter 4*, even if no client is accessing the Mailbox Server directly.

As I mentioned, Storage Groups no longer exist in Exchange Server 2010 SP1, but mailboxes are still stored in databases, just like in Exchange Server 2007. Although rumors have been circulating for more than ten years that the database engine used in Exchange Server will be replaced by a SQL Server engine, it has not happened yet. Just as in earlier versions of Exchange Server, the Extensible Storage Engine (ESE) is still being used, although major changes have been made to the database and the database schema.

By default, the first database on a server will be installed in the directory: `C:\Program Files\Microsoft\Exchange Server\V14\Mailbox\Mailbox Database <<identifier>>`.

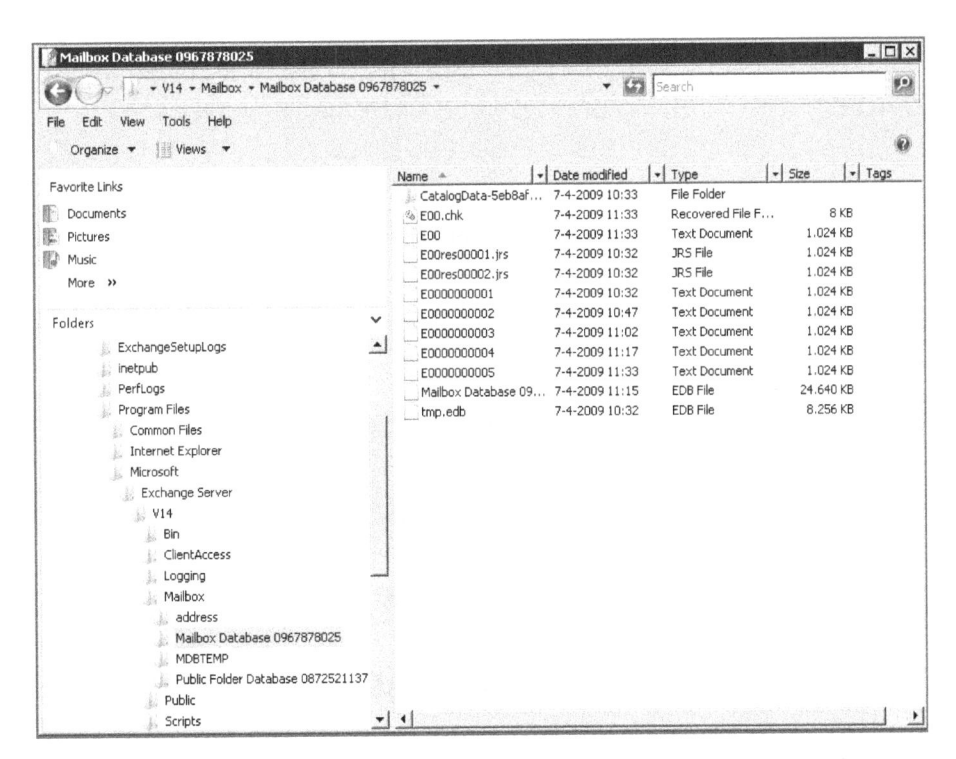

Figure 1.7: The default location for the Mailbox Databases and the log files.

The <<identifier>> is a unique number to make sure that the Mailbox Database name is unique within the Exchange organization.

It is a best practice, from both a performance and a recovery perspective, to place the database and the accompanying log files on a dedicated disk. This disk can be on a Fiber Channel SAN (Storage Area Network), an iSCSI SAN, or on a Direct Attached Storage (DAS) solution. Whilst it was a design goal to limit the amount of disk I/O to a level where both the database and the log files could be installed on a 1 TB SATA disk, this is only an option if Database Copies are configured and you have at least three copies of the Mailbox Database, in order to avoid a single point of failure.

1.7.2 Client Access Server Role

The Client Access Server Role offers access to the mailboxes for all available protocols. In Exchange Server 2003, Microsoft introduced the concept of "front-end" and "back-end" servers, and the Client Access Server Role is comparable to an Exchange Server 2003 Front-End Server.

All clients connect to the Client Access Server and after authentication the requests are proxied to the appropriate Mailbox Server. Communication between the client and the Client Access Server is via the normal protocols (HTTP, IMAP4, POP3 and MAPI), and communication between the Client Access Server and the Mailbox Server is via Remote Procedure Calls (RPC).

The following functionality is provided by the Exchange Server 2010 SP1 Client Access Server:

- HTTP for Outlook Web App
- Outlook Anywhere (formerly known as RPC/HTTP) for Outlook 2003, Outlook 2007 and Outlook 2010

- ActiveSync for (Windows Mobile) PDAs
- Internet protocols POP3 and IMAP4
- RPC Client Access
- Availability Service, Autodiscovery and Exchange Web Services. These services are offered to Outlook 2007 or higher clients and provide free/busy information, automatic configuration of the Outlook 2007 or higher client and the Offline Address Book downloads and Out-of-Office functionality. The Exchange Web Services offer an XML-based interface that can be used by other applications to access the messaging infrastructure. A good example of such an application is the latest version of Entourage, which is completely built on Exchange Server 2010 Web Services.

Note

SMTP Services are not offered by the Client Access Server. All SMTP Services are handled by the Hub Transport Server.

At least one Client Access Server is needed for each Mailbox Server in an Active Directory site, as well as a fast connection between the Client Access Server and the Mailbox Server. The Client Access Server also needs a fast connection to a Global Catalog Server.

The Client Access Server should be deployed on the internal network and *not* in the network's DMZ. In order to access a Client Access Server from the Internet, a Microsoft Internet Security and Acceleration (ISA) Server or Threat Management Gateway (TMG) should be installed in the DMZ. All necessary Exchange services should be "published" to the Internet, on this ISA Server or TMG.

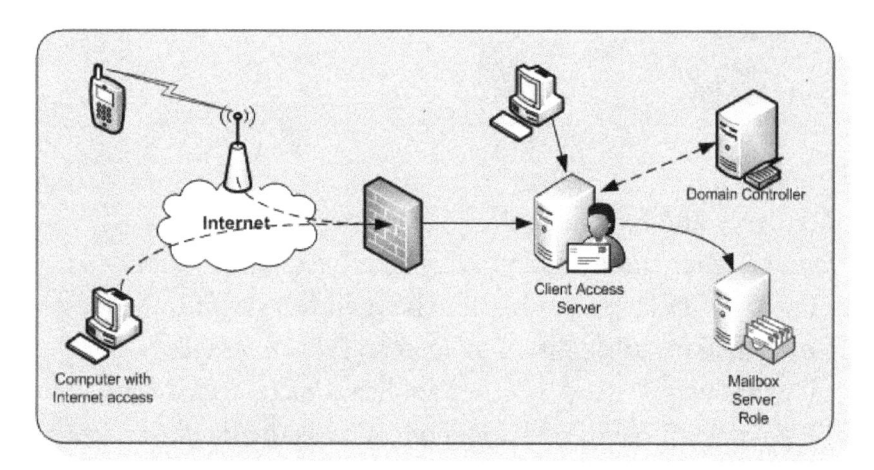

Figure 1.8: The Client Access Server is responsible for providing access to (Internet) clients. The ISA/TMG Server is not in this picture.

1.7.3　Hub Transport Server Role

The Hub Transport Server Role is responsible for routing messages, not only between the Internet and the Exchange organization, but also between Exchange Servers within your organization.

All messages are routed via the Hub Transport Server Role, even if the source and the destination mailbox are on the same server, and even if the source and the destination mailbox are in the same Mailbox Database. For example, in Figure 1.9:

- Step 1: a message is sent to the Hub Transport Server
- Step 2: a recipient on the same server as the sender means the message is sent back
- Step 3: when the recipient is on another Mailbox Server, the message is routed to the appropriate Hub Transport Server; this is then followed by...
- Step 4: the second Hub Transport Server delivers the message to the Mailbox Server of the recipient.

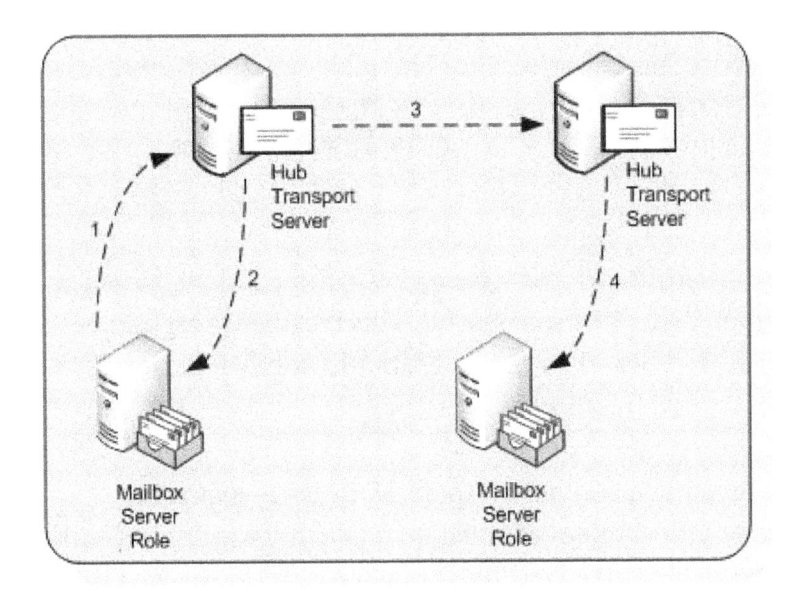

Chapter 1: Introduction to Exchange Server 2010

Figure 1.9: The Hub Transport Server is responsible for routing all messages.

The reason for routing all messages through the Hub Transport Server is simply compliancy. Using the Hub Transport Server, it is possible to track all messaging flowing through the Exchange organization and to take appropriate action if needed (legal requirements, HIPAA (Health Insurance Portability and Accountability Act), Sarbanes-Oxley, etc.). On the Hub Transport Server the following agents can be configured for compliancy purposes:

- **Transport Rule agents** – using Transport Rules, all kinds of actions can be applied to messages according to the rule's filter or conditions. Rules can be applied to internal messages, external messages or both.

- **Journaling agents** – using the journaling agent, it is possible to save a copy of every message sent or received by a particular recipient.

Since a Mailbox Server does not deliver any messages, every Mailbox Server in an Active Directory site requires a Hub Transport Server in that site. The Hub Transport Server also needs a fast connection to a Global Catalog Server for querying Active Directory. This Global Catalog Server should be in the same Active Directory site as the Hub Transport Server.

When a message has an external destination, i.e. a recipient on the Internet, the message is sent from the Hub Transport Server to the "outside world." This may be via an Exchange Server 2010 SP1 Edge Transport Server in the DMZ, but the Hub Transport Server can also deliver messages directly to the Internet.

Optionally, the Hub Transport Server can be configured to deal with anti-spam and antivirus functions. The anti-spam services are not enabled on a Hub Transport Server by default, since this service is intended to be run on an Edge Transport Service in the DMZ. Microsoft has supplied a script on every Hub Transport Server that can be used to enable anti-spam services if desired.

Antivirus services can be achieved by installing the Microsoft Forefront for Exchange software. The antivirus software on the Hub Transport Server will scan inbound and outbound SMTP traffic, whereas antivirus software on the Mailbox Server will scan the contents of a Mailbox Database, providing a double layer of security.

1.7.4   Edge Server Role

The Edge Server Role was introduced with Exchange Server 2007, and provides an extra layer of message hygiene. The Edge Transport Server Role is typically installed as an SMTP gateway in the network's DMZ. Messages from the Internet are delivered to the Edge Transport Server Role and, after anti-spam and antivirus services, the messages are forwarded to a Hub Transport Server on the internal network.

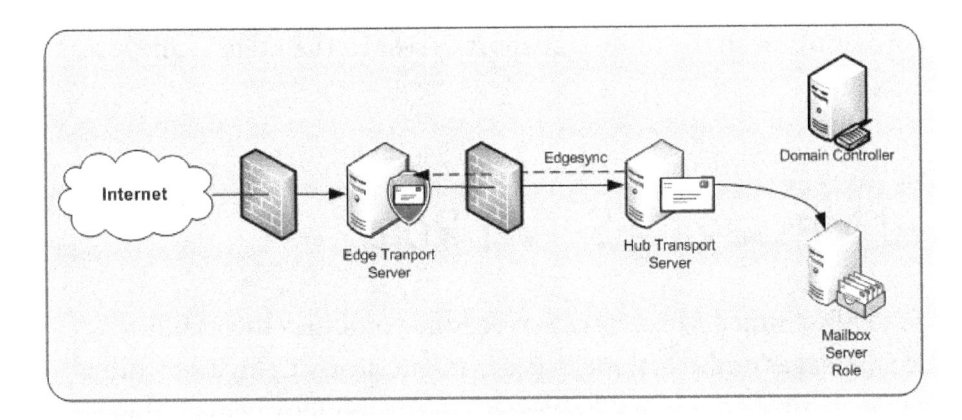

Figure 1.10: The Edge Transport Server is installed between the Internet and the Hub Transport Server.

The Edge Transport Server can also provide the following services:

- **Edge Transport Rules** – like the Transport Rules on the Hub Transport Server, these rules can also control the flow of messages that are sent to or received from the Internet when they meet a certain condition.
- **Address rewriting** – with address rewriting, the SMTP address of messages sent to or received from the Internet can be changed. This can be useful for hiding internal domains, for example, after a merger of two companies but before a merged Active Directory and Exchange organization is created.

The Edge Transport Server is installed in the DMZ and cannot be a member of the company's internal Active Directory domain and Exchange Server 2010 organization. The Edge Transport Server uses the Active Directory Lightweight Directory Services (AD LDS) to store all information. In previous versions of Windows this service was called Active Directory Application Mode (ADAM). Basic information regarding the Exchange infrastructure is stored in the AD LDS, like the recipients and the Hub Transport Server which the Edge Transport Server is sending its messages to.

To keep the AD LDS database up to date, a synchronization feature called EdgeSync is used, which pushes information from the Hub Transport Server to the Edge Transport Server at regular intervals.

1.7.5 Unified Messaging Server Role

The Exchange Server 2010 SP1 Unified Messaging Server Role combines the Mailbox Database and both voice messages and email messages into one store. Using the Unified Messaging Server Role it is possible to access all messages in the mailbox using either a telephone or a computer.

The phone system can be an IP-based system or a "classical" analog PBX system although, in the latter case, a special Unified Messaging IP Gateway is needed to connect the two.

The Unified Messaging Server Role provides users with the features below.

- **Call Answering** – this feature acts as an answering machine. When somebody cannot answer the phone, a personal message can be played, after which a caller can leave a message. The message will be recorded and sent to the recipient's mailbox as an mp3 file.

- **Subscriber Access** – sometimes referred to as "Outlook Voice Access." Using Subscriber Access, users can access their mailbox using a normal phone line and listen to their voicemail messages. It is also possible to access regular mailbox items like messages and calendar items, and even reschedule appointments in the calendar.

- **Auto Attendant** – using the Auto Attendant, it is possible to create a custom menu in the Unified Messaging system using voice prompts. A caller can use either the telephone keypad or his or her voice to navigate through the menu.

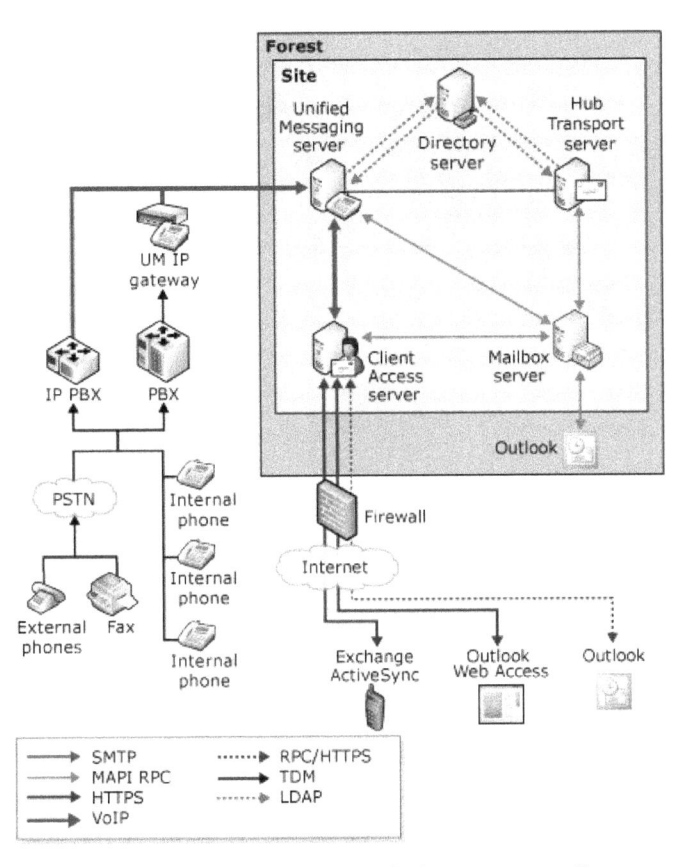

Figure 1.11: Overview of the Unified Messaging infrastructure.

The Unified Messaging service installed on the Unified Messaging Server Role works closely with the Microsoft Exchange Speech Engine Service. This Speech Engine Service provides the services below.

- **Dual Tone Multi-Frequency (DTMF)** also referred to as the touch tone (the beeps you hear when dialing a phone number or accessing a menu).

- **Automatic Speech Recognition**.

- **Text to Speech service**, responsible for reading mailbox items and reading the voice menus.

The Unified Messaging Server Role should be installed in an Active Directory site together with a Hub Transport Server, since this latter server is responsible for routing messaging to the Mailbox Servers. It should also have a fast connection to a Global Catalog Server. If possible, the Mailbox Server Role should be installed as close as possible to the Unified Messaging Server Role, preferably in the same site, and with a decent network connection. I'll cover this Unified Messaging Role in more detail in *Chapter 6*.

1.8 Summary

Exchange Server 2010 SP1 is the new Messaging and Collaboration platform from Microsoft, and it has a lot of new, compelling features. The new High Availability, management, and compliancy features make Exchange Server 2010 a very interesting product for the Exchange administrator. In fact, the new features in Exchange Server 2010 will generally result in *less* complexity, which is always a good thing! As far as Service Pack 1 is concerned, this completes the implementation of quite a lot of functionality that Microsoft was not able to finish in the RTM version of Exchange Server 2010. Think about the performance of the Exchange Management Console, import and export Mailbox, and the most important, the personal archive improvements!

In the next chapter, I will give you a more detailed walk-through of installing Exchange Server 2010. Furthermore, the remainder of this book deals with Exchange Server 2010 Service Pack 1.

Chapter 2: Installing Exchange Server 2010 SP1

In the previous chapter, I took you through a brief description of what's new in Exchange Server 2010 and Exchange Server 2010 SP1, and what has been removed from the product. Now it's time to install Exchange Server 2010 SP1 and get a handle on the real look and feel. In this chapter, we will install it in a "greenfield" scenario, meaning we'll be working with a fresh Active Directory environment, and the Exchange organization we'll install will be the first Exchange installation in that environment. This chapter will be a fairly straightforward, step-by-step guide to the installation process, and will cover both the prerequisites of the installation environment and the post-installation configuration of various features. In short, you should have everything you need here to get up and running, and I'll refer to aspects of this process when I take you through coexistence with Exchange Server 2003 and 2007 in the next chapter.

So, before installing Exchange Server 2010 SP1, several prerequisites have to be met.

- Exchange Server 2010 SP1 runs **only** on Windows Server 2008 SP2 and Windows Server 2008 R2. Since Windows Server 2008 SP2 also needs some additional software to be installed, and bearing in mind the improvements in Windows Server 2008 R2, the latter is the better option.

- Any Active Directory domain containing Exchange objects has to be running (at the very least) Windows 2003 domain functionality level.

- The Active Directory forest also has to be running in at least Windows 2003 forest functionality level. Actually, running the forest in Windows 2003 forest functionality level automatically implies that all domains are running (at least) at Windows 2003 domain functionality level.

- The Schema Master and the Global Catalog Server(s) have to have a minimum level of Windows Server 2003 R2.

- Exchange Server 2010 SP1 **cannot** be installed in an organization where an Exchange Server 2000 exists. This is hard-coded blocked in the setup application.

2.1 Exchange Pre-Deployment Analyzer

The Exchange Pre-Deployment Analyzer is a tool provided by Microsoft which you can use to perform a scan of the overall readiness of your environment. If you are familiar with the **Exchange Best Practices Analyzer** (ExBPA), then the Pre-Deployment Analyzer is a bit like the **Exchange 2007 readiness** option in older versions of the ExBPA.

After starting the Pre-Deployment Analyzer, just follow the wizard and create a new scan.

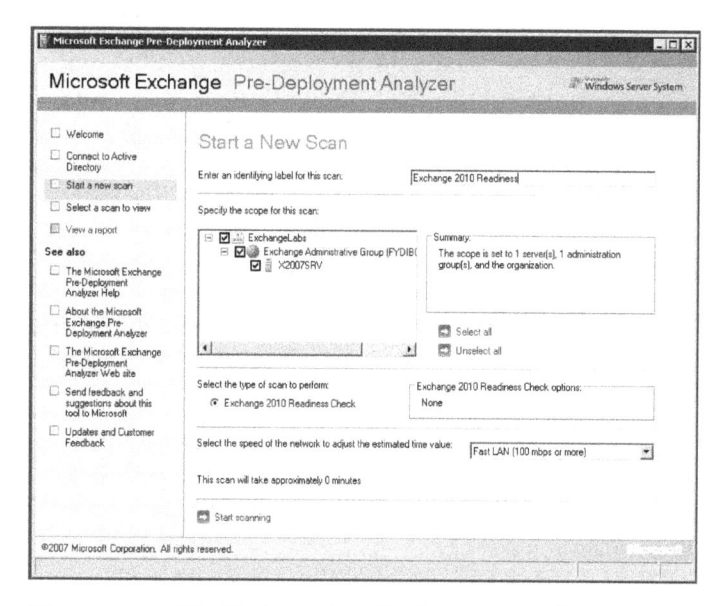

Figure 2.1: The Exchange Pre-Deployment Analyzer in an Exchange 2007 environment.

The Pre-Deployment Analyzer will analyze the existing Exchange environment and, when finished, will return a list of any issues that are found, together with the corresponding fixes. This is a perfect tool to see if your existing organization is ready for Exchange Server 2010 SP1.

The Pre-Deployment Analyzer can be downloaded from the Microsoft website at: HTTP://TINYURL.COM/YCORLVP.

2.2 Installing Exchange Server 2010 SP1 prerequisites

When installing Exchange Server 2010 SP1 on Windows Server 2008 SP2, some additional software needs to be installed first:

- Microsoft .NET Framework 3.5 SP1

- Microsoft .NET Framework 3.5 Family update for Windows Vista x64, and Windows Server 2008 x64

- Windows Remote Management (WinRM) and Windows PowerShell 2.0

- Internet Information Server 7.0

- Office 2007 Filter Pack (for the Hub Transport Server and Mailbox Server Role).

The installation program will give you the option to install .NET 3.5 and PowerShell V2 when you begin the installation, but you'll need to install the rest of the prerequisites yourself. The Internet Information Server Role is now needed on *all* the Server Roles of Exchange Server 2010 SP1, but there are some fine-grained differences between the various Server Roles, as you can see in Table 2.1.

Chapter 2: Installing Exchange Server 2010 SP1

Description	Mgmt Tools	Mail-box	Hub Transport	Client Access	UM	Edge
.NET Framework 3.5	Yes	Yes	Yes	Yes	Yes	Yes
PowerShell 2.0	Yes	Yes	Yes	Yes	Yes	Yes
Windows Remote Management	Yes	Yes	Yes	Yes	Yes	Yes
Hot-fix KB 951725	Yes	Yes	Yes	Yes	Yes	Yes
MS Filter Pack		Yes				
ServerManagerCmd -i Web-Server		Yes	Yes	Yes	Yes	
ServerManagerCmd -i Web-Metabase	Yes	Yes	Yes	Yes	Yes	
ServerManagerCmd -i Web-Lgcy-Mgmt-Console	Yes	Yes	Yes	Yes	Yes	
ServerManagerCmd -i Web-Basic-Auth		Yes	Yes	Yes	Yes	
ServerManagerCmd -i Web-Windows-Auth		Yes	Yes	Yes	Yes	
ServerManagerCmd -i Web-Net-Ext		Yes	Yes	Yes	Yes	
ServerManagerCmd -i Web-Digest-Auth				Yes		
ServerManagerCmd -i Web-Dyn-Compression				Yes		

Description	Mgmt Tools	Mail-box	Hub Transport	Client Access	UM	Edge
ServerManagerCmd -i NET-HTTP-Activation				Yes		
ServerManagerCmd -i Web-ISAPI-Ext				Yes		
ServerManagerCmd -i RPC-over-HTTP-proxy (only needed for Outlook Anywhere)				Yes		
ServerManagerCmd -i Desktop-Experience					Yes	
ServerManagerCmd -i ADLDS						Yes
ServerManagerCmd -i fail-over-clustering (only needed for database availability)		Yes				
ServerManagerCmd -i RSAT-ADDS	Yes	Yes	Yes	Yes	Yes	

Table 2.1: Internet Information Server settings for all Exchange Server 2010 SP1 Server Roles.

Note

When you use `ServerManagerCmd.exe` *a warning messages is shown about the supportability of this command. While Microsoft has plans to discontinue this feature, its future is still undecided. But I still use it, and I think I'll keep using it as long as possible.*

Chapter 2: Installing Exchange Server 2010 SP1

If you want to install the Exchange Server 2010 SP1 Management Tools on a Windows Vista SP2 workstation, you'll have to install the following software:

- Microsoft .NET Framework 3.5 SP1

- Microsoft .NET Framework 3.5 Family update for Windows Vista x64, and Windows Server 2008 x64 updates

- Windows Remote Management (WinRM) and Windows PowerShell 2.0

- some basic parts of the Internet Information Server: the IIS Web Metabase and the IIS Legacy Management Console.

If you want to install the Exchange Server 2010 SP1 Management Tools on a Windows 7 workstation, you'll have to install the following software beforehand:

- Microsoft .NET Framework 3.5.1

- The Web Management Tools and the IIS 6 Management Compatibility as part of the Internet Information Server.

Note

When installing Exchange Server 2010 SP1 on a Windows Server 2008 R2 server, almost all the prerequisite software is already included in the product. You only have to install Windows Server 2008 R2, install Internet Information Server (as outlined below), and you're ready to go!

The .NET Framework 3.5 can be automatically downloaded the first time you use Windows Update, but do *not* install PowerShell using the Windows Server 2008 Server Manager. This installs PowerShell Version 1, and Exchange Server 2010 SP1 needs PowerShell Version 2, which you can download from the Microsoft website.

The various configurations of Internet Information Server 7 can be easily installed using the `ServerManagerCmd.exe` application, which is a command-line version of the Windows Server 2008 Server Manager. To make it possible to change the Active Directory schema on a non-domain controller before this process, enter the following command on the server you want to install Exchange Server 2010 on: `ServerManagerCmd -i RSAT-ADDS`.

Note

When the –`Restart` option is added to `ServerManagerCmd.exe` the server will automatically restart as necessary.

This command will add the Active Directory Management Tools on your Windows 2008 Server to make it possible to change the Active Directory schema from this particular server.

Once that process is finished, enter the commands below to install the various components of Internet Information Server 7.

```
ServerManagerCmd -i Web-Server
ServerManagerCmd -i Web-ISAPI-Ext
ServerManagerCmd -i Web-Metabase
ServerManagerCmd -i Web-Lgcy-Mgmt-Console
ServerManagerCmd -i Web-Basic-Auth
ServerManagerCmd -i Web-Digest-Auth
ServerManagerCmd -i Web-Windows-Auth
ServerManagerCmd -i Web-Dyn-Compression
ServerManagerCmd -i Web-Net-Ext
ServerManagerCmd -i RPC-over-HTTP-proxy (when Outlook
                    Anywhere is used)
ServerManagerCmd -i Net-HTTP-Activation
ServerManagerCmd -i Desktop-Experience (when the UM Role is
                    required)
```

Chapter 2: Installing Exchange Server 2010 SP1

If you want to speed up the process, or your fingers get tired and you don't want to enter that many commands, you can enter various options in one `ServerManagerCmd` cmdlet, like this:

```
ServerManagerCmd -i Web-Server Web-ISAPI-Ext Web-Metabase Web-Lgcy-Mgmt-Console
Web-Basic-Auth Web-Digest-Auth Web-Windows-Auth Web-Dyn-Compression Web-Net-Ext
RPC-over-HTTP-proxy Net-HTTP-Activation Desktop-Experience
```

Just make sure you change these commands according to the information in Table 2.1. And here's some more good news: Microsoft makes an Exchange administrator's life easier! With Exchange Server 2010 SP1, Microsoft supplies a number of XML files (one for every Server Role) that automate all prerequisite software installation.

Navigate to the \setup\serverRoles\common directory on the installation media; there, you'll find a number of XML files, like Exchange-Hub.XML, Exchange-CAS.XML and Exchange-MBX.XML. Any of these can be used as an input file for the ServerManagerCmd.exe application, as appropriate.

To install the prerequisite software for a typical Exchange 2010 Server installation, just enter the following commands: ServerManagerCmd.exe –InputPath Exchange-Typical.XML.

As you can see in Figure 2.2 (this is on Windows Server 2008 R2), there is a message saying that ServerManagerCmd.exe is deprecated and is not guaranteed to be supported in future releases of Windows. Don't let this message scare you; it does work right now, and if it won't be supported in future releases of Windows, then the Exchange team will certainly take care of this.

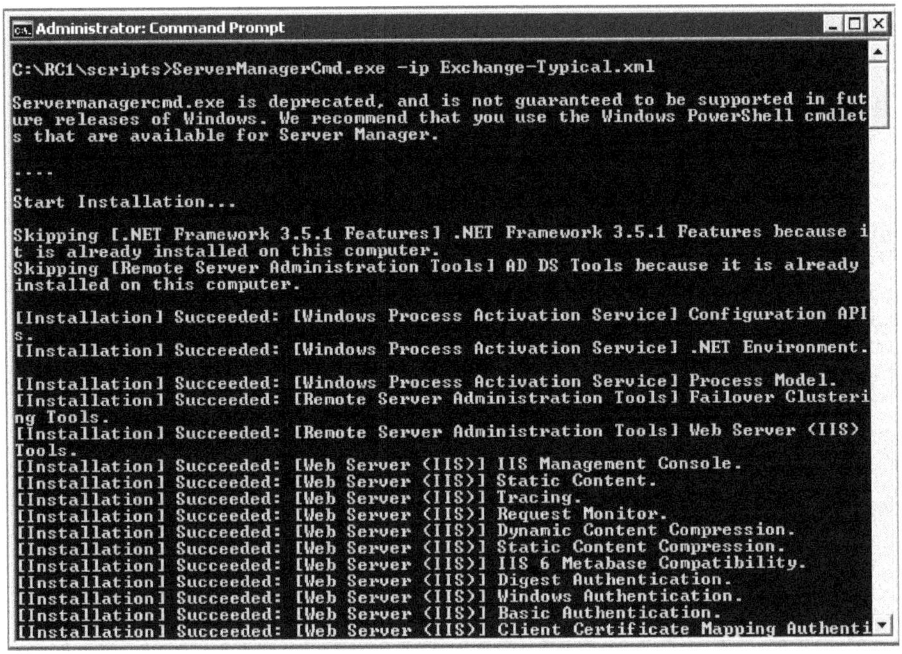

Figure 2.2: The installation of the prerequisite software is fully automated.

You can also use PowerShell to install the prerequisite software. Open a PowerShell command prompt and enter the following command: `ServerManagerCmd.exe –IP <path to xml file>\Exchange-Typical.xml`.

If you don't want to install the .NET Framework and Internet Information Server at this point, the Exchange Server 2010 setup program now has the ability to install the prerequisite software automatically during the setup of Exchange Server 2010. There is more information on this in Section 2.3, Item 10, later in this chapter.

Another thing to be aware of is the NET.TCP port sharing service. This service has to start automatically, but it is set to start manually by default; you can change this setting by opening a command prompt and entering the following command: `sc config NetTcpPortSharing start= auto`.

Chapter 2: Installing Exchange Server 2010 SP1

Note

The space after `start=` *is required! In addition, if the service is not started at all, you have to start it using the* `net start NetTcpPortSharing` *command from the command line.*

Of course, it is also possible to change this setting using the Services MMC snap-in.

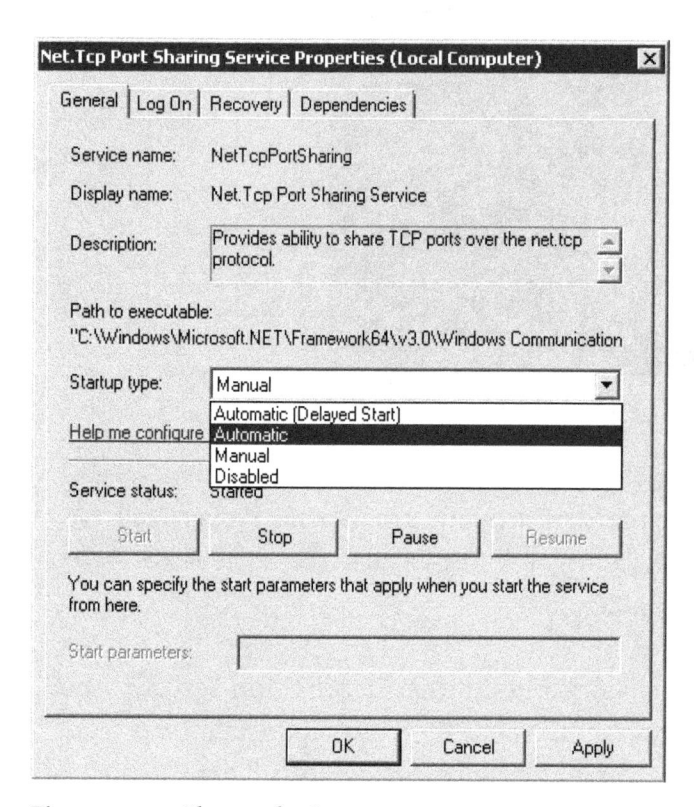

Figure 2.3:   Change the Startup type to Automatic.

But there's even more good news regarding the prerequisite roles and features installation in Service Pack 1: now you can have the setup application, both the graphical and command-line versions, take care of this for you. I'll get back on this later in the setup process (see Figure 2.5 for an example).

Chapter 2: Installing Exchange Server 2010 SP1

Most of the Exchange Server 2010 SP1 Server Roles can be combined on a single server, just as in Exchange Server 2007. Specifically, the Mailbox Server, Client Access Server, Hub Transport Server and Unified Messaging Server can be installed together on one machine. However, none of these Server Roles can be installed alongside the Exchange Server 2010 SP1 Edge Transport Server Role, as this is a completely standalone role. I'll cover the installation of the Exchange Server 2010 SP1 Edge Transport Server Role in Section 2.7.

2.3 Performing a typical Exchange Server 2010 install

When performing a typical server install, the account that's used for the installation process needs to be a member of the Schema Administrators group in Active Directory, as well as a member of the Enterprise Administrators. Membership of these groups automatically inherits membership of the local administrators group (on the server itself) as well as Domain Administrators membership. This is true for an upgrade from Exchange Server 2010 RTM to Exchange Server 2010 SP1 *as well as* for a completely new installation.

To install Exchange Server 2010 SP1, just follow the steps below.

1. Log on to the server on which you want to install Exchange Server 2010 SP1.
2. Navigate to the installation (DVD, local directory or a network share) and double-click the **setup.exe** program. This will start the setup splash screen.
3. If you haven't already installed the Exchange Server 2010 SP1 prerequisites, the setup program offers the possibility to install them using the menu:
   a. Install Microsoft .NET Framework 3.5 SP1
   b. Install Windows PowerShell V2 .

4. You have to select the **Language Options** for Exchange Server 2010 SP1. You can download all language files from the Language Bundle (locally stored or on the Internet) or continue with the language packs that are on your DVD. If you select this option, only the default language will be used, not only for the setup application, but also, for example, for the Outlook Web App.

5. When all prerequisite software is installed you can select **Step 4: Install Microsoft Exchange**.

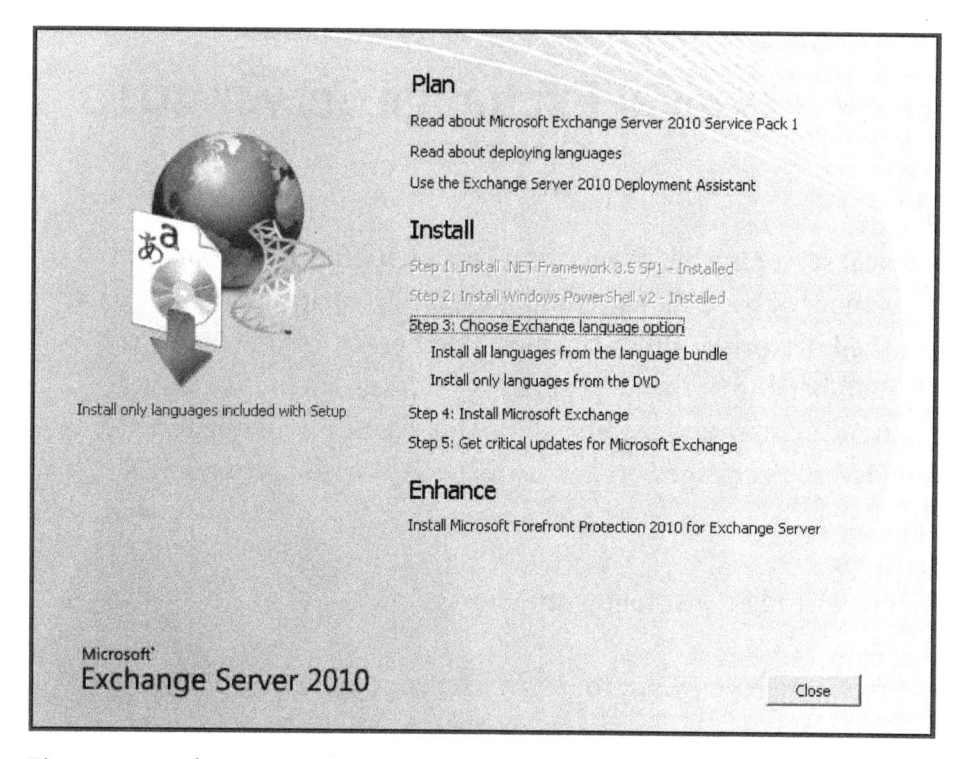

Figure 2.4: The setup application Welcome screen.

6. On the **Introduction** and **Confirmation** pages you can just click **Next** after you've read the messages.

7. You'll need to accept the terms in the license agreement – select the appropriate radio button, and click **Next**.

Chapter 2: Installing Exchange Server 2010 SP1

8. Depending on your company policy, select whether or not you want to enable the **Error Reporting** feature, and click **Next** to continue.

9. The next page asks for the **Installation Type**. You can select a typical Exchange Server installation, where the Hub Transport Server Role, Client Access Server Role, Mailbox Server Role and the Exchange Management Tools are all installed on the same server. The second option is a custom Exchange Server installation, where you can select which individual roles to install.

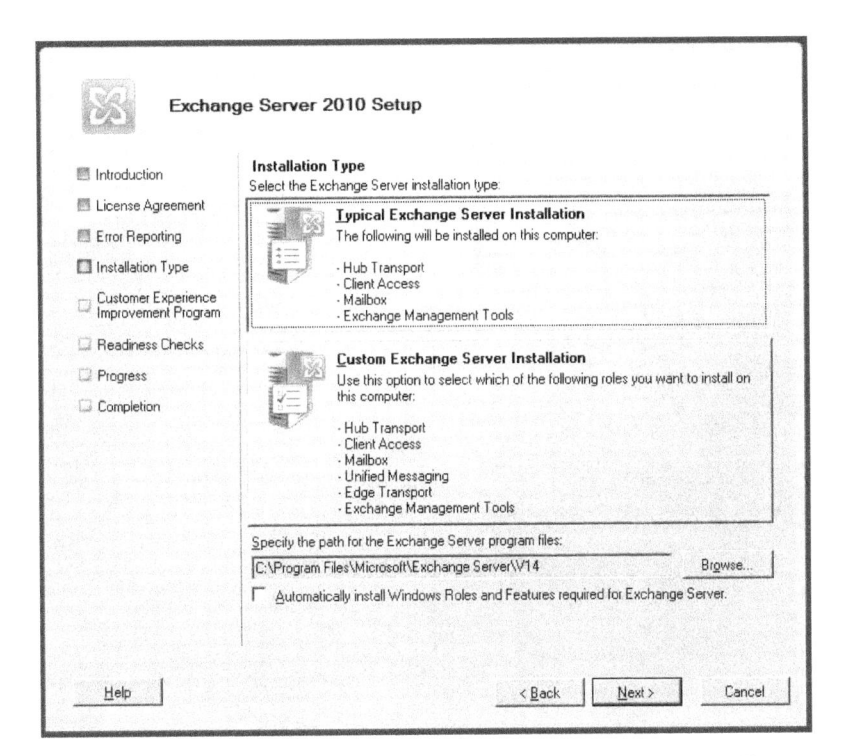

Figure 2.5: Select a Typical or a Custom Exchange Server installation.

10. New in Service Pack 1 is the **Automatically install Windows Roles and Features required for Exchange Server** option. When you check this option, the prerequisite software, like the Microsoft .NET Framework and Internet Information Server, will be automatically installed.

11. Select the **Typical Exchange Server Installation** and click **Next** to continue.

59

Chapter 2: Installing Exchange Server 2010 SP1

12. Since this is a fresh installation, an Exchange organization doesn't exist yet, so you'll need to enter a name for the Exchange Server organization. The default name is "First Organization" but any name can be used, as long as the following are the only characters used:

    a. A through Z

    b. a through z

    c. 0 through 9

    d. space (not leading or trailing)

    e. hyphen or dash.

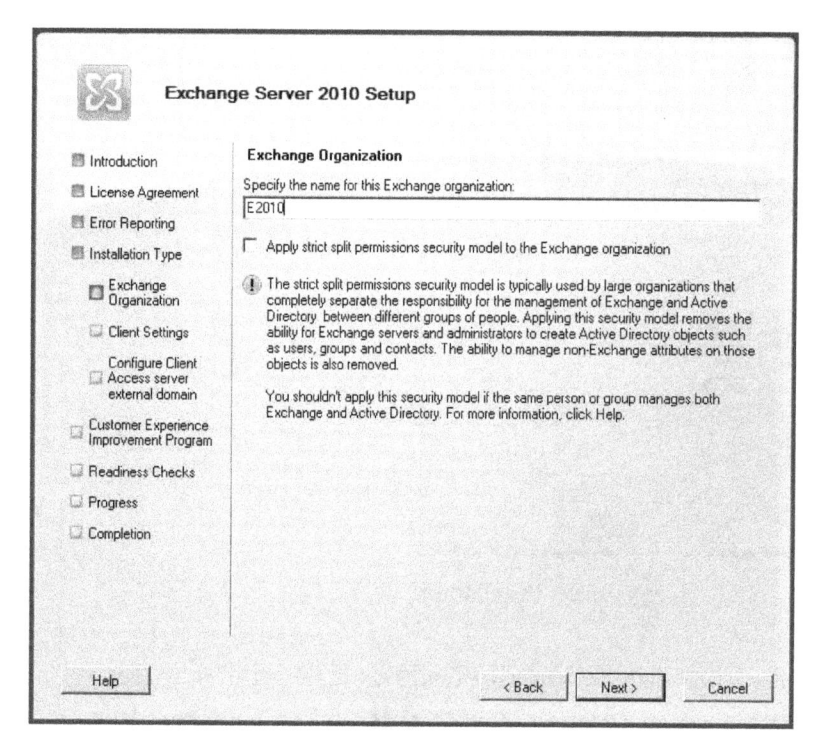

Figure 2.6: Enter the organization name. Note the strict split permissions security model check box.

Chapter 2: Installing Exchange Server 2010 SP1

Note

Just so you know, throughout this book I'll use the organization name "E2010." New in Service Pack 1 is the option to implement split permissions for Active Directory and Exchange. This can be useful for large organizations with separate Active Directory and Exchange Server administrators. If this is not the case, leave this in its default state (unchecked), and click **Next** *to continue;*

13. The next window is the **Client Settings** window, and this is very important. Your selection needs to be based on the email clients used in your organization. Outlook 2003 or earlier and Entourage clients depend on Public Folders for Free/Busy information (i.e. calendaring) and Offline Address Book downloads. On the other hand, Outlook 2007 and Outlook 2010 can both use the Availability Services and Web-based Offline Address Book Download features in Exchange Server 2007 and later. If you do not install Public Folders at this time, it's always possible to install them later to support Outlook 2003 or Entourage clients in your Exchange environment. Click **Next** to continue.

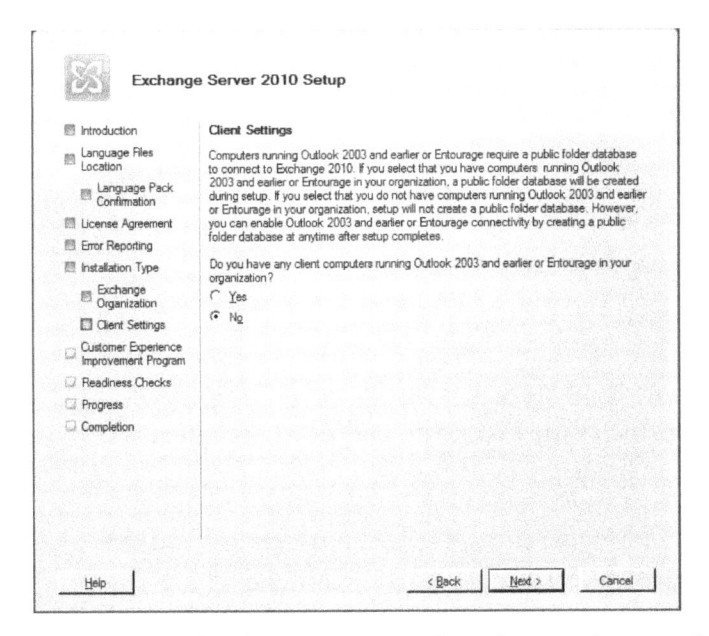

Figure 2.7: The client settings are dependent on the type of clients used in your organization.

Chapter 2: Installing Exchange Server 2010 SP1

14. A new aspect of the Exchange Server 2010 setup process is the option to enter the external domain name. If you *do* enter an external domain name, the Exchange Server 2010 Client Access Server Role will be configured smoothly and automatically with the appropriate settings. If you do not enter an external domain name during the setup, you'll have to configure the settings manually after the setup has finished.

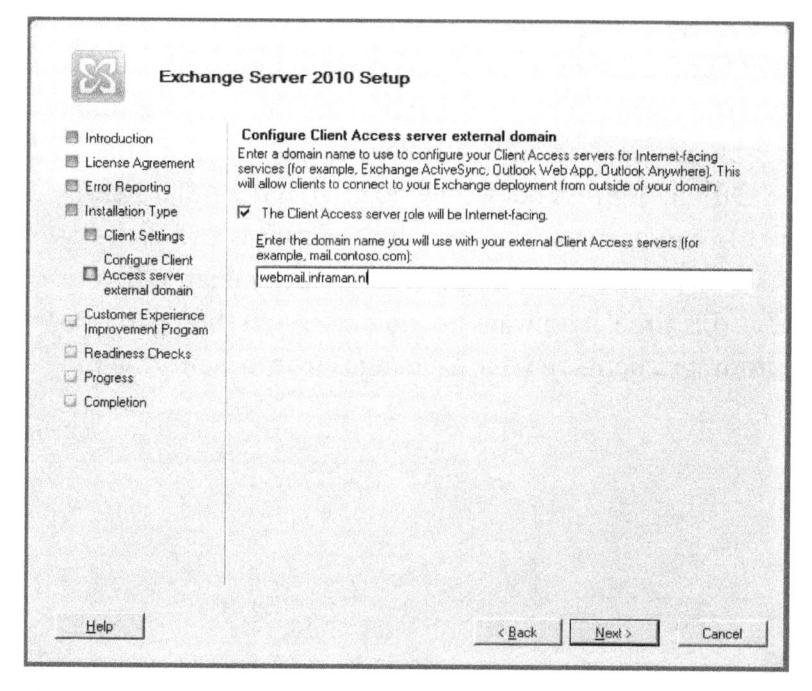

Figure 2.8: Enter the external domain name for automatically configuring the Client Access Server.

15. Depending on your company policy, you can choose whether or not to join the **Exchange Customer Experience Improvement Program**, and then click **Next**.

16. The next step is the **Readiness Check**. The setup program will run a final check on the server's readiness for the Exchange organization, the language packs, and the Server Roles. If any prerequisite is missing, it's displayed here and you'll have the option to correct the issues. If all the checks come back OK, you can finally click that inviting **Install** button.

17. During the installation, the progress is shown for each part of the process. This whole affair can take a considerable amount of time, depending on the hardware being used for the Exchange Server, so you'll need to be patient. Once the setup program is finished, you'll have the option to view the setup log, just in case of problems (which, if you've followed these steps, there shouldn't be). When you click on **Finish**, the setup program is done, and the Exchange Management Console is opened to finalize the new Exchange Server.

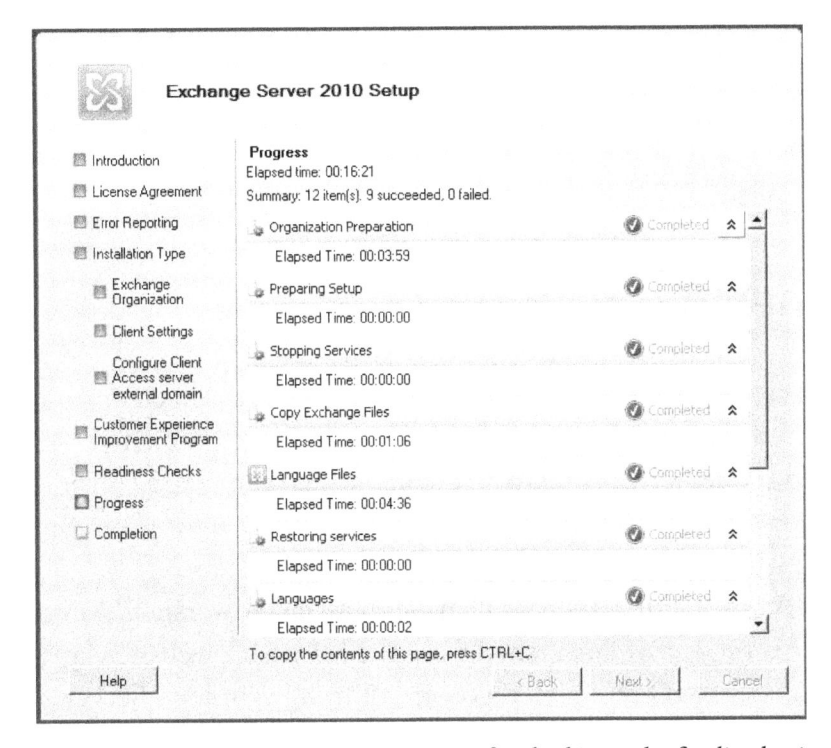

Figure 2.9: When the setup program is finished it can be finalized using the Exchange Management Console.

2.4 Unattended setup

It is also possible to install Exchange Server 2010 SP1 fully unattended. This may be useful when installing multiple servers. Also, when something goes wrong, you know exactly in which step it went wrong. This process assumes that all the prerequisite software has been installed, including Internet Information Server and the **LDIFDE** program (HTTP://TINY.CC/LDIFDE) to prepare the schema.

> *Note*
>
> *LDIFDE is installed when installing the RSAT-ADDS tools using* `ServerManagerCmd.exe`.

2.4.1 PrepareSchema

The first step in an unattended setup is to prepare the schema. This basically means upgrading the schema to an Exchange Server 2010 SP1 level. Several Exchange-related objects and attributes are added to the Active Directory schema, which can take a considerable amount of time. You'll need to be patient, again.

If you are running Windows Server 2008 (R1), then you'll have to install Powershell 2.0 on the server. You can download this version of Powershell from the Microsoft website via HTTP://GO.MICROSOFT.COM/FWLINK/?LINKID=151321. If you are running Windows Server 2008 R2, you're lucky; this version of Windows has Powershell 2.0 already installed.

For extending the schema, you'll also need the Active Directory Services remote administration tools, which make it possible to access the schema and make all the necessary changes. You can install the Remote Administration Tools by opening a command prompt and entering: `ServerManagerCmd.exe –i RSAT-ADDS`.

Chapter 2: Installing Exchange Server 2010 SP1

When finished, reboot the servers as requested. To prepare the schema, log on to the server as an administrator who is a member of both the schema Admins and Enterprise Admins Security Groups. Open a command prompt, navigate to the Exchange Server 2010 SP1 installation media and type the following command: `Setup.com /PrepareSchema`.

The command-line setup program will start and upgrade the Active Directory schema to an Exchange Server 2010 SP1 level. If you have multiple Domain Controllers, wait until the schema changes have been replicated to all Domain Controllers in the forest before continuing with the next step.

2.4.2 PrepareAD

After preparing the schema, Active Directory now has to be prepared for Exchange Server 2010 SP1 because, as I explained in *Chapter 1*, the Exchange Server organization is installed in the Configuration Partition of Active Directory. This is why the account used for the installation needs to be a member of the Enterprise Admins Security Group (Domain Administrators cannot write in the Configuration Partition).

Log on to the server, open a command prompt, navigate to the Exchange Server 2010 SP1 installation media, and enter in this command: `Setup.com /PrepareAD /OrganizationName:E2010`.

Note

The `/OrganizationName` parameter is only needed when implementing Exchange Server 2010 in a greenfield scenario. When an Exchange organization is already present in your Active Directory environment there's no need to include the `/OrganizationName` option (in fact, it will fail when you do).

Chapter 2: Installing Exchange Server 2010 SP1

The Active Directory Configuration Partition will now be prepared for Exchange Server 2010 SP1 using the previously-mentioned "E2010" organization name.

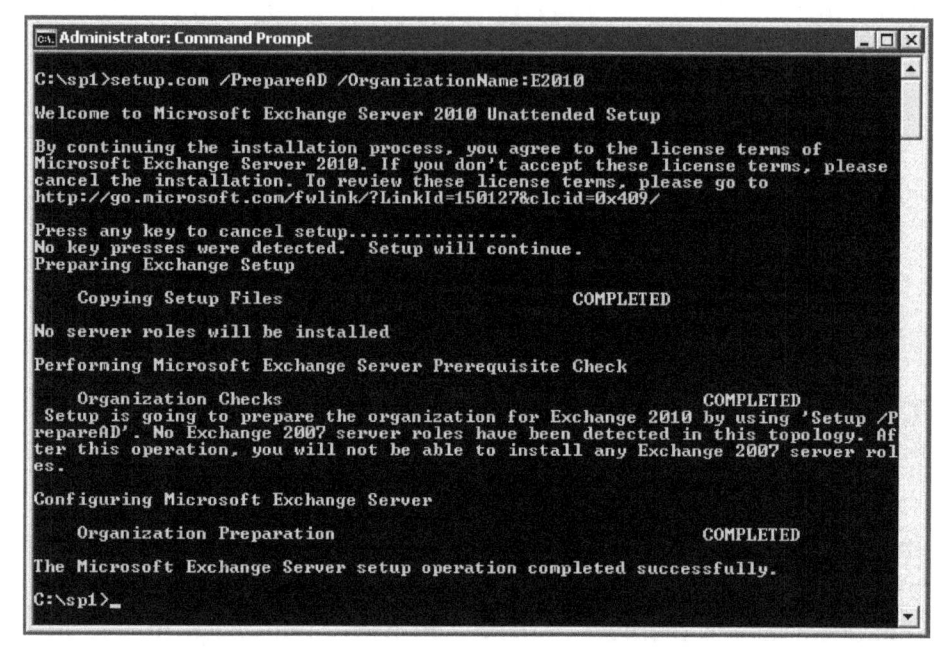

```
C:\sp1>setup.com /PrepareAD /OrganizationName:E2010
Welcome to Microsoft Exchange Server 2010 Unattended Setup

By continuing the installation process, you agree to the license terms of
Microsoft Exchange Server 2010. If you don't accept these license terms, please
cancel the installation. To review these license terms, please go to
http://go.microsoft.com/fwlink/?LinkId=150127&clcid=0x409/

Press any key to cancel setup................
No key presses were detected. Setup will continue.
Preparing Exchange Setup

    Copying Setup Files                                 COMPLETED
No server roles will be installed
Performing Microsoft Exchange Server Prerequisite Check

    Organization Checks                                 COMPLETED
 Setup is going to prepare the organization for Exchange 2010 by using 'Setup /P
repareAD'. No Exchange 2007 server roles have been detected in this topology. Af
ter this operation, you will not be able to install any Exchange 2007 server rol
es.

Configuring Microsoft Exchange Server

    Organization Preparation                            COMPLETED

The Microsoft Exchange Server setup operation completed successfully.
C:\sp1>_
```

Figure 2.10: Preparing the Active Directory Configuration Partition for Exchange Server 2010.

Please note the warning during setup! If you create an Exchange Server 2010 SP1 organization, you are not able to add any Exchange Server 2007 Server Roles to it.

If you want to check the creation of the Exchange Server 2010 SP1 organization you can use **ADSIEdit** and navigate to the Configuration container. Open **CN=Configuration > CN=Services > CN=Microsoft Exchange**. Right here, a new entry, **CN=E2010**, holding the Exchange Server 2010 SP1 configuration, should be created.

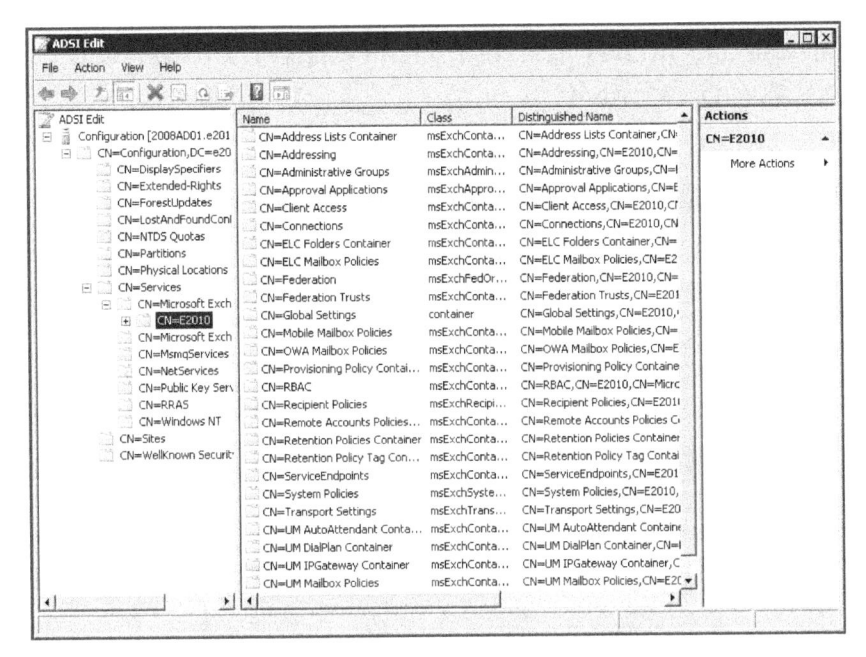

Figure 2.11: Check the creation of the Exchange organization in Active Directory using ADSIEdit.

If you have multiple Domain Controllers, wait until the schema changes have been replicated to all Domain Controllers in the forest before continuing with the next step.

2.4.3 PrepareDomain

The last step in preparing the Active Directory environment is to prepare the domain that is going to host Exchange Server 2010 SP1.

Log on to the server using an administrator account, open a command prompt and navigate to the Exchange Server 2010 installation media. Type the following command: `Setup.com /PrepareDomain`.

Chapter 2: Installing Exchange Server 2010 SP1

The current domain will now be prepared for the introduction of Exchange Server 2010 SP1. If you want to prepare all domains in the forest for Exchange Server 2010 SP1, you can also use the `/PrepareAllDomains` switch.

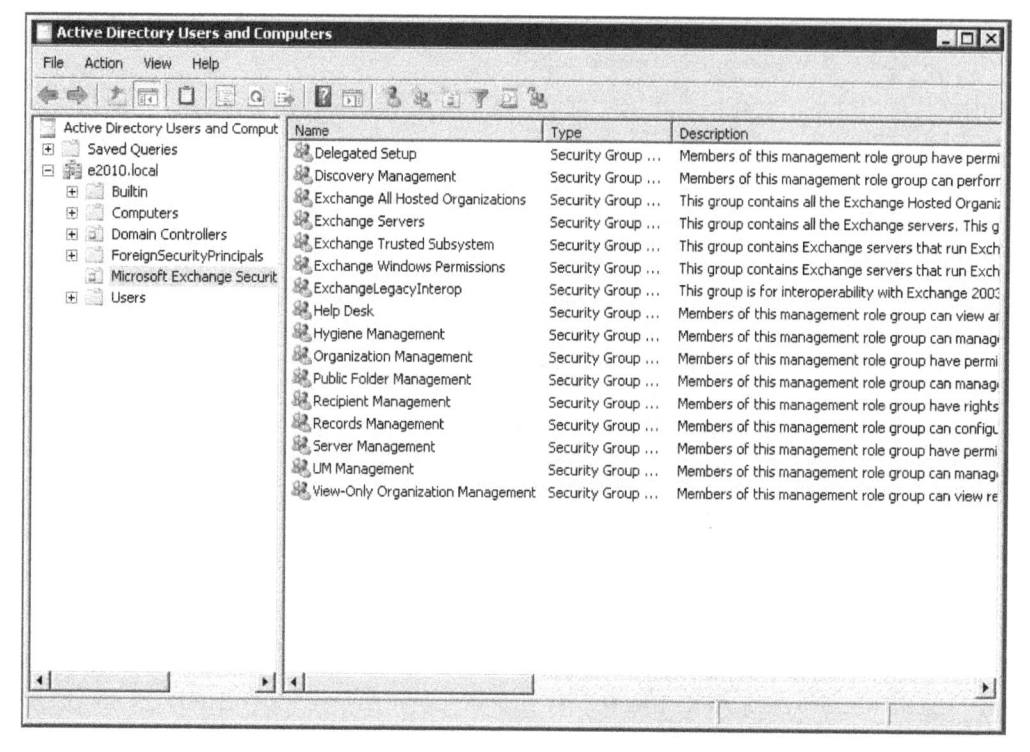

Figure 2.12: The Security Groups created after preparing the domain for Exchange Server 2010.

During the preparation of the domain, a container is created in the root of the domain called **Microsoft Exchange Security Groups**. This container holds the following Security Groups:

- Delegated Setup
- Discovery Management
- Exchange All Hosted Organizations

- Exchange Servers
- Exchange Trusted Subsystem
- Exchange Windows Permissions
- ExchangeLegacyInterop
- Help Desk
- Hygiene Management
- Organization Management
- Public Folder Management
- Recipient Management
- Records Management
- Server Management
- UM Management
- View-Only Organization Management.

When the preparation of the domain (or domains) is finished, just make sure you wait until replication to all the Domain Controllers is completed.

2.4.4 Install Server Roles

The very last step is to install the actual Server Roles. This can be done using the `setup.com` program with the `/mode` and `/Roles` switches. The `/mode` switch is used to select the **Install** option, the `/Roles` switch is used to select which Server Roles are installed.

Chapter 2: Installing Exchange Server 2010 SP1

For an unattended typical server setup, log on to the server and open a command prompt. Navigate to the Exchange Server 2010 SP1 installation media (one last time) and enter the following command:

```
Setup.com /mode:install /Roles:ht,ca,mb /InstallWindowsComponents /
EnableLegacyOutlook /LanguagePack:C:\Download\LanguagePackBundle.exe
```

New in Service Pack 1 is the `/InstallWindowsComponents` parameter, which can be added to the setup program. This will install the prerequisite roles and features needed for the specific Exchange Server Roles you're installing.

The `/EnableLegacyOutlook` option will create a Public Folder Database for Outlook 2003 and Entourage Clients, and the `/LanguagePack` option will use the Language Pack Bundle file specified during installation.

The Exchange Server 2010 SP1 Hub Transport Server, Client Access Server and Mailbox Server Role will now be installed in the default location, which is `C:\Program Files\Microsoft\Exchange\v14`.

When entered, the details in Figure 2.13 will be shown on the screen.

Chapter 2: Installing Exchange Server 2010 SP1

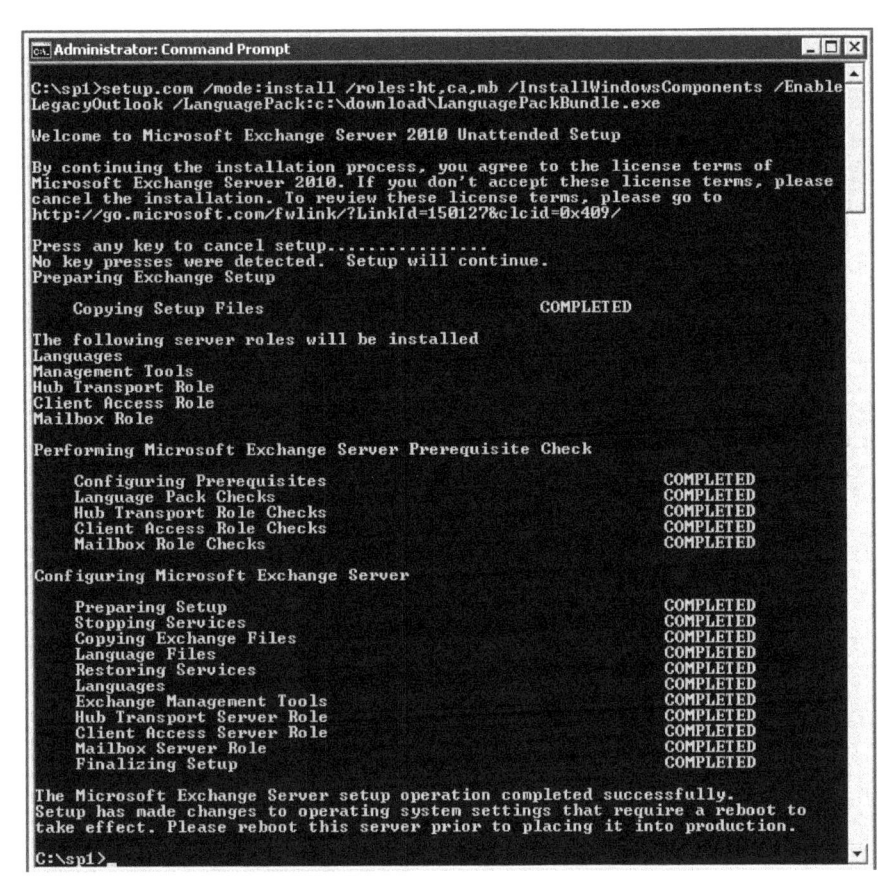

Figure 2.13: Unattended setup of a typical Exchange Server 2010 SP1 server.

2.5 Check the Exchange installation

After installing Exchange Server 2010 SP1, it's time to check if that installation was successful.

To start with, you should have noticed if anything went wrong during the installation because an error message would have been raised, and the setup program would probably have aborted. If not, the installation program finished successfully.

Chapter 2: Installing Exchange Server 2010 SP1

Check if you can log on using Outlook Web App, by typing HTTPS://LOCALHOST/OWA into your web browser. When Exchange Server 2010 SP1 is running fine, you should first see a certificate error message. This is normal behavior the first time you log on; it's because, if the Client Access Server is installed, a self-signed certificate comes along with it. This security certificate is not issued by a trusted certificate authority, hence the error, but in this case it is safe to continue. A logon page should be presented and, after entering the Administrator's credentials you should have access to the Administrator's mailbox as shown in Figure 2.14.

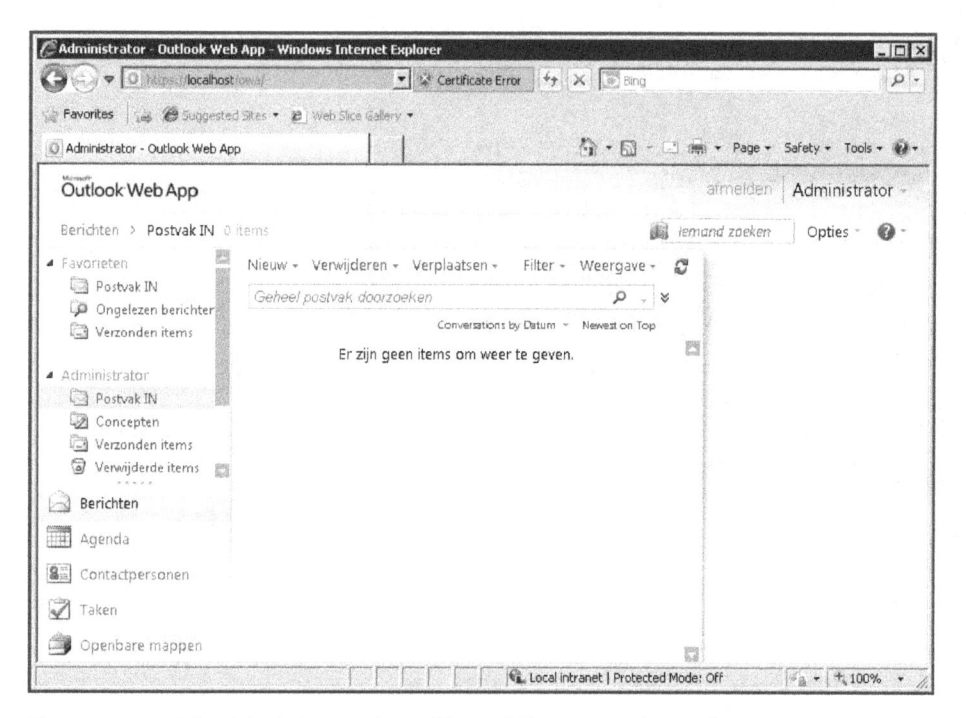

Figure 2.14: The Administrator's mailbox while testing the Exchange Server 2010 SP1 installation. Please note that this OWA is in Dutch, and in this way we know that the language pack was applied successfully.

You can also check the Services MMC snap-in on the newly installed Exchange Server. It should contain all Exchange services as shown in Figure 2.15.

Chapter 2: Installing Exchange Server 2010 SP1

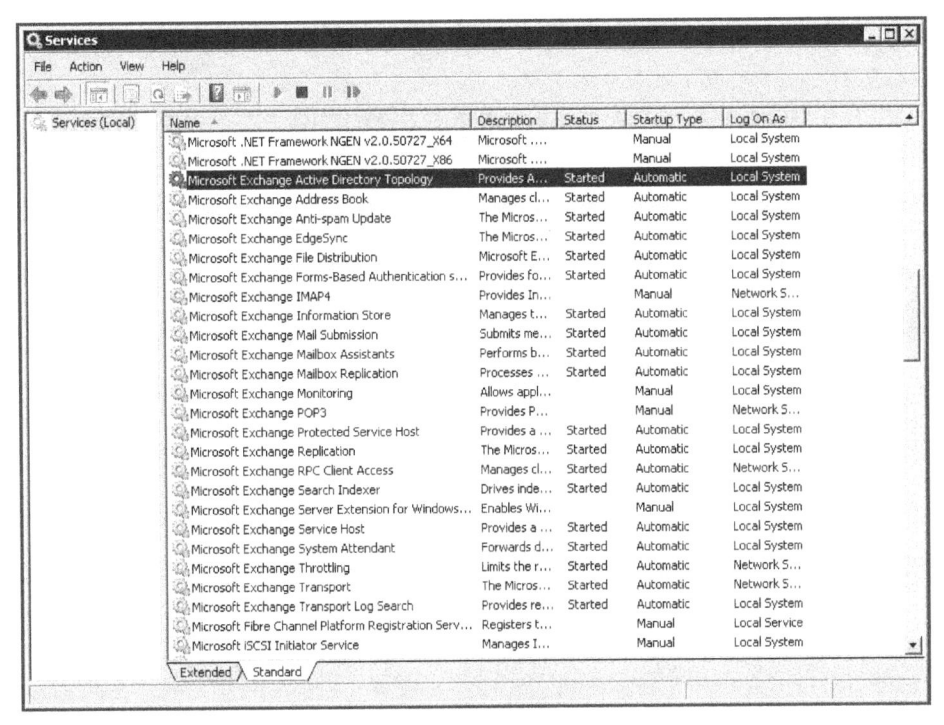

Figure 2.15: Services installed on the Exchange Server during installation of a typical server.

Another step in troubleshooting is to check the event log of the Exchange Server, and this should not give any indications that something went wrong during the installation.

The last resort of troubleshooting a failed Exchange Server 2010 installation is the log files, located in the `C:\ExchangeSetupLogs` directory. I have to warn you, these are hard to read for the typical SysAdmin. But they are more or less meant to be sent to Microsoft when a call is logged about a failed installation.

2.6 Installing dedicated Server Roles

For scalability and availability reasons it can be useful to separate the various Exchange Server 2010 SP1 Server Roles onto different machines, giving you dedicated Mailbox Servers, Hub Transport Servers, Client Access Servers and Unified Messaging Servers. I'll cover the benefits of this kind of setup later in the book.

The prerequisites for a dedicated Exchange Server 2010 SP1 installation are exactly the same as for a typical installation with multiple roles installed on one server. Just make sure you follow the guidelines from Section 2.2 to install the proper parts of Internet Information Server for the Server Role you want.

When installing a dedicated Exchange Server 2010 SP1 Mailbox Server Role, start the `setup.exe` application from the installation media. When reaching the **Installation Type** window, you should now select the **Custom Exchange Server Installation**. At this stage, you'll be able to select the Server Role you want (such as, for example the **Mailbox Role** as can be seen in Figure 2.16).

It is also possible to install a dedicated Server Role using the command-line setup. When entering the setup command, just use the appropriate switch to enter the roles you want to install. For example, if you want to install the Mailbox Server Role using the command-line setup, enter the following command: `Setup.com /mode:install /Roles:mb /EnableLegacyOutlook`.

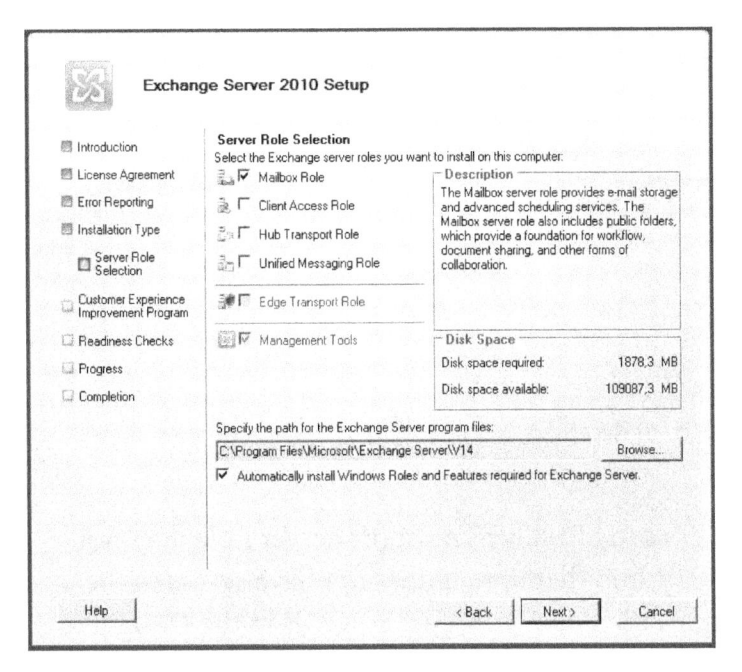

Figure 2.16: Installing a dedicated Exchange Server 2010 SP1 Mailbox Server Role.

2.7 Installing the Edge Transport Server

In order to offer Exchange services, the Edge Transport Server has a local copy of the most significant information of the company's Active Directory. This is stored in a Lightweight Directory Services database, which was formerly known as **Active Directory Application Mode** or ADAM. This database only stores a subset of the Active Directory information, and only informational items like recipients that exist in the internal Exchange organization. No information is stored that can compromise the company's Active Directory security.

Note

The Edge Transport Server should not be a member of the forest that holds the Exchange organization.

Chapter 2: Installing Exchange Server 2010 SP1

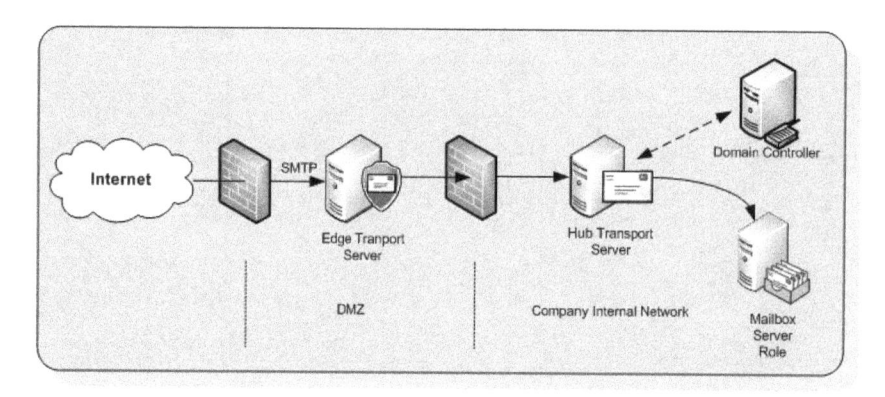

Figure 2.17: The Edge Transport Server located in the DMZ.

Being in the DMZ, the Exchange Server 2010 SP1 Edge Transport Server Role does not have full access to the corporate network, and therefore it does not have access to the corporate Domain Controllers; and since the Edge Transport Server is in the DMZ, it cannot use the company's internal DNS servers, and so needs to use external DNS servers instead. The Edge Transport Server must always be able to resolve external SMTP hosts for delivering messages; hence the external DNS server entries.

As part of its role, the Edge Transport Server also needs to deliver SMTP messages to the internal Hub Transport Server. To resolve these servers, they have to be added to the Edge Transport Server's **HOSTS** file.

Chapter 2: Installing Exchange Server 2010 SP1

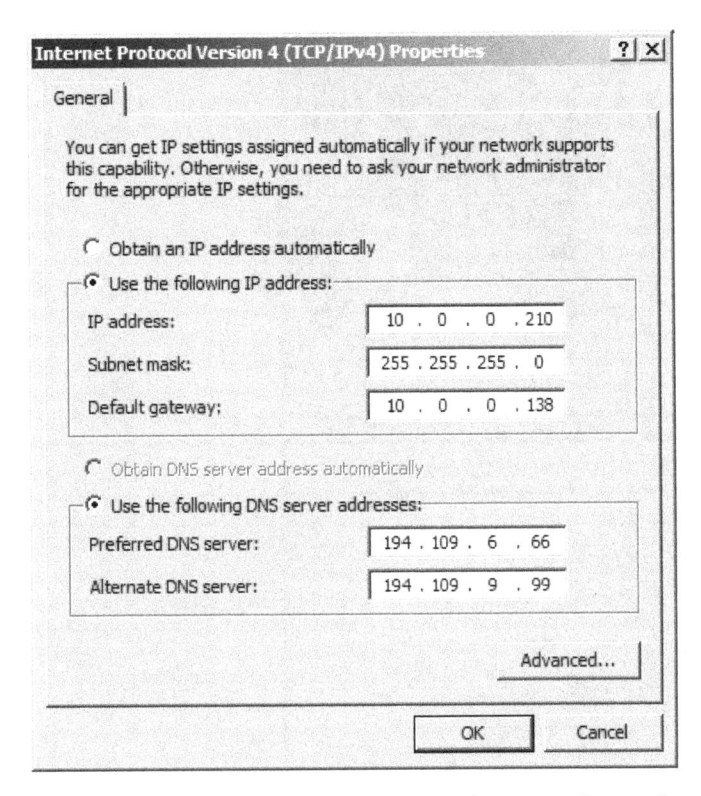

Figure 2.18: External DNS settings on the network interface of the Edge Transport Server.

Being in the DMZ (and therefore *not* a part of the internal domain) the Edge Transport Server's DNS suffix has to be configured manually. To do this, follow the steps below.

- Open the properties of **My Computer** on the Edge Transport Server.
- Select **Computer Name** and click on the **Change** button.
- On the **Computer Name** tab, click the **More** button.
- In the **Primary DNS Suffix for this computer** field, enter your external DNS Suffix.
- Click **OK** and reboot your computer.

Chapter 2: Installing Exchange Server 2010 SP1

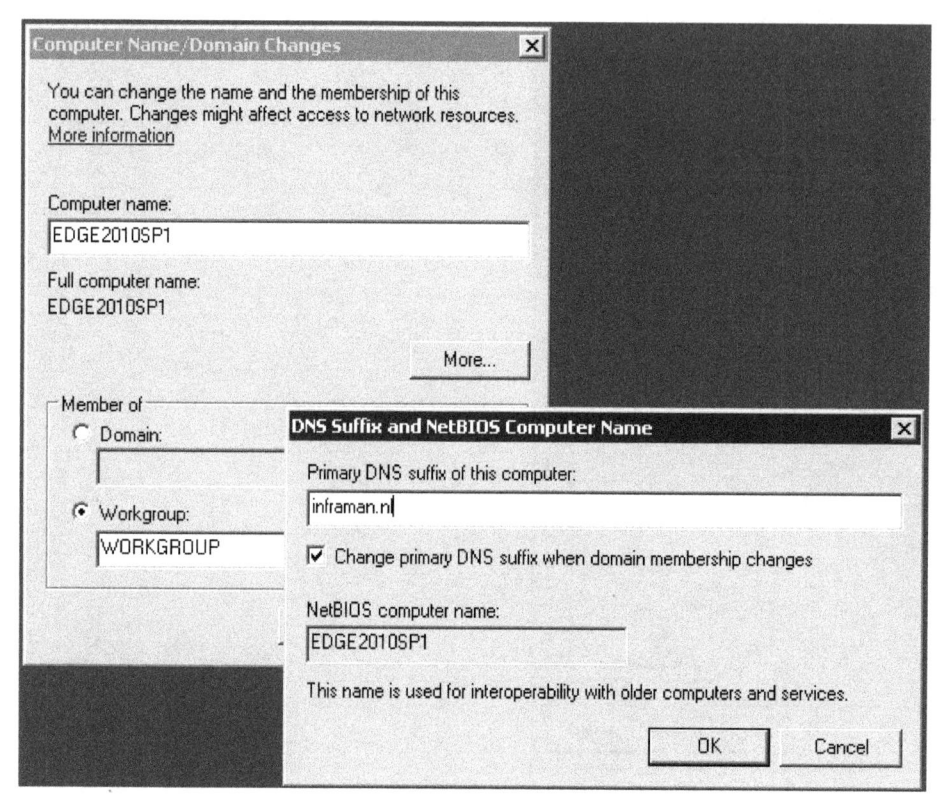

Figure 2.19: Setting the DNS suffix on an Edge Transport Server.

As can be derived from Table 2.1, the Exchange Server 2010 SP1 Edge Transport Server Role has the following prerequisites:

- Windows Server 2008 SP2 x64 or Windows Server 2008 R2
- .NET Framework 3.5 SP1
- PowerShell 2.0
- Active Directory Lightweight Directory Services.

2.7.1 Installing Active Directory Lightweight Directory Services

The Active Directory Lightweight Directory Services (AD LDS), previously known as Active Directory Application Mode or ADAM, can be installed using the Windows Server 2008 Server Manager. To install the AD LDS follow the steps below.

- Log on to the server, click the **Start** button and select the **Server Manager**.
- In the **Server Manager**, click **Roles** and in the **Action** pane click **Add Roles**.
- Click **Next** on the **Before you begin** page.
- On the **Select Server Role** page, select the **Active Directory Lightweight Directory Services** and click **Next**.
- On the **Introduction** page, click **Next**.
- On the **Confirmation** page, click **Install**.
- On the **Installation Results** page, click **Finish**.

The Active Directory Lightweight Directory Services Role is now installed and the server is ready for the Edge Transport Server Role.

2.7.2 Installing the Edge Transport Server Role

When all the prerequisite software for the Exchange Server 2010 Edge Transport Server Role is installed, you can move on to the Exchange Server itself.

- Log on to the server with local administrator credentials, go to the installation media and start the `setup.exe` installation program.

Chapter 2: Installing Exchange Server 2010 SP1

- Once all prerequisite software is installed correctly, the first two options are grayed out.

- Select the language you want to use. It is possible to download the Language Pack Bundle or use an earlier download of this file.

- After the language selection, select **Install Microsoft Exchange**.

- On the **Introduction** page click **Next**.

- Accept the License Agreement and click **Next**.

- Select whether you want to participate in the **Error Reporting Feature** and click **Next**.

- On the **Installation Type** page select **Custom Installation**. If you haven't installed the prerequisite software, you can check the **Automatically install Windows Roles and Features required for Exchange Server** option and, if needed, you can select another directory where the Exchange software is installed. Click **Next** to continue.

- On the **Server Role Selection** page, select the Edge Transport Server Role. Notice that when you select this role the other roles (Mailbox, Client Access, etc.) are grayed out immediately. Click **Next** to continue.

- The setup program will now perform a Readiness Check to see if your server is capable of running the Edge Transport Server Role. When successfully completed, click **Install** to continue.

- The Exchange binaries will now be copied to the local disk, the Management Tools will be installed and the Edge Transport Server will be installed. This can take quite some time to finish.

- When finished you can continue configuring the Edge Transport Server using the Exchange Management Console.

The Edge Transport Server is now installed, but not yet configured. It is possible to configure everything, like the Accepted Domains and the Send Connectors, manually using the Exchange Management Console. An easier way is to use a synchronization process which synchronizes information from the Hub Transport Server within the company's Active Directory and Exchange organization with the Edge Transport Server in the DMZ. This process is called Edge Transport Synchronization, or **EdgeSync**.

2.7.3 Configuring Edge Transport Synchronization

As I mentioned, the Exchange Server 2010 SP1 Edge Transport Server is not part of the internal Active Directory and Exchange organization, and is typically installed in the network's DMZ. A mechanism obviously needs to be in place for keeping the server up to date with information.

For example, for the recipient filtering in the Edge Transport Server to take place, the server needs to know which recipients exist in the internal Exchange environment. The Edge Transport Server also needs to have knowledge about the existing Hub Transport Server in the internal Exchange organization, where the Edge Transport Server has to deliver its SMTP messages.

This information is pushed from an internal Hub Transport Server to the Edge Transport Server by the EdgeSync process mentioned earlier. Please note that, for a successful synchronization from the Hub Transport Server to the Edge Transport Server, you have to open Port 50636 on the internal firewall. This port has to be opened from the internal network to the Edge Transport Servers in the DMZ and *not* vice versa.

Chapter 2: Installing Exchange Server 2010 SP1

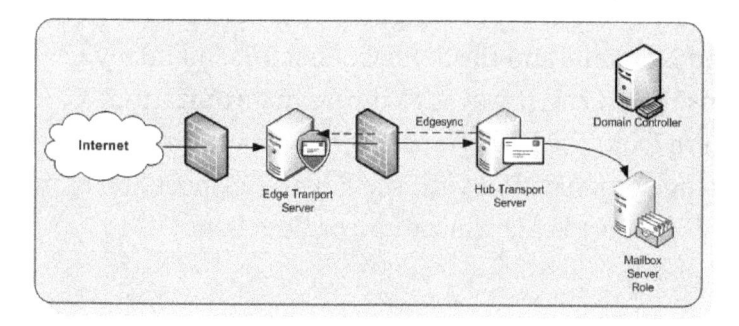

Figure 2.20: The Edge Transport Server in the DMZ is kept up to date via the EdgeSync process.

To set up an Edge Synchronization, a special XML file has to be created on the Edge Transport Server. This XML file has to be imported to a Hub Transport Server on the internal network creating a relationship between the Edge Transport Server and the respective Hub Transport Server. Once that relationship is created, the EdgeSync service can be started. To set up the EdgeSync service, follow the steps below.

1. Log on to the Edge Transport Server using an administrator account and open an **Exchange Management Shell**.

2. Enter the following command `New-EdgeSubscription –Filename <<filename.xml>>`.

3. You'll get a confirmation message. Note that the XML file that will be created is only valid for 1,440 minutes (i.e. 24 hours). If you don't process the XML file within this time, you will have to create a new XML file. Click **Y** to continue.

4. Copy the `<<filename.xml>>` to a directory on the Hub Transport Server.

5. Log on to the Hub Transport Server using an administrator account and open an **Exchange Management Shell** command prompt.

6. Enter the following command: `New-EdgeSubscription -FileData ([byte[]]$(Get-Content -Path "filename.xml" -Encoding Byte -ReadCount 0)) -Site "Default-First-Site-Name"`.

7. When successfully finished on the Exchange Management Shell command prompt, enter the following command `Start-EdgeSynchronization`.

8. The Edge Synchronization process should now successfully start. If you get a `Could-NotConnect` error message, make sure that the Hub Transport Server is able to resolve the Edge Transport Server.

9. On the Edge Transport Server, open the **Exchange Management Shell** and check if the settings are identical to the settings on the Hub Transport Server.

When making changes to the internal Exchange organization, these changes will automatically replicate to the Edge Transport Server in the DMZ.

2.8 Post-setup configuration

When the installations of both the internal Exchange organization and the Edge Transport Server are finished, the post-setup configuration can be started. As in Exchange Server 2007, there are a few additions and changes in the configuration that have to be made to the Exchange Server 2010 SP1 instance before mail can be sent or received from the Internet.

- Enter an Exchange Server 2010 SP1 license key.
- Enter Accepted Domains and set up email address policies.
- Configure a Send Connector to send email to the Internet.
- Configure the Hub Transport Server to accept anonymous SMTP if an Edge Transport Server is not used.
- Add a Certificate to the Client Access Server Role.
- Configure the Client Access Server Role.

2.8.1 Exchange Server 2010 SP1 license key

After successfully installing Exchange Server 2010 SP1, you can enter the license key.

- Log on to the Exchange Server and open the **Exchange Management Console**.
- In the Navigation pane, expand **Microsoft Exchange On-Premises**.
- In the Navigation pane, select **Server Configuration** and, in the Results pane, select your just-installed Exchange server.
- In the Actions pane, click on **Enter Product Key** and, in the resulting window, enter your Product Key. Depending on the Server Roles you installed, you may have to restart several Exchange services, but I normally find it easier to just reboot the Exchange Server.

2.8.2 Accepted Domains

The first thing for Exchange Server 2010 SP1 to configure is the Accepted Domains. In order to receive SMTP messages from the Internet, an Exchange Server has to know what domains it will be receiving email *for*, as well as which domains it is responsible for. These are called "Accepted Domains," and there are three types.

1. **Authoritative Domain** – for this type of domain, the Exchange organization is fully responsible and there will be no other messaging environment responsible. This Exchange organization will also generate NDR (Non Delivery Report) messages when mailboxes are not available.
2. **Internal Relay Domain** – the Exchange organization will receive mail for this type of domain, but it will relay all messages to an Exchange organization within the company.

3. **External Relay Domain** – and for this type of domain, the Exchange organization will receive mail, but it will relay all messages to a messaging platform outside the company.

For all three scenarios the MX records for the domain will be pointing to your Exchange organization, and mail will be initially delivered to your Exchange Servers.

Accepted domains are configured on the organization level and, as such, are known by all Hub Transport Servers. If you are using an Edge Transport Server as well, the Accepted Domain information will also be synchronized to the Edge Transport Servers.

To configure Accepted Domains follow the steps below.

- Log on to an Exchange Server 2010 SP1 server with domain administrator credentials and open the **Exchange Management Console**.
- Expand the **Microsoft Exchange On-Premises**.
- Expand the **Organization Configuration**.
- Click on **Hub Transport** in the left-hand pane.
- In the middle pane there are eight tabs; click on the **Accepted Domains** tab.
- One entry will appear, and the name will be the local domain (FQDN) that's used when installing the Active Directory. In the Actions pane click on **New Accepted Domain**.
- In the **New Accepted Domain Wizard**, enter a (friendly) name and the Accepted Domain itself, for example *yourdomain.com*. When entered, select the type of **Accepted Domain** in your **Exchange organization**. In this example, select the **Authoritative Domain**, and then click **New** to continue.
- The Accepted Domain will now be created, and you can now click **Finish** in the **Completion** window.

You have just created an Accepted Domain in your Exchange organization; the Exchange Server will accept messages for this domain and, if no recipients are found, an NDR (Non Delivery Report) will be generated.

2.8.3 Email Address Policies

Exchange recipients clearly need an email address for receiving email. For receiving email from the Internet, recipients need an email address that corresponds to an Accepted Domain. Recipients are either assigned an email address using an Email Address Policy, or it is also possible to manually assign email addresses to recipients.

To configure email address policies follow the steps below.

- Log on to an Exchange Server 2010 SP1 server with domain administrator credentials and open the **Exchange Management Console**.
- Expand the **Microsoft Exchange On-Premises**.
- Expand the **Organization Configuration**.
- Click on **Hub Transport** in the left-hand pane.
- In the middle pane there are eight tabs; click on the one labeled **Email Address Policies**.
- There will be one default policy that will be applied to all recipients in your organization. For now, the default policy will be changed so that recipients will have the email address corresponding to your Accepted Domain. Click on **New Email Address policy** to create a new policy.
- On the **Introduction** page, enter a new Friendly Name. Click the **Browse** button to select a container or Organizational Unit in Active Directory where you want to apply the filter. Select the **Users** container. Click **Next** to continue.

- On the **Conditions** page you can select conditions on how the recipients in the container will be queried; for example, on State, Province, Department, Company, etc. Do not select anything for this demonstration, but just click **Next** to continue.

- On the **Email Addresses** tab, click the **Add** button, and the **SMTP Email Address** pop-up will be shown. Leave the local part as default (**Use Alias**), select the **Select the Accepted Domain for the email address** option, and click **Browse**.

- Select the **Accepted Domain** you entered earlier (in Section 2.8.2), click **OK** twice, and then click **Next** to continue.

- On the **Schedule** page, you have the option to apply the policy immediately or schedule it to apply during, for example, non-office hours. This is useful when you have to change thousands of recipients. For now, leave it on **Immediately** and click **Next** to continue.

- Review the settings and, if everything is OK, click **New** to create the policy and apply it immediately.

- When finished successfully, click the **Finish** button.

You can check the email address on a recipient through the EMC to confirm your policy has been correctly applied.

- Expand the **Recipient Configuration** in the left pane of the **Exchange Management Console** and click on **Mailbox**.

- In the middle pane, a list of recipients should show up, although right after installation only an administrator mailbox should be visible.

- Double-click on the administrator mailbox and select the **Email Addresses** tab. *Administrator@yourdomain.com* should be the primary SMTP address.

2.8.4 Configure a Send Connector to the Internet

Exchange Server 2010 SP1 cannot send out SMTP messages to the Internet by default. To achieve this you'll need to create an SMTP connector, which is a connector between one or more Hub Transport Server and the Internet. Since this information is stored in Active Directory, all Hub Transport Servers in the organization know of its existence and know how to route messages via the SMTP connector to the Internet.

To create an SMTP connector to the Internet, follow the steps below.

- Log on to the Exchange Server 2010 SP1 server using a domain administrator account, and open the **Exchange Management Console**.

- Expand **Microsoft Exchange On-Premises** and then expand the **Organization Configuration**.

- Click on **Hub Transport**, and then click on the **Send Connectors** tab in the middle pane.

- In the **Actions Pane**, click on **New Send Connector**.

- On the **Introduction** page, enter a Friendly Name, "Internet Connector" for example, and in the **Select the intended use for this Send Connector** drop-down box, select the **Internet** option. Click **Next** to continue.

- On the **Address Space** page, click on the **Add** button to add an address space for the Internet Connector. In the address field, enter an asterisk, leave the cost on default, and click **OK**. Click **Next** to continue.

- On the **Network Settings** page you can select if the Send Connector will use its own network DNS settings to route email to other organizations, or to use a smart host. Change this according to your own environment, and click **Next** to continue.

- On the **Source Server** page you can choose multiple source servers for the Send Connector. You can compare this to Bridgehead Servers in Exchange Server 2003. When you enter multiple Hub Transport Servers, the Exchange organization will automatically load balance the SMTP traffic between the Hub Transport Servers. Since we have only one Hub Transport Server installed, we can leave this as default. Click **Next** to continue.

- Check the **Configuration Summary** and, if everything is OK, click on **New** to create the Send Connector.

- On the Completion page, just click **Finish**.

You have now created a Send Connector that routes messages from the internal Exchange Server 2010 SP1 organization to the Internet.

2.8.5 Add a Certificate to the Client Access Server Role

When the Exchange Server 2010 SP1 Client Access Server Role is installed, a self-signed certificate is installed automatically, primarily for testing purposes. However, as soon as the installation is finished, a real certificate should be acquired and installed. Exchange Server 2010 SP1 uses a Unified Messaging certificate which, besides its Subject Name holds other names as well, called the **Subject Alternative Names** (**SAN**). For example, the Subject Name could be `webmail.yourdomain.com` and Subject Alternative Names could be `autodiscover.yourdomain.com` and `mail.yourdomain.com`.

To request a certificate you can either use the Exchange Management Console or the Exchange Management Shell. When using the Exchange Management Console (after all, we are Windows administrators, right?) use the following steps.

- Log on to the Exchange Server 2010 SP1 Client Access Server and open the **Exchange Management Console**.

- In the **Navigation** pane, expand **Microsoft Exchange On-Premises**, and then click on **Server Configuration**.

- In the top half of the middle pane, you'll see your Exchange Servers, including your Edge Transport Server, and in the bottom half you'll see the corresponding certificate. This is the self-signed certificate that's created during the installation of your Exchange Server.

- In the **Actions** pane click on **New Exchange Certificate**, and the **New Exchange Certificate** wizard is shown. Enter a Friendly Name, for example "Exchange Server," and click **Next** to continue.

- With Exchange Server 2010 you have the option to enable a wildcard certificate, and this is fully supported by Microsoft. For this chapter, a wildcard certificate is not used, so this option is left blank.

- The next page is the **Exchange Configuration**, where you can determine the usage of the certificate. Select the following services:

  - Client Access Server (Outlook Web App)
  - Client Access Server (Exchange ActiveSync)
  - Client Access Server (Web Services, Outlook Anywhere and Autodiscover).

- In all three options, enter the external hostname for your organization. In the last option, also select **Autodiscover used on the Internet** and select the proper URL. The default is the long URL, like `autodiscover.yourdomain.com`. Click **Next** to continue.

- In the **Organization and Location** page you have to enter your company-specific details, like Organization, Organizational Unit, Country, and so on. In the **Certificate Request File Path** click **Browse** to enter a location for the Certificate Request File. Enter a filename like `C:\Exch-Cert.req` and click **Save**. If you request a certificate with a third-party vendor, make sure that the information entered here is the same as the information registered in the WHOIS records. The vendor will check this information and, if there's a mismatch, they will contact you for additional information. Click **Next** to continue.

- On the **Certificate Configuration** page check your certificate request details and, if all is OK, click **New** to generate the request file.

- On the **Completion** page you'll see the PowerShell command that was used for generating this certificate request. If needed you can use **CTRL+C** to copy the contents of this page to the server's clipboard. Click **Finish** to continue.

You can find the file `C:\Exch-Cert.req` on your server, and it should look something like this:

```
-----BEGIN NEW CERTIFICATE REQUEST-----
MIIEPzCCAycCAQAwfjEcMBoGA1UEAwwTd2VibWFpbC5pbmZyYW1hbi5ubDEMMAoG
A1UECwwDUk5EMSIwIAYDVQQKDBlXZXNzWxpdXMgQmVoZWVyIEdyb2VwIGJ2MRIw
EAYDVQQHDAlFTU1FTE9PUkQxCzAJBgNVBAgMAkZMMQswCQYDVQQGEwJOTDCCASIw
DQYJKoZIhvcNAQEBBQADggEPADCCAQoCggEBAJ3nH2tgA3U8vpX+jioMmcxcIHye
6EYt4trSWqtnenKHMlQsJJzq30plAMeiBsRWtb+mD59esi+NorY711c3rgvpIoQ0
cobG8UUQzkOpm1FMpx3kCrQ1J/ZGke/9RdW2XyRSaalGqLDo1QtBJ73Mrm2hOvtU
KvD2hbgEb0JazlSyTjwtQy8bkfddkbLm932DwHfw89tLwpS5jhmTKE1T4CwzmWow
GtBAae+j71pHcfnb7OYwp0tAxRUQNzCV3AxUKePjj+z/Aph6MHlrWNuDpNJ16woi
zXx9zTXvfDJlzk89nZ1JH0amMYBHPjeTyaOcuPCC9gk0Wq3v29/8v5XR55sCAwEA
AaCCAXowGgYKKwYBBAGCNw0CAzEMFgo2LjAuNjAwMi4yMF8GCSsGAQQBgjcVFDFS
MFACAQUMFTIwMDhYU1JWUi51MjAxMC5sb2NhbAwQRTIwMTBcMjAwOFhTU1ZSSJAwi
TW1jcm9zb2Z0LkV4Y2hhbmdlLlNlcnZpY2Vib3N0LmV4ZTByBgorBgEEAYI3DQIC
MWQwYgIBAR5aAE0AaQBjAHIAbwBzAG8AZgBgOACAAUgBTAEEAIABTAEMAaABhAG4A
bgBlAGwAIABDAHIAeQBwAHQAbwBnAHIAYQBwAGgAaQBjACAAUABYAG8AdgBpAGQA
ZQByAwEAMIGGBgkqhkiG9w0BCQ4xeTB3MA4GA1UdDwEB/wQEAwIFoDA4BgNVHREE
MTAvghN3ZWJtYWlsLmluZnJhbWFuLm5sghhhdXRvZGlzY292ZXIuaWFuZmcmFtYW4u
bmwwDAYDVR0TAQH/BAIwADAdBgNVHQ4EFgQUZF1UxjwlMO6oecHerppFMwrX9T4w
DQYJKoZIhvcNAQEFBQADggEBAIyguUWHMtPK519krPaC/gDwLdAqj6/KheNlEyqT
iS2pn8QOhpuePtTKCUgpbuGXVtJowQrrGoK3Spbk6BWZhcdhYiq1ieyJFL96ocCZ
rtI5I8n8o8X99XunsRQkHBeqEVhP0Ih5DjUYdhk5BUJBpXYW51ArxYwvp8sW918q
Xj9JRROalISbBTQufalO3sg2FGozdkgFodLjZKsgi1MaxLkeBCAoNss5Y2BQPJ5i
p6sEqMhxI5Z/VYPkvUToxEwg9NzqP6x/UabAMKFIfKNHzNn59O7sOjk8v9QBNAeM
LljEr6KjACOYE83Ey+30fowze0ST1d7SZDoUw8fqnZsxKM0=
-----END NEW CERTIFICATE REQUEST-----
```

To request a new certificate, you have to submit this file to your certificate authority. This can be any vendor that supports Unified Communications certificates.

Chapter 2: Installing Exchange Server 2010 SP1

On the **Exchange Certificates** tab in the **Exchange Management Console**, you'll see a new entry, and the parameters you entered in the previous step can be identified here.

When you receive the certificate from your authority follow the steps below.

- Save the certificate on the hard disk of your server.
- In the **Exchange Management Console**, on the **Exchange Certificates** tab, right-click the new certificate and select **Complete Pending Request**.
- Browse to the file you stored on the hard disk in the first step.
- Follow the wizard to complete the certificate request and finish the installation.
- In the **Exchange Management Console**, on the **Exchange Certificates** tab, select the original self-signed certificate, right-click on it, and select **Remove** to remove this certificate from the Exchange Server 2010 SP1 server.
- Using Internet Explorer, open Outlook Web App (using HTTPS://LOCALHOST/OWA) and check the new certificate. Never mind the error message you will receive; this is just because the name `localhost` is not in the certificate.

You can also use the Exchange Management Shell to request a new certificate:

- log on to the Exchange Server 2010 SP1 server with domain administrator credentials and open the **Exchange Management Shell**
- Since the –Path option is no longer supported in Exchange Server 2010 SP1, you first have to use a variable and you even have to write the actual file below:

```
$CertData = New-ExchangeCertificate -FriendlyName 'Exchange Server'
-GenerateRequest -PrivateKeyExportable:$TRUE -DomainName:webmail.inframan.
nl,autodiscover.inframan.nl -SubjectName "C=NL,S=FL,L=Emmeloord,O=Wesselius Beheer
Groep,OU=RND, CN=webmail.inframan.nl"

Set-Content -Path c:\cert-req.txt -Value $CertData
```

This command will generate a Certificate Request File identical to the request you created in the GUI, which can be submitted at your own certificate authority.

A certificate will be sent by your certificate authority that can be imported on the Client Access Server by using the `Import-ExchangeCertificate` commandlet in the Exchange Management Shell. The output of this commandlet can be piped into the `Enable-ExchangeCertificate` to enable the certificate after importing it.

- Log on to the Exchange Server 2010 SP1 server with domain administrator credentials and open the **Exchange Management Shell**
- Enter the following command:

```
Import-ExchangeCertificate -FileData ($(Get-Content -Path c:\cert-new.cer -Encoding byte)) | Enable-ExchangeCertificate -Services POP,IMAP,IIS,SMTP
```

2.8.6 Configure the Client Access Server Role

The Client Access Server Role is responsible for handling all client requests with respect to mailbox access. This means that Outlook Web App, POP3 and IMAP4, Outlook Anywhere and ActiveSync all have to be configured on the Client Access Server Role. New in Exchange Server 2010 SP1 is the fact that the Client Access Server now also handles all MAPI requests. So Outlook clients no longer connect to the Mailbox Server Role directory, but rather to the Client Access Server. This functionality is called **RPC Client Access**.

In this section I will briefly focus on Outlook Web App, Outlook Anywhere and ActiveSync. A prerequisite for proper functioning of these services is that a valid Unified Communications certificate from a trusted vendor, with proper Subject Alternative Names is installed, as described in Section 2.8.5.

> **Note**
>
> *The configuration steps mentioned below are already defined when you've entered the Client Access Server external domain, as outlined in Section 2.3 (Figure 2.7).*

- Log on to the Exchange Server 2010 SP1 server with domain administrator credentials and open the **Exchange Management Console**.
- In the Navigation pane expand **Microsoft Exchange On-Premises**, and then expand **Server Configuration**.
- Click on **Client Access**.
- In the lower part of the Results pane, you can select the tabs for **Outlook Web App**, **Exchange ActiveSync**, **Offline Address Book Distribution** and **POP3** and **IMAP4**. From here, you can now configure the various aspects of the Client Access Server.

2.8.6.1 Outlook Web App

- To configure Outlook Web App select the **Outlook Web App** tab, right-click on **OWA (Default Website)** and select its properties.
- In the **External URL** field, enter the URL that users will use when connecting to the OWA site from the Internet. Make sure that this name corresponds to the name used in the certificate you installed in the previous section.
- Click **OK** to close the Properties page.

2.8.6.2 Exchange ActiveSync

- On the **Exchange ActiveSync** tab, right-click **Microsoft Server ActiveSync** and select its properties.

Chapter 2: Installing Exchange Server 2010 SP1

- In the **External URL** field, enter the URL that users will use when connecting to the OWA site from the Internet. Make sure that this name corresponds to the name used in the certificate you installed in the previous section.

- Click **OK** to close the Properties page.

Note

Testing your Exchange Server 2010 SP1 ActiveSync setup is always difficult. To avoid needing a real mobile device you can use an emulator for testing purposes. Microsoft has several emulators available on the Microsoft download site, and you can download the Windows Mobile 6.5 emulator from HTTP://TINY.CC/EMULATOR135. *Just install it on your computer or laptop, connect it to your local network adapter and start configuring the device. When you have the proper connectivity you can even test it from home; this works great!*

Figure 2.21: Windows Mobile 6.5 working with an Exchange Server 2010 SP1.

2.8.6.3 Outlook Anywhere

Outlook Anywhere uses the HTTP protocol to encapsulate RPC information for sending between the Outlook client (version 2003 and 2007) and the Exchange Server 2010 SP1 server. For this service to run properly, the RPC over HTTP Proxy service has to be installed on the Client Access Server. This can be achieved either by adding this as a feature via the Server Manager, or by entering the following command on a PowerShell command prompt: `ServerManagerCmd.exe -i RPC-over-HTTP-proxy`.

When the RPC over HTTP Proxy is installed, use the steps below to configure Outlook Anywhere.

- Open the **Exchange Management Console**.

- In the Navigation pane, expand **Microsoft Exchange On-Premises**, and then expand **Server Configuration**.

- Click on **Client Access** and select your Client Access Server.

- In the **Actions** pane, click on **Enable Outlook Anywhere**.

- On the **Enable Outlook Anywhere** page enter the External host name. Make sure that this name is also available in the certificate you created previously. You'll need to select the authentication methods used by clients (i.e. **Basic Authentication** or **NTLM Authentication**), but for now just leave these settings on default and click **Enable** to continue.

- This will activate the Outlook Anywhere service on this service, and it may take up to 15 minutes before the service is actually useable on the Client Access Server. Click **Finish** to close the wizard.

2.9 Upgrading Exchange Server 2010

Starting with Exchange Server 2007, a Service Pack is no longer an add-on to the original product, but is now a complete reinstall of the "original" product; this is still true for Exchange Server 2010 Service Pack 1. When upgrading an existing Exchange Server 2010 server to Exchange Server 2010 Service Pack 1, the original Exchange Server is uninstalled, and this is immediately followed by an installation of Exchange Server 2010 Service Pack 1. Needless to say, all settings of this Exchange Server 2010 server are maintained throughout the upgrade.

Note

It is only possible to do an in-place upgrade of an existing Exchange Server 2010 server. This is not possible with an Exchange Server 2003 or an Exchange Server 2007 server.

When upgrading an existing Exchange Server 2010 installation, you should work from the outside in. So, upgrade the Client Access Server and Hub Transport Server first, followed by the Mailbox Server and the Unified Messaging Server. An Exchange Server 2010 Service Pack 1 Client Access Server and Hub Transport Server will work with an original Exchange Server 2010 Mailbox Server Role, so there's no need to perform a side-by-side installation.

The Edge Transport Server can be upgraded at any time; the Edge Synchronization works fine between Exchange 2010 RTM and Exchange 2010 SP1 and there's no particular best order for it to be upgraded, with regard to the other roles.

- To upgrade your existing Exchange Server 2010 installation, navigate to the installation media and start `setup.exe`.
- The splash screen will appear. Since this is an upgrade, fewer options are available; for example, the prerequisite software is already installed on the Exchange Server.

Chapter 2: Installing Exchange Server 2010 SP1

- When you upgrade the Language Pack Bundle, a new file will be downloaded from the Microsoft website and stored in the directory `C:\ExchangeSetupLogs\ExchangeLanguagePack\`. This Language Pack Bundle file can be copied to a file share on your network for subsequent installations of Exchange Server 2010 Service Pack 1.

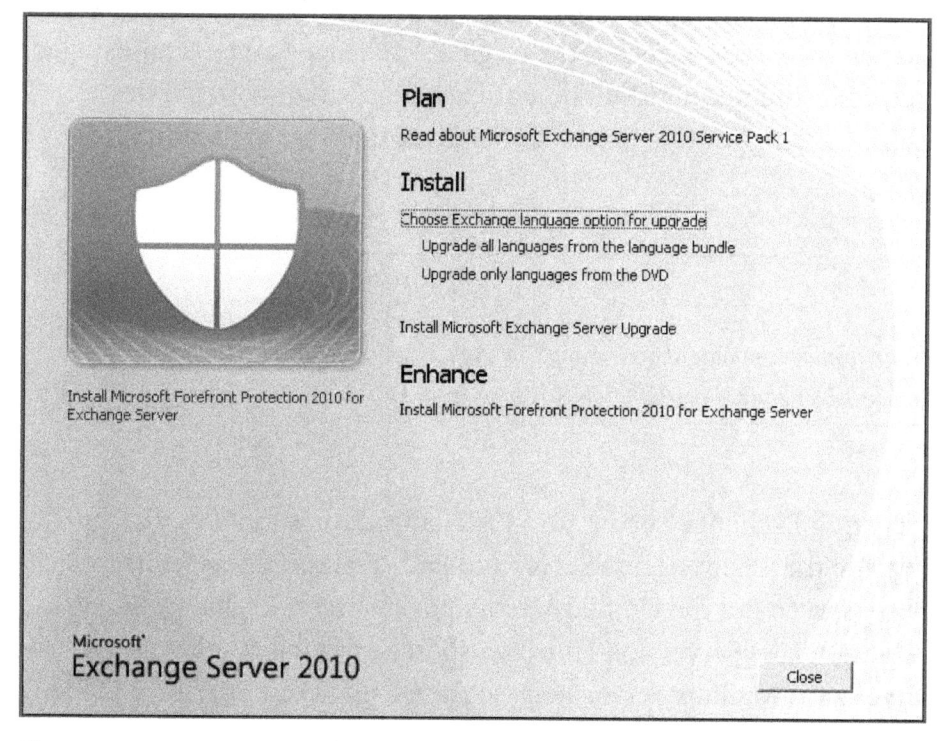

Figure 2.22: Fewer options during an upgrade. The setup program will automatically detect whether to do a fresh install or an upgrade.

- When the Language Pack Bundle is downloaded, continue with the next step, "**Install Microsoft Exchange Server Upgrade.**"

- During the actual upgrade you'll see the original binaries being uninstalled and the new binaries being installed.

Chapter 2: Installing Exchange Server 2010 SP1

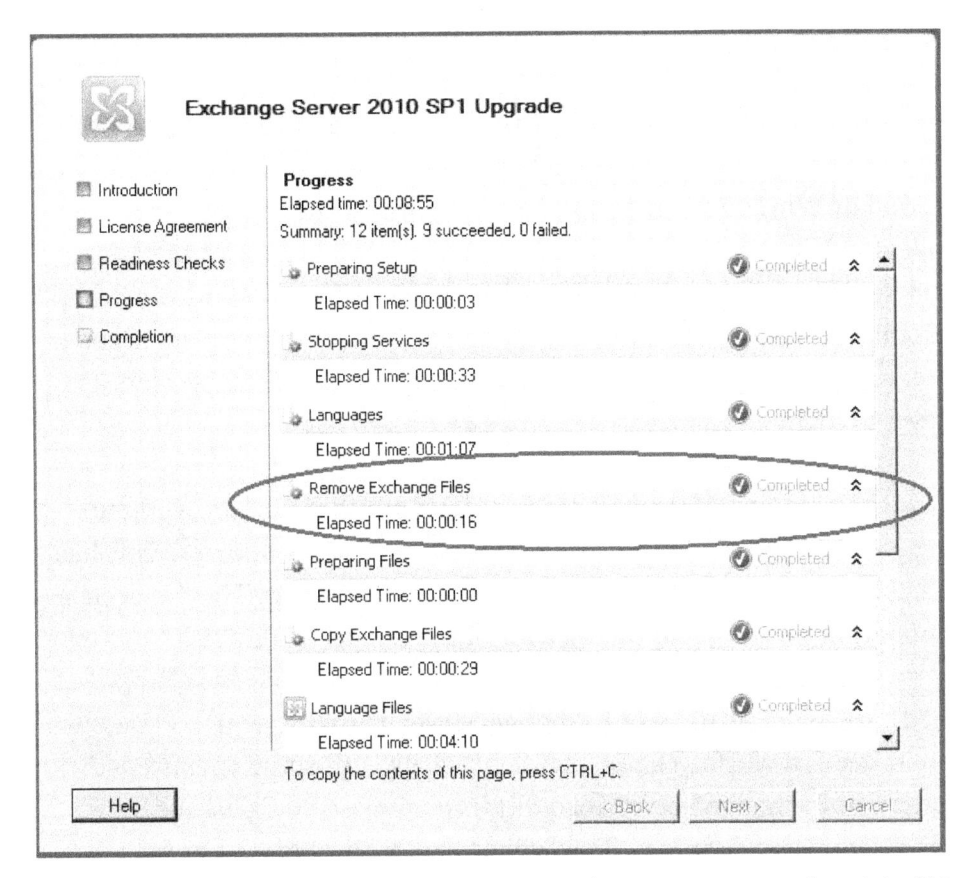

Figure 2.23: The Exchange Server 2010 SP1 Upgrade process removes the original binaries before the new ones are installed.

- When the upgrade has finished, click the **Finish** button to end the setup program and start the Exchange Management Console.

Chapter 2: Installing Exchange Server 2010 SP1

2.9 Summary

Installing Exchange Server 2010 SP1 is really quite easy. There are a number of prerequisites, like the .NET Framework 3.5 and PowerShell Version 2, which should all be running on Windows Server 2008 or Windows Server 2008 R2. Looking at the prerequisites that need to be installed on Windows Server 2008, which are available out of the box in Windows Server 2008 R2, in my humble opinion it's a no-brainer to use Windows Server 2008 R2. Although Exchange Server 2010 SP1 is not supported on Windows Server 2003, the Active Directory can be running on Windows Server 2003, as long as the servers are on a Service Pack 1 level or higher.

Compared to Exchange Server 2007, Microsoft made quite a number of improvements to the Exchange Management Console, especially when it comes to certificates. This has always been a serious pain for most Exchange administrators in the past. They've done a good job of streamlining that process, and taking a lot of the headache out of it.

This chapter described a fresh installation of Exchange Server 2010 SP1, which I guess will not happen too often in the real world. The next chapter deals with some coexistence scenarios, i.e. installation of Exchange Server 2010 SP1 into an existing Exchange Server 2003 or Exchange Server 2007 environment. This will probably be by far the more common situation SysAdmins will find themselves in, although I will be referring back to this chapter when discussing the basic installation steps.

Chapter 3: Exchange Server 2010 SP1 Coexistence

As we've seen, installing Exchange Server 2010 SP1 in a greenfield situation and configuring it correctly isn't that difficult. However, there is a distinct possibility that you already have an Exchange organization deployed, be it Exchange Server 2007 or Exchange Server 2003.

In fact, a large portion of Exchange Server customers in the last few years have decided that they are *not* going to upgrade from their existing Exchange Server 2003 infrastructure to a new Exchange Server 2007 one. A commonly heard reason for this is that 2003 "is good enough." To be fair, if the scalability, Unified Messaging or High Availability options in Exchange Server 2007 don't offer you a solid business case for upgrading, this decision is perfectly understandable.

But with Exchange Server 2010 things changed. Besides all of the new functionality, if you are still running Exchange Server 2003, you'll find that Microsoft will deprecate the support on it. It will not stop immediately, but Microsoft's focus will be on Exchange Server 2010 and Exchange Server 2007. So, if you want to make sure you're fully supported, upgrading to Exchange Server 2010 SP1 can be done in two ways.

- **Integrate Exchange Server 2010 SP1 into your existing Exchange infrastructure and transition your mailboxes to the new Exchange Servers**.
  This method can be done when you are running on Exchange Server 2007 or Exchange Server 2003.
- **Build a new Active Directory and a new Exchange Server 2010 SP1 organization and migrate your mailboxes to the new environment.**
  This is the preferred method if your current environment is not compatible with Exchange Server 2010 SP1.

Chapter 3: Exchange Server 2010 SP1 Coexistence

I've chosen my terminology carefully here, so as to be consistent with other documentation you may encounter. Moving mailboxes from Exchange Server 2003 to Exchange Server 2010 SP1 in one organization is called **transitioning**. If Exchange Server 2010 SP1 is installed in a new Active Directory forest and mailboxes are moved from one Active Directory forest to another, it's called a **migration**.

This chapter will focus on integrating Exchange Server 2010 SP1 into an existing Exchange Server 2003 or Exchange Server 2007 environment (the first method), but bear in mind that Exchange Server 2010 SP1 *cannot* be installed into an existing Exchange Server 2000 environment. This is enforced in the Exchange setup programs, which will check on the current version of all Exchange Servers. If Exchange Server 2000 is detected on *any* server, the setup program will display an error and abort.

Exchange Server 2010 SP1 *does* support the following scenarios:

- single forest, single Active Directory site
- single forest, multiple Active Directory sites
- multiple forest, multiple Active Directory sites
- coexistence with Exchange Server 2003 SP2; older versions of Exchange Server are not supported in an Exchange Server 2010 coexistence scenario
- coexistence with Exchange Server 2007 SP2; older versions of Exchange Server 2007 are not supported in an Exchange Server 2010 coexistence scenario.

Note

When transitioning to Exchange Server 2010 SP1, you must start with the Internet-facing Active Directory site. Other Active Directory sites will be moved later on in the transition process. Starting with internal Active Directory sites is not supported.

The rest of this chapter is split into two sections, each of which will aim to get you running Exchange Server 2010 SP1 in coexistence with the respective older environments. In each section, I'll cover:

- the order in which the different servers should be installed
- Active Directory upgrades and prerequisite considerations
- the actual installation process for Exchange Server 2010 SP1
- the SMTP infrastructure
- moving mailboxes.

You'll notice a certain amount of replication between the two sections (if you read them both), but I've tried to minimize that where possible, by referring to instructions rather than duplicating them. In any case, you should be able to pick the section most relevant to you and find everything you need to get you started.

3.1 Coexistence with Exchange Server 2003

You won't be too surprised to hear that there are a lot of differences between Exchange Server 2003 and Exchange Server 2010 SP1. The most important are listed below.

- Exchange Server 2010 is available only in a 64-bit version.
- Exchange Server 2010 does not use Administrative Groups for delegation of control.
- Exchange Server 2010 does not use Routing Groups for routing messages.
- Exchange Server 2010 does not use Link State Routing for updating the Routing Table.
- Exchange Server 2010 does not use the Recipient Update Service for setting Exchange properties on recipient objects.

This is a much more extensive list than the differences with Exchange Server 2007, and the differences themselves are also more significant. Just to make sure everyone is on the same proverbial page as I go through this, I'll lay down a little background information on each of these legacy systems (e.g. Administrative Groups) before I explain what's changed.

3.1.1 64-bit support

Exchange Server 2010 SP1 is only available in a 64-bit version, as the Exchange Product Group at Microsoft is taking full advantage of the hardware advances since Exchange Server 2007 was released. The old 32-bit (X86) platform was developed in the mid-eighties, and has a 4 GB memory limit. In those days, 4 GB of memory was beyond everyone's imagination; today, 4 GB of memory is commonly installed in a laptop.

As the successor of the 32-bit platform, one of the clear advantages of 64-bit is a theoretical memory limit of 2^{64} bytes, or 16 PB (Petabytes). Windows obviously cannot *address* this amount of memory at this time, but the current memory limit of Windows Server 2008 R2 Enterprise is 2 TB (Terabytes). Naturally, current processors just cannot address anything like that much physical memory, but Moore's law and the inexorable march of technological progress mean that this limit will keep being pushed back in the future.

Whilst 4 GB of memory might be enough for a laptop or workstation, for large server applications like Exchange Server, a mere 4 GB of memory is a huge limitation. This fact can be clearly illustrated in Exchange Server 2003, when having more than 2,000 mailboxes on one Exchange Server will result in a severe disk I/O penalty, which typically results in an expensive storage solution.

There are special techniques for addressing more than 4 GB of memory on the 32-bit platform, like Physical Address Extensions (PAE), which you can read more about at HTTP://SUPPORT.MICROSOFT.COM/KB/291988.

However, Exchange Server 2003 does not use this technique, and so is stuck with the 4 GB memory limit (and you can read more about *that* at HTTP://SUPPORT.MICROSOFT.COM/KB/823440). Given that Exchange Server 2010 SP1 is 64-bit-only, this automatically implies that an in-place upgrade of Exchange Server 2003 server to Exchange Server 2010 SP1 is impossible. *A new Exchange Server 2010 SP1 server in a 2003 environment always needs to be installed on separate hardware.* You should also bear in mind that the same is true for Exchange Server 2007; although it is also a 64-bit application, Microsoft does not support an in-place upgrade due to technical complexity in both products.

3.1.2 Administrative Groups are no longer used for delegation of control

Exchange Server 2003 uses Administrative Groups for delegation of control, allowing you to create multiple Administrative Groups and delegate control of them to different administrators. For example, a large multinational company could create multiple Administrative Groups, one for each country, and each country could have its own Exchange administration department, responsible for maintaining their local Exchange Servers. This could be achieved by delegating control of the appropriate Administrative Group to specific Universal Security Groups, which these Exchange administrators are, in turn, assigned to. This sounds pretty complicated and, after seeing such a scenario in real life, I can assure you that it *is* complicated. And besides being complicated, it is prone to error and I've seen it bring a world-wide deployment to its knees. It's a good thing Microsoft is not continuing this path!

Exchange Server 2010 SP1 no longer uses Administrative Groups. During installation of the *first* Exchange Server 2010 SP1 server, a new Administrative Group will be created in Active Directory, called **Exchange Administrative Group (FYDIBOHF23SPDLT)**. All subsequent servers will be installed in this Administrative Group. Delegation of control in Exchange Server 2010 SP1 is achieved by implementing a Role Based Access Control (RBAC) model. This won't really affect the installation process, so I will explain the RBAC model in more detail in *Chapter 4*.

3.1.3 Routing Groups are no longer used for routing messages

For routing messages between different locations, Exchange Server 2003 uses a concept called Routing Groups. A Routing Group can be identified as a location with a high bandwidth and low latency network, such as an office with a 100 Mbps internal network where all Exchange Server 2003 servers have full access to each other all the time. When multiple locations are present, each has their own Routing Group, and each Routing Group is connected with each other using "slow links." These Routing Groups in an Exchange organization are connected using Routing Group Connectors, and so Routing Groups are very similar to sites in Active Directory. Active Directory sites already exist since Windows 2000 Active Directory, but Exchange Server 2003 just didn't use them and relied on their own mechanism. And to be honest, this really didn't make sense.

Instead of Routing Groups, Exchange Server 2010 SP1 now uses Active Directory sites to route messages to Exchange Servers in other locations. To connect Exchange Server 2010 SP1 with an Exchange Server 2003 environment in the same Active Directory forest (and thus the same Exchange organization), a special Routing Group, called **Exchange Routing Group (DWBGZMFD01QNBJR)**, will be created during the installation of the first Exchange Server 2010 SP1 server. A special Interop Routing Group Connector will also be created during the setup of that initial server, in order to route messages between Exchange Server 2003 and Exchange Server 2010 SP1.

It's also worth bearing in mind that, amongst other reasons, since Exchange Server 2010 SP1 uses Active Directory sites for routing SMTP messages, every site that contains an Exchange Server 2010 SP1 Mailbox Server Role will also need an Exchange Server 2010 Hub Transport Server Role to be installed, when a Mailbox Server is installed in that particular site, of course.

3.1.4 Link State is no longer used for updating the routing table

To keep routing information up to date in Exchange Server 2003, a process called Link State is used. When a connector in Exchange Server 2003 changes its state, the Routing Table used by the Routing Group Connectors is updated, and this Routing Table is immediately sent to other Exchange Servers in the same Routing Group. When an Exchange Server 2003 server initiates an SMTP connection to a similar server in another Routing Group, the Routing Tables on both servers are compared and, if needed, the newer version of the Routing Table is sent to the other server.

This works fine as long as the Routing Table is not very large, but there are known cases, with over 75 Routing Groups and hundreds of Routing Group Connectors, where the Routing Table was between 750 KB and 1 MB in size. It might not sound like much, but when a Routing Table is being exchanged frequently, this will have a noticeable negative impact on the network traffic across the WAN.

> **Note**
>
> *More information regarding message routing in Exchange Server 2003 can be found in the "Exchange Server Transport and Routing Guide" which is on the Microsoft TechNet site (HTTP://TINYURL.COM/ROUTINGGUIDE). When you want to take a closer look at the Routing Table in your own Exchange Server 2003 environment, you can download the WinRoute tool from the Microsoft website at HTTP://TINYURL.COM/WINROUTE.*

Exchange Server 2010 SP1 has replaced this whole system with Active Directory site links (as explained above) and thus leverages Active Directory information to determine an alternate route when a specific link is no longer available. Before installing the first Exchange Server 2010 SP1 server into an existing Exchange Server 2003 environment, Link State Updates need to be suppressed to avoid routing conflicts between the Exchange versions.

3.1.5 Recipient Update Service versus Email Address Policies

The Recipient Update Service (RUS) in Exchange Server 2003 is the service that is responsible for updating the Exchange-specific properties of Exchange recipients in Active Directory. When a user is created with Active Directory Users and Computers, the RUS will pick up the user account and "stamp" it with Exchange specific attributes, such as the `homeserver`, `homeMTA`, `homeMDB` and email addresses. It can take some time for a user to be fully provisioned and available, especially on busy servers. The RUS is part of the System Attendant, and only one instance is running in each Active Directory domain.

Exchange Server 2010 SP1 no longer uses the Recipient Update Service, but uses Email Address Policies instead. When a mailbox-enabled user is created, an Email Address Policy is applied immediately, and the mailbox is therefore available instantly though, of course, the user object needs to be replicated between all Domain Controllers in your environment to be fully available at all locations. In a coexistence scenario, the Recipient Update Service and the accompanying Recipient Policies can only be managed from the Exchange Server 2003 System Manager, and the Exchange Server 2010 SP1 Address List Policies can only be managed from the Exchange Management Console or the Exchange Management Shell. The only time a Recipient Policy is accessed using the Exchange Management Shell is when upgrading the Recipient Policy to an Email Address Policy.

3.2 Installing into an existing Exchange Server 2003 environment

Before installing the first Exchange Server 2010 SP1 server into an existing Exchange Server 2003 environment, a number of prerequisites have to be met.

- All domains in the existing Active Directory forest containing Exchange Recipients have to be running in native mode.
- The Active Directory forest has to be running on a Windows Server 2003 or higher forest functionality level.
- Each site in Active Directory should have at least one Domain Controller, and the Global Catalog Server needs to be at least on a Windows Server 2003 SP2 level. Although not required, it is recommended to have 64-bit type Domain Controllers and Global Catalog Servers for best performance.
- The Schema Master of the Active Directory needs to be a Windows Server 2003 SP2 or higher server. This can be either a 64-bit or a 32-bit server.
- All Exchange 2003 servers must have Service Pack 2 installed.

In addition to that, the server where Exchange Server will be installed also needs to meet the prerequisites below.

- The server needs to be a 64-bit computer.
- Windows Server 2008 SP2 or Windows Server 2008 R2 64-bit needs to be installed.
- Internet Information Server 7 needs to be installed.
- Windows Remote Management (WinRM) 2.0 needs to be installed.
- PowerShell 2.0 needs to be installed.
- .NET Framework 3.5 SP1 needs to be installed.

Chapter 3: Exchange Server 2010 SP1 Coexistence

Depending on the version of Windows 2008 you're using (i.e. Service Pack 2 or R2), a number of hot-fixes will also need to be installed. I would strongly recommend that you bring your server up to date with the latest hot-fixes from Microsoft Update, preferably before you perform this installation.

To make the process of installing prerequisites as painless as possible, the Exchange Server product group has created a series of XML files that can be used to automatically install Internet Information Server on your computer, together with the other prerequisites for Exchange Server 2010 SP1. These files are located on your installation media in the \setup\serverRoles\common directory.

To install the Internet Information Server (and other prerequisites) in a configuration needed to support, for example, an Exchange Server 2010 SP1 Client Access Server, you can use the Exchange-CAS.xml file with the following command: ServerManagerCmd.exe —inputpath Exchange-CAS.xml.

If you are using Windows Server 2008 R2, you will get a warning about ServermanagerCmd.exe being deprecated under Windows Server 2008 R2, but it still works fine, so go ahead and run it.

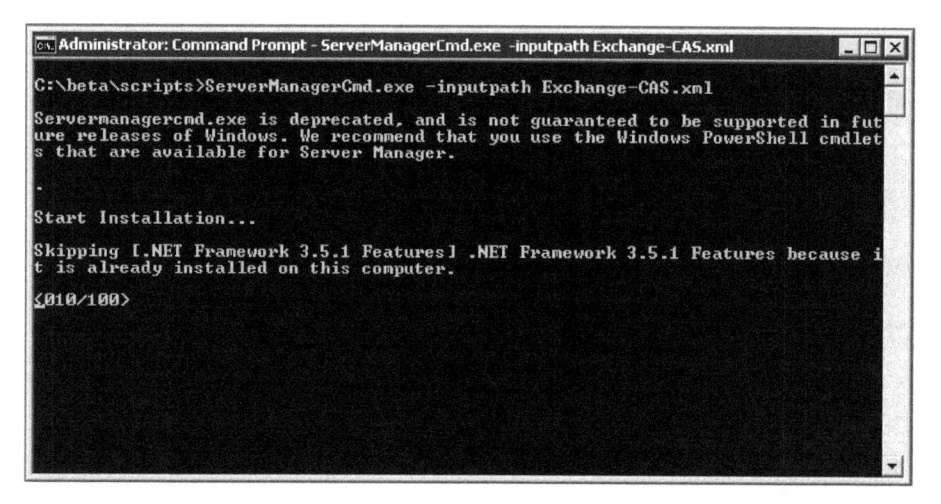

Figure 3.1: Use ServerManagerCmd.exe to install Internet Information Server.

However, starting with Service Pack 1, there's the option to have the setup application install the prerequisite Server Roles and features. This is the recommended way to install the prerequisite software, as it will install the minimum amount of software on your server.

3.2.1 Exchange Server 2010 SP1 Order of Installation

Although Exchange Server 2010 SP1 can be installed into an existing Exchange Server 2003 environment – in the same forest and the same domain – there are some issues with compatibility, and the various clients behave in a different manner in a coexistence scenario. For example, when you have a combined Exchange Server 2003 and Exchange Server 2010 environment, the situations below will occur.

- An Exchange Server 2010 Client Access Server will not always work directly with an Exchange Server 2003 Mailbox Server when a particular mailbox is located on this Exchange Server 2003 Mailbox Server.

- An Exchange Server 2003 Front-End Server will never communicate with an Exchange Server 2010 Mailbox Server.

- An Outlook Web App client will initially connect to the Exchange Server 2010 Client Access Server. This Client Access Server will not communicate directly with the Exchange Server 2003 Mailbox Server, therefore the OWA client will be redirected to the Exchange Server 2003 Front-End Server. The Exchange Server 2003 Front-End Server will handle the request and communicate with the Exchange Server 2003 Mailbox Server using the HTTP protocol.

- A Windows Mobile Device will connect to the ActiveSync service on the Exchange Server 2010 Client Access Server. The Client Access Server will service the request and forward it to the appropriate Exchange Server 2003 Mailbox Server using the HTTP protocol.

Chapter 3: Exchange Server 2010 SP1 Coexistence

- An Outlook client using Outlook Anywhere will connect to the Exchange Server 2010 Client Access Server. This is an RPC over HTTPS connection, so the RPC Proxy Service on the Client Access Server will handle the request and will retrieve the RPC information from the HTTPS packets. The Client Access Server will communicate directly with the Exchange Server 2003 Mailbox Server using RPC.

- An Exchange Server 2010 Hub Transport Server will not communicate directly with an Exchange Server 2003 Front-End Server. A Legacy or Interop Routing Group Connector needs to be in place to route SMTP messages between Exchange Server 2003 and Exchange Server 2010 and vice versa.

This behavior has its consequences on the order of installation of the various Server Roles, but it also has an impact on the way clients are redirected or proxied. I will explain this now.

The order of installation of Exchange Server 2010 Server Roles and prerequisites in an existing Exchange Server 2003 environment is as shown below.

- **First** – You have to upgrade the Internet-facing site.

- **Second** – Exchange Server 2010 SP1 Client Access Server.

- **Third** – Exchange Server 2010 SP1 Hub Transport Server.

- **Fourth** – Exchange Server 2010 SP1 Mailbox Server Role. After you've installed the Mailbox Server Role and established a proper Public Folder replication between Exchange Server 2003 and Exchange Server 2010, you can start moving mailboxes to the new Mailbox Server.

- The Exchange Server 2010 SP1 Edge Transport Server Role can be installed at any time during the upgrade, but the Edge Transport Server features are only fully available when the Exchange Server 2010 SP1 Hub Transport Server is installed.

Note

An in-place upgrade to Exchange Server 2010 SP1 is not supported in any scenario!

3.2.2 Installing Exchange Server 2010 SP1

Although you will need to install each of the Exchange Server 2010 SP1 Server Roles in a specific order, these roles can of course be combined on one machine.

Installing Exchange Server 2010 SP1 into an existing Exchange Server 2003 environment is pretty straightforward. The process can be broken down into the following easy steps.

- Exchange Server Readiness Check (as part of the Best Practices Analyzer).
- Upgrading the Active Directory schema.
- Upgrading the Exchange organization.
- Upgrading the Active Directory domain.
- Install the first Exchange Server 2010 SP1 server.

When you start the GUI setup application of Exchange Server 2010 SP1 (`setup.exe`), all these steps will be performed automatically in the correct order. I'll go through them in more detail here, because you can use the command-line version of setup if you want to fully control the options and execution of the setup program. Another important reason for using the command-line version is when using separation of permissions in Exchange Management departments.

Note

It is also possible to run the Exchange Server Pre-Deployment Analyzer as part of the Readiness Check. You can download the Exchange Server Pre-Deployment Analyzer from the Microsoft download site at HTTP://TINYURL.COM/DEPANALYZER.

3.2.2.1 Upgrading the Active Directory

The first step in changing your configuration for Exchange Server 2010 SP1 is upgrading the Active Directory schema to the Exchange Server 2010 SP1 level. You can achieve this by opening a command prompt on the Active Directory schema master from the Exchange Server 2010 SP1 installation media, and running the following commands:

```
Setup.com /PrepareLegacyExchangePermissions <<domainname>>
Setup.com /PrepareSchema
```

The first command, with `/PrepareLegacyExchangePermissions`, grants new permissions to ensure that the Recipient Update Service in Exchange Server 2003 continues to run correctly after the schema change to Exchange Server 2010 (which is performed in the second step). The `/PrepareLegacyExchangePermissions` must be performed before the actual upgrade of the schema, which is what the *second* command does.

If you want to change the schema on a computer that's not the Schema Master, you have to make sure that the LDIFDE application is available on that computer. You can install this by opening a command prompt and entering: `ServerManagerCmd.exe –I RSAT-ADDS`.

You can check what version your schema is, or check if the upgrade was successful, using a tool like `ADSIEDIT` or `LDP.EXE` and checking the `CN=ms-Exch-Schema-Version-Pt` object in the Active Directory schema. After the schema change, its `rangeUpper` property should have the value 14726. Just so you know, the property can have the values in the table below.

Chapter 3: Exchange Server 2010 SP1 Coexistence

Value	Corresponding Exchange version
6870	Exchange Server 2003 RTM
6936	Exchange Server 2003 Service Pack 2
10628	Exchange Server 2007
11116	Exchange Server 2007 Service Pack 1
14622	Exchange Server 2007 Service Pack 2
14622	Exchange Server 2010
14726	Exchange Server 2010 SP1 (likely to change)

Note

If you have multiple Domain Controllers in your Exchange Server environment, you'll have wait for the Domain Controller replication to finish before you continue to the next step.

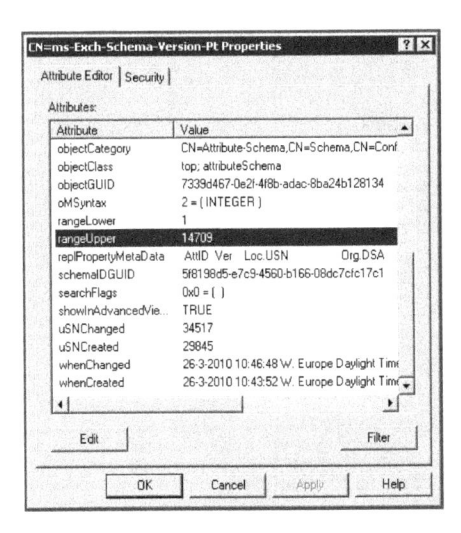

Figure 3.2: Check the schema version. This schema is on the Exchange Server 2010 level.

115

Chapter 3: Exchange Server 2010 SP1 Coexistence

After upgrading the schema, the current Exchange Server 2003 organization can be upgraded to support Exchange Server 2010 SP1. To do this, run the following command from the Exchange Server 2010 installation media: `Setup.com /PrepareAD`.

This simple command automatically configures the global Exchange objects in Active Directory (residing in the Active Directory Configuration Container), creates the Exchange Universal Security Groups in the root of the domain, and prepares the current domain for Exchange Server 2010 SP1.

It also creates the Exchange 2010 SP1 Administrative Group called **Exchange Administrative Group (FYDIBOHF23SPDLT)** and Exchange 2010 SP1 Routing Group called **Exchange Routing Group (DWBGZMFD01QNBJR)**, if they didn't already exist (see Sections 3.1.2. and 3.1.3 if you missed the significance of this).

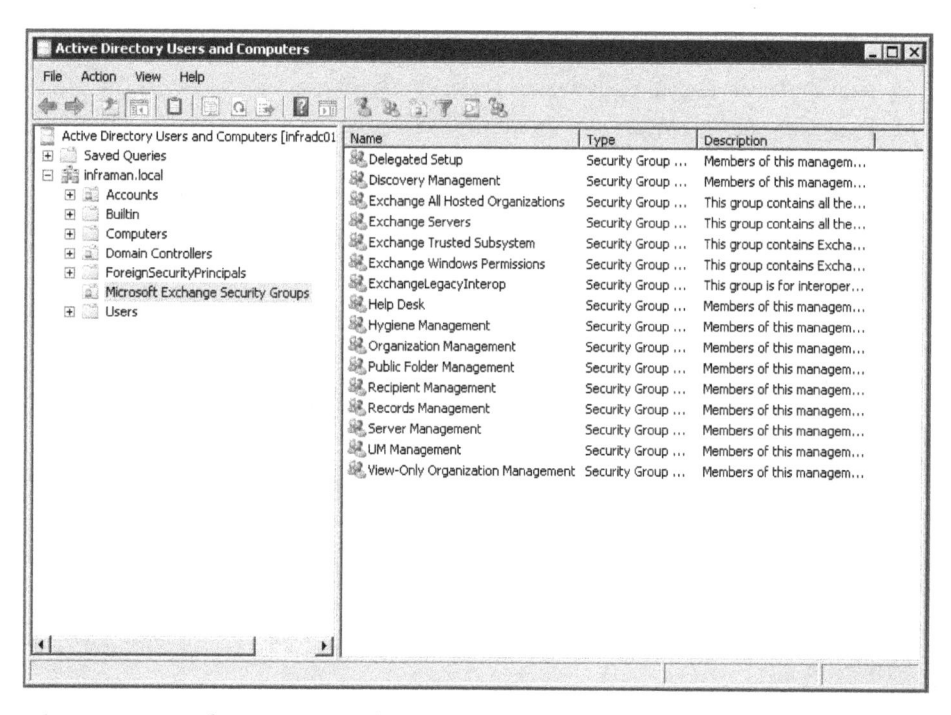

Figure 3.3: Exchange Universal Security Groups created during the `/PrepareAD` option.

Chapter 3: Exchange Server 2010 SP1 Coexistence

To verify that this step completed successfully, make sure that there is a new Organizational Unit (OU) in the root domain called **Microsoft Exchange Security Groups** and that this container contains the groups shown in Figure 3.3.

After running the `setup.com` application with the `/PrepareAD` switch, the newly created Administrative Group will show up in the Exchange Server 2003 System Manager, as you can see in Figure 3.4.

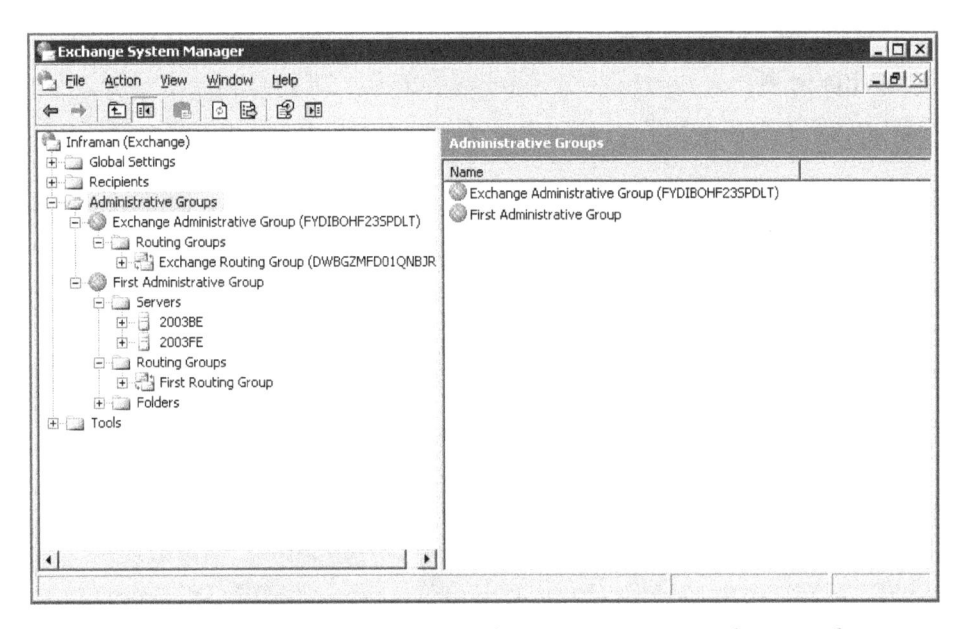

Figure 3.4: The Exchange Server 2010 Administrative Groups show up after running `setup.com /PrepareAD`.

The last step in preparing your environment for the implementation of Exchange Server 2010 SP1 is to prepare the Active Directory domain (or domains) for Exchange Server 2010 SP1. The domain is prepared by running the following command from the Exchange Server 2010 SP1 installation media: `Setup.com /PrepareDomain`.

When you have multiple domains holding Exchange objects in your Active Directory forest, and you want to prepare all domains in one step you can replace the `/PrepareDomain` with `/PrepareAllDomains`.

This sets the necessary permissions on the Exchange Server container in Active Directory, as well as for the Exchange Servers, the Exchange Administrators and Authenticated Users. It also creates a new Global Group called **Exchange Install Domain Servers** in the domain where the command is run. This Global Group is only used for installing Exchange Server 2010 servers in a child domain, in a domain other than the root domain. The setup program uses this to avoid installation issues when the Domain Controllers haven't yet fully replicated all the updated information.

After performing these easy steps, the Active Directory and Exchange Server environment is fully prepared for the installation of the first Exchange Server 2010 server.

3.2.2.2 Installing the first Exchange Server 2010 SP1 server.

In our example Exchange Server 2003 environment, we will implement a combined Exchange Server 2010 SP1 Hub Transport and Client Access Server, and a dedicated Exchange Server 2010 SP1 Mailbox Server. Both the Client Access and Hub Transport Servers will need to have Internet Information Server installed.

To install a combined Exchange Server 2010 SP1 Hub Transport and Client Access Server into the nicely prepared Exchange Server 2003 environment, follow the steps below.

- Log on to the new server where you want to install Exchange Server 2010 SP1. Make sure that the server is a member of the domain where Exchange Server 2003 is installed, and that all the prerequisite software is installed.

- Go to the installation media and start the `setup.exe` installation program. The setup splash screen appears and, if all prerequisite software is installed correctly, the first three steps are grayed out.

- If needed, download the language files, or else just use the languages provided on the DVD. You have to select one of these options to proceed.

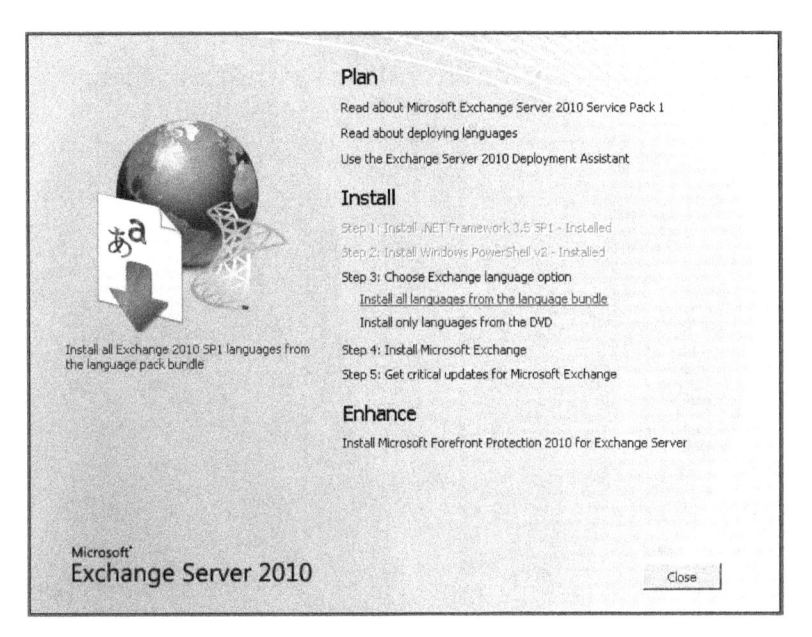

Figure 3.5: Choose Step 4 if you want to install non-English language packs.

- If you select **Install all languages from the language bundle**, you have the option to download the latest Language Pack Bundle from the Internet or specify a location where an earlier download of this file can be found. This can be a local hard drive or a network share.

- When finished downloading the language files, select **Step 4: Install Microsoft Exchange** and click **Next** to move past the **Introduction** page.

- Accept the license agreement and click **Next**.

- If wanted, you can select the **Error Reporting** option. Click **Next**.

Chapter 3: Exchange Server 2010 SP1 Coexistence

- In the **Installation Type** screen, you can choose between a **Typical Installation** or a **Custom Installation**, which is identical to the installation process in *Chapter 2*. For now, select **Custom Exchange Server Installation**. If you want to let the installation take care of the prerequisite software, you can check the **Automatically install Windows Roles and Features required for Exchange Server** and then click **Next**.

- As we're only installing the Hub Transport Server and Client Access Server Roles, you need to ensure that those are the only two options selected from the component list. The Exchange Management Tools will be automatically installed with any Exchange Server Role. Click **Next** to continue.

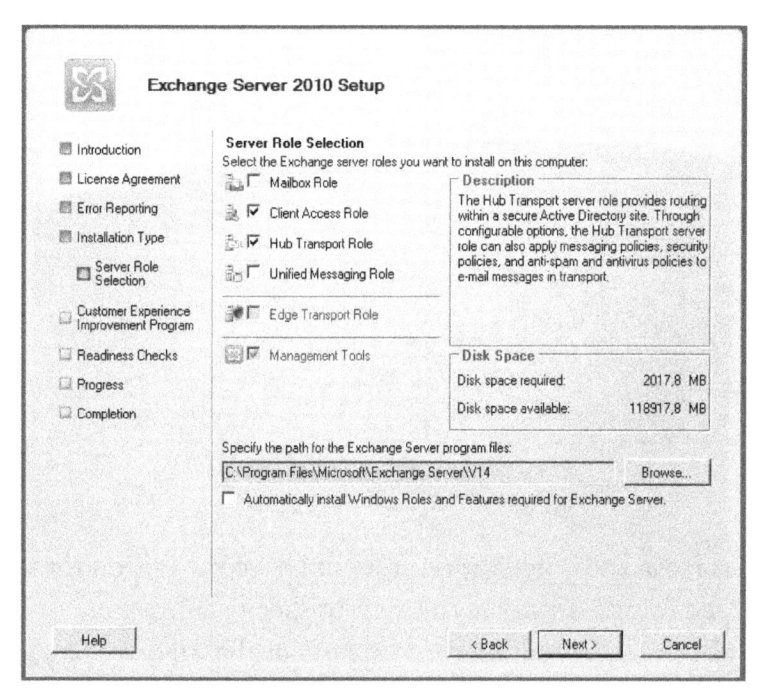

Figure 3.6: Select the Client Access Role and the Hub Transport Role.

- With the Exchange Server 2010 SP1 setup program, there's the option to configure the Client Access Server Role as an Internet-facing server. If that's what you want, you can just tick the relevant check box and enter the domain name you want to use when accessing the Client Access Server from the Internet.

Chapter 3: Exchange Server 2010 SP1 Coexistence

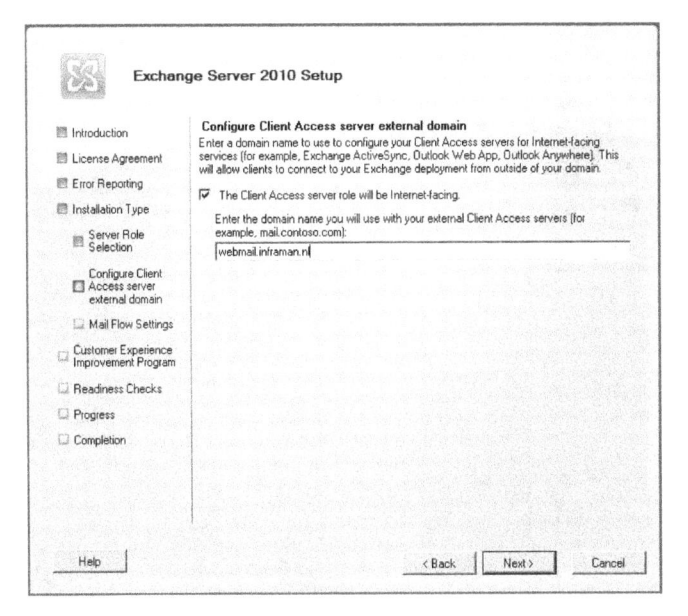

Figure 3.7: Enter the external domain for your Client Access Server.

- It is also possible to leave this field blank and enter the parameters during the later configuration of the servers. For now, we'll use this option, so enter your own domain name and click **Next** to continue.

- The **Mail Flow Settings** screen will only appear when performing a transition from Exchange Server 2003 to Exchange Server 2010. Using the **Browse** button, you can select which 2003 Exchange Server will be assigned as a hub server for an Interop Routing Group Connector, which both Exchange Server 2003 and Exchange Server 2010 use for sending messages to each other (see Section 3.1.3).

Chapter 3: Exchange Server 2010 SP1 Coexistence

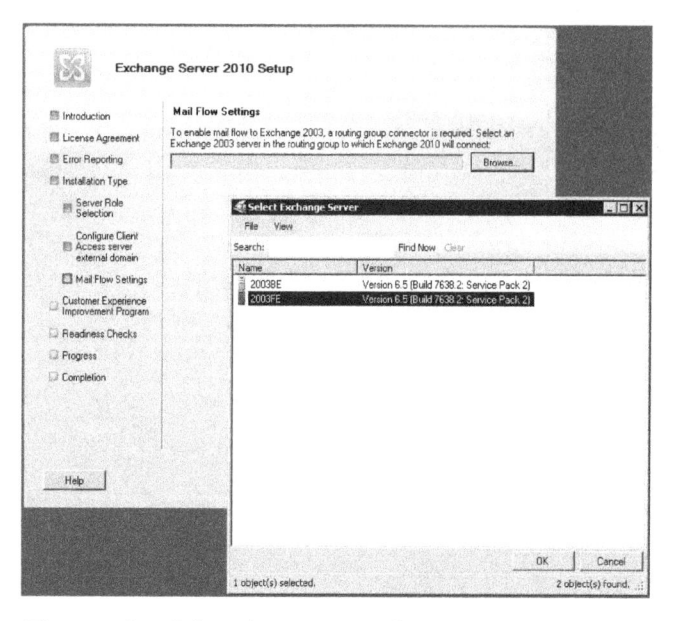

Figure 3.8: Select the proper Exchange Server 2003 server for the Interop Routing Group Connector.

- As explained earlier in this chapter, Exchange Server 2003 uses Routing Groups for routing email messages, whereas Exchange Server 2010 uses Active Directory sites. Routing Groups and Active Directory sites are not compatible with each other for the purposes of routing messages. As a result, Exchange Server 2010 has only one Routing Group, where all Exchange Server 2010 Hub Transport Servers are located.

- To establish message flow from the Exchange Server 2010 Routing Group to the Exchange Server 2003 Routing Group, a Routing Group Connector is created, and that's what happens in Figure 3.8.

- This Routing Group Connector is visible in the Exchange Server Manager in Exchange Server 2003 but, since this is an Exchange Server 2010 object, it is not manageable from the Exchange System Manager. The Routing Group Connector is actually not visible in the Exchange Server 2010 Management Console, so you have to use the `Get-RoutingGroupConnector` and `Set-RoutingGroupConnector` commands in the **Exchange Management Shell** for managing the Connector.

- Using these commands, it is possible to assign multiple Hub Transport Servers or multiple Front-End Servers to the Routing Group Connector for scalability or redundancy purposes. In this example, we'll select the **2003FE** server, which is an Exchange Server 2003 Front-End Server. Click **OK** and then **Next**.

- In the **Customer Experience Improvement Program** screen, you can select whether or not you want to participate in this program. There's no trick to this, so you can just make your selection and click **Next**.

- The setup application will now check the readiness of the Exchange configuration. If issues are found, they are presented at this stage and you'll have the opportunity to resolve them. If no issues are found, just click **Install**.

- The Exchange Server 2010 server will now be installed. For every step, a progress bar is shown.

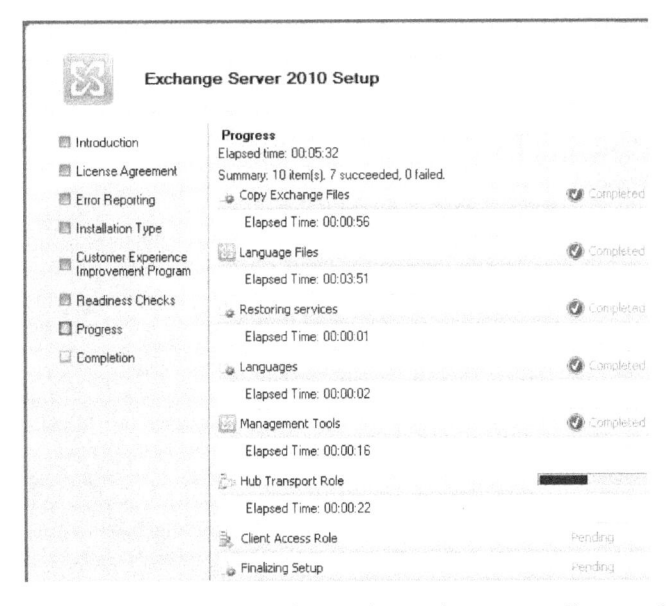

Figure 3.9: A progress bar is shown during installation of Exchange Server 2010 SP1.

- When all steps are completed, click **Finish**, and then click **Close** on the **Welcome** screen to end the setup program. You can continue to check the installation using the **Exchange Management Console** which is automatically opened after the setup.

Chapter 3: Exchange Server 2010 SP1 Coexistence

3.2.2.3 Installing the Exchange Server 2010 SP1 Mailbox Server Role

As we've only installed a Client Access Server and Hub Transport Server, we still need to go through the installation process for an Exchange Server 2010 Mailbox Server. The steps are very similar, but there *are* some small differences.

- Log on to the server that will hold the Mailbox Server Role. Make sure that it is a member of the domain and that all prerequisite software is installed.

- If you haven't done so already, install Internet Information Server for the Mailbox Server Role by going to the \Setup\ServerRoles\Common directory on the installation media, and entering the following command: ServerManagerCmd.exe – inputpath Exchange-MBX.xml.

- This will install Internet Information Server and the fail-over clustering software components according to the Mailbox Server Role prerequisites.

- Open the graphical setup program (setup.exe) and follow the steps as outlined earlier, making sure that you select the **Custom Exchange Server Installation** and select *only* the **Mailbox Server Role**.

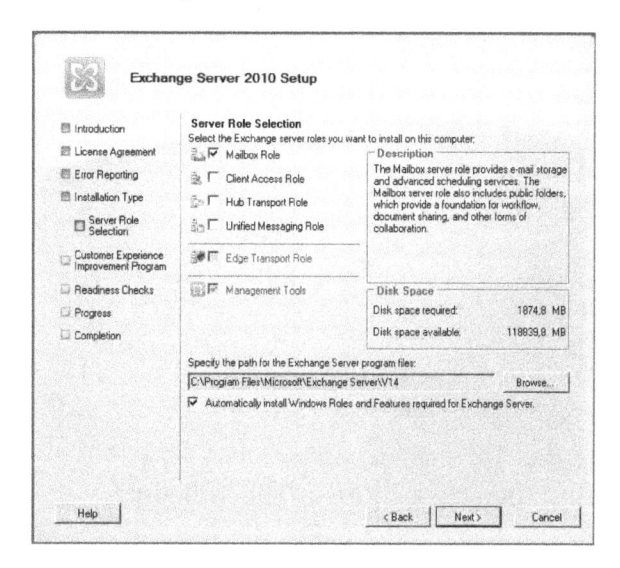

Figure 3.10: Select only the Mailbox Server Role.

- During the Readiness Check, a warning message will be displayed about Public Folder Replication as the setup application automatically detects the Exchange Server 2003 environment and the Public Folder existence. Don't worry about this, as Public Folder replication between Exchange Server 2003 and Exchange Server 2010 SP1 will have to be configured manually when setup is finished.

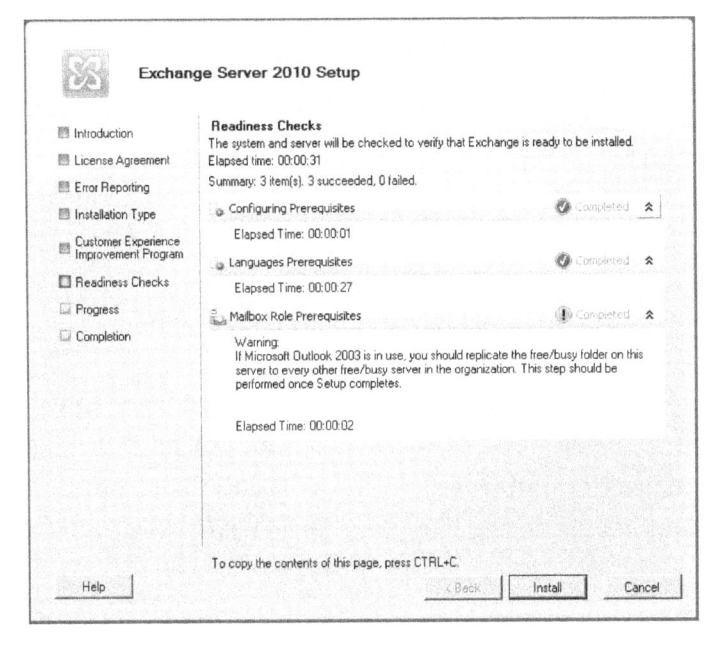

Figure 3.11: When finished you have to configure Public Folder replication.

- Click **Install** to complete the installation process, then click **Close** on the **Welcome** screen to end the setup program. As before, you can continue to check the installation using the **Exchange Management Console**, which is automatically opened after the setup.

3.2.3 Finishing the installation

Now that we have successfully installed two Exchange Server 2010 SP1 servers, it's time to configure the environment and finish the setup. We're now going to have to make sure the items below are taken care of.

- Public Folder Replication.
- Certificate installation on the Client Access Server.
- Configure Exchange Server 2010 Web Services.

3.2.3.1 Public Folder Replication

During the Mailbox Server Role Readiness Check, you saw a warning message regarding the Public Folder replication (see Figure 3.11). You don't need to worry about this, but you *are* going to have to take steps to ensure that Public Folder information from the Exchange Server 2003 Public Folders is replicated to the Exchange Server 2010 SP1 Public Folders, and vice versa.

So, to make sure this happens smoothly, log on to the Exchange Server 2003 server and open the Exchange System Manager. Browse to the Public Folders in the First Administrative Group and, if needed, right-click on **Public Folders** and select **View System Folders**. Select the Offline Address Book **/o=<<yourorg>>/cn=addrlists/cn=oabs/cn=Default Offline Address Book** and open its properties. Click **Add** on the **Replication** tab, and add the Public Folder Database on the Exchange Server 2010 SP1 Mailbox Server.

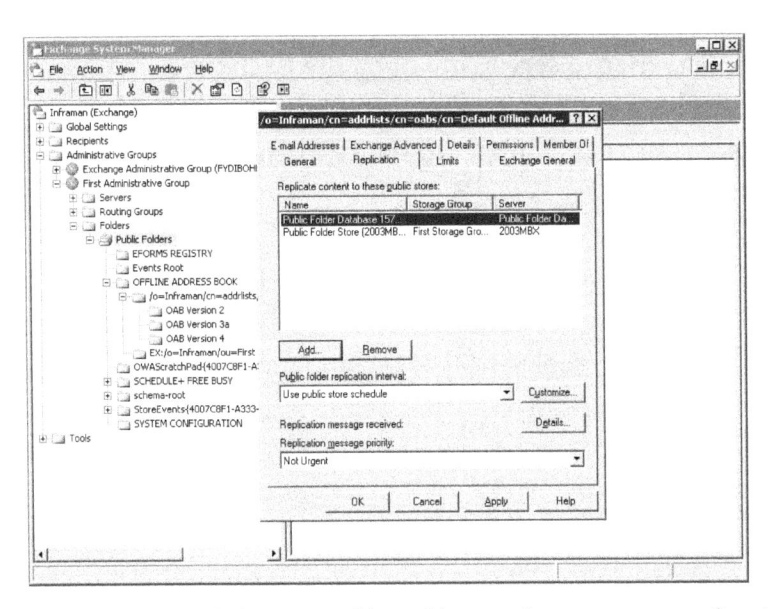

Figure 3.12: Add the 2010 Public Folder Database to set up replication.

Repeat these steps for:

- OAB Version 2
- OAB Version 3a
- OAB Version 4
- EX:/o=<<yourorg>>/ou=First Administrative Group
- Schedule+ Free Busy: EX:/o=<<yourorg>>/ou=First Administrative Group.

And that's all of your Exchange Server 2003 to Exchange Server 2010 SP1 Public Folder Replication set up!

In Exchange Server 2003 you can also use the **Manage Settings** options and perform the above steps at once in a single step.

Chapter 3: Exchange Server 2010 SP1 Coexistence

To set up Public Folder replication from Exchange Server 2010 SP1 back to Exchange Server 2003, log on to the Exchange Server 2010 server and open the **Exchange Management Console**. In the left-hand pane, select **Toolbox**, open the **Public Folder Management Console** in the **Results** pane, then connect to the Exchange Server 2010 Mailbox Server.

In the Public Folder Management Console, expand the **System Public Folders**, and then expand the Offline Address Book. For all Offline Address Books located in the Results pane, select their properties and configure the replication to include the Exchange Server 2003 Public Folder Database, as shown in Figure 3.13.

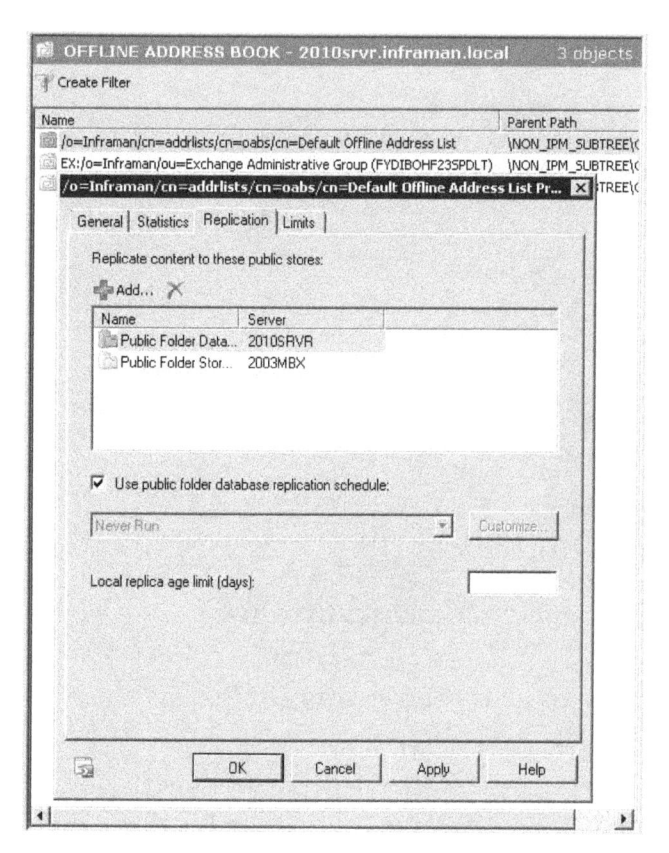

Figure 3.13: Configure Public Folder Replication to the Exchange Server 2003 server.

All you need to do to finalize your Replication configuration is repeat these steps for:

- OAB Version 2
- OAB Version 3a
- OAB Version 4
- EX:/o=<<yourorg>>/ou=Exchange Administrative Group (FYDIBOHF23SPDLT)
- EX:/o=<<yourorg>>/ou=First Administrative Group
- Schedule+ Free Busy: EX:/o=<<yourorg>>/ou= Exchange Administrative Group (FYDIBOHF23SPDLT)
- Schedule+ Free Busy: EX:/o=<<yourorg>>/ou=First Administrative Group.

These are only the System Public Folders. It is likely that organizations also use User Public Folders, and these can number in the thousands. These have to be replicated as well.

Bear in mind that, depending on the size of your Public Folder database, you may have to wait a considerable amount of time for Public Folder replication to finish.

3.2.3.1 Certificate installation

After installation of the Client Access Server, a new certificate also needs to be installed. By default, a self-signed certificate is created during setup but, for production purposes, a third-party certificate is needed. For Exchange Server 2010, a Unified Communication (UC) certificate is used, and these have their own Subject Name (like `webmail.inframan.nl`) as well as Subject Alternative Names like `autodiscover.inframan.nl` and `mail.inframan.nl`. Check out Microsoft Knowledge Base Article 929395 (HTTP://SUPPORT.MICROSOFT.COM/KB/929395) for more information regarding UC certificates and a list of supported Certification Authorities that can issue them.

Chapter 3: Exchange Server 2010 SP1 Coexistence

Suppose we have a domain called `inframan.nl` – our Outlook Web App name can be `webmail.inframan.nl`. A second namespace used in Exchange Server 2010 is Autodiscover, which resolves, in our example, to `autodiscover.inframan.nl`. So far this is the same as it was in Exchange Server 2007. New in Exchange Server 2010 is a third name called `legacy`, which results in `legacy.inframan.nl`. This legacy namespace is used for interoperability between Outlook Web Access in Exchange Server 2003 and Exchange Server 2010 Outlook Web App. As explained in the beginning of this chapter, some clients are handled directly by the Exchange Server 2010 Client Access Server, while other clients are forwarded to the Exchange Server 2003 Front-End Server. OWA, for example, is a service that is redirected to the old Exchange Server 2003 Front-End Server.

When all Exchange Server 2010 servers are up and running, it's time to have the clients connect to the new Client Access Server instead of the old Front-End Server so that, when a web browser enters HTTPS://WEBMAIL.INFRAMAN.NL/EXCHANGE, the client contacts the Exchange Server 2010 Client Access Server. The user's credentials are entered and the Client Access Server accesses the Active Directory to determine the location of the actual Mailbox. When the Client Access Server determines that the Mailbox Server is an Exchange Server 2003 Mailbox Server, the OWA client is redirected to the old Exchange Server 2003 Front-End Server. Since two web servers cannot have the same Fully Qualified Domain Name (FQDN) the old Exchange Server 2003 Front-End Server will get a new FQDN. This will be the `legacy.inframan.nl` domain name; of course, it can have any FQDN, but the legacy name is generally used in Microsoft Knowledgebase articles and white papers.

The FQDN of the old Exchange Server 2003 Front-End Server is a property of the OWA Virtual Directory on the Exchange Server 2010 Client Access Server. To set this property, open an Exchange Management Shell on the Exchange Server 2010 Client Access Server and enter the following command:

```
Set-OWAVirtualDirectory <2010CASHUB01>\OWA* `
    -ExternalURL https://webmail.inframan.nl/OWA `
    -Exchange2003URL https://legacy.inframan.nl/exchange
```

Now, when an OWA client enters a request to an Exchange Server 2010 Client Access Server, and the actual Mailbox is still on the Exchange Server 2003 Mailbox Server, the client is automatically redirected to the old Exchange Server 2003 Front-End Server.

Therefore three domain names will be used on the Exchange Server 2010 Client Access Server certificate:

- `Webmail.inframan.nl` (primary OWA access point).
- `Autodiscover.inframan.nl`.
- `Legacy.inframan.nl` (OWA access for Exchange Server 2003 mailboxes).

To ensure the Exchange Server 2010 Client Access Server Role functions correctly, the various settings need to be configured, which is what I'll explain in the next section.

3.2.3.3 Configure Exchange Web Services

Like its predecessors, Exchange Server 2010 SP1 uses the Client Access Server to offer Offline Address Book downloads and Free/Busy information using the HTTP protocol, and these can be used by Outlook 2007 and Outlook 2010. However, Outlook 2003 uses the Public Folder architecture to get the Offline Address Book and Free/Busy information.

As explained in Section 3.2.2.2 (see Figure 3.7), you can enter the external domain that the Client Access Server is using, for example `webmail.inframan.nl`.

If you haven't configured the external domain during setup, you have to configure the following settings using the Exchange Management Shell command below.

Chapter 3: Exchange Server 2010 SP1 Coexistence

```
Offline Address Book:
   Set-OABVirtualDirectory <2010CASHUB01>\OAB* `
      -ExternalURL https://webmail.inframan.nl/OAB

Web Services:
   Set-WebServicesVirtualDirectory <2010CASHUB01>\EWS* `
      -ExternalURL https://webmail.inframan.nl/ews/exchange.asmx

ActiveSync:
   Set-ActiveSyncVirtualDirectory <2010CASHUB01>\Microsoft-Server-ActiveSync`
      -ExternalURL https://webmail.inframan.nl/Microsoft-Server-ActiveSync

Set-ECPVirtualDirectory <2010CASHUB01>\ECP* `
   -ExternalURL https://webmail.inframan.nl/ECP
```

Before the Offline Address Book can be distributed by the Client Access Server, the Generation Server needs be changed from Exchange Server 2003 to Exchange Server 2010 SP1. This can be achieved by using the **Exchange Management Console** as below.

- Log on to the Exchange Server 2010 SP1 server and open the **Exchange Management Console**.

- Expand **Microsoft Exchange on-Premises** and expand the **Organization** container.

- Click the **Mailbox** option and, in the **Results** pane, select the **Offline Address Book** tab. The **Default Offline Address List** will appear, and the **Generation Server** will be the current Exchange Server 2003 server.

- Right-click the **Default Offline Address Book** and select **Move**. The **Move Offline Address Book** wizard will appear. Use the **Browse** button to select the new Exchange Server 2010 SP1 Mailbox Server and, when finished, click **Move** again. When the move to the new Mailbox Server is complete, click **Finish**.

Note

You can also use the **Exchange Management Shell** *to move the Generation Server to Exchange Server 2010 by using the following command:* `Move-OfflineAddressBook 'Default Offline Address Book' -Server 2010MBX`.

Even once you've gone through these steps, the distribution itself is still using the Public Folder Mechanism. To change this to Web-based distribution, use the procedure below.

- Log on to the Exchange Server 2010 SP1 server and open the **Exchange Management Console**.

- Expand **Microsoft Exchange on-Premises**, and expand the **Organization** container.

- Click the **Mailbox** option and select the **Offline Address Book** tab in the **Results** pane. The **Default Offline Address List** will appear. Right-click this and select **Properties**.

- Select the **Distribution** tab and tick the **Enable Web-based Distribution** check box. Click **Add** to select the **Client Access Server Virtual Directory** used for distribution and, when finished, click **OK**.

The Exchange Server 2010 SP1 Client Access Server will now start distributing the Offline Address Book using a virtual directory, using the HTTP protocol that can be used by Microsoft Outlook 2007 or Outlook 2010 clients.

Users with mailboxes still on Exchange Server 2003, and who access their mailbox using a Windows Mobile device, will get an error when they use the Exchange Server 2010 SP1 Client Access Server. These users will be able to synchronize their device when the Microsoft-Server-ActiveSync virtual directory on the Exchange Server 2003 back-end server has **Integrated Windows Authentication** enabled. This will allow the Client Access Server and the Exchange Server 2003 back-end server to use Kerberos for authentication.

Chapter 3: Exchange Server 2010 SP1 Coexistence

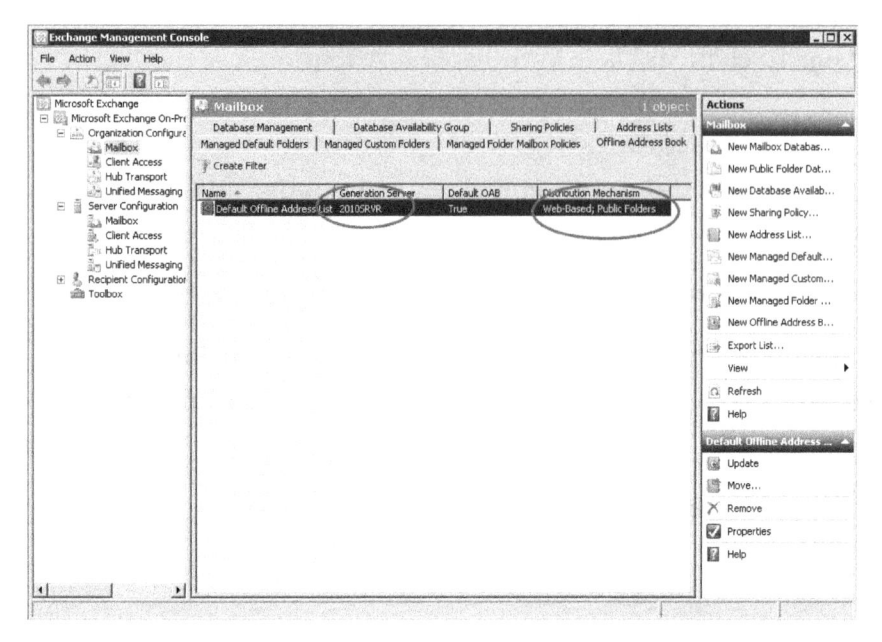

Figure 3.14: After configuring the Offline Address Book generation server you can check the configuration using the Exchange Management Console.

Now that you've got your Public Folder replication, Certificates and Web Services all configured, it's time to change your Internet access infrastructure. You need to make sure that users who try to access HTTPS://WEBMAIL.INFRAMAN.NL (the example we've been using so far) are redirected to the new Exchange Server 2010 Client Access Server. So I'll quickly outline the SMTP Infrastructure for this coexistence scenario.

3.2.4 SMTP Infrastructure

As discussed earlier, when an Exchange Server 2010 SP1 Hub Transport Server is installed into an existing Exchange Server 2003 environment, it installs a special Legacy, or Interop, Routing Group Connector. This Interop Routing Group Connector is responsible for sending messages between Exchange Server 2003 and Exchange Server 2010 SP1 and vice versa.

When you move mailboxes to Exchange Server 2010 SP1 and a new message arrives on the Exchange Server 2003 Front-End Server, this server will check Active Directory and find the intended user's mailbox is on Exchange Server 2010 SP1. The message will be routed through the Interop Routing Group Connector to the new Hub Transport Server, and the message will be delivered in the Exchange Server 2010 SP1 Mailbox Server – nice and simple.

Similarly, when a user with a mailbox on Exchange Server 2010 SP1 composes a message for a mailbox on Exchange Server 2003, the message is routed from the Hub Transport Server, through the Interop Routing Group Connector, to the Exchange Server 2003 Front-End Server. From there it will be delivered to the user's mailbox on the Exchange Server 2003 Mailbox Server – *also* nice and simple.

As this is a completely stable system, it is up to the system administrator to decide when the mail flow is switched from delivery at the Exchange Server 2003 server to the Exchange Server 2010 SP1 Hub Transport Server. There are no hard requirements when to switch the message flow.

3.2.4.1 Edge Transport Server

An Exchange Server 2010 SP1 Edge Transport Server is used for message hygiene purposes; it will be used as an anti-spam and antivirus solution. The anti-spam solution is built in to the product, and Microsoft Forefront Protection for Exchange Server can be used for antivirus.

An Exchange Server 2010 SP1 Edge Transport Server can also be used, together with a pure Exchange Server 2003 environment. The Edge Transport Server is used as a smart host for the Exchange Server 2003 server, and can still act as an anti-spam and antivirus solution. The full feature set of an Edge Transport Server is, of course, not available in an Exchange Server 2003 environment.

Chapter 3: Exchange Server 2010 SP1 Coexistence

The full feature set of the Exchange Server 2010 SP1 Edge Transport Server becomes available when you transition to the Exchange Server 2010 SP1 Hub Transport Server, subscribe the Edge Transport Server to the Hub Transport Server, and switch the mail flow from the Exchange Server 2003 environment to the Exchange Server 2010 SP1 environment.

If you want to install the Exchange Server 2010 SP1 Edge Transport Server and subscribe it to the Exchange Server 2010 SP1 Hub Transport Server, follow the installation guidelines as outlined in *Chapter 2*. The question is, do you *want* to install the Edge Transport Server? There's no definitive answer to this, and a consultant's answer would be "It depends." An Edge Transport Server does a great job in offering antivirus and anti-spam functionality and, as such, I can really recommend it. But a lot of customers already have other anti-spam and antivirus solutions that perform very well. If this is the case, you have to make a decision based on experience, pricing, manageability, and so on.

3.2.5   Final Exchange 2003 coexistence notes

So, at the end of that, you should have everything you need to configure your own Exchange Server 2003 coexistence scenario. Just to finish off, there are a few things I want to recap for when you are running this kind of scenario.

- An Exchange Server 2003 and Exchange Server 2010 SP1 coexistence scenario has two management interfaces:
  - the Exchange Server 2003 System Manager can *only* be used to manage Exchange Server 2003 objects
  - the Exchange Server 2010 SP1 Management Console and Management Shell can *only* be used to manage Exchange Server 2010 SP1 objects.
- If mailboxes running on Exchange Server 2003 need to be moved to Exchange Server 2010 SP1, this can *only* be achieved using the Exchange Server 2010 SP1 tools.

- When shared mailboxes are moved from Exchange Server 2003 to Exchange Server 2010 SP1, they will continue to run as shared mailboxes. They can be converted to Resource Mailboxes at a later stage.

- Mailboxes can be moved from Exchange Server 2010 SP1 to Exchange Server 2003 using the Exchange Management Console or the Exchange Management Shell on Exchange Server 2010 SP1. When a mailbox on Exchange Server 2010 SP1 has an archive associated with it, the archive naturally has to be removed before the move to Exchange Server 2003.

3.3 Coexistence with Exchange Server 2007

The differences between Exchange Server 2007 and Exchange Server 2010 SP1 aren't that large. All the Server Roles have new or altered functionality, but it isn't as drastic as the differences with Exchange Server 2003. One of the important changes between Exchange Server 2007 and Exchange Server 2010 SP1 is in the replication technology.

The "old" replication technology, like Cluster Continuous Replication (CCR), Local Continuous Replication (LCR) and Stand-by Continuous Replication (SCR) is no longer available in Exchange Server 2010 SP1. Additionally, in the Client Access Server, the RPC Client Access functionality is new when compared to Exchange Server 2007.

When building a coexistence scenario with Exchange Server 2007 the most important issues are Management interfaces and Server Role features.

- **Management interfaces** – Exchange Server 2010 SP1 objects can be managed by the Exchange Management Console (EMC) or the Exchange Management Shell (EMS). Some attributes of an Exchange Server 2007 can be viewed as well, but Exchange Server 2007 objects should be managed using the Exchange Server 2007 Management Tools.

- **Server Role features** – Exchange Server 2010 SP1 has the same Server Roles as Exchange Server 2007, but the functionality that's available to end-users depends on the location of their mailbox. Not all features are available when the user's mailbox is still hosted on Exchange Server 2007.

If you've already read the section about a coexistence scenario with Exchange Server 2003, then some of the more fine-grained details of this process will seem fairly familiar. Nevertheless, this section of the chapter should give you everything you need to configure a coexistence scenario between Exchange Servers 2007 and 2010. Before I dive into the installation details, I'd just like to make a brief comment regarding 64-bit systems.

3.3.1 64-Bit in Exchange Server 2007

Exchange Server 2007 was the first Exchange version available in a 64-bit version, and indeed the 64-bit version is the *only* version that is supported in a production environment. The Information Store of Exchange Server 2007 will use as much memory as is available to cache mailbox information which, in turn, can result in a dramatic reduction of disk I/O. As long as there is sufficient memory available in the Exchange Server, of course.

As a result (and to be fair, this is somewhat true for *any* server) an Exchange Server 2007 server that is not properly designed will still result in a poorly performing server. A best practice for designing a well performing Exchange Server is to use the Exchange 2010 Mailbox Server Role Requirements Calculator, which is available on the Microsoft Exchange Team Blog at HTTP://WWW.TINYURL.COM/REQCALC.

There is a 32-bit version available of Exchange Server 2007, but this version is not supported in a production environment and should only be used in test and development environments. To enforce this, it is time-bombed, and will officially only run for 120 days. But now, on to the installation! And once again, remember that, as mentioned before, there is *not* a 32-bit version available of Exchange Server 2010.

3.4 Installing into an existing Exchange Server 2007 environment

Before installing the first Exchange Server 2010 SP1 server into an existing Exchange Server 2007 environment, a number of prerequisites have to be met.

- All domains in an existing Active Directory forest have to be running in native mode.

- The Active Directory forest has to be running on a Windows Server 2003 forest functionality level.

- Each site in Active Directory should have at least one Domain Controller and the Global Catalog Server on a Windows Server 2003 SP2 level. Although not enforced, it is recommended to have 64-bit type Domain Controllers and Global Catalog Servers for optimal performance.

- The Schema Master of the Active Directory needs to be a Windows Server 2003 SP2 or a Windows Server 2008 SP1 server. This can either be a 64-bit or a 32-bit server.

- All Exchange Server 2007 servers must have Service Pack 2 installed.

- The Internet-facing Active Directory sites must be the first sites that will be upgraded to Exchange Server 2010.

Likewise, the physical server where Exchange Server will be installed needs to meet the prerequisites below.

- The server needs to be a 64-bit (64-bit Itanium is not supported!) based computer.
- Windows Server 2008 SP 2 or Windows Server 2008 R2 64-bit needs to be installed.
- Internet Information Server needs to be installed.
- Windows Remote Management (WinRM) 2.0 needs to be installed.
- PowerShell 2.0 needs to be installed.
- .NET Framework 3.51 needs to be installed.

Depending on the version of Windows 2008 you're using (i.e. Service Pack 2 or R2) a number of hot-fixes need to be installed. I strongly recommend you bring your server up to date with the latest hot-fixes from Windows Update.

3.4.1 Exchange Server 2010 SP1 order of installation

Exchange Server 2010 can be installed into an existing Exchange Server 2007 environment in the same forest and the same domain, but there are some issues with compatibility. You have to take the installation order of the Exchange Server 2010 servers into account to minimize the impact of this.

- **First** – you have to upgrade the Internet-facing sites in Exchange Server 2007.
- **Second** – Exchange Server 2010 SP1 Client Access Server. The Client Access Server can work with an Exchange Server 2007 Mailbox Server as well as an Exchange Server 2010 Mailbox Server.
- **Third** – Exchange Server 2010 SP1 Hub Transport Server.
- **Fourth** – Exchange Server 2010 SP1 Mailbox Server.
- The Edge Transport Server can be installed at any time, since an Exchange Server 2010 SP1 Edge Transport Server can be subscribed to an Exchange Server 2007 SP2 Hub Transport Server.

After you've installed the Mailbox Server Role and established a proper Public Folder replication between Exchange Server 2007 and Exchange Server 2010 SP1, you can start moving mailboxes to the new Mailbox Server. Of course, the Public Folder replication needs only to be configured when Public Folders are used in Exchange Server 2007.

Please bear in mind that an in-place upgrade to Exchange Server 2010 SP1 is not supported *in any scenario*!

3.4.2 Installing Exchange Server 2010 SP1

Although there's a specific order to the installation of Server Roles, these roles can, of course, be combined on one server.

When upgrading to Exchange Server 2010 SP1 the following steps need to be performed:

- upgrade the Active Directory schema
- upgrade the Active Directory configuration
- upgrade the Active Directory domain
- install the Exchange Server 2010 SP1 Server Roles.

So, let's get started with the upgrade.

3.4.2.1 Upgrading Active Directory

Before you even think about installing Server Roles, the first step in upgrading the Exchange Server 2007 environment to Exchange Server 2010 SP1 is upgrading the Active Directory schema. Bear in mind that it is also possible to use the graphical setup program, as this can be found on the installation media as `setup.exe`. When you use this program, all steps below are automatically performed. The command prompt system is mainly for people who want to retain more fine-grained control over their transition.

This is not different from the procedure described in Section 3.2.2, and can also be achieved by entering the following into a command prompt: `Setup.com /PrepareSchema`.

Once the schema has been upgraded, the Configuration (which is stored in the Active Directory Configuration Container) can follow.

Chapter 3: Exchange Server 2010 SP1 Coexistence

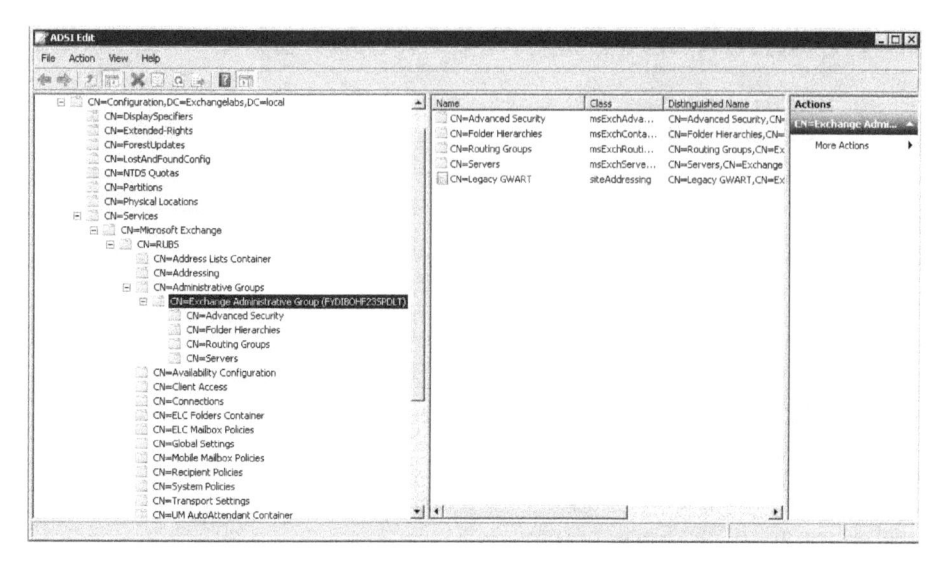

Figure 3.15: The Exchange Organization in the Configuration Partition of a pure Exchange Server 2007 environment.

The Exchange Server 2007 organization called "RUBS" can be seen in Figure 3.15. All Exchange Server 2007 servers are stored in the default Administrative Group **Exchange Administrative Group (FYDIBOHF23SPDLT)**. If your Exchange 2007 has previously been upgraded from Exchange Server 2003, then it's very likely that you will see a **First Administrative Group** as well. If the upgrade was finished correctly, this First Administrative Group should be empty, or almost empty.

Exchange Server 2010 SP1 *also* uses the **Exchange Administrative Group (FYDIBOHF-23SPDLT)**, but there are differences in how Exchange Server 2010 works, for example, with databases. In Exchange Server 2007, a database is bound to a Mailbox Server while, in Exchange Server 2010 SP1, databases exist on the organization level, independent of any Mailbox Server. So, when upgrading the Exchange configuration, the Administrative Group is changed to facilitate both the Exchange Server 2007 environment as well as the Exchange Server 2010 SP1 environment.

When you want to change the Exchange configuration, open a command prompt, navigate to the Exchange Server 2010 SP1 installation media, and enter the following command: `Setup.com /PrepareAD`.

After upgrading the Exchange configuration, some Exchange Server 2010 SP1 specific entries appear in the Exchange Administrative Group, like the Database Availability Group and the Databases container. Figure 3.16 shows more or less what you should see.

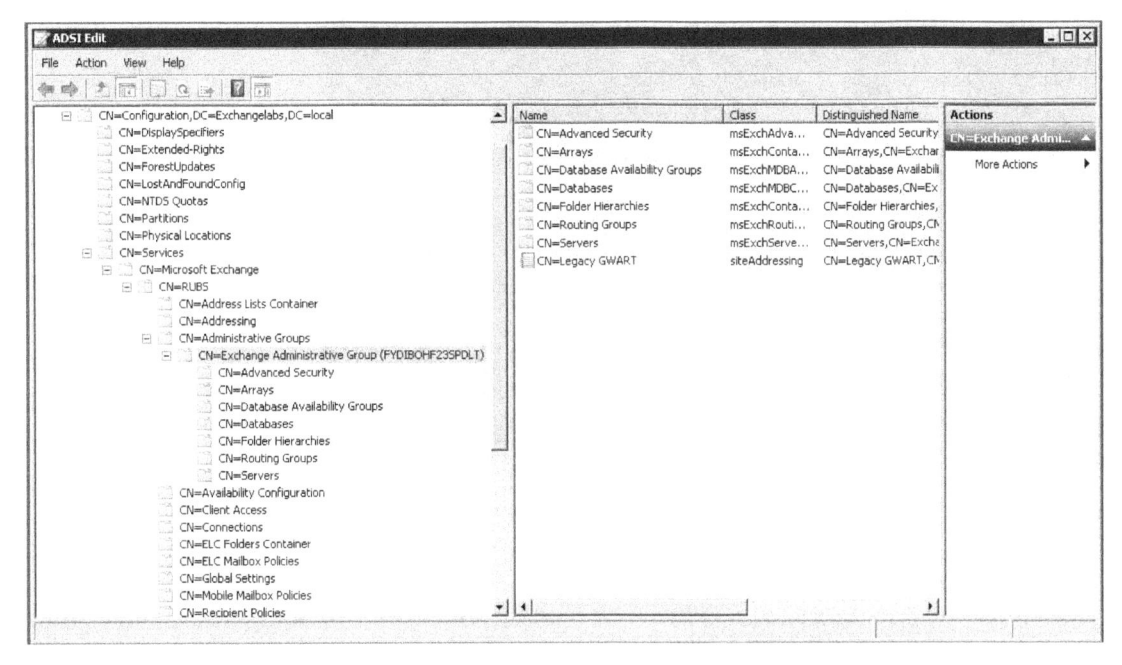

Figure 3.16: The Configuration Container after upgrading the Active Directory. The Exchange Server 2010 SP1 specific entries are clearly visible.

The next step is to prepare the domain (or domains if you have multiple domains that host user accounts with Exchange Server mailboxes) for use with Exchange Server 2010 SP1. To do this, open a command prompt, navigate to the installation media and enter the following command: `Setup.com /PrepareDomain`.

Chapter 3: Exchange Server 2010 SP1 Coexistence

And if you want to prepare *all* domains in your environment, enter: `Setup.com /PrepareAllDomains`.

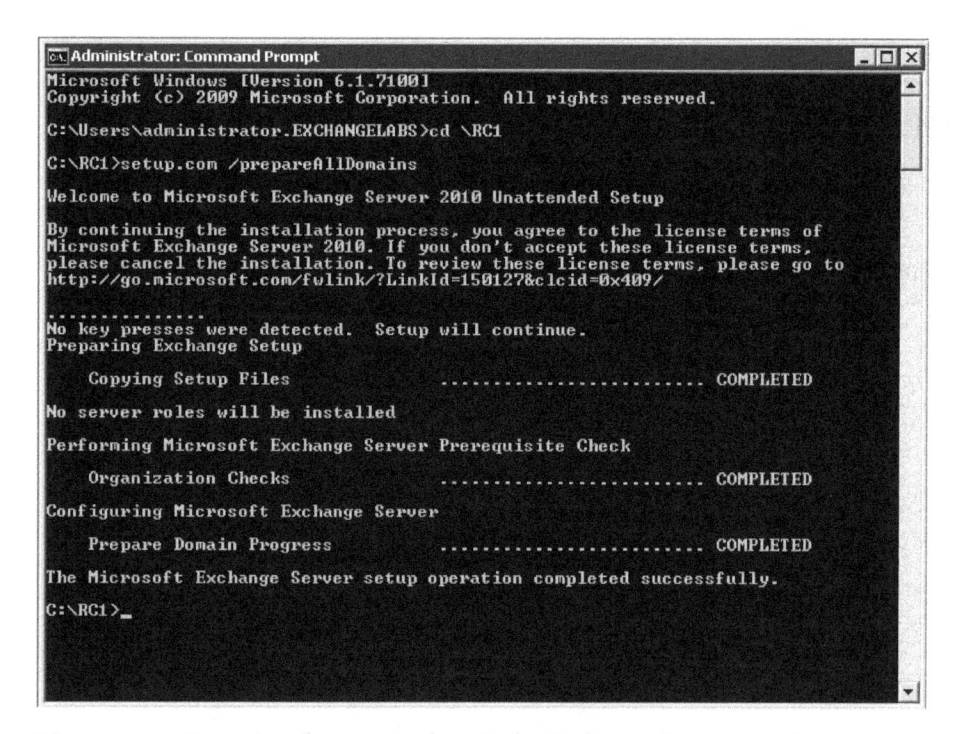

Figure 3.17: Preparing the current domain for Exchange Server 2010 SP1.

When the setup `/PrepareDomain` is finished the Active Directory is now ready to install the first Exchange Server 2010 SP1 server.

3.4.2.2   Installing the Exchange Server 2010 SP1 servers

As mentioned earlier, the *only* supported order of installation of Exchange Server 2010 SP1 Server Roles into an existing Exchange Server 2007 environment is as follows:

- Client Access Servers
- Hub Transport Servers
- Mailbox Servers.

Also, the Internet-facing Active Directory site, the site associated with your external Autodiscover record, should be the *first* to be transitioned. Then you should transition other Internet-facing Active Directory sites, sometimes referred to as "regional sites." The last sites you should transition are the internal Active Directory sites. Transitioning internal Active Directory sites before the Internet-facing Active Directory sites have been transitioned is not supported.

In our test environment, we are installing a combined Exchange Server 2010 SP1 Client Access Server Role and Hub Transport Server Role, and one dedicated Exchange Server 2010 SP1 Mailbox Server Role.

The procedure to install Exchange Server 2010 SP1 in an existing Exchange Server 2007 environment is not very different from when installing into an existing Exchange Server 2003 environment, as described in Section 3.2.2.2.

First, ensure that Windows Server 2008 Server and all the prerequisite software is installed on the target server. To install Internet Information Server 7 (or 7.5 in the case of Windows Server 2008 R2) and other prerequisites, open a command prompt, navigate to the `\setup\serverRoles\common` directory in the installation media and enter the following command: `ServerManagerCmd.exe -ip Exchange-CAS.XML`.

This will install Internet Information Server, as well as other prerequisites, with the right configuration for the Client Access Server and the Hub Transport Server. However, it is recommended to have the setup application install all prerequisite Roles and features as outlined both earlier and later in this chapter.

To install the actual Exchange Server Roles you can use either the command-line setup or the graphical setup. Right now, we will use the graphical setup program, and to open this setup application you just need to start the `setup.exe` program in the installation media.

- During the setup, choose the Exchange language option. You can choose to download additional language packs from the Microsoft website, or use the language as available on the DVD. Select **Install all languages from the language bundle** to download additional language information.

- Follow the setup wizard, and at the **Installation Type** windows select **Custom Exchange Server Installation** in order to select the Server Roles that need to be installed. Select the **Client Access Server Role** and the **Hub Transport Server Role**. When you check the **Automatically install Windows Roles and Features required for Exchange Server** check box, all prerequisite software, like the various Internet Information Server parts, will be installed automatically.

- In contrast with what I wrote in Section 3.2.2.2, you are not asked to select a Hub Transport Server in the Exchange Server 2007 environment. This is because both versions use Active Directory sites for routing messages, and so this *should* work right away.

- Once everything is OK and the **Readiness Checks** are successful, you can start the actual installation of the Exchange Server 2010 SP1 Client Access Server and Hub Transport Server Roles. When the setup is finished, close the setup application and reboot the server (if the setup asks you to do so).

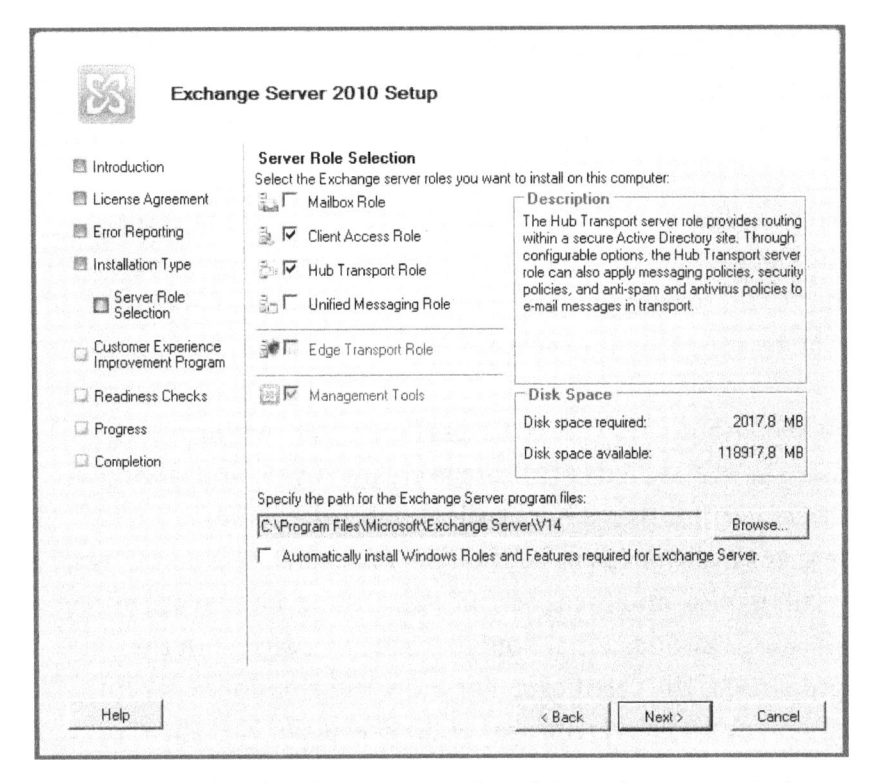

Figure 3.18: Select the Client Access Role and the Hub Transport Role.

- To install the Exchange Server 2010 SP1 Mailbox Server Role into the existing Exchange Server 2007 environment you can follow the procedure as outlined in Section 3.2.2.3. This is exactly the same, so there's no point in me giving it its own subheading!

3.4.2.3 Certificate installation

After the installation of the Exchange Server 2010 SP1 Client Access Server, the coexistence still has to be configured. Eventually, users will connect to the new Client Access Server and, if a user's mailbox exists on the new Exchange Server 2010 SP1 Mailbox Server, the request will be processed as usual. When the user's mailbox still exists on the Exchange Server 2007 Mailbox Server, however, the request is either forwarded to the

Exchange Server 2007 Client Access Server, or processed by the Exchange Server 2010 SP1 Client Access Server, and the information retrieved from the Exchange Server 2007 Mailbox Server. This all depends on the protocol that's being used, but is important for determining the certificates being used on the Client Access Server, as explained below.

Outlook Web Access clients naturally connect to the Exchange Server 2010 SP1 Client Access Server. After validating the user's credentials, the Client Access Server checks the Mailbox Server and, if this is still running on Exchange Server 2007, the request is redirected to the Exchange Server 2007 Client Access Server.

After installing the Exchange Server 2010 SP1 Client Access Server, a new third-party certificate needs to be requested. A self-signed certificate is created by default during the setup of the Client Access Server, but this is not at all useable for a production environment. The certificate that ideally needs to be used on a Client Access Server is a certificate with multiple domain names, and these certificates are also known as Unified Communications (UC) certificates. The additional domain names are stored in the Subject Alternative Names property of the certificate. For more information regarding these certificates and a list of supported UC certificate vendors, you can visit the Microsoft website at HTTP://SUPPORT.MICROSOFT.COM/KB/929395.

As explained in Section 3.2.3.1, Outlook Web Access clients are redirected from the Exchange Server 2010 Client Access Server to the Exchange Server 2003 Front-End Server when the actual Mailbox is located on the Exchange Server 2003 Mailbox Server. This is also true when the actual Mailbox is still located on an Exchange Server 2007 Mailbox Server though, of course, the OWA client is now redirected to the Exchange Server 2007 Client Access Server, which will contact the Exchange Server 2007 Mailbox Server to process the request.

This UC certificate should contain at least the following domain names:

- **Webmail.inframan.nl** – this is the primary entry point for all Outlook Web Access, Exchange Active Sync (EAS) and Exchange Web Services (EWS) requests
- **Autodiscover.inframan.nl**
- **Legacy.inframan.nl** – this is the namespace for the Exchange Server 2007 Client Access Server.

If you chose not to enter the external domain during setup (in the case of an Internet-facing Client Access Server) a number of external URLs will also need to be configured as explained in the next section.

3.4.2.4 Configure Exchange Web Services

Exchange Server 2010 SP1 uses the Client Access Server to offer the Offline Address Book and Free/Busy information using the HTTP protocol, and these can therefore be used by Outlook 2007 and Outlook 2010. To configure the Exchange services, open an Exchange Management Shell and enter the commands below.

```
Set-OWAVirtualDirectory —Identity 2010CASHUB\OWA* `
   -ExternalURL https://webmail.inframan.nl/OWA

Set-OABVirtualDirectory —Identity 2010CASHUB\OAB* `
   -ExternalURL https://webmail.inframan.nl/OAB

Set-WebServicesVirtualDirectory —Identity 2010CASHUB\EWS* `
   -ExternalURL https://webmail.inframan.nl/ews/exchange.asmx

Set-ActiveSyncVirtualDirectory `
   —Identity 2010CASHUB\Microsoft-Server-ActiveSync `
   —ExternalURL https://webmail.inframan.nl/Microsoft-Server-ActiveSync

Set-ECPVirtualDirectory —Identity 2010CASHUB\ECP* `
   -ExternalURL https://webmail.inframan.nl/ECP
```

In the coexistence scenario, the Offline Address Book Generation Server is still the Exchange Server 2007 Mailbox Server. We want to move this to the Exchange Server 2010 SP1 Mailbox Server, so we follow these steps:

- log on to an Exchange Server 2010 SP1 server and open the **Exchange Management Console**
- expand the **Microsoft Exchange On-Premises (SERVERNAME)** option
- expand the **Organization Configuration** container and select the **Mailbox** option; click the **Offline Address Book** tab
- right-click the **Default Offline Address Book** and select **Move**
- use the **Browse** button to select the new Exchange Server 2010 SP1 Mailbox Server, and click **Move**.

It is also possible to move the Generation Server to Exchange Server 2010 SP1 using the Exchange Server 2010 Management Shell. On an Exchange Server 2010 SP1 server, open the Exchange Management Shell and enter the command: `Move-OfflineAddressBook 'Default Offline Address Book' –Server 2010MBX`.

If your Exchange Server 2007 environment has Public Folders, it is likely that you will want these on your Exchange Server 2010 SP1 Mailbox Server as well. The Public Folder database is, in this case, automatically created, but you have to manually configure replication, which is a bit of a hassle, and time consuming if you have a lot of User Public Folders.

- Log on to an Exchange Server 2007 Mailbox Server and open the **Exchange Management Console**.
- In the Exchange Management Console, double-click the **Toolbox**. Double-click the **Public Folder Management Console** in the **Results** pane.
- Select the **Offline Address Book** and, in the **Results** pane, right-click the /o=<<organization>>/cn=addrlists/cn=oabs/cn=Default Offline Address Book and then select the **Replication** tab. Use the **Add** button to add the Exchange Server 2010 SP1 Public Folder Database, and then click **OK** to close the Properties window.

Chapter 3: Exchange Server 2010 SP1 Coexistence

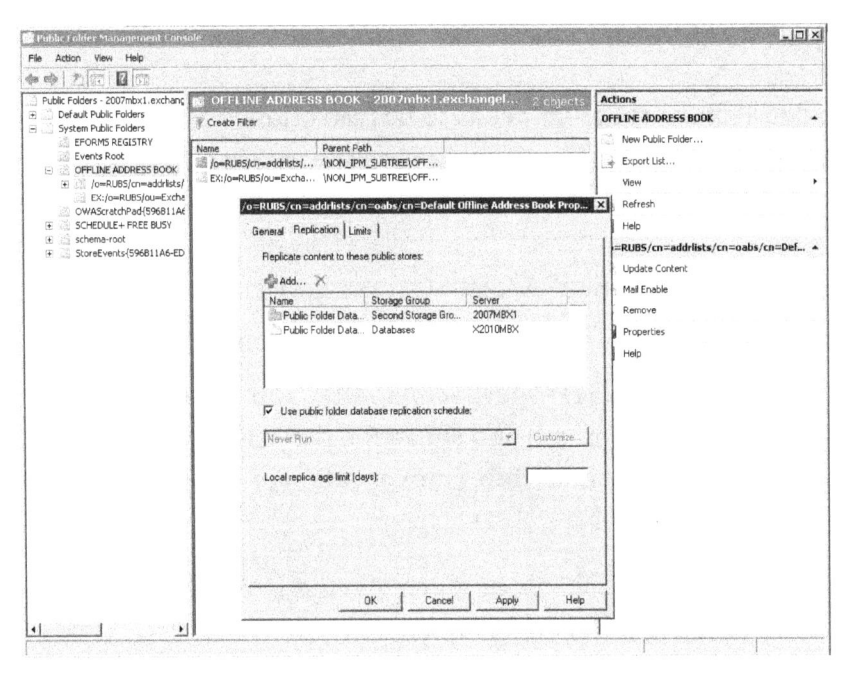

Figure 3.19: Add the Exchange Server 2010 Public Folder database to the replication list.

Repeat these steps for:

- EX:/o=<<organization>>/ou=Exchange Administrative Group (FYDIBOHF23SPDLT)
- OAB Version 2
- OAB Version 3a
- OAB Version 4
- EX:/o=<<yourorg>>/ou=Exchange Administrative Group (FYDIBOHF23SPDLT)
- Schedule+ Free Busy: EX:/o=<<yourorg>>/ou= Exchange Administrative Group (FYDIBOHF23SPDLT).

3.4.3 SMTP Infrastructure

The Exchange Server 2007 Edge Transport Server needs to be transitioned to Exchange Server 2010 SP1 as well. Before doing so, you need to make sure the Active Directory has been transitioned first.

- Install Exchange Server 2007 SP2 on all Client Access Servers in the entire Exchange organization.

- Install the Exchange Server 2010 SP1 Hub Transport Server (after you've installed the Exchange Server 2010 SP1 Client Access Server!) and subscribe the existing Exchange Server 2007 Edge Transport Server to this new Hub Transport Server. This can coexist for some time if needed.

- Install the Exchange Server 2010 SP1 Edge Transport Server in the DMZ. You can follow the procedure for doing this as outlined in *Chapter 2*.

- Remove the subscription from the Exchange Server 2007 Edge Transport Server, and subscribe the new Exchange Server 2010 SP1 Edge Transport Server to the Exchange Server 2010 Hub Transport Server.

It's actually rather simple, although you should bear in mind that this is one of the rare cases when the relationship between Exchange Servers 2007 and 2010 SP1 is asymmetric! Specifically, an Exchange Server 2010 SP1 Edge Transport Server cannot be subscribed to an Exchange Server 2007 Hub Transport Server.

3.4.4 Moving Mailboxes to Exchange Server 2010 SP1

Mailboxes should be moved from Exchange Server 2007 to Exchange Server 2010 SP1 using the 2010 version of the Exchange Management Console, or the Exchange Management Shell. Even more interesting, the new online move-mailbox functionality (with the `New-MoveRequest` command) can be used, which results in a minimal downtime for the users, even when they have a multi-Gigabyte mailbox!

During an online move-mailbox, a new mailbox is created on the Exchange Server 2010 SP1 Mailbox Server and the contents between the old (on Exchange Server 2007) and the new mailbox are synchronized. The user is *still working* with the old mailbox and new messages still arrive at the old mailbox. When both mailboxes are in sync the old mailbox is closed, Active Directory is updated with information regarding the new mailbox location and the new mailbox on Exchange Server 2010 SP1 is fully up and running.

Lastly, note that the online move-mailbox functionality only works between Exchange Server 2010 SP1 servers, and when moving from Exchange Server 2007 to Exchange Server 2010 SP1. When moving from Exchange Server 2010 SP1 to Exchange Server 2007, the move is offline. It also doesn't work with Exchange Server 2003, which is a shame.

Either way, congratulations! You should now have Exchange Server 2010 SP1 running in coexistence with either your Exchange Server 2003 or 2007 environment!

3.5 Summary

As you've seen in this chapter, Exchange Server 2010 SP1 can coexist perfectly into an existing Exchange Server 2003 or Exchange Server 2007 organization. There's no in-place upgrade possibility, so you have to use other (new) hardware to do the actual Exchange Server 2010 SP1 installation. When you transition from either version of Exchange Server, be aware that you have to think about the external namespaces, i.e. `webmail`, `Autodiscover` and `legacy`, in advance to get a smooth transition path. In the next chapter I will focus more on the administration part of Exchange Server 2010 SP1.

Chapter 4: Managing Exchange Server 2010 SP1

Exchange Server 2010 and Active Directory have a closely intertwined relationship. Managing an Exchange Server 2010 SP1 environment automatically implies managing, to some degree, aspects of an Active Directory environment.

For those not familiar with it, Active Directory can be managed using the default tools, such as:

- the Active Directory Users and Computers MMC snap-in
- the Active Directory Sites and Services MMC snap-in
- the Active Directory domains and trusts MMC snap-in.

Exchange Server 2010 can be managed using:

- Exchange Management Console (EMC)
- Exchange Management Shell (EMS)
- Exchange Control Panel (ECP).

In this chapter, I'm going to focus primarily on getting to grips with the three Exchange Server 2010 SP1 Management Tools, and touch upon the Active Directory methods where relevant.

The Exchange Management Console is the GUI for managing an Exchange environment. In a Windows environment, especially smaller environments, lots of Exchange administrators are used to GUIs and, as such, the EMC will almost certainly be the primary (though not exclusive) means of Exchange Management.

Chapter 4: Managing Exchange Server 2010 SP1

Alternatively, the Exchange Management Shell is a complete management interface, and can manage all aspects of an Exchange organization. The EMS is actually also the primary management interface, as the EMC is built on top of it. Every action taken in the EMC is translated on the fly into an EMS command and executed. Under the hood, the EMS uses Windows PowerShell 2.0 which, combined with the remote management capabilities in Windows Server 2008 SP2 and Windows Server 2008 R2, gives Exchange administrators the ability to remotely manage their Exchange environment. As an aside, a combination of the EMC and EMS is a great environment for learning more about using PowerShell 2.0 in Exchange Server 2010 SP1, and I'll explain this later when I go into detail about the Management Console.

Exchange Server 2010 also has a new management feature, called the Exchange Control Panel (ECP). The ECP is a part of the Outlook Web App which gives both users and administrators some administrative control. Regular users can, of course, do as much as they were able to in the Outlook Web Access options page in Exchange Server 2007, but Exchange administrators and users with appropriate delegated permissions now have the additional ability to manage some basic information in their Exchange environment.

In this chapter, I'll go through each of these management tools in enough detail for you to pick them up and use them in your own environment as soon as you put this book down. Once I've done that, I'll also take you through some of the finer points of the new Role Based Access Control system, and give you a deeper understanding of the (changed) Archiving and Compliancy features in Exchange Server 2010 SP1. So, without further ado, let's get started.

4.1 The Exchange Management Shell

Windows Server 2008 was the first operating system that came with PowerShell 1.0 by default, although it was available as a download as far back as Windows Server 2003. In case you don't know about it, PowerShell is a very potent command-line interface which can be used to manage your Windows Server, and the first Microsoft application to

Chapter 4: Managing Exchange Server 2010 SP1

fully utilize it was Exchange Server 2007; the Exchange Management Shell is actually a superset of commands built on top of PowerShell. Product Teams within Microsoft create their own Management Shell solutions, and the Exchange Server team was one of the first product teams building theirs. Naturally, there are other tools with Management Shells, such as the System Center products, for example, and many of them are also built on top of PowerShell.

Exchange Server 2010 SP1 uses PowerShell Version 2 (as can Exchange Server 2007 SP2, although it actually uses Version 1 by default), and in addition to the command-line interface this version also has an Integrated Scripting Environment, which is an integrated GUI that can be used to easily create PowerShell scripts. As I mentioned earlier, PowerShell 2.0 is also integrated with Windows Remote Management (WinRM), making it possible to use PowerShell to remotely manage your Exchange 2010 SP1 environment using the standard HTTP protocol. All that's needed is a workstation or a server that has PowerShell Version 2 installed on the workstation.

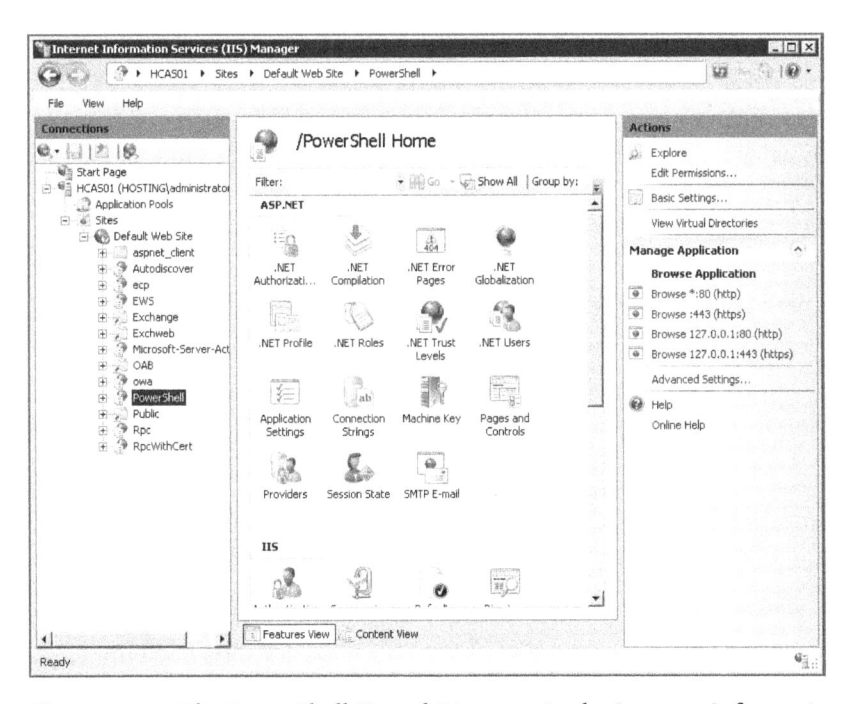

Figure 4.1: The PowerShell Virtual Directory in the Internet Information snap-in.

Chapter 4: Managing Exchange Server 2010 SP1

Even the Exchange Management Console uses the Management Shell (i.e. is written on top of it), and so there are some functions which are not available in the Console but *are* available in the Shell, such as Attachment Filtering in the anti-spam options. Since the Exchange Management Shell is the primary management tool in Exchange Server 2010 SP1 (as it was in Exchange Server 2007), this development direction may hurt a little bit if you're a die-hard GUI administrator.

When the Exchange Management Shell is started, you'll basically see an empty box with just a command prompt – exactly like the Windows command prompt. You can get a list of all available commands at this stage by entering `Get-Command`.

For the benefit of the afore-mentioned die-hard GUI administrators, a PowerShell command consists of two parts: a Noun and a Verb. Verbs can be instructions like **get**, **set**, **new**, **remove**, **enable**, **disable**, and the Noun component can be any objects in Exchange Server. Just combine the Noun and the Verb, as shown below.

- **Get-ExchangeServer** – retrieves a list of all Exchange 2010 Servers in the organization.
- **Set-MailboxDatabase** – sets a property on a Mailbox Database.
- **New-Mailbox** – creates a new mailbox-enabled user.
- **Remove-Mailbox** – deletes a user object and its mailbox.

If you want to learn more about PowerShell commands, a quick web search will turn up scores and scores of learning resources.

> **Note**
>
> *Besides the Exchange Management Shell, there's also the Windows 2008 PowerShell on your server or workstation. If you start the PowerShell instead of the Exchange Management Shell, you'll see a command prompt with a blue background, and the Exchange Server 2010 SP1 cmdlets won't be available. If you are new to PowerShell and the Exchange Management Shell, there will come a day when you will start the wrong Shell.*

4.1.1 Exchange Management Shell help

If there's anything you're not sure about when you're using the EMS, you have a friend in the form of the Quick Reference Guide, located in `C:\Program Files\Microsoft\ExchangeServer\v14\bin\en\ExQuick.htm`. This contains the most important and most-used cmdlets, and their variables.

If you need help on the fly, it's also possible to use the Shell's built-in help function. To get a list of all available help items, just type `help *`. If you need help about a *specific* cmdlet, just type `help` and the name of the cmdlet. To get help about mail-enabling an existing user, for example, just type `help enable-mailbox`.

4.1.2 Pipelining

Another great feature in PowerShell and the Exchange Management Shell is the pipelining function, which uses the output of one cmdlet as the input for a second command. This can drastically reduce the amount of work you need to put in to accomplish relatively complex tasks, and is more or less limited only by your own ingenuity.

For example, if you want to move all mailboxes in a Mailbox Database called `Mailbox Database 1988197524` to another Mailbox Database called `Mailbox Database 0823751426`, you can use the following command:

```
Get-Mailbox –Database "Mailbox Database 1988197524" | New-MoveRequest –TargetDatabase "Mailbox Database 0823751426"
```

This is what happens: `Get-Mailbox –Database "Mailbox Database 1988197524"` retrieves a list of all mailboxes in this particular database. The output of this cmdlet is used as the input of the second cmdlet, the request to online-move mailboxes to the other database.

Chapter 4: Managing Exchange Server 2010 SP1

It's also possible to use more specific queries; for example, to get a list of all mailboxes whose name starts with "Chris" you would use the command: `Get-Mailbox | where-object {$_.name –like "Chris*"}`.

You can then use this as the input for a request to move all these mailboxes to another database:

```
Get-Mailbox | where-object {$_.name –like "Chris*"} | New-MoveRequest '
–TargetDatabase "Mailbox Database 0823751426"
```

It's possible to return only certain properties when using PowerShell commands by using the `Select` option in combination with the technology's pipelining functionality. For example, to return a list of mailboxes and only display the Identity, the Mailbox Database and the Archive Mailbox, just enter the following command:

```
Get-Mailbox –Identity J.Wesselius | Select Name,Alias,DisplayName,GrantSendOnBehalf
To,ArchiveDatabase
```

You'll get an output like that shown in Figure 4.2.

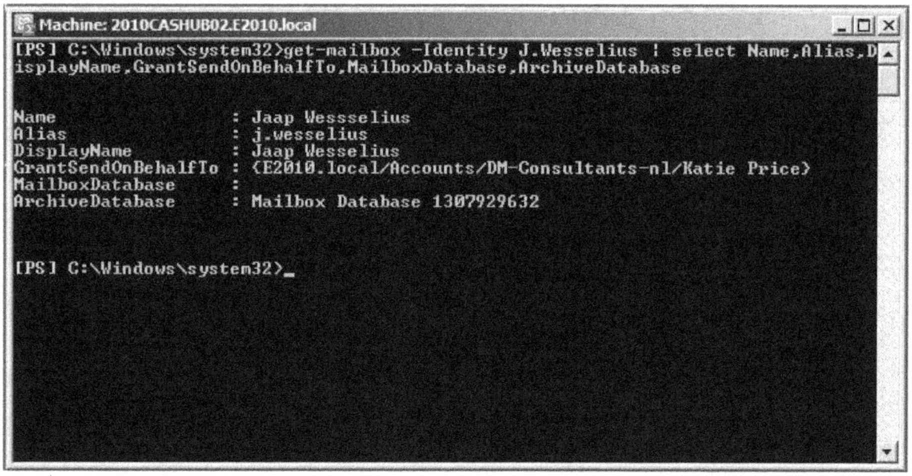

Figure 4.2: Query only a specific set of properties.

4.1.3 Bulk user creation in the Exchange Management Shell

This can be very useful, particularly when you need to create a lot of mailboxes in a hurry. Suppose you have an Organizational Unit named `Sales` in Active Directory, where 100 user objects reside. This command will create a mailbox for each user in this Organizational Unit:

```
Get-User —OrganizationalUnit "Sales" | Enable-Mailbox —Database "Mailbox Database 0823751426"
```

When there are multiple Organizational Units called `Sales` you have to specify the complete path of the Organizational Unit:

```
Get-User —OrganizationalUnit "E14.local/Account/Sales" | Enable-Mailbox —Database "Mailbox Database 0823751426"
```

It's also possible to filter the output of the `Get-User` command with the `—Filter` parameter. For example, to Mailbox-Enable all users whose company attribute is set to `Inframan`, enter the following command:

```
Get-User —Filter {Company —eq "Inframan" } | Enable-Mailbox —Database "Mailbox Database 0823751426"
```

If you want to be even more specific, for example to Mailbox-Enable all users whose company attribute is set to `Inframan` and whose department attribute is set to `Intern`, enter the following command:

```
Get-User —Filter {(Company —eq "Inframan") -AND (Department —eq "Intern")} | Enable-Mailbox —Database "Mailbox Database 0823751426"
```

Chapter 4: Managing Exchange Server 2010 SP1

The following operations are available for the `-Filter` option:

- `-and`
- `-or`
- `-not`
- `-eq` (equals)
- `-ne` (does not equal)
- `-lt` (less than)
- `-gt` (greater than)
- `-like` (compare strings by using wildcard rules)
- `-notlike` (compare strings by using wildcard rules).

In some cases, you'll find it useful to import a list of users from a .CSV file. This list can be exported from another Active Directory or even from an HR (Human Resources) application. It is actually relatively easy to import a .CSV file using PowerShell; the only thing that you need to be mindful of is that the `-Password` option doesn't accept clear text input. The input to this field has to be converted to a secure string:

```
$Database="Mailbox Database 1563944384"
$UPN="e2010.local"
$users = import-csv $args[0]
function SecurePassword([string]$password)
{
    $secure = new-object System.Security.SecureString
    $password.ToCharArray() | % { $secure.AppendChar($_) }
    return $secure
}
foreach ($i in $users)
  {
  $sp = SecurePassword $i.password
  $upn = $i.FirstName + "@"+ $upn
```

```
    $DisplayName = $i.FirstName + " "+ $i.LastName
    New-Mailbox -Password $sp -Database $Database `
    -UserPrincipalName $UPN
    -Name $i.DisplayName
    -FirstName $i.FirstName `
    -LastName $i.LastName
    -OrganizationalUnit $i.OU
}
```

On the first three lines, three parameters are set that are used during the actual creation of the user and the mailbox. The file is read in a `ForEach` loop, and the actual users and the mailboxes are created as this loop progresses.

The `SecurePassword` function reads the password from the output .CSV file and converts it into a secure string which is used, in turn, as the password input during the creation of the users. The .CSV file itself is formatted like this:

```
FirstName,LastName,Password,OU
Jaap,Wesselius,Pass1word,Accounts
Michael,Francis,Pass1word,Accounts
Michael,Smith,Pass1word,Accounts
John,Doe,Pass1word,Accounts
```

To make this script usable, save the script file as `create.ps1` in a directory like `C:\scripts`. You'll also need to save the .CSV output file as `users.csv` in the same directory. To actually use the script, open a PowerShell command prompt, navigate to the `C:\scripts` directory and enter the following command: `.\create.ps1 users.csv`.

4.1.4 Remote PowerShell

As I keep saying (I'll stop soon), the Remote PowerShell is new in Exchange Server 2010, making it possible to connect to an Exchange Server 2010 server at a remote location, and this hasn't changed in Exchange Server 2010 SP1. The workstation doesn't have to be in the same domain or even have the Exchange Management Tools installed – as long as the proper credentials are used, it will work. With this kind of functionality, it's now as easy to manage your Exchange Servers in another part of the building as your Exchange Server in a datacenter in another part of the country. Needless to say, if you are using a non-domain client for Remote PowerShell you cannot use Kerberos. You have to change the authentication to Basic for this to happen.

When the Exchange Management Shell is opened via **Start Menu > All Programs > Exchange Server 2010**, the Exchange Management Shell will automatically connect to the Exchange 2010 SP1 Server you're logged in to. However, this is only true if you are logged in to an Exchange Server (Console or RDP) at the time. If you are on a management workstation, it will choose an arbitrary Exchange Server within your AD site. Alternatively, using the remote options, it's also possible to connect to a remote Exchange Server at this stage.

To use Remote PowerShell, you'll need to log on to a Windows Server 2008 (R2) server or Windows 7 workstation that has the Windows Management Framework installed. The Management Framework consists of PowerShell 2.0 and Windows Remote Management (WinRM) 2.0, and can be downloaded from the Microsoft website at HTTP://TINYURL.COM/POWERSHELL2.

Make sure that the workstation (or server) supports remote signed scripts. Due to security constraints, this is disabled by default. You can enable this support by opening a Windows PowerShell command prompt and entering: `Set-ExecutionPolicy RemoteSigned`.

The next step is to create a session that will connect to the remote Exchange Server. When the session is created it can be imported into PowerShell:

```
$Session = New-PSSession `
 —ConfigurationName Microsoft.Exchange `
 —ConnectionUri http://E2010MBX01.E2010.local/PowerShell `
 -Authentication Kerberos
Import-PSSession $Session
```

The PowerShell on the workstation will now connect to the remote Exchange Server using a default SSL connection and, RBAC permitting, all Exchange cmdlets will be available. It's incredibly easy.

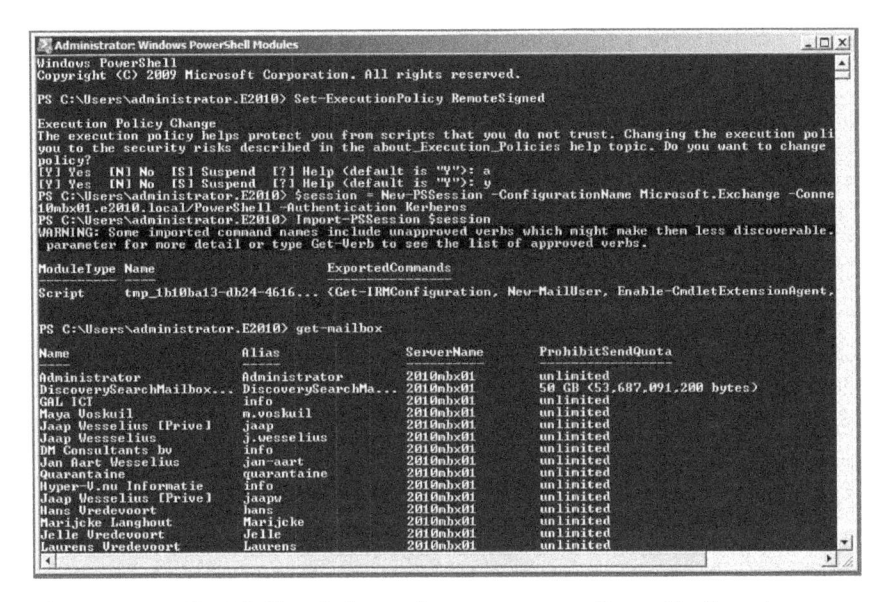

Figure 4.3: Get Mailbox information on a remote PowerShell session.

To end the remote PowerShell session, just enter: `Remove-PSSession $session`.

Admittedly, the above example is from a server that's also a member of the same Active Directory domain. To connect to a remote Exchange Server 2010 server that's available over the Internet, multiple steps are required. The first step is to create a variable in the PowerShell command prompt that contains the username and password for the remote session: `$Credential = Get-Credential`.

A pop-up box will appear, requesting a username and password for the remote Exchange environment. Once you've filled in the credentials, the following command will create a new session that will set up a connection to the Exchange environment. The `$Credential` variable is used to pass the credentials to the Exchange environment, and then the session is imported into PowerShell.

Chapter 4: Managing Exchange Server 2010 SP1

```
$Session = New-PSSession `
  -ConfigurationName Microsoft.Exchange `
  -ConnectionUri https://www.exchange14.nl/PowerShell `
  -Authentication Basic -Credential $Credential

Import-PSSession $Session
```

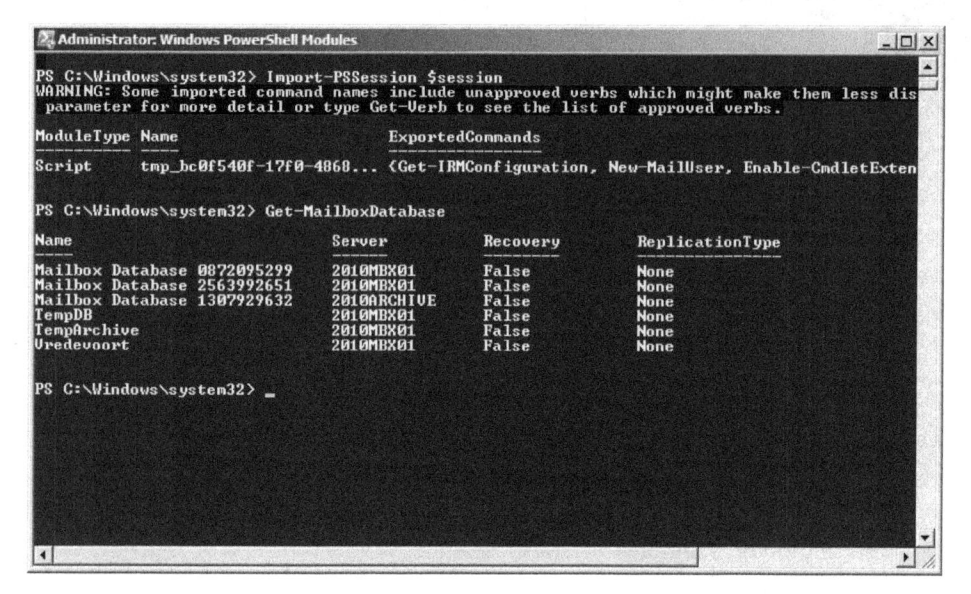

Figure 4.4: Getting Mailbox Database information using the remote PowerShell from my laptop at home.

Note

If you want to connect to a remote Exchange Server 2010 SP1 server over the Internet, remember to enable Basic Authentication on the remote server. Open the Internet Information Services (IIS) Manager on the server, navigate to the default website and select the /PowerShell Virtual Directory. In the **Results** *pane, under IIS double-click on* **Authentication***. Here you can enable Basic Authentication.*

The examples were for the Active Directory domain administrator, who automatically has the remote management option enabled. To enable another user for remote management, enter: `Set-User <<username>> -RemotePowerShellEnabled $True`.

4.1.5 Reporting with the Exchange Management Shell

The Exchange Management Shell can actually be very effectively used for creating reports. The EMS has quite a lot of powerful cmdlets, and with the pipelining option it is possible to create all kinds of reporting. I'll give you a few examples, although please bear in mind that the outputs for many of these examples have been **edited for readability**.

The `Get-ExchangeServer` cmdlet will return a list of all Exchange 2010 servers in the organization.

```
PS C:\Windows\system32> Get-ExchangeServer

Name            Site          ServerRole    Edition     AdminDisplayVe
----            ----          ----------    -------     --------------

2010CASHUB02    E2010.loc...  ClientAc...   Enterprise  Version 14.1
2010MBX01       E2010.loc...  Mailbox       Enterprise  Version 14.1
2010ARCHIVE     E2010.loc...  Mailbox       Enterprise  Version 14.1

PS C:\Windows\system32>
```

With the `-Identity` option it is possible to retrieve the information for only one Exchange server, and when the `Get-ExchangeServer` cmdlet is used in a pipeline with the `Format-List` command, all the detailed information for the server in question is shown.

Chapter 4: Managing Exchange Server 2010 SP1

```
PS C:\Windows\system32> Get-ExchangeServer -Identity 2010CASHUB02 | fl


RunspaceId             : fe882992-164b-46bf-b077-396ffb9d01a2
Name                   : 2010CASHUB02
DataPath               : C:\Program Files\Microsoft\Exchange
                         Server\V14\Mailbox
Domain                 : E2010.local
Edition                : Enterprise
ExchangeLegacyDN       : /o=E2010/ou=Exchange Administrative
                         Group (FYDIBOHF23SPDLT)/
                         cn=Configuration/cn=Severs/
                         cn=2010CASHUB02
ExchangeLegacyServerRole : 0
Fqdn                   : 2010CASHUB02.E2010.local
CustomerFeedbackEnabled : False
InternetWebProxy       :
IsHubTransportServer   : True
IsClientAccessServer   : True
IsExchange2007OrLater  : True
IsEdgeServer           : False
IsMailboxServer        : False
IsE14OrLater           : True
IsProvisionedServer    : False
IsUnifiedMessagingServer : False
OrganizationalUnit     : E2010.local/2010CASHUB02
AdminDisplayVersion    : Version 14.1 (Build 180.1)
Site                   : E2010.local/Configuration/
                         Sites/Default-First-Site-Name
ServerRole             : ClientAccess, HubTransport
Identity               : 2010CASHUB02
OriginatingServer      : 2010AD02.E2010.local
```

Chapter 4: Managing Exchange Server 2010 SP1

If you want to retrieve mailbox information from your Exchange Server, the `Get-Mailbox` and `Get-MailboxStatistics` cmdlets can be used:

```
PS C:\Windows\system32> get-mailbox

Name                 Alias           ServerName  ProhibitSendQuota
----                 -----           ----------  -----------------
Administrator        Administrator   2010mbx01   unlimited
GAL ICT              info            2010mbx01   unlimited
Maya Voskuil         m.voskuil       2010mbx01   unlimited
Jaap Wesselius       jaap            2010mbx01   unlimited
Jaap Wessselius      j.wesselius     2010mbx01   unlimited
DM Consultants       info            2010mbx01   unlimited
Jan Aart Wesse..     jan-aart        2010mbx01   unlimited
Quarantaine          quarantaine     2010mbx01   unlimited
Hyper-V.nu Inf..     info            2010mbx01   unlimited
Jaap Wesselius       jaapw           2010mbx01   unlimited
Hans Vredevoort      hans            2010mbx01   unlimited
Marijcke Langh..     Marijcke        2010mbx01   unlimited
Jelle Vredevoo..     Jelle           2010mbx01   unlimited
Laurens Vredev..     Laurens         2010mbx01   unlimited
Steven Vredevo..     Steven          2010mbx01   unlimited
Jos Vredevoort       Jos             2010mbx01   unlimited
Ineke Vredevoo..     Ineke           2010mbx01   unlimited
Bram Wesselius       bram            2010mbx01   unlimited
TAP                  tap             2010mbx01   unlimited
Albert Alberts       a.alberts       2010mbx01   unlimited
Joe Lawyer           J.Lawyer        2010mbx01   unlimited
Katie Price          K.Price         2010mbx01   unlimited
Michael Francis      M.Francis       2010mbx01   unlimited
Marina Wesseli..     marina          2010mbx01   unlimited
ExAdmin              ExAdmin         2010mbx01   unlimited

PS C:\Windows\system32>
```

To get detailed information about a particular mailbox, the output of that mailbox's identity can be piped to the `Format-List` command.

Chapter 4: Managing Exchange Server 2010 SP1

```
PS C:\Windows\system32> get-mailbox -Identity J.Wesselius | fl

RunspaceId                          : fe882992-164b-46bf-b077-
                                      396ffb9d01a2
Database                            : TempDB
UseDatabaseRetentionDefaults        : True
RetainDeletedItemsUntilBackup       : False
DeliverToMailboxAndForward          : True
LitigationHoldEnabled               : True
SingleItemRecoveryEnabled           : False
RetentionHoldEnabled                : False
LitigationHoldDate                  : 26-4-2010 20:24:34
LitigationHoldOwner                 : Administrator
ManagedFolderMailboxPolicy          :
RetentionPolicy                     :
CalendarRepairDisabled              : False
IsMailboxEnabled                    : True
Languages                           : {en-US}
ProhibitSendQuota                   : unlimited
ProhibitSendReceiveQuota            : unlimited
RecoverableItemsQuota               : unlimited
RecoverableItemsWarningQuota        : unlimited
SamAccountName                      : J.Wesselius
ServerName                          : 2010mbx01
UseDatabaseQuotaDefaults            : False
IssueWarningQuota                   : 4 GB (4,294,967,296 bytes)
RulesQuota                          : 64 KB (65,536 bytes)
ArchiveDatabase                     : Mailbox Database 1307929632
ArchiveGuid                         : ad5140e7-4985-49a1-9411-
                                      f88773395375
ArchiveName                         : {Online Archive -
                                        Jaap Wesselius}
ArchiveQuota                        : unlimited
ArchiveWarningQuota                 : unlimited
CalendarVersionStoreDisabled        : False
Alias                               : j.wesselius
GrantSendOnBehalfTo                 : {E2010.local/Accounts/
                                        DM-Consultants-nl/
                                        Katie Price}
Name                                : Jaap Wessselius
OriginatingServer                   : 2010AD02.E2010.local

PS C:\Windows\system32>
```

The `Get-MailboxStatistics` cmdlet retrieves detailed information about Mailbox usage from an Exchange Server.

```
[PS] C:\Windows\system32>Get-MailboxStatistics -server 2010MBX01

DisplayName          ItemCount    StorageLimitStatus    LastLogonTime
-----------          ---------    ------------------    -------------
Discovery Search     974          BelowLimit            20-5-2010...
Hyper-V.nu In..      1496         BelowLimit            26-4-2010...
Maya Voskuil         2704         BelowLimit            8-6-2010...
GAL ICT              211          BelowLimit            8-6-2010...
DM Consultants ..    1062         BelowLimit            27-5-2010...
Microsoft Excha..    15           NoChecking
Joe Lawyer [Leg..    16           BelowLimit            4-6-2010...
Jos Vredevoort       2329         BelowLimit            8-6-2010...
Jaap Wesselius       6438         BelowLimit            8-6-2010...
Katie Price [HR..    1            BelowLimit            13-4-2010...
Quarantaine          337          BelowLimit            6-6-2010...
Albert Alberts       7            BelowLimit            25-3-2010...
Hans Vredevoort      1338         BelowLimit            8-6-2010...
Administrator        5            BelowLimit            7-6-2010...
Marijcke Langho..    1784         BelowLimit            8-6-2010...
Marina Wesseliu..    4483         BelowLimit            8-6-2010...
Jan Aart Wessel..    113          BelowLimit            12-6-2010...
Hyper-V.nu Info..    1497         BelowLimit            11-6-2010...

PS C:\Windows\system32>

[PS] C:\Windows\system32>
```

So the `Get-MailboxStatistics` cmdlet gives lots of information about usage. To get some real reporting information, PowerShell has an option to convert its output to HTML. So, when you enter the following command:

```
Get-MailboxStatistics -Server 2010MBX01 | ConvertTo-HTML DisplayName > 2010MBX01.html
```

… nothing is logged to the screen, but an HTML file is created in the directory where the PowerShell is running. Use Internet Explorer to open the output file (see Figure 4.5).

Chapter 4: Managing Exchange Server 2010 SP1

```
DisplayName
Discovery Search Mailbox
student7
Microsoft Exchange Approval Assistant
student22
SystemMailbox{0a1620a9-c22d-49ce-9536-6b5e902d15a5}
Hyper-V.nu Informatie
Maya Voskuil
student8
GAL ICT
student16
DM Consultants bv
Microsoft Exchange
Joe Lawyer [Legal Department]
Jos Vredevoort
Jaap Wesselius
Katie Price [HR Deplartment]
```

Figure 4.5: Output of the Get-MailboxStatistics cmdlet redirected to an HTML file.

Using just the `DisplayName` is not really useful, so let's add some more parameters:

```
Get-MailboxStatistics —Server 2010MBX01 | ConvertTo-HTML DisplayName,ServerName,
DatabaseName,ItemCount,
TotalItemSize, LastLoggedOnUserAccount  > MbxInfo.html
```

This will give the HMTL file shown in Figure 4.6.

Chapter 4: Managing Exchange Server 2010 SP1

DisplayName	ServerName	DatabaseName	ItemCount	TotalItemSize	LastLoggedOnUserAccount
Discovery Search Mailbox	2010MBX01	Mailbox Database 0872095299	974	92.52 MB (97,017,454 bytes)	E2010\J.Lawyer
student7	2010MBX01	Mailbox Database 0872095299	1	134 B (134 bytes)	
Microsoft Exchange Approval Assistant	2010MBX01	Mailbox Database 0872095299	3	113.5 KB (116,196 bytes)	
student22	2010MBX01	Mailbox Database 0872095299	1	134 B (134 bytes)	
SystemMailbox {0a1620a9-c22d-49ce-9536-6b5e902d15a5}	2010MBX01	Mailbox Database 0872095299	2	889 B (889 bytes)	
Hyper-V.nu Informatie	2010MBX01	Mailbox Database 0872095299	1496	29.44 MB (30,867,225 bytes)	E2010\info-hv
Maya Voskuil	2010MBX01	Mailbox Database 0872095299	2704	45.36 MB (47,560,813 bytes)	E2010\m.voskuil

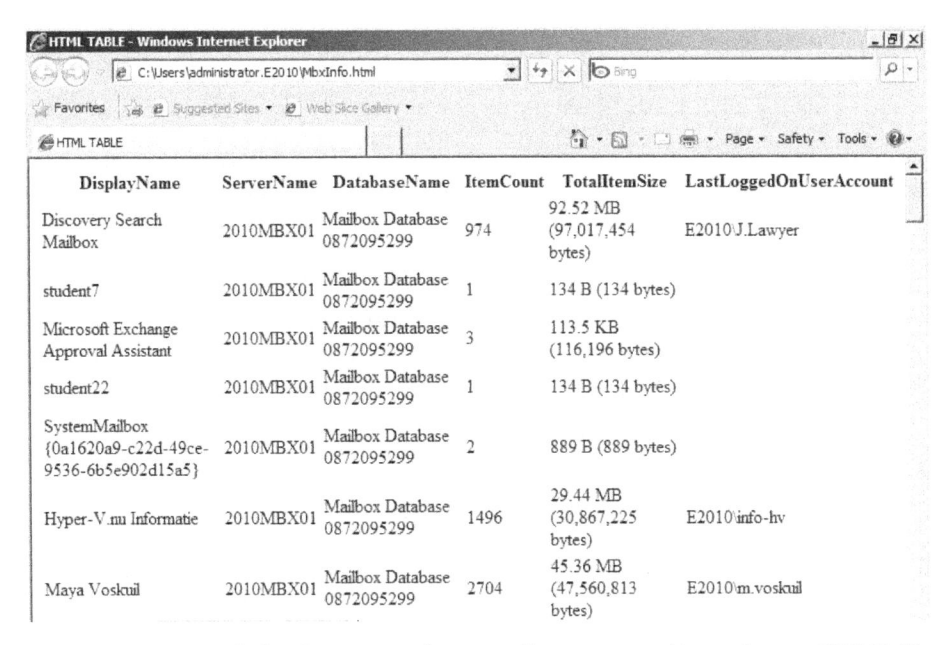

Figure 4.6: Detailed information about mailbox usage redirected to an HTML file.

Much nicer!

> **Note**
>
> *If you're enjoying pipelining, it's also possible to use the PowerShell* Out-File *option instead of redirecting using the ">".*

Now let's create a small script with some variables:

- **$Now** contains the date and time the script runs
- **$BodyStyle** contains a value used to retrieve a stylesheet to customize the HMTL file
- **$MBXOutput** contains the actual output from the Get-MailboxStatistics cmdlet.

Your script should look something like this:

```
$Now=Get-Date
$BodyStyle="<link rel='stylesheet' type='text/css' href= 'http://www.domain.com/
styles/reporting.css' />"
$BodyStyle=$BodyStyle + "<title>Exchange 2010 Mailbox Reporting</title>"
$MBXOutput = Get-MailboxStatistics -Server 2010MBX01 |
ConvertTo-HTML  DisplayName,ServerName,DatabaseName,ItemCount,TotalItemSize,LastLog
gedOnUserAccount -Title "Mailbox Overview"  -Head $BodyStyle

$MBXoutput = $MBXoutput -replace "<BODY>", "<BODY><div id='midden'> <h3>Report
$($now)</h3>"
$MBXoutput = $MBXoutput -replace "</BODY>", "</DIV></BODY>"
$MBXoutput | Out-File MailboxInfo.html
```

Save this file as `reporting.ps1` and run the script. It will still show the output of the query, but now it'll be beautifully formatted according the CSS style sheet.
This methodology will allow you to create some really cool custom reporting setups.

4.2 The Exchange Management Console

As discussed earlier, the Exchange Management Console is the GUI for managing the Exchange Server 2010 SP1 environment. The Exchange Management Console is an MMC 3.0 snap-in and consists of several panes, as shown in Figure 4.7.

- **Navigation pane** – this is the left-hand pane where the Exchange organization is visible, and features different leaves like the Organization Configuration, the Server Configuration, the Recipient Configuration and the Toolbox.
- **Results pane** – this is the middle pane where the results about the selection in the Navigation pane are visible.
- **Actions pane** – this is the right-hand pane, where actions are chosen that need to be performed against the selections made in the other two panes.

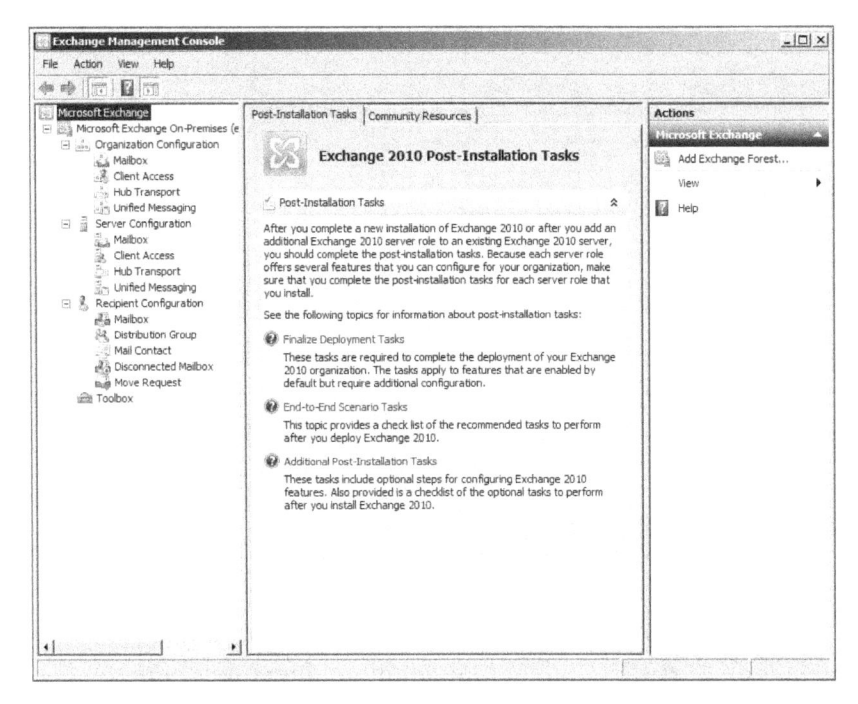

Figure 4.7: The Exchange Management Console with the three panes.

When the Organization Configuration in the Navigation Pane is selected, the organization-wide configuration of the Exchange organization can be managed, which all the Exchange Servers in the entire organization will share. In the organizational configuration, information can be set for example about Send Connectors, Accepted Domains, Email Address Policies, Database Availability Group, Mailboxes, etc. The Server Configuration in the Navigation pane contains all the server-specific configuration options, such as a particular server's Receive Connectors, Outlook Web App settings or Outlook Anywhere settings.

Lastly, the Recipient Configuration contains some of the configuration options regarding the following recipients:

- Mailbox
- Distribution Group
- Mail Contact
- Disconnected Mailbox
- Move Request.

4.2.1 PowerShell and the EMC

The easiest way to learn the PowerShell commands you'll need to manage Exchange Server 2010 SP1 is to remember that, as the Exchange Management Console is written on top of the Exchange Management Shell, every action in the Management Console is translated to a Management Shell command. This is important because it's possible to take an action in the EMC, and then *see its PowerShell equivalent*.

For example, to mail-enable a user in the Management Console:

- in the **Navigation** pane, select the **Recipients** configuration and select **Mailbox**; in the Actions pane select **New Mailbox**
- in the **New Mailbox** Wizard select **User Mailbox**, and then click **Next**
- in the **User Type** windows, select **Existing user** and click the **Add** button; select an available user object (this user object must be already created) and click **OK**, then click **Next** to continue

- in the **Mailbox Settings** windows, enter an appropriate alias for the new mailbox and click **Next** to continue

- in the **New Mailbox** window, verify the configuration that's entered, and click **New** to create the new mailbox.

All of the configuration information that you've just entered is being translated to a Management Shell command on the fly, and this command is then executed. When the command is executed the window shown in Figure 4.8 appears.

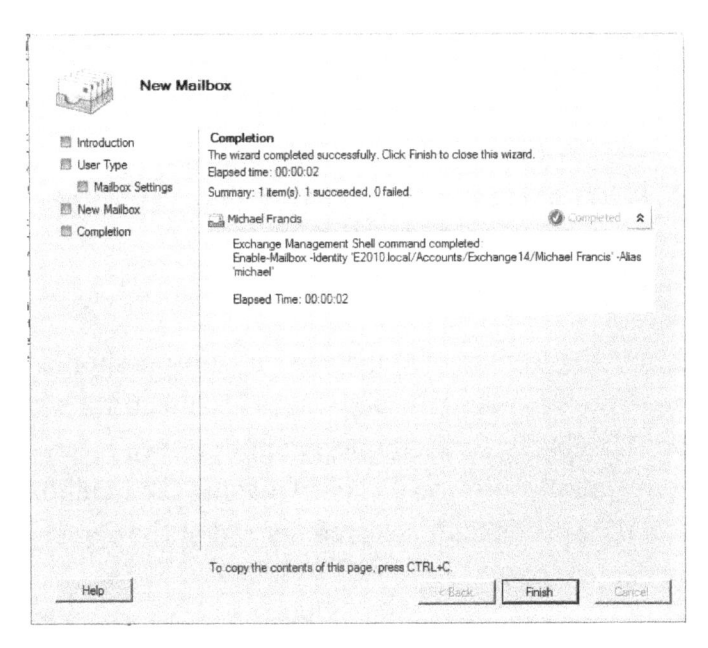

Figure 4.8: The results of mail-enabling a user.

In the lower part you see **To copy the contents of this page, press CTRL+C**. If you press **CTRL+C**, the contents of this dialog are copied to the Windows clipboard, which then contains the output below.

Chapter 4: Managing Exchange Server 2010 SP1

```
Summary: 1 item(s). 1 succeeded, 0 failed.
Elapsed time: 00:00:02

Michael Francis
Completed

Exchange Management Shell command completed:
Enable-Mailbox -Identity 'E2010.local/Accounts/Exchange14/Michael Francis'
    -Alias 'michael'

Elapsed Time: 00:00:02
```

Included in the output is the actual command that was executed, and this is by far the easiest way to learn the PowerShell commands.

4.2.2 Evolution of the Exchange Management Console

If you're familiar with Exchange Server 2007, the Exchange Management Console should be familiar as well. There *are* some changes, though primarily because of architectural changes in Exchange Server 2010. Mailbox Databases, for example, are not on the server level as in Exchange Server 2007, but on the organization level. For managing the Mailbox Database, the Organization Configuration now needs to be selected instead of the Server Configuration (as is the case in Exchange Server 2007).

Since Mailbox Databases are on the organization level, individual Mailbox Database names must be unique across the entire organization. This is the reason why default Mailbox Databases are created with names like Mailbox Database 0889073255 and Mailbox Database 1563944384.

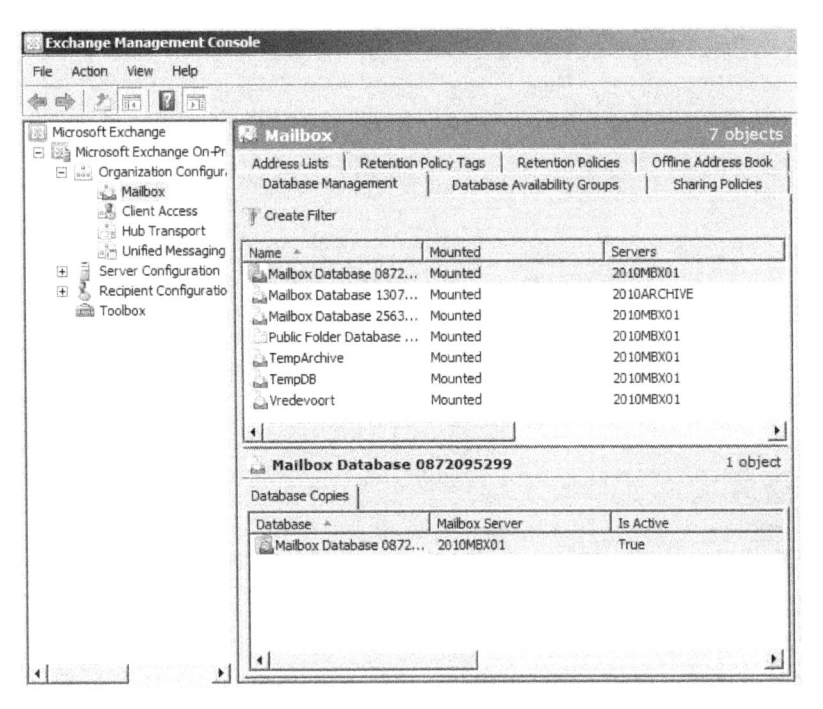

Figure 4.9: Mailbox databases are on an organization level in Exchange Server 2010 SP1.

A new feature in the Exchange Management Console is the option to manage multiple Exchange organizations in a single console. If you open the Exchange Management Console, by default the Exchange On-Premises organization which the Exchange Server is a member of is shown. In the **Actions** pane, click **Add Exchange Forest** and enter the Fully Qualified Domain Name (FQDN) of another Exchange organization you have access to. Enter the proper credentials, and two separate Exchange organizations can be managed at once from a single console. The ability to manage multiple locations and multiple organizations is one of the things that Exchange Server 2010 now does very well.

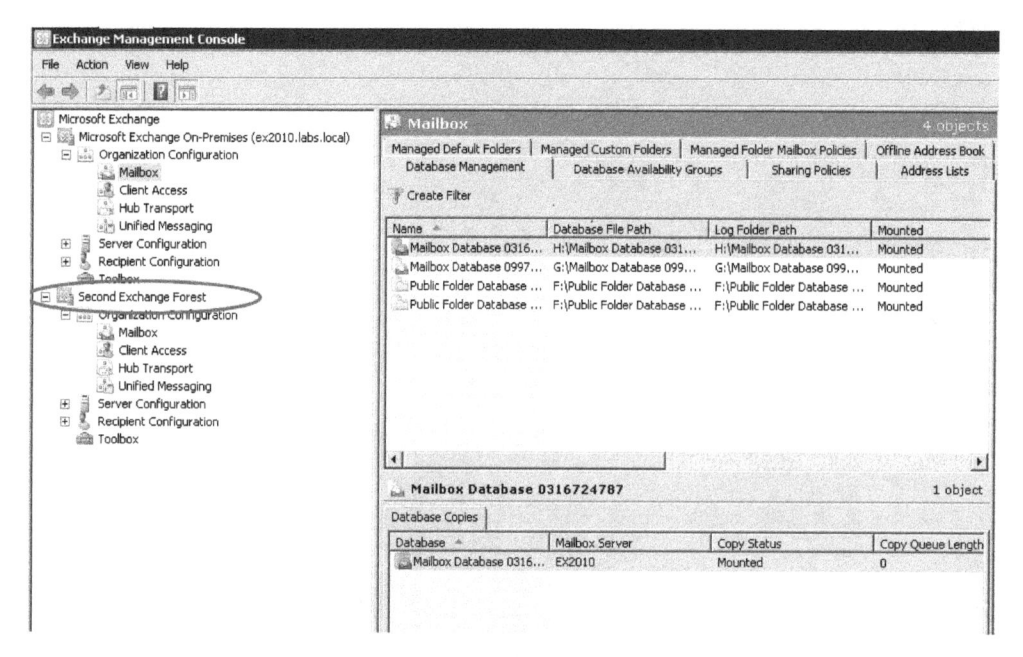

Figure 4.10: Managing two Exchange organizations from one Management Console!

4.3 The Exchange Control Panel (ECP)

The Exchange Control Panel (ECP) was new in Exchange Server 2010, and has now been significantly enhanced in Exchange Server 2010 SP1. It's a self-service Control Panel for both end-users *and* Exchange administrators, accessible through the Outlook Web App interface. The management possibilities available in the ECP naturally depend on the management rights an individual user has in the Exchange organization.

When logged on to the Outlook Web App, click the **Options** button in the upper right corner to access the Exchange Control Panel. A typical user enters a page where only their individual settings can be changed, as in Figure 4.11.

Chapter 4: Managing Exchange Server 2010 SP1

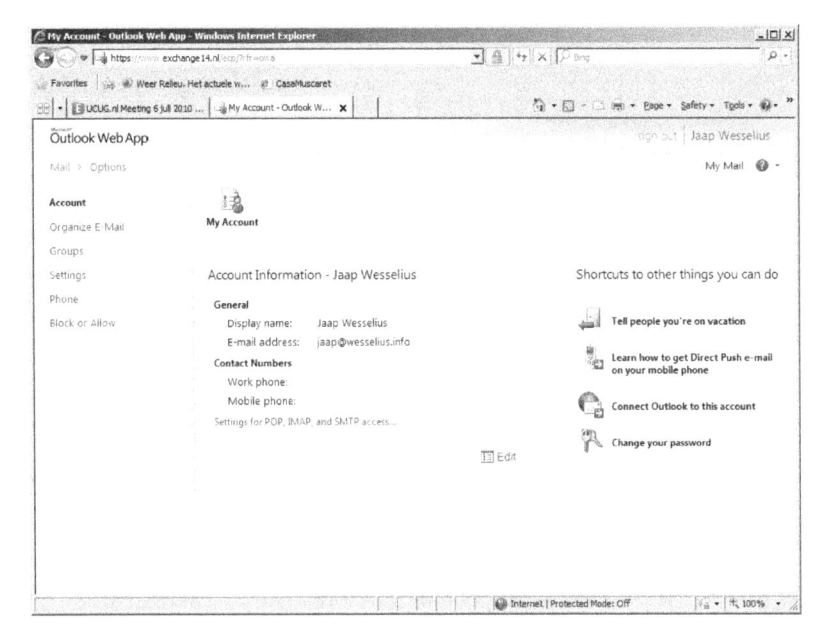

Figure 4.11: The Exchange Control Panel for a regular user.

Also new in Exchange Server 2010 is the option for the user to change his or her own attributes in Active Directory, such as address, location or phone number. A user just has to click on the Edit button as shown in Figure 4.11 above, and their personal properties can be changed.

For a typical user, the ECP is the replacement of the **Options** page in Exchange Server 2007 OWA and earlier, with the additional capability of modifying their personal attributes. However, when a user has administrative privileges, the ECP has much more potential. In the upper left corner there's an additional option, **Select what to manage**, and the available options are:

- Myself
- My Organization
- Another User.

181

Chapter 4: Managing Exchange Server 2010 SP1

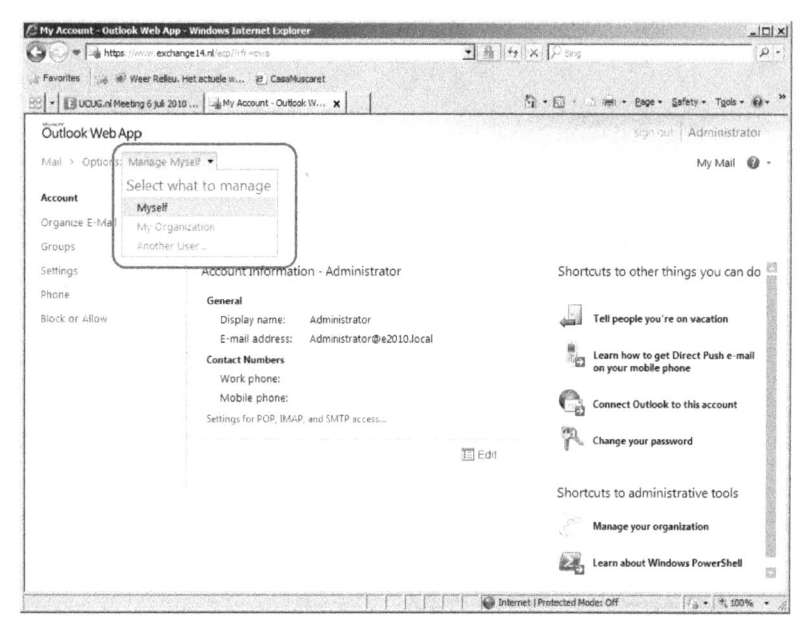

Figure 4.12: The Exchange Control Panel for an administrative user.

When **My Organization** is selected, the admin user has the ability to perform basic administrative tasks like Managing Mailboxes, Public Groups, External Contacts, Administrative Roles and User Roles. Using the ECP it is even possible to create, modify or delete Mailboxes, Groups or External Contacts.

Chapter 4: Managing Exchange Server 2010 SP1

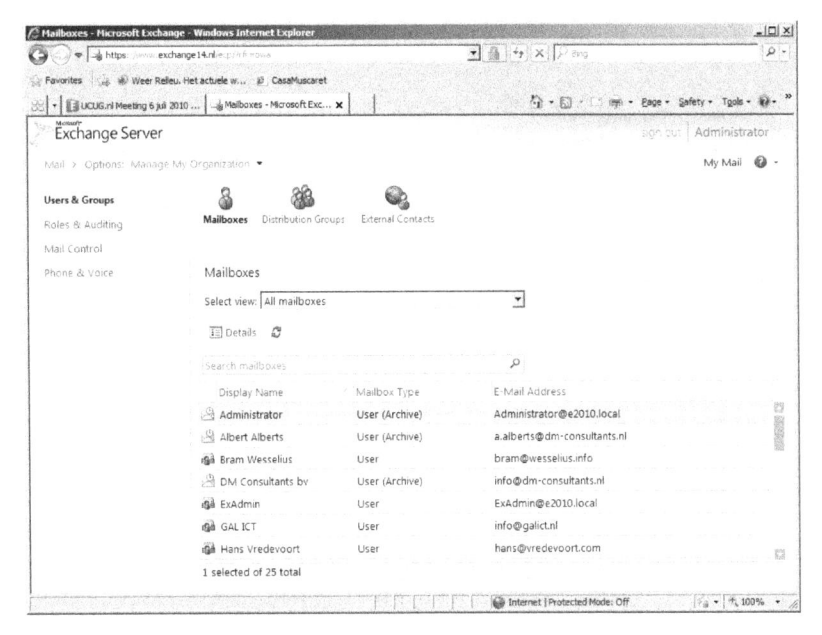

Figure 4.13: Available administrative tasks in the Exchange Control Panel.

Besides **Users & Groups** there is also a **Reporting** option available in the Exchange Control Panel, and this gives access to a tool which is the successor of the **Message Tracking** Tool in Exchange Server 2007. Using the **Reporting** options it is possible to retrieve information about the message flow in Exchange Server 2010.

To try it out, select the mailbox to search for information, select the **Recipient** (messages sent to or messages received from) and information for the **Subject Line**. The Exchange Control Panel will show a list of messages that comply with the search options.

183

Chapter 4: Managing Exchange Server 2010 SP1

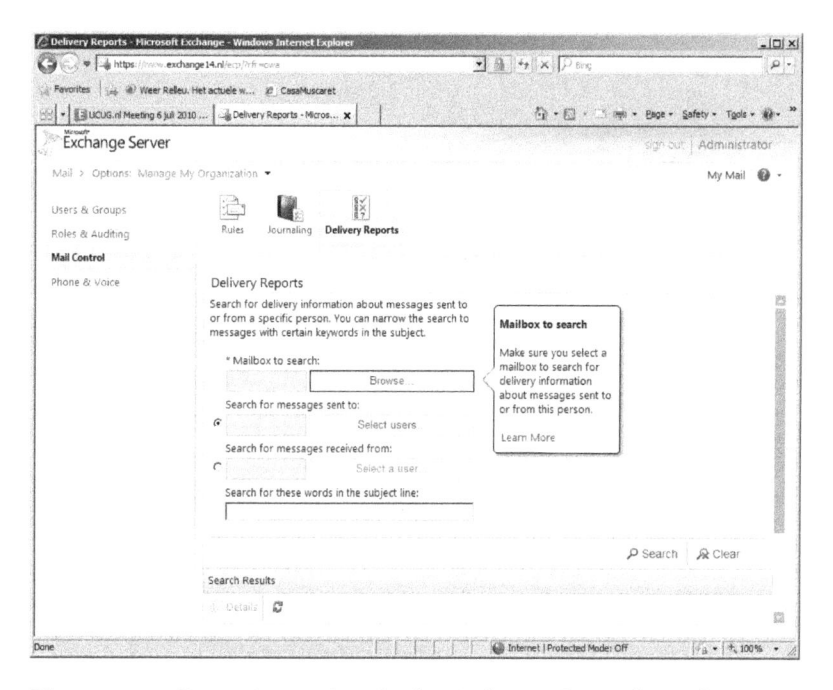

Figure 4.14: Reporting options in the Exchange Control Panel.

4.4 Role Based Access Control (RBAC)

In Exchange Server 2003 and Exchange Server 2007, the Exchange Administrator has the ability to perform some **delegation of control**. This way it is possible to grant other users or Security Groups more privileges in the Exchange organization, allowing them to perform some administrative tasks as well.

In Exchange Server 2010 this has changed into a Role Based Access model, where users can be added to predefined Role Groups. When a user or a security group is added to such a Role Group they automatically inherit the security rights assigned to it.

The following default Role Groups are available:

- Delegated Setup
- Discovery Management
- Help Desk
- Hygiene Management
- Organization Management
- Public Folder Management
- Recipient Management
- Records Management
- Server Management
- UM Management
- View-Only Organization Management.

To give a user additional permissions on the Exchange organization, you really do just need to add the user to the appropriate Role Group. This can be achieved using:

- Exchange Management Console – the RBAC Editor can be found in the tools section but, when selected, you're redirected to the Exchange Control Panel
- Exchange Management Shell
- Exchange Control Panel.

To add a user to the Recipient Management Role Group in the Exchange Management Shell, enter the following command: `Add-RoleGroupMember "Recipient Management" -Member J.Wesselius`.

Chapter 4: Managing Exchange Server 2010 SP1

To add a user to the Recipient Management Role Group using the Exchange Control Panel, open the ECP and select **My Organization** in the **Select what to manage** drop-down box. Click the **Administrator Roles** tab, and double-click the **Recipient Management** Role Group, then click **Add** and select the user.

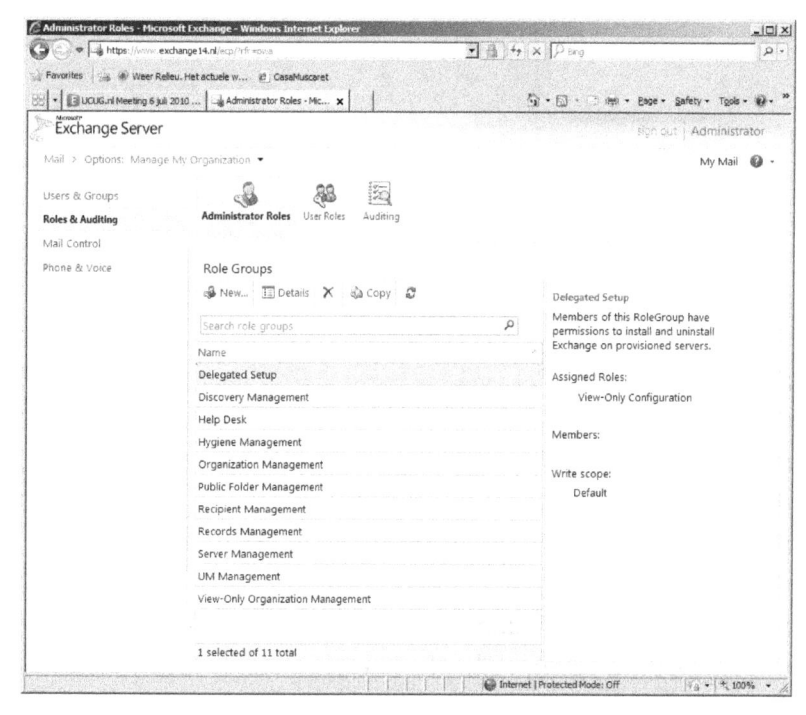

Figure 4.15: Managing RBAC Administrative Roles using the Exchange Control Panel.

One of the major benefits of using Role Based Access Control is that it is possible to give very granular permissions to users or Security Groups. Although this was possible in Exchange Server 2007 as well, you had to work with Access Control Lists (ACLs) to get the same results, and the downside of changing ACLs is that it can give unwanted results due to unexpected restrictions.

4.4.1 RBAC architecture

Role Based Access Control, or RBAC, is a management model that can be used to delegate control in your Exchange organization. RBAC consists of Management Roles, Role Entries and Role Scopes.

- A **Management Role** is a configuration object, stored in Active Directory, which defines management tasks. These tasks are made available to any users to which the Management Role has been assigned. There are two types of Management Roles, the Built-in Management Roles, as shown in Figure 4.15, and Custom Management Roles.

- **Management Role Entries** are, in essence, just a list of Exchange Tasks that can be performed. You can see this list as the equivalent Exchange Management Shell cmdlets that can be run.

- The **Management Role Scope** is the boundary of control for a Management Role Assignment.

- A **Management Role Assignment** is a configuration object, also stored in Active Directory, which links a particular Management Role to a user or Universal Security Group (USG), also known as the "assignee."

- The **Role Assignment Policy** allows the assignment of Management Roles to a Mailbox, and is linked to a particular Mailbox using a property (`RoleAssignmentPolicy`) on the Mailbox.

- A **Role Group** is a Universal Security Group in Active Directory, stored in the **Microsoft Exchange Security Group** Organizational Unit.

Chapter 4: Managing Exchange Server 2010 SP1

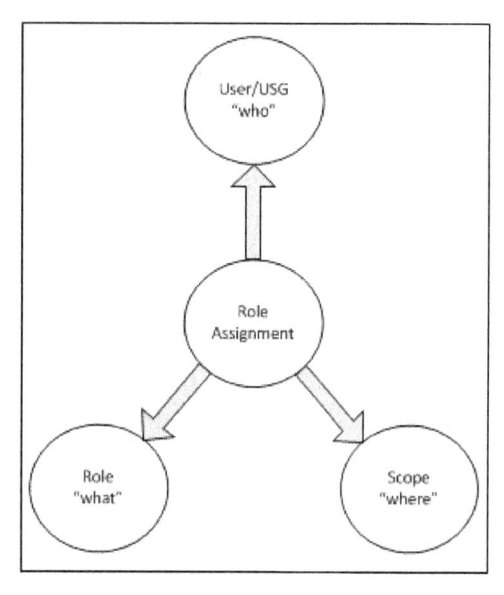

Figure 4.16: Schematic overview of the RBAC architecture.

Out of the box, Exchange Server 2010 only has one Role Assignment Policy, the **Default Role Assignment Policy**, which you can view using the `Get-RoleAssignmentPolicy` cmdlet.

```
PS C:\Windows\system32> Get-RoleAssignmentPolicy

RunspaceId      : ae7eaeff-a2be-4957-9505-d2387c4cbeeb
IsDefault       : True
Description     : This policy grants end users
                  permissions to set their Outlook Web
                  App options and perform other
                  self-administration tasks.
RoleAssignments : {MyBaseOptions-Default Role Assignment
                   Policy, MyContactInformation-Default
                   Role Assignment Policy, MyVoiceMail-
                   Default Role Assignment Policy,
                   MyTextMessaging-Default Role
                   Assignment Policy...}
AssignedRoles   : {MyBaseOptions, MyContactInformation,
```

```
                      MyVoiceMail, MyTextMessaging...}
AdminDisplayName  :
ExchangeVersion   : 0.11 (14.0.509.0)
Name              : Default Role Assignment Policy
DistinguishedName : CN=Default Role Assignment Policy,
                    CN=Policies,CN=RBAC,CN=E2010,
                    CN=Microsoft Exchange,CN=Services,
                    CN=Configuration,DC=E2010,DC=local
Identity          : Default Role Assignment Policy
Guid              : a2ed89da-59b3-40ec-84a9-0321ef100b80
ObjectCategory    : E2010.local/Configuration/Schema/
                    ms-Exch-RBAC-Policy
ObjectClass       : {top, msExchRBACPolicy}
WhenChanged       : 19-8-2009 14:56:19
WhenCreated       : 18-7-2009 19:57:36
WhenChangedUTC    : 19-8-2009 12:56:19
WhenCreatedUTC    : 18-7-2009 17:57:36
OrganizationId    :
OriginatingServer : 2010AD02.E2010.local
IsValid           : True

PS C:\Windows\system32>
```

This Role Assignment Policy is assigned to all users by default, and makes sure that the users can manage their own properties. The only other user that's a member of one of the Role Groups is the Administrator who has installed Exchange Server 2010, who is a member of the **Organization Management** Management Role.

When you want to add the mailbox-enabled user name "Support Desk" to the **Help Desk** Management Group, follow the steps below.

- Log on as an Exchange Administrator to OWA and open the **Exchange Control Panel**.

- In the **Options** drop-down menu, select **Manage My Organization**.

- In the **Navigation** pane, select the **Roles & Auditing** option. The Role Groups will appear in the **Results** pane.

Chapter 4: Managing Exchange Server 2010 SP1

- In the **Results** pane, select the **Help Desk** Role Group and click the **Details** button. The Role Group window will appear. In the **Members** area, click the **Add** button and select the **Support Desk** mailbox. Click **Add** and click **OK** to finish the **Add Member** wizard.

- Click **Save** to save the new settings.

When you check the members of the Universal Security Group called **Help Desk** in Active Directory Users and Computers, you'll see that the **Support Desk** user is now a member of this Group. You might ask yourself, "Can I just add users to this, or other Security Groups to achieve this functionality?" The answer is "Yes." You can add other users to these Security Groups to achieve the same Role Based Access Control functionality. Only when you want to change very specific settings, for example, the possibility of importing and exporting mailboxes you have to use the native RBAC options.

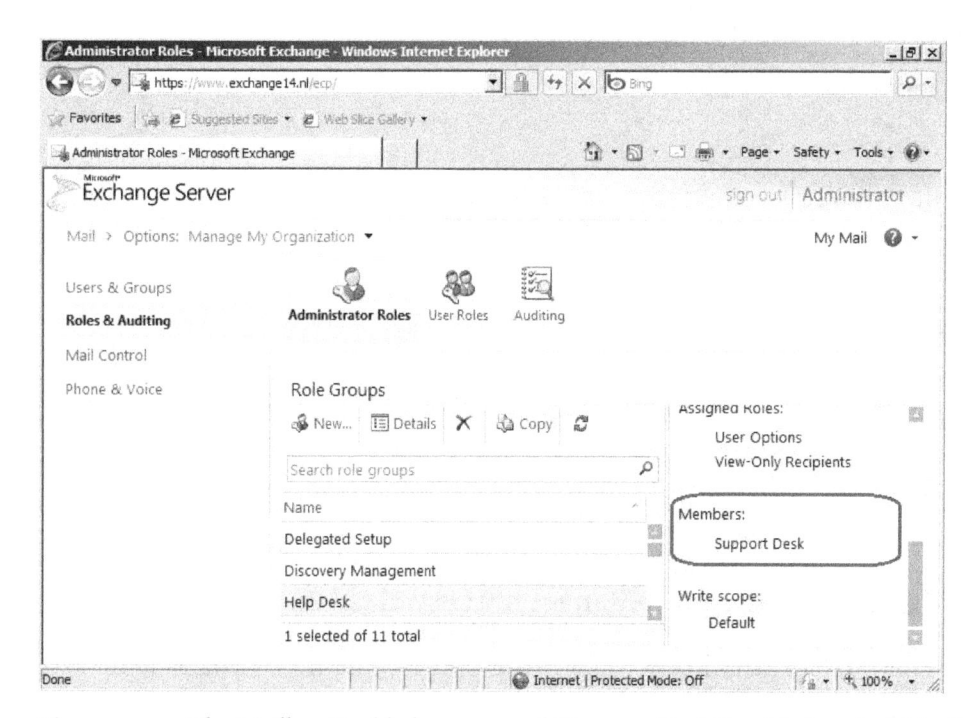

Figure 4.17: The Mailbox-Enabled user named "Support Desk" is added to the Help Desk Management Role.

Chapter 4: Managing Exchange Server 2010 SP1

The next time the Support Desk user logs on and opens the Exchange Control Panel, he/she will be able to manage other users and their mailboxes.

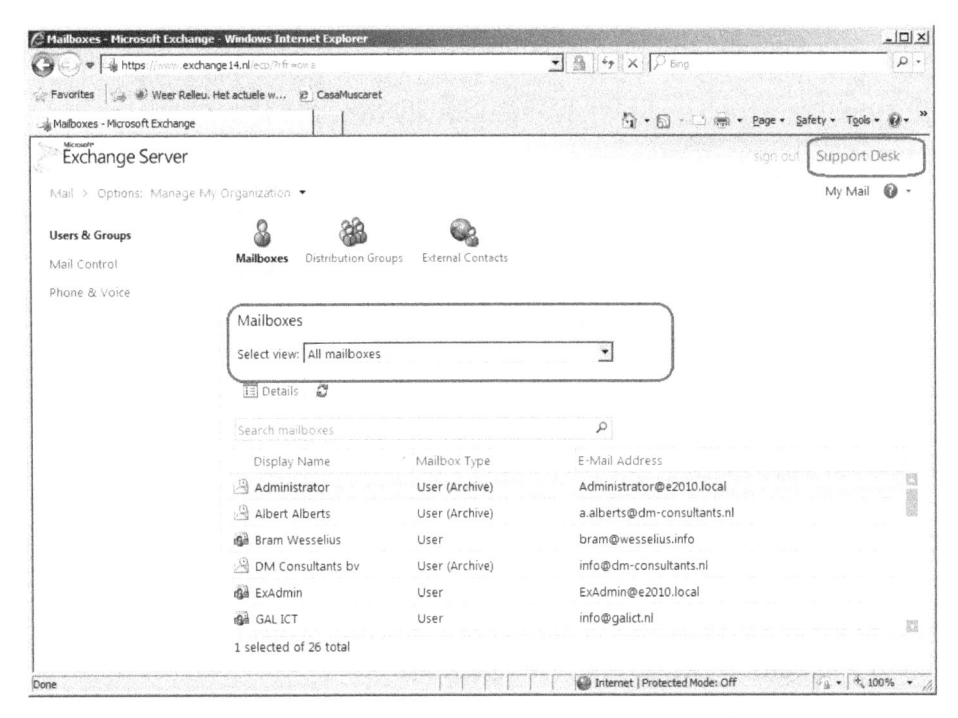

Figure 4.18: The Support Desk user can now manage users/mailboxes.

It is also possible to add a specific role to a user. For example, nobody can import or export mailboxes immediately; permissions must first be granted. To grant this option to the Support Desk user, the Management Role has to be assigned. Open the **Exchange Management Shell** and enter the following command:

```
New-ManagementRoleAssignment -Role "Mailbox Import Export" -User "Support Desk"
```

The Support Desk user now has the ability to start the `New-MailboxExportRequest` and `New-MailboxExportRequest` cmdlets.

4.5 Archiving and Compliancy

One important aspect of managing your Exchange environment is obviously managing the email; both the amount of email, and how email is treated.

The amount of email people receive has grown tremendously over the last couple of years. It is not uncommon any more for people to have a multi-gigabyte mailbox, plus a number of PST files where they keep all kinds of information.

Exchange used to be dependent upon an expensive storage solution, although this became less important with Exchange Server 2007. But managing an environment with multi-gigabyte mailboxes brings its own challenges with respect to storage. PST files are a different story again; they're unsafe to use because they are usually stored on a desktop or laptop. If this is stolen, the information is lost and, potentially, compromised. PST files are sometimes stored on network shares, but this is not actually supported by Microsoft.

Third-party archiving solutions are often implemented, which are a particularly good idea when they're part of an Information Lifecycle Management policy. An Information Lifecycle Management policy is a procedural solution that describes how an organization deals with information (i.e. email). It includes details such as:

- how organizations stick to compliancy regulations
- how long email is stored (retention times)
- where email is stored (location and folders)
- how email is backed up.

An Information Lifecycle Management solution is a proper business case for an archiving solution. Sometimes "cheap storage" is mentioned, but there's no such thing as cheap storage. Of course, a 500 GB SATA disk is less expensive than a 320 GB SAS disk, but SATA disks need power, cooling and, most importantly, management. An archiving solution will also need to be managed, backed up, and properly provisioned with hardware (but maybe not as often as a regular Exchange system).

4.5.1   Exchange 2010 Archiving

New in Exchange Server 2010 RTM was the built-in archiving solution, which made it possible to create a personal archive mailbox within the Exchange organization. The downside of Exchange Server 2010 RTM was the fact that the personal archive was created in the same Mailbox Database as the user's primary mailbox. This wasn't a real archiving solution, as it failed offload the large amounts of legacy data to a less important server.

New in Exchange Server 2010 SP1 is the fact that you can now create a personal archive on a separate Mailbox Database, which can even be located on a separate Mailbox Server. So, it's now possible to create your primary mailboxes on a Mailbox Server that's part of a DAG (I'll discuss this more in *Chapter 5*) and achieve High Availability at the primary mailbox level. In addition, you can create the personal archive on a separate server, without a DAG, and potentially even an alternative storage solution.

To create a dedicated Mailbox Server for hosting personal archives, the only thing you have to do is to install an Exchange Server 2010 SP1 Mailbox Server and create one (or more) Mailbox Databases on this server.

What you don't want to happen is for any primary mailboxes to be provisioned on this Mailbox Database. To prevent this, you can exclude this particular Mailbox Database from provisioning mailboxes. After installing Exchange Server 2010 SP1, open the Exchange Management Shell and enter the following command:

```
set-mailboxdatabase –Identity <<mailbox database>>
-isexcludedfromprovisioning:$true
```

To create a personal archive mailbox, follow the steps below.

- Log on to an Exchange Server and open the **Exchange Management Console**.
- Expand the **Exchange On-Premise**, expand the **Recipient Configuration** and select **Mailbox**.
- In the **Results** pane select one or more users that need to have an Archive.
- Right-click the selected user(s) and select **Enable Archive**. The **Enable Archive** wizard will appear. By default it will create a local archive, which means in your own Exchange organization, but you can enter another database to locate the personal archive on. A slick feature is to have a remote Archive, which means in the "Cloud." At the moment of printing (Summer 2011) this was not available, but for sure the new Microsoft Online offering (Office 365) will include this. Click **OK** to continue and the archive will be created.

Except for the icon changing, nothing special happens in the Exchange Management Console. You can request the mailbox properties and select the Mailbox Features tab to check if the Archive is enabled (see Figure 4.19).

The archive is actually just a secondary mailbox which is created in the same Mailbox Database or, my personal preference, in a separate Mailbox Database as the primary mailbox. But remember, the default still is adding the personal archive to the same Database! As mentioned earlier, if you're using a separate Mailbox Database for your archive mailboxes, this database can also be running on an entirely separate Mailbox Server. To request more information about the Mailbox Archive, open the Exchange Management Shell and enter the following command:

```
Get-Mailbox -Identity <<mailbox>> -Archive | `
    ft ArchiveGuid, ArchiveName, ArchiveQuota, '
    ArchiveDatabase
```

Chapter 4: Managing Exchange Server 2010 SP1

The default Mailbox Quota is 2 GB, and the default Quota for the Mailbox Archive is unlimited (although a warning is issued at 50 GB), but these quotes are not set in stone.

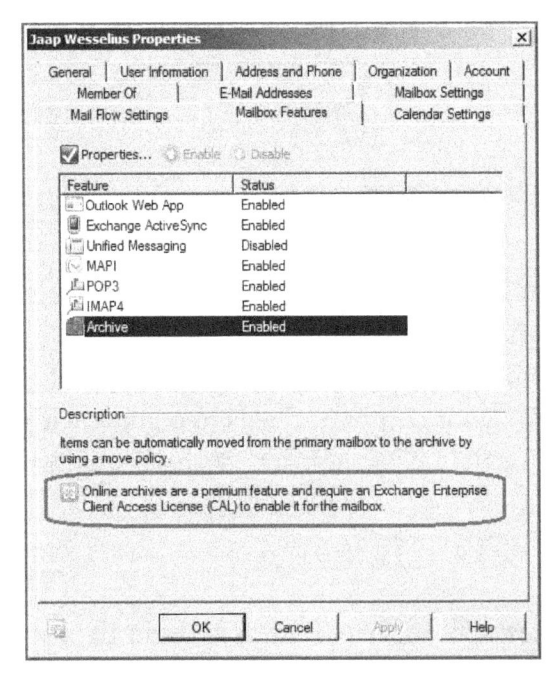

Figure 4.19: The archive is enabled on this particular mailbox.

For example, to set the Mailbox Archive Quota to 10 GB, use the Exchange Management Shell and enter: `Set-Mailbox –Identity <<mailbox>> –ArchiveQuota 10GB`.

The `ArchiveQuota` value can be entered using B (Bytes), KB (Kilobytes), MB (Megabytes), GB (Gigabytes) or TB (Terabytes), and the value itself can range from 1 to 9223372036854775807 bytes.

Chapter 4: Managing Exchange Server 2010 SP1

Note

The maximum recommended database size in Exchange Server 2010 is 2 TB, so special care needs to be taken with the amount of mailboxes per database and the Archive Quota per Mailbox to prevent unlimited growth of the database.

4.5.2 Messaging Records Management

Messaging Records Management (MRM) policies in Exchange Server 2010 are comparable to rules in an Outlook client. With these policies, an Exchange administrator has the ability to automate the processing of email and simplify message retention. Examples of reasons for implementing MRM rules are things like: your company needs to comply with requirements from Sarbanes-Oxley (SOX), HIPAA, or the US Patriot Act. With Messaging Records Management it is possible to:

- configure Retention Policies on users' mailboxes
- configure settings on specified folders so that messages in these folders are sent to another recipient.

One way to implement MRM is by using Managed Folders, which involve an Exchange administrator creating one or more custom folders and an associated custom folder policy. This policy can be responsible for, as an example, messages being deleted after 180 or 360 days, but the user is still responsible for moving the individual messages to the custom folder.

Note

Managed Folders and an Archive Mailbox are not compatible. If you are using Managed Folders on a particular mailbox and you want to create an Archive, the creation will fail (see Figure 4.20). You have to migrate the Managed Folder solution to a Retention Policy solution before implementing an Archive Mailbox.

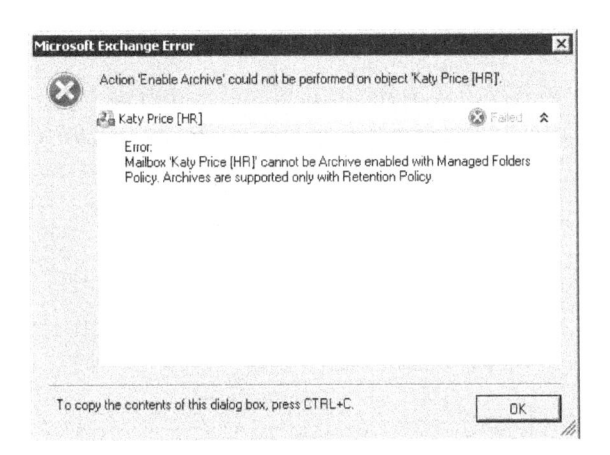

Figure 4.20: Error message arising from a conflict between Managed Folders and Archiving.

Managed Folders first appeared in Exchange Server 2007, and they have continued in Exchange Server 2010. However, Microsoft is focusing more on the Retention Policies as part of the MRM Version 2, than on the Managed Folders. In Service Pack 1 of Exchange Server 2010, you'll see that the Retention Policies can now be managed from the Exchange Management Console, but the Managed Folders can now *only* be managed from the Exchange Management Shell – i.e. the ability to control Managed Folders has been removed from the Management Console.

If you are new to Messaging Records Management, I wouldn't bet on Managed Folders, and would instead start implementing Retention Policies.

As you might have guessed, new in Exchange Server 2010 is the implementation of MRM 2.0 using Retention Policies and Retention Tags. Retention Tags specify if retention is enabled, how long a message (which can be a note or a contact as well) should be retained, and what action will be performed when the retention age is reached.

Chapter 4: Managing Exchange Server 2010 SP1

There are three types of Retention Tags:

1. **Retention Policy Tags** – these are tags that are applied to default folders such as the Inbox, Junk Email, Sent Items or Deleted Items. These are set by the Exchange administrator and cannot be changed by the individual user. An example of a Retention Policy Tag could be "Delete all items from the Deleted Items folder after 30 days."
2. **Default Policy Tags** – these are tags that are applied to items that are not subject to any other Policy Tags. You can create multiple Default Policy Tags, but a Retention Policy can only have one Default Policy Tag.
3. **Personal Tags** – these are tags that are created by the Exchange administrator, and which can be applied by individual users to Folders or Messages in their Mailbox.

Messages are processed by the Exchange Mailbox Server based on the Retention Tags and the content settings of those tags. When a message reaches the retention age limit specified in the tag, it can be archived, deleted, or flagged for user attention.

Using Retention Policies, it is now also possible to store only messages with a maximum age of 3 months in the user's mailbox, and store messages older than 3 months in the Archive Mailbox. Suppose there's a Human Resources department within your organization, and all messages older than 3 months should be stored into the user's Archive. The following steps have to be followed:

- create the necessary Retention Tags which define when an action should be taken (i.e. when the retention time of 3 months has passed)
- create the Retention Policy that defines what needs to be done when the retention time has passed (i.e. move to the Archive)
- apply the policy to the mailbox.

In Exchange Server 2010 RTM you could only use the Exchange Management Shell when creating Retention Policy Tags and Retention Policies. In Exchange Server 2010 SP1, you can now use the Management Console for these actions.

As an example, we'll create a Retention Policy Tag that will move all items older than 180 days (6 months) to the user's personal archive. Follow the steps below to create this Retention Policy Tag.

- Log on to an Exchange Server 2010 SP1 server and open the **Exchange Management Console**.
- Expand the **Microsoft Exchange On-Premises (SERVERNAME)**.
- Expand the **Organization Configuration** container and select the **Mailbox** option and click the **Retention Policy Tags** tab.
- In the **New Retention Policy Tag** wizard, enter a **Tag Name**, and for the **Tag Type**, select **All other folders in the mailbox**. Enter 180 as the number of days for the **Age Limit**, and select **Move to Archive** as the action to take.
- Click **New**, and when the Retention Policy Tag is created, click **Finish**.

Conversely, in Exchange Server 2010, the same Retention Policy Tag could only be created using the Exchange Management Shell using the command below.

```
New-RetentionPolicyTag -Name '180 Days - Move To The
Archive' -Type 'All' -Comment ''
-AgeLimitForRetention '180.00:00:00'
-RetentionAction 'MoveToArchive'
-RetentionEnabled $true
```

As a further demonstration, it is also possible to create a Retention Policy Tag that automatically deletes all items from the Deleted Items folder in the mailbox. In the **Retention Policy Tags** tab, select **New Retention Policy Tag...** and enter the values shown in Figure 4.21.

Chapter 4: Managing Exchange Server 2010 SP1

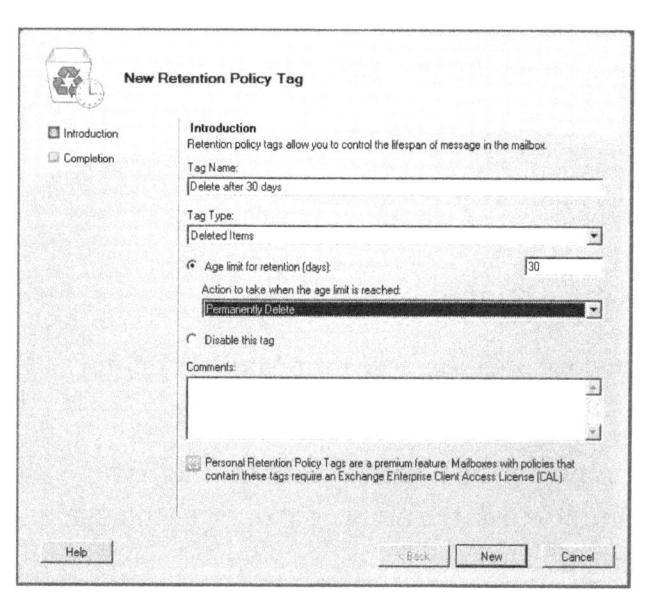

Figure 4.21: Create a new Retention Policy Tag that cleans up the deleted Items after 30 days.

The next step is to combine one or more Retention Policy Tags into a Retention Policy.

- Log on to an Exchange Server 2010 SP1 server and open the **Exchange Management Console**.

- Expand the **Microsoft Exchange On-Premises (SERVERNAME)**.

- Expand the **Organization Configuration** container and select the **Mailbox** option, and click the **Retention Policies** tab.

- In the **Actions pane**, select **New Retention Policy** and follow the wizard.

- Add the **Retention Policy Tags** that were created in the previous step, and click **Next** to continue.

- Click **Next** again, and add one or more mailboxes to which you want to apply this Retention Policy. Click **Next** to continue, and click **Finish** when the Retention Policy is created.

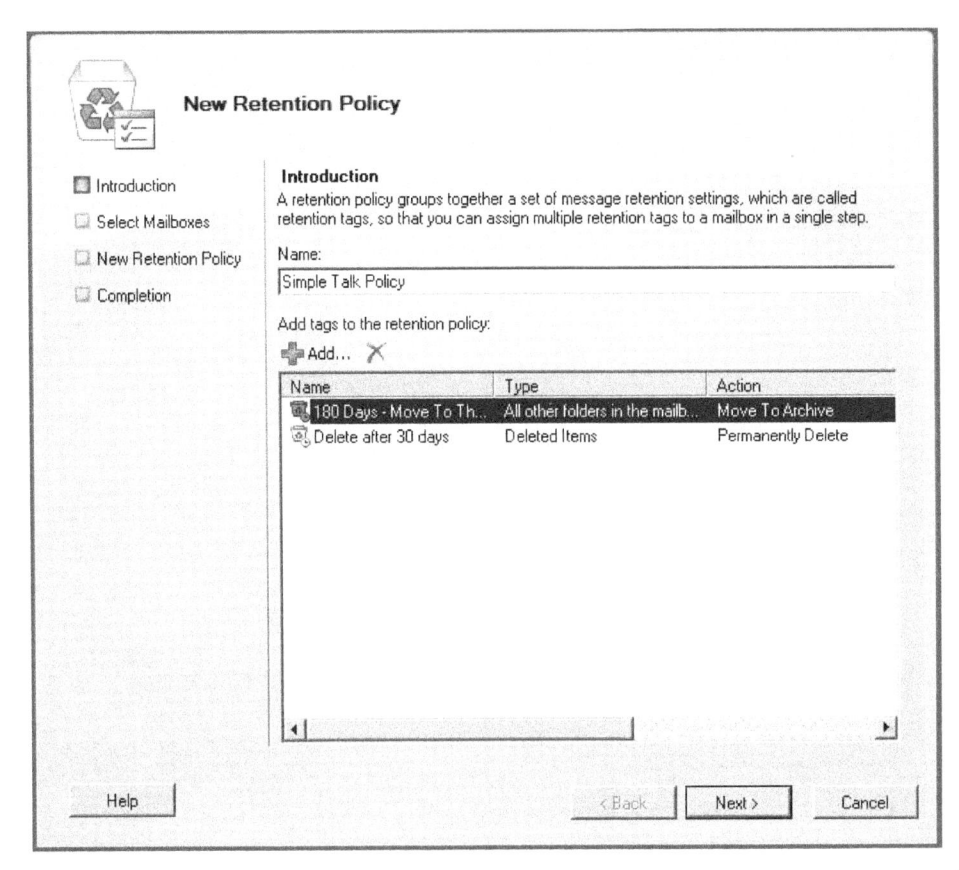

Figure 4.22: Create a new Retention Policy with the previously created Retention Policy Tags.

As we've just seen, during the creation of the Retention Policy it is possible to select one or more mailboxes to which the Retention Policy will be immediately applied. It is also possible to assign a Retention Policy to existing mailboxes. To do this, in the **Exchange Management Console**, open the **Retention Policy Properties** and select the **Mailboxes** tab; you can add Mailboxes to the Retention Policy right here.

Chapter 4: Managing Exchange Server 2010 SP1

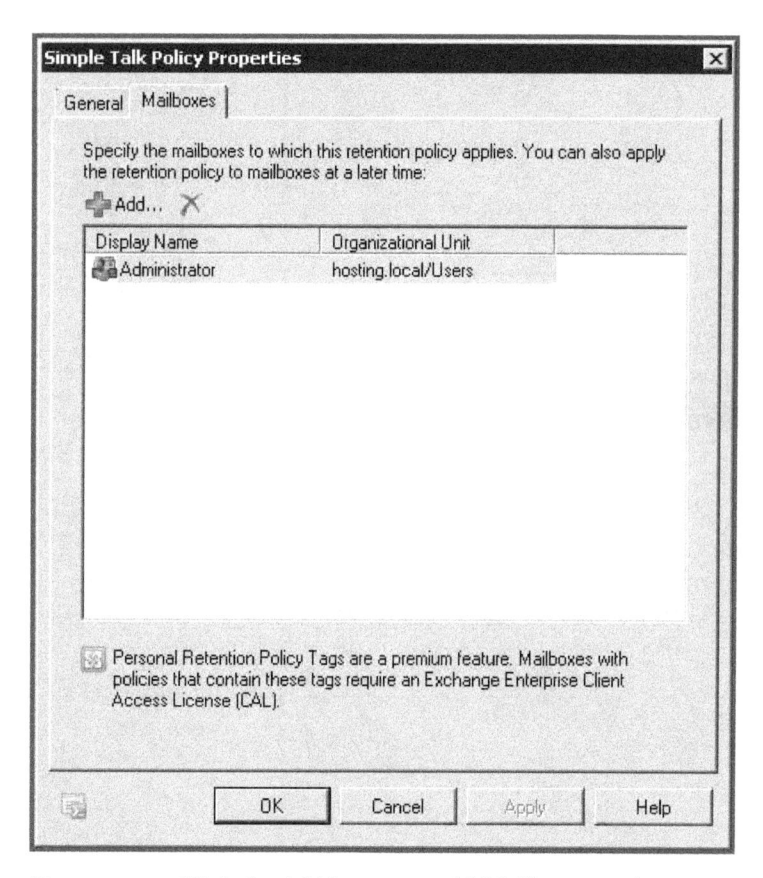

Figure 4.23: Click the Add button to add Mailboxes to the Retention Policy.

Alternatively, you can also select the **Mailbox** in the **Exchange Management Console**, open its properties and select the **Mailbox Settings** tab. Select the properties of the **Messaging Records Management** and add the desired Retention Policy.

Chapter 4: Managing Exchange Server 2010 SP1

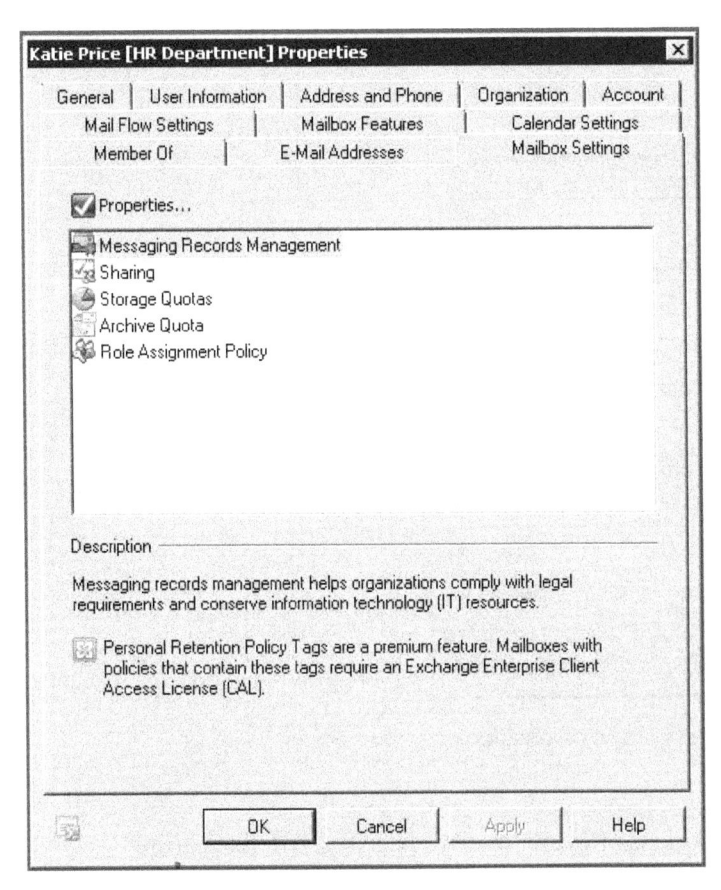

Figure 4.24: Add the Retention Policy in the Mailbox Properties.

You can even add a Retention Policy during the creation of a mailbox, as in Figure 4.25.

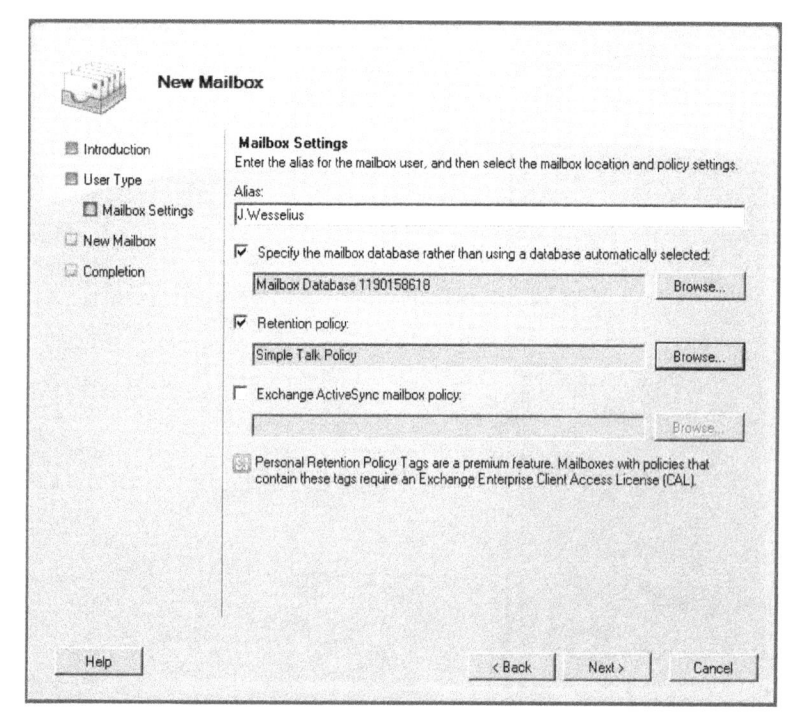

Figure 4.25: Assign a Retention Policy during creation of a mailbox.

The last option available to you is to add the Retention Policy using the Exchange Management Shell, by entering: `Set-Mailbox –Identity "user" –Retention-Policy "Simple Talk Policy"`.

The Managed Folder Assistant (which we'll look at in just a moment) is responsible for applying the Retention Policy to the Mailbox, and when the Managed Folder Assistant is finished processing the Mailbox, you'll see content older than 180 days appear in the Personal Archive, as in Figure 4.26.

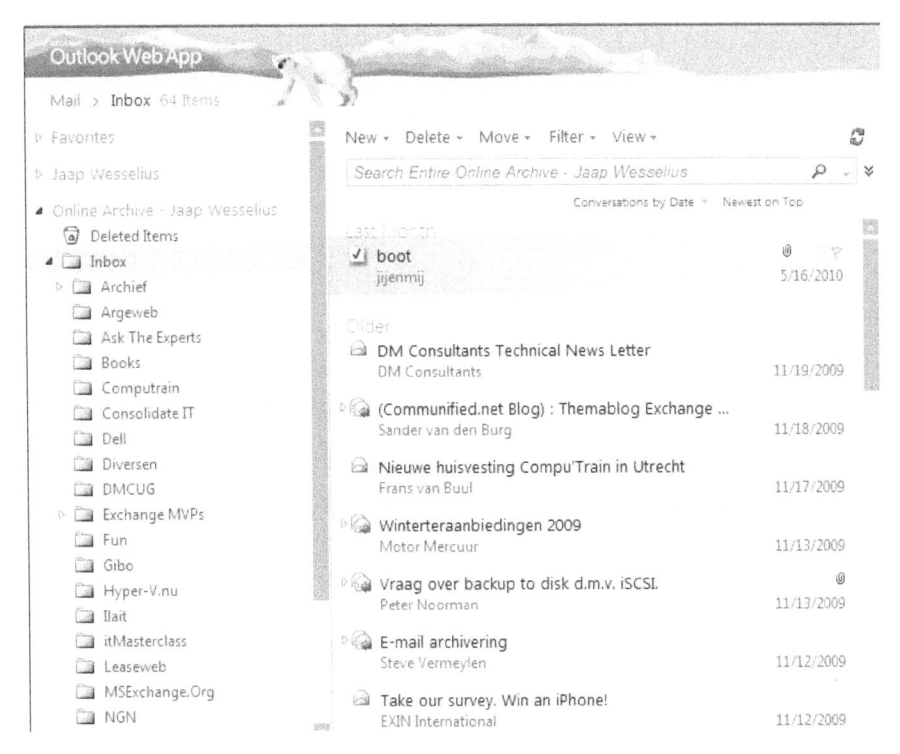

Figure 4.26: The Personal Archive after the Retention Policy is applied. The "jijenmij" email was moved manually to the Archive.

The Managed Folder Assistant is running on the Mailbox Server where the user's mailbox resides. In Exchange Server 2010 RTM, the Managed Folder Assistant runs at specified times, by default, between 01:00 and 05:00. You can change these values by requesting the properties of the Exchange Server in the Exchange Management Console.

In Exchange Server 2010 SP1, the Managed Folder Assistant is a throttle-based assistant. It doesn't run on a set schedule, but it runs (on a Mailbox Server) within a certain period of time known as the Work Cycle. At specific times, the Managed Folder Assistant refreshes the list of mailboxes that need to be processed, and these points in time are known as the Work Cycle Checkpoints. During these Checkpoints, new mailboxes, or mailboxes that are moved to this Mailbox Server, are added to the queue of mailboxes to be processed.

4.5.3 Discovery search functionality

Exchange Server 2010 Discovery is the process of searching relevant content in Exchange Server 2010 mailboxes. Reasons for using the Exchange Server 2010 Discovery can be:

- legal discovery
- internal investigations
- Human Resources.

Exchange Server 2010 Discovery leverages the content indexes that are created as part of the Exchange Search engine and no doubt, as you use Exchange Server 2010, you'll find plenty more reasons to use this powerful search technology.

To create and manage a Discovery search, a user needs to be a member of the Discovery Management Role Group, which is one of the default RBAC Roles. This is an explicit right and Exchange administrators do not have sufficient rights to create and manage discovery searches.

Note

Exchange Server 2010 Discovery is a very powerful feature. Users who are member of the Discovery Management Role Group can search through all content in all mailboxes on all Exchange Server 2010 Mailbox Servers.

To add a user named Joe Lawyer to the Discovery Management Role Group, follow the steps below.

- Log on as an administrator to the **Exchange Control Panel**.
- In the ECP options, select **Manage My Organization**.
- In the **Navigation** pane, select **Roles & Auditing**.
- In the **Administrator Roles** section of the **Results** pane, select **Discovery Management** and click on **Details**.
- In the **Members** section, click **Add** and add **Joe Lawyer** as a member of the **Discovery Management Role Group**.
- Exit the Exchange Control Panel.

You can also add Joe Lawyer to the Discovery Management Role Group using the **Exchange Management Shell** by entering the following command:

```
Add-RoleGroupMember "Discovery Management" `
   -User "Joe Lawyer"
```

Now this user can create queries to find relevant information if there are suspicions about another employee. To create a Discovery Search, Joe Lawyer has to follow the steps below.

- Log on to the Exchange Control Panel as the user **Joe Lawyer**.
- In the ECP Options, select **Manage My Organization**. (Having added Joe Lawyer to the Discovery Management Role Group, you'll notice that Joe now has the **Manage My Organization** option as well, but it isn't as powerful as the ECP that's available to an Exchange administrator).
- In the **Navigation** pane, select **Mail Control**.

Chapter 4: Managing Exchange Server 2010 SP1

- In the **Results** pane, select **New** to create a new Discovery Search, and then select one or more keywords to search for, and enter email addresses received from, or sent to, as search filters.

- In the **Mailboxes to Search**, you can enter one or more mailboxes in your Exchange organization. Be cautious here, because if you select **Search All Mailboxes**, then the result set that will be returned could be tremendous!

- In the **Search Name, Type, and Storage Location** option, you have to give the search a specific name. In this example, the name will be **Exchange Search Functionality**. Now is a good time to mention a couple of new features in Exchange Server 2010 SP1. There is the option to do an estimation of the actual search, and there is also a de-duplication functionality in the Discovery search. So, if a particular item is returned multiple times, then it will be shown only once.

- When you're done, select **Save** and the query will be run.

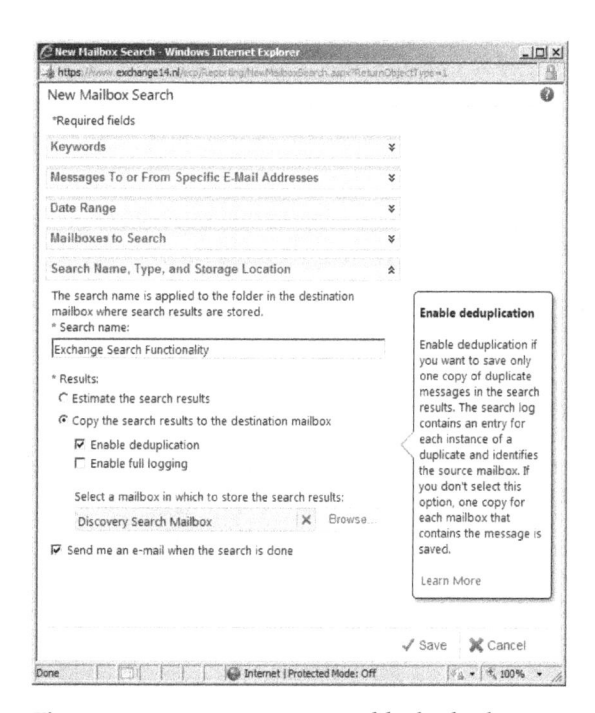

Figure 4.27: Enter a name, enable de-duplication and enter a mailbox where the search results will be stored.

When the search is completed, the results are stored in the Discovery Search Mailbox. Members of the Discovery Search Role Group automatically inherit permissions to access this particular Mailbox, and Joe Lawyer will have to do so in order to investigate the results. You can check the **Send me an e-mail when the search is done** option so you can leave the Exchange Control Panel. When the search is completed you'll be notified automatically.

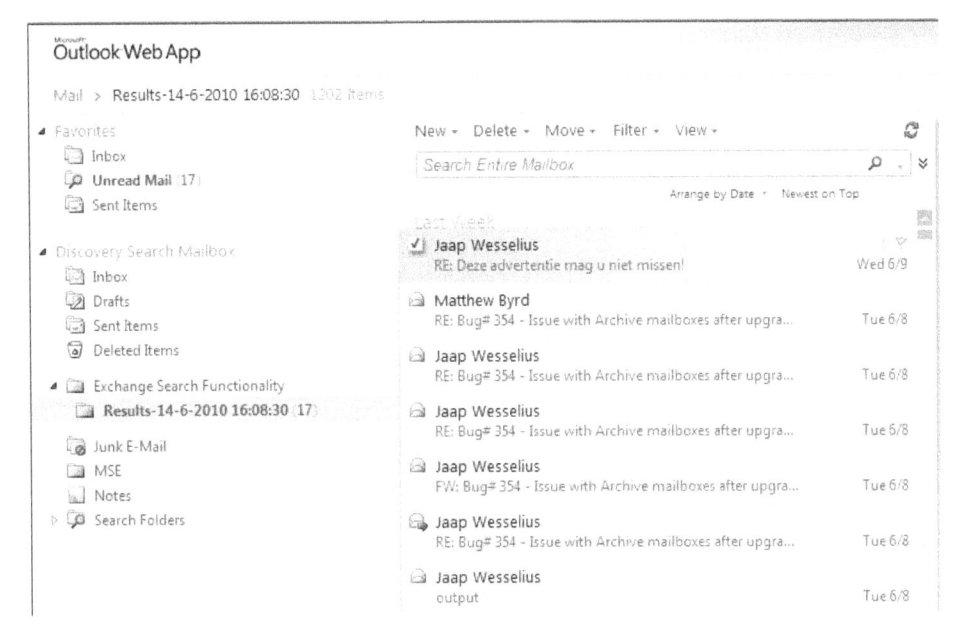

Figure 4.28: The results of the Discovery Search are stored in a dedicated folder in the Discovery Search Mailbox.

A special folder for this Discovery search is created in the Discovery Search Mailbox, and this is where the results are stored. In this example, the search was named **Exchange Search Functionality** and you can see a folder appear in the Discovery Search Mailbox with the same name (see Figure 4.28).

When Joe Lawyer deletes the search in his Control Panel, the search results will be deleted from the Discovery Search Mailbox as well.

Chapter 4: Managing Exchange Server 2010 SP1

> **Note**
>
> *To use the Discovery Search functionality you need the Enterprise Client Access License (eCAL) for Exchange Server 2010.*

It is also possible to perform a Discovery search in the Exchange Management Shell by entering the following command:

```
New-MailboxSearch -Name "Search From the Shell" -TargetMailbox "Discovery Search Mailbox"
-SearchQuery "Simple Talk" -MessageTypes Email —SourceMailbox "J.Wesselius"
—IncludeUnsearchableItems
```

If the `—SourceMailbox` option is omitted, all Mailbox Databases in the entire Exchange organization will be searched. This can create an enormous result set, creating an unexpected growth of the target mailbox.

```
[PS] C:\Windows\system32>New-MailboxSearch -Name "Search From the Shell"
-SearchQuery "Simple Talk" -MessageTypes Email -SourceMailboxes J.Wesselius
-TargetMailbox "Discovery Search Mailbox"

RunspaceId              : d867feb7-ecdf-4724-b472-
                          66b2fccad259
Identity                : cb51d495-58b6-4bad-932d-
                          9080ef8f7088
Name                    : Search From the Shell
CreatedBy               : Administrator
SourceMailboxes         : {E2010.local/Accounts/DM-
                          Consultants-nl/Jaap Wessselius}
TargetMailbox           : E2010.local/Users/
                          DiscoverySearchMailbox{D919BA05-
                          46A6-415f-80AD-7E09334BB852}
SearchQuery             : Simple Talk
Language                : nl-NL
Senders                 : {}
Recipients              : {}
StartDate               :
```

```
EndDate                     :
MessageTypes                : {email}
SearchDumpster              : True
IncludeUnsearchableItems    : False
DoNotIncludeArchive         : False
EstimateOnly                : False
ExcludeDuplicateMessages    : True
Resume                      : False
LogLevel                    : Basic
StatusMailRecipients        : {}
Status                      : InProgress
LastRunBy                   : Administrator
LastStartTime               : 14-6-2010 16:27:01
LastEndTime                 :
NumberMailboxesToSearch     : 1
PercentComplete             : 0
ResultNumber                : 0
ResultNumberEstimate        : 0
ResultSize                  : 0 B (0 bytes)
ResultSizeEstimate          : 0 B (0 bytes)
ResultSizeCopied            : 0 B (0 bytes)
ResultsLink                 :
Errors                      : {}
KeywordHits                 : {}

[PS] C:\Windows\system32>
```

Edited for readability.

The progress of the Discovery search can be monitored using the `Get-MailboxSearch` cmdlet.

When the search is complete you can log on to the Discovery Search Mailbox again, and the results will be shown in a new folder in the Mailbox, as you can see in Figure 4.29.

Chapter 4: Managing Exchange Server 2010 SP1

Outlook Web App

Mail > Search From the Shell 1 Items

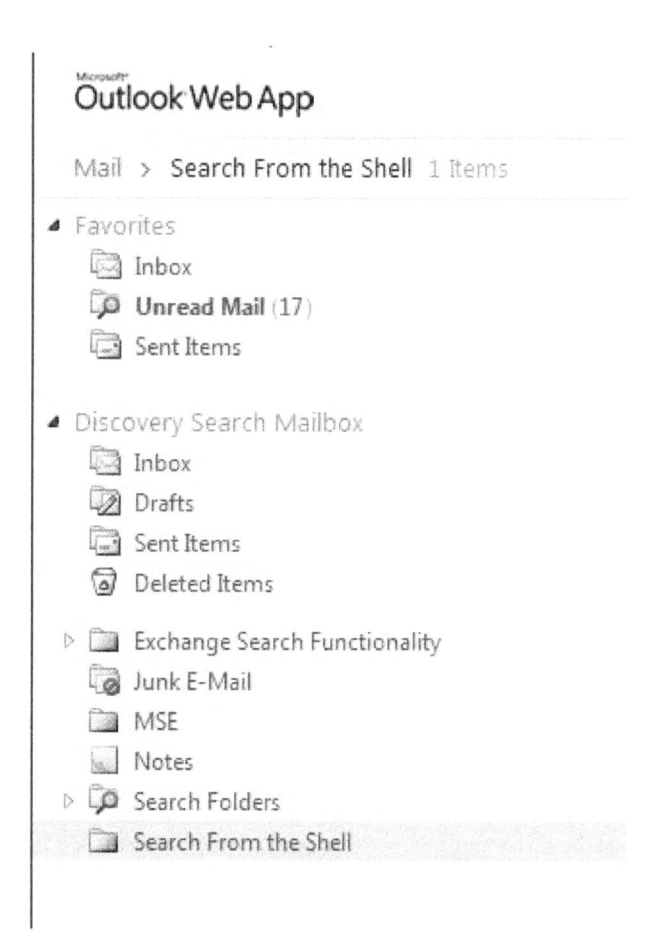

- Favorites
  - Inbox
  - **Unread Mail** (17)
  - Sent Items

- Discovery Search Mailbox
  - Inbox
  - Drafts
  - Sent Items
  - Deleted Items
  - Exchange Search Functionality
  - Junk E-Mail
  - MSE
  - Notes
  - Search Folders
  - Search From the Shell

Figure 4.29: The results of the Mailbox search performed from the Exchange Management Shell.

When the Mailbox search is removed using the `Remove-MailboxSearch` cmdlet the folders in the target mailbox will be deleted as well.

4.5.4 Litigation Hold

In Exchange Server 2010 it is possible to configure a mailbox to be in Litigation Hold. Litigation Hold is a feature of the Dumpster in the Exchange Server 2010 Mailbox Server Role, and when a particular mailbox has the Litigation Hold enabled, all actions performed on items in that mailbox are stored in the Dumpster. For example, when a user deletes a message, and tries to permanently delete it, the message is still kept in the Dumpster; messages are even kept in the Dumpster when they are beyond the retention time.

Version Control is also part of the Litigation Hold. When a user receives a message and subsequently changes its contents, for example when it's a compromising message, both the original message as well as the changed message are kept in the Dumpster. This is fully transparent to the user, who doesn't notice any of this process, but their results will be shown in a Discovery Search.

This is true for both the primary Mailbox as well as the personal archive.

To place a mailbox in Litigation Hold, enter the following Exchange Management Shell command: `Set-Mailbox J.Wesselius -LitigationHoldEnabled $true`.

Please note that the Litigation Hold is part of the Dumpster 2.0 functionality in Exchange Server 2010.

4.6 Summary

There are multiple ways to manage your Exchange Server 2010 SP1 environment, and you'll have to see for yourself which is the most comfortable for your own situation. The Exchange Management Console is the most convenient, but for the nitty gritty details you really do have to use the Exchange Management Shell, and for some functionality, like the Discovery Search, the Exchange Control is the best solution.

This chapter should give you everything you need to start managing your Exchange Server 2010 SP1 environment as effectively and smoothly as possible. I've covered the steps you'll need to take to use the more prominent features, and hopefully given you enough tips and helpful notes that you'll have a really good understanding of what's happening to your system. I'd love to be able to dive into really deep detail on all the management and messaging features in Exchange Server 2010 SP1, like the improved Messaging Records Management, but if I did that this book would be a real door-stop! I'll just say that everything I've touched upon, such as the personal archive and the retention options, give you unprecedented possibilities for managing your messaging environment.

Chapter 5: High Availability in Exchange Server 2010 SP1

5.1 High Availability

There are several options in Exchange Server 2010 SP1 that can be configured as a High Availability solution. New in Exchange Server 2010 is the Database Availability Group offering high availability on the Mailbox Server Role. If you want a full High Availability solution, then the Client Access (CA) Server and the Hub Transport Server need to be configured as a High Availability solution, and you need to be using Network Load Balancing and a Client Access Array as well. This chapter focuses on configuring the Mailbox Server and the CA Server Roles, as these contain a lot of new features and technologies. There's not too much focus on configuring the Hub Transport Server Role, as High Availability options for this role haven't changed significantly since Exchange Server 2007.

New in Exchange Server 2010 is the fact that the Exchange Server 2010 Standard Edition now also supports the Database Availability Group, just like the Exchange Server 2010 Enterprise Edition. The only difference is that the Standard Edition only supports up to 5 databases, while the Enterprise Edition supports up to 100 databases per server. This is a perfect development for organizations that do not have thousands of mailboxes, and therefore do not need to create a lot of Mailbox Databases.

Before I start with the Database Availability Group topic, I want to give a database technology primer, just to make the Database Availability Group more understandable.

5.2 Exchange Server Database Technologies

Before we start talking about high availability on the Mailbox Server Role, we have to discuss some database technologies used in Exchange Server 2010. Exchange Server 2010 uses a database to store the primary data, i.e. the messages you send and receive. This database technology is a transactional system, which is pretty common, but Exchange Server uses its own technology, built on the Extensible Storage Engine (ESE), sometimes referred to as a JET database.

When installing an Exchange Server 2010 Mailbox Server, the initial mailbox database is, by default, stored on the installation drive; assuming that's the `C:\` drive, then more specifically on `C:\Program Files\Microsoft\Exchange Server\V14\Mailbox\Mailbox Database <<random number>>\`. This random number is generated by Exchange Server during the initial configuration because the database names on Exchange 2010 and higher servers *must* be unique within the Exchange organization.

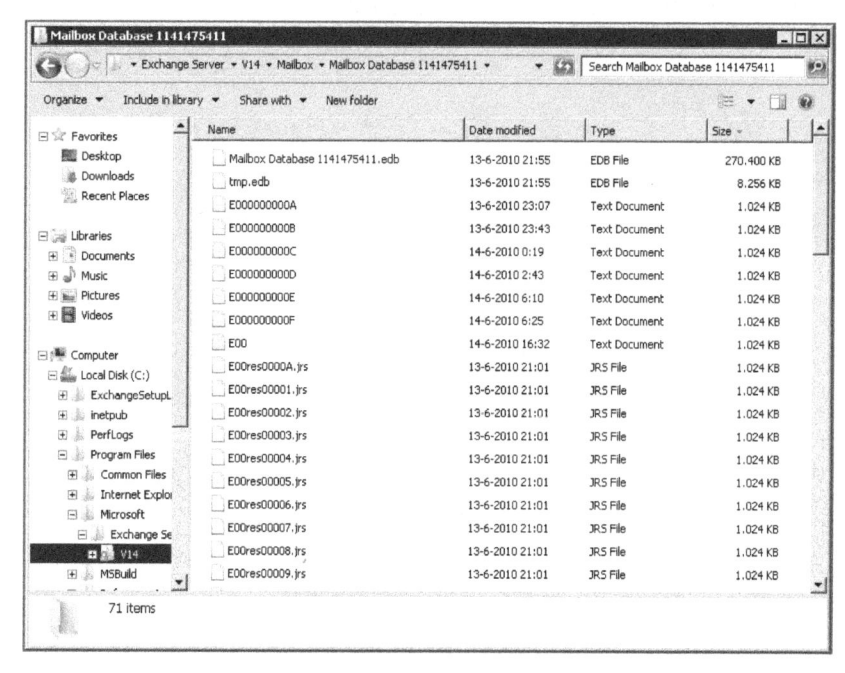

Figure 5.1:   By default the database and log files are placed on the C:\ drive.

A number of files make up the Exchange 2010 database environment:

- `mailbox database 1141475411.edb`
- `E00.log`
- `E00000003a.log`, `E000000003b.log`, `E00000003c.log`, etc.
- `E00.chk`
- `E00res00001.jrs` through `E00res0000A.jrs`
- `E00tmp.log`
- `Tmp.edb`.

> *Note*
>
> The random number in this example is *1141475411*, which is why the name of the Mailbox Database is `Mailbox Database 1141475411.edb`. All names in the above mentioned list start with the same three digits: E00, called the database prefix. The first database in the Exchange organization has a prefix of E00, the second database has a prefix E01, and so on. All of these files play a crucial role in the correct functioning of Exchange Server.

A crucial step in understanding Exchange database technology is understanding the flow of data between the Exchange Server and the database itself. Data is processed in 32 KB blocks, also called "pages." When Exchange is finished processing such a page it is immediately written to a log file if it was updated. The page is still kept in memory until Exchange needs this memory again but, when the page isn't used for some time, or when Exchange needs to force an update during a checkpoint, the page is written to the database file. So, the data in the log files is always in advance of the data in the database. This is an important step to remember when troubleshooting database issues!

Chapter 5: High Availability in Exchange Server 2010 SP1

Note

Exchange Server 2010 uses 32 KB pages, Exchange Server 2007 uses 8 KB pages, Exchange Server 2003 and earlier use 4 KB pages when processing data. The parts of the server memory that are used by these pages are referred to as the "Version Store."

As data is written to the database, a pointer called the checkpoint is updated to reflect the new or updated page that was written to the database. The checkpoint is stored in a special file called the checkpoint file, which Exchange Server uses to make sure it knows what data has been written to the database, and what data is in the log files and not yet written to the database. So, in short:

1. mail data is initially processed in memory, separated into pages
2. updated pages are written to the log file
3. if pages are no longer needed by Exchange these pages are written to the database
4. the checkpoint file is updated to reflect the new location of the checkpoint.

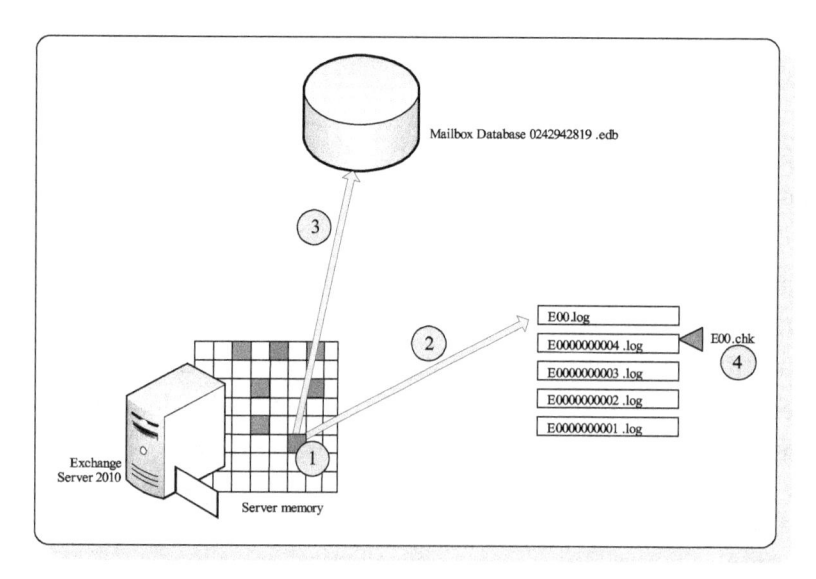

Figure 5.2: Processing of mail data in Exchange Server 2010.

5.2.1 Extensible Storage Engine

The database engine used by Exchange Server is quite special, and is built on the Extensible Storage Engine, or ESE. ESE exists in several flavors:

- ESE97 for Exchange Server 5.5
- ESE98 for Exchange Server 2000/2003
- ESENT for Active Directory
- ESE for Exchange Server 2007 and Exchange Server 2010.

ESE is a low-level database engine. This means it knows all about "base types," such as `short`, `string`, `long`, `longlong`, `systime`, etc., but it has no knowledge of any structure or schema. The schema is defined by the Information Store in the application. This is in contrast to a relational database like Microsoft SQL Server, where all the database structures are just meta-data (i.e. they are part of the database itself).

ESE is optimized for handling large amounts of semi-structured data, as it is impossible for an Exchange Server to predict what kind of data will be received, how large the data will be, or what attachments messages will have.

> **Note**
>
> *Ever since the early days of Exchange, rumors have been going around about the use of Microsoft SQL Server as the database engine for Exchange Server. Microsoft tried this for Exchange Server 2010 and actually got it working. However, the decision was made to stay on the ESE database. More information about this can be found on the Microsoft Exchange Product Group blog at* HTTP://MSEXCHANGETEAM.COM/ARCHIVE/2009/07/16/451784.ASPX.

5.2.2 Log files

When Exchange Server is working with a page, and that page's status is changed from dirty to clean, the page is written to the log file almost immediately. Data held in memory is fast to access, but it is volatile; all it takes is a minor hiccup in the server, and data in memory is lost. When it is saved in the log file, the whole server could burn down and, as long as you keep the disk, you also keep the data. Thankfully, saving to the log file is normally a matter of milliseconds. The log files are numbered internally, and this number (referred to as the `lGeneration`) is used for identifying the log files, and for storing them on the disk when they are completely filled with data.

The current log file, or the "log file in use" is `E00.log`, and while Exchange is filling this log file with data, a temporary `E00tmp.log` file is already created (or is in the process of being created) in the background. When the `E00.log` is eventually filled with data, it is saved under another name. The name is derived from the log file's prefix (E00, E01, E02, etc.) and the `lGeneration` value, which is a sequential hexadecimal notation. So, for example, when the `lGeneration` value is 1, the `E00.log` is saved as `E0000000001.log`. Alternatively, the last time this process happened in Figure 5.1, the `lGeneration` value was 3E, so the log file was saved as `E000000003E.log`. Since the `lGeneration` is a sequential number, we know that the *next* `lGeneration` of the E00.log must be 3F, and the next time this log file roll-over process takes place, the log file will be saved as `E000000003F.log`.

Although it's not directly visible, the `lGeneration` is stored inside the log file, and can be checked by dumping the header information of the log file with the **ESEUTIL** utility. When you use the `ESEUTIL /ML E00.LOG` command, the first few lines of the log file's header should read something like:

```
Base name: E00
Log file: E00.log
lGeneration: 63 (0x3F)
Checkpoint: (0x3F,8,16)
```

The `lGeneration` value is listed on the third line, both in decimal and hexadecimal notation. Unfortunately, this is very confusing, and there *will* be a day that an Exchange administrator mixes up these notations and starts working with the wrong log file.

After the pages are written to the log file, they are kept in memory, thereby saving an expensive read from disk action when Exchange Server needs the page again. When the Mailbox Server needs that memory for other pages, or when the page stays in memory for a long time, it is written to the database file. This is also known as the "lazy writer mechanism." A common misbelief is that data is read from the log files and written to the database file, but this is not the case. It is written directly from memory to the database, and log files are generally only read in recovery scenarios (with a few exceptions) for example, after an improper shutdown of the server. Under normal circumstances, the log files are 100% write, whereas the database is a random mix between read and write actions.

To be honest, it would be possible to write an entire book just about the storage technologies involved, but I think that level of detail generally isn't necessary for the average SysAdmin. However, if you're feeling particularly advanced I can recommend the book *Mission-Critical Microsoft Exchange 2003: Designing and Building Reliable Exchange Servers* by Jerry Cochran. You can find it on Amazon, and Jerry has an article on WindowsITPro.com (HTTP://TINYURL.COM/JERRYCOCHRAN) which also covers the topic.

5.2.3 Checkpoint file

The relationship between writing data in the log files and writing data into the database itself is managed by the checkpoint file, `E00.chk`. The checkpoint file points to the page in the database that was last written, and is advanced as soon as Exchange writes another page from memory to the database.

The difference between the data in the database and the data in the log files is referred to as **checkpoint depth**. This checkpoint depth can be several log files; in fact the default checkpoint depth is 20 log files. By using the checkpoint, Exchange waits before writing to the database, and tries to combine several write actions so that the database write operations can be performed more efficiently.

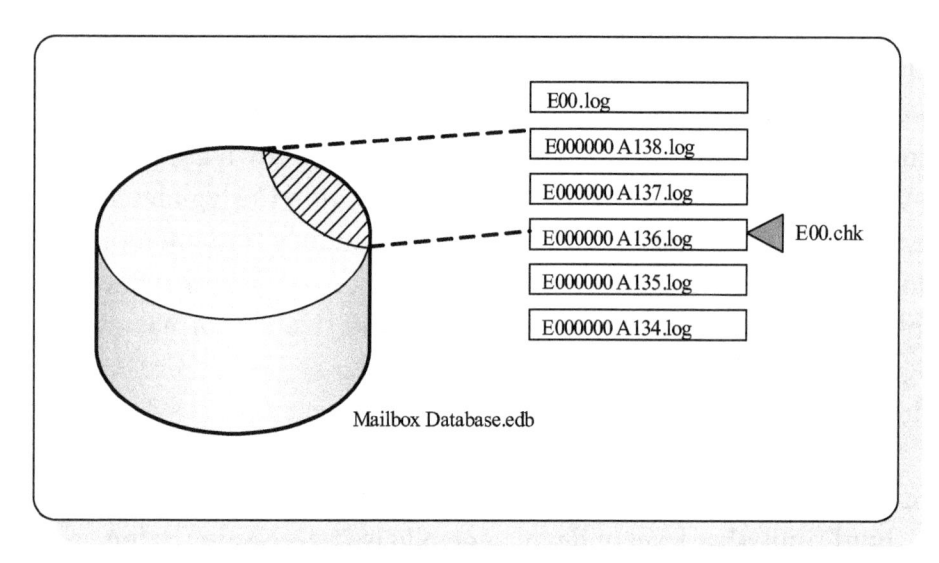

Figure 5.3: All data below the checkpoint is written to the database.

Checkpoint depth is also a per database setting. So when a database's checkpoint depth is 20 log files, a minimum of 20 MB of data is kept in memory for that specific database. When using 30 databases in Exchange Server 2010, each at its default checkpoint depth, approximately 600 MB of Exchange data is kept in memory.

5.2.4 The Mailbox Database

The `Mailbox Database 0242942819.edb` file is the primary repository of the Exchange Server 2010 Mailbox Server Role. In Exchange Server 2007 this file was called `Mailbox Database.edb`, whereas in Exchange 2003 and Exchange 2000 the database was comprised of two files: `priv1.edb` and `priv1.stm`. In Exchange Server 2010

Enterprise Edition, a Mailbox Server can now hold up to 100 databases and, as mentioned earlier, an Exchange Server 2010 Standard Edition Server is limited to only 5 databases.

The maximum size of an ESE database can be huge. The upper limit of a file on NTFS is 64 Exabytes, and this is generally considered sufficient to host large Mailbox Database files. The Microsoft-recommended maximum file size of the Mailbox Database on Exchange Server 2010 is 2 TB. Compared to the 200 GB file-size limit in Exchange 2007 (using Continuous Cluster Replication) this is a tremendous increase. Bear in mind that a prerequisite for using this sizing is that you have to configure multiple database copies to achieve a Highly Available solution. Please note that, unlike in some previous versions of Exchange Server, there's no hard-coded limit on the database sizing of Exchange Server 2010 Standard Edition. The size of your databases is limited by your SLA and how your Exchange environment is set up. Microsoft recommends using 2 TB Mailbox Databases *only* if you have multiple copies (at least three) of your Mailbox Databases running with a DAG (Database Availability Group) configuration.

5.3 High Availability in Exchange Server

Ever since Exchange Server 5.5, Microsoft has offered the option to use Windows clustering to create a highly available Exchange Mailbox environment. In a typical shared storage cluster environment, there are two server nodes available, both running Exchange Server, and both connected to a shared storage solution. In the early days, this shared storage was built on a shared SCSI bus and, later, on SANs with a Fiber Channel or iSCSI network connection were used. The important part was the shared storage where the Exchange Server databases were located.

At any given point in time, only one server node is the *owner* of this shared data, and it is this server node that is providing the client services; this server node is also known as the *active node*. The other node was not able to access this data, and was therefore the *passive node*. A private network between the two server nodes is used for intra-cluster

Chapter 5: High Availability in Exchange Server 2010 SP1

communications, such as a heartbeat signal, allowing both nodes to determine the state of the cluster and if the other node (or nodes if you're using a larger cluster) are still alive.

In addition to the two nodes, an *Exchange Virtual Server* was created as a cluster resource (note that this has nothing to do with virtual machines!). This is the resource that (Outlook) clients connect to in order to get access to their mailbox. When the active node fails, the passive node takes over the Exchange Virtual Server, which then continues to run. Although users will notice a short downtime during the fail-over, it is an otherwise seamless experience, and no action is needed from an end-user perspective.

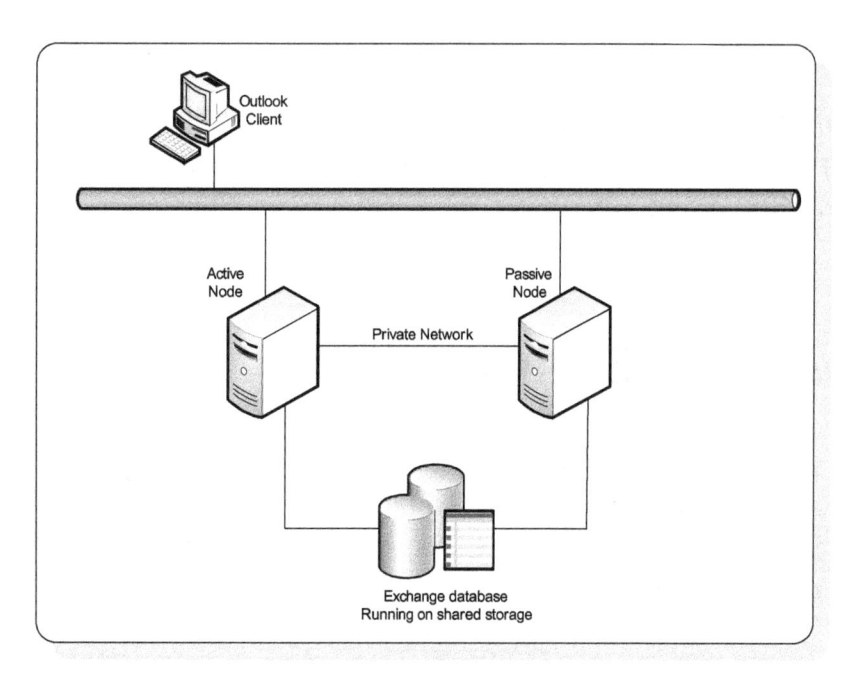

Figure 5.4: A two-node cluster with shared storage.

Although this solution offers redundancy, there's still a single point of failure: the shared database of the Exchange Server. In a typical environment this database is stored on a SAN and, by its nature, a SAN is a highly available environment. But when something *does* happen to the database, a logical failure for example, the database is no longer available for *both* nodes, resulting in total unavailability.

5.3.1 Exchange database replication

Microsoft offered a new solution in Exchange Server 2007 to create highly available Exchange environments: database replication. When using database replication, a copy of a database was created, resulting in database redundancy. This technology was available in three flavors:

- **Local Continuous Replication** (LCR) – a copy of the database is created on the same server
- **Cluster Continuous Replication** (CCR) – a copy of the database is created on another node in a Windows fail-over cluster (there can only be two nodes in a CCR cluster)
- **Stand-by Continuous Replication** (SCR) – this came with Exchange Server 2007 SP1; a copy of a database is created on any other Exchange Server (i.e. not necessarily in the cluster); this is not meant as a High Availability solution, but more as a disaster recovery solution.

This is how database replication works in a CCR clustered environment. Exchange Server 2007 is installed on a Windows Server 2003 or Windows Server 2008 fail-over cluster. There's no shared storage in use within the cluster, but each node has its own storage. This can be either on a SAN (fiber channel or iSCSI) or Direct Attached Storage (DAS), i.e. local physical disks.

As mentioned earlier, the active node in the cluster is servicing client requests, and Exchange Server uses the standard database technology with a database, log files, and a checkpoint file. When Exchange Server is finished with a log file, the log file is sent immediately to the passive node of the cluster. This can either be via a normal network connection or via a dedicated replication network.

The passive node receives the log file and checks it for errors. If none are found, the data in the log file is replayed into the passive copy of the database. This is an asynchronous

Chapter 5: High Availability in Exchange Server 2010 SP1

process, meaning the passive copy is always a couple of log files behind the active copy, and so information is "missing" in the passive copy.

All messages are always sent via a Hub Transport Server, even internal messages. The Hub Transport Server keeps track of these messages, and can therefore send missing information (which the passive node actually requests) to the passive copy of the cluster in case of a cluster fail-over. This is called the "Transport Dumpster" in a Hub Transport Server.

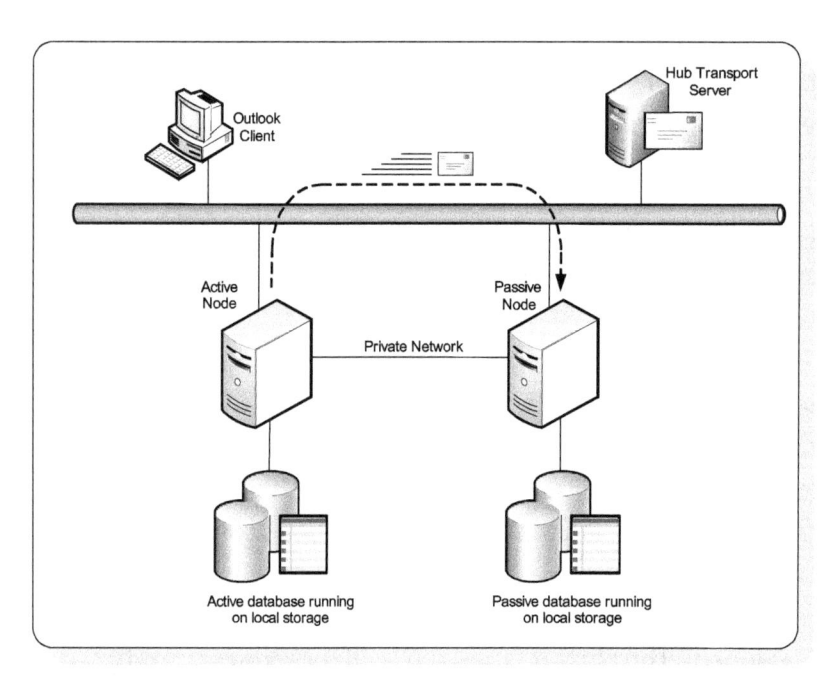

Figure 5.5: A fail-over cluster with Exchange Server 2007 Continuous Cluster Replication.

This kind of replication works very well; a lot of System Administrators are using CCR replication and are very satisfied with it. There are a few drawbacks, though.

- If an Exchange Server 2007 CCR environment is running on Windows Server 2003 or Windows Server 2008 clustering, this brings a lot of additional complexity to the environment for many Exchange administrators.

- Windows Server 2003 clustering in a multi-subnet environment is nearly impossible, although this has improved (but is still not perfect) in Windows Server 2008 fail-over clustering.

- Site Resilience is not seamless.

- CCR clustering is only possible for two nodes.

- All three kinds of replication (LCR, CCR, and SCR) are managed differently.

To overcome these issues, Microsoft has dramatically improved the replication technology, and reduced the administrative overhead at the same time. This is achieved by completely hiding the cluster components behind the implementation of Exchange Server 2010. The cluster components are still there, but the administration is completely done with the Exchange Management Console or the Exchange Management Shell.

5.3.2 Database Availability Group and Continuous Replication

In Exchange Server 2010, Microsoft introduced the concept of a Database Availability Group (DAG), which is a logical unit of Exchange Server 2010 Mailbox Servers. All Mailbox Servers within a DAG can replicate databases to each other, and a single DAG can hold up to 16 Mailbox Servers and up to 16 copies of a database. The idea of multiple copies of a database in one Exchange organization is called Exchange Mobility; one database exists on multiple servers, each instance of which is 100% identical and thus has the same GUID.

In Exchange Server 2010, all clients, including all MAPI clients like Microsoft Outlook, connect to the CA Server. Supported Outlook clients in Exchange Server 2010 include Outlook 2003, Outlook 2007, and Outlook 2010. So, the Outlook client connects to the CA Server which, in turn, connects to the mailbox in the active copy of the database, as you can see in Figure 5.6. Unfortunately, this is only true for Mailbox Databases. When

Chapter 5: High Availability in Exchange Server 2010 SP1

an Outlook client needs to access a Public Folder Database, the client still accesses the Mailbox Server directly, but only for Public Folder information.

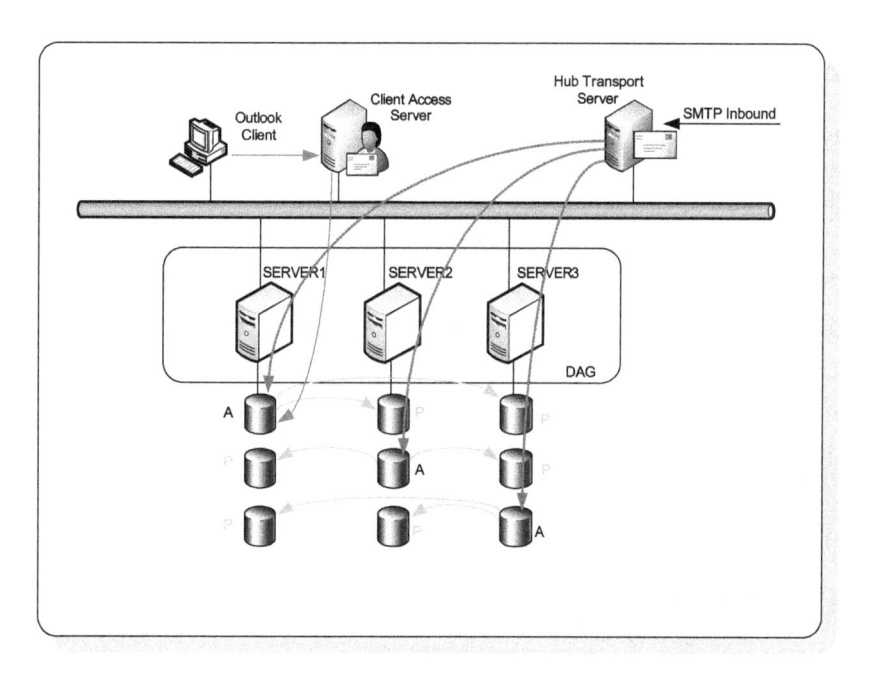

Figure 5.6: A Database Availability Group with three servers; each server holds one active and two passive databases.

5.3.3 DAG architecture

So, the continuous replication used inside the Database Availability Group is based on log shipping technology. The Exchange Replication Service on an Exchange Mailbox Server is responsible for sending the log files from the active copy of a Mailbox Database to the passive copies of a Mailbox Database (of which there can be one or several). In Exchange Server 2007 Cluster Continuous Replication (CCR), where the DAG is derived from, this log shipping was a pull model. In Exchange Server 2010 the log shipping is a push model, so the log files are pushed from the active copy of a Mailbox Database to the passive copies of a Mailbox Database.

Now let's go back to Figure 5.2 (which is also seen as a component of Figure 5.7). As soon as the database engine is finished processing the current log file (E00.log), the log file roll-over takes place and the log file is saved with another name (in this example, E0000000004.log, as seen in Step 2 in Figure 5.7, below). As soon as this log file is saved, the Exchange Replication Service copies the file to the other server in the DAG, where the passive copy of the Mailbox Database resides. On this server, it is placed into the inspector directory, which you'll find on all Mailbox Servers that are a member of the DAG and that have a passive copy of a given Mailbox Database.

The replication service then inspects the log file to make sure it isn't corrupt and, if the log file is OK, it is copied to the log file directory of the Mailbox Database. When the log file is in this directory, it is picked up by the Information Store service (MSExchangeIS.exe) and replayed into the Mailbox Database.

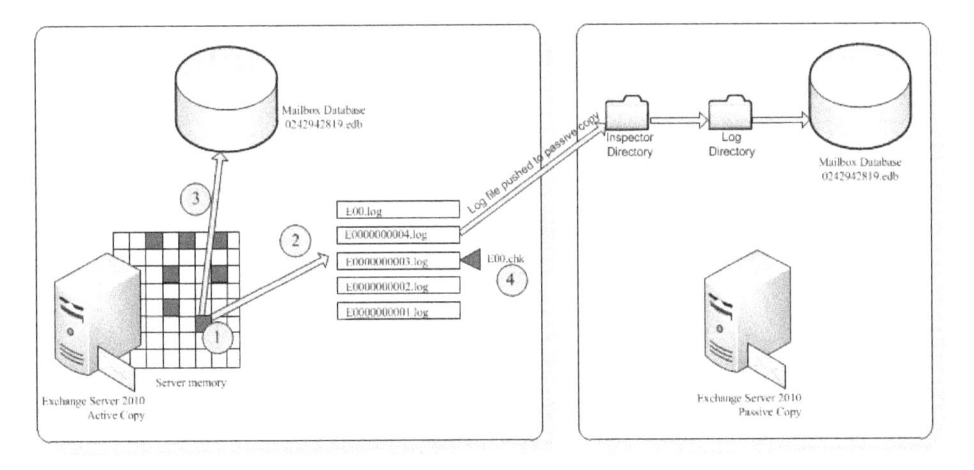

Figure 5.7: Log shipping from the active copy to a passive copy of a Mailbox Database.

Shipping log files from the active copy of a Mailbox Database to the passive copies of a Mailbox Database is an asynchronous process. This means that there's always a delay, and therefore a difference, between the active copy and the passive copies of a Mailbox Database. This form of replication is called **continuous replication – file mode**.

New in Exchange Server 2010 Service Pack 1 is a technology called **continuous replication – block mode**. In block mode, when Exchange is finished with a transaction in memory, that transaction is copied to the memory of the Exchange Mailbox Server holding a passive copy of the Mailbox Database. When log buffers in memory are full, they are written to the log file of the Mailbox Database, on the active, as well as on the passive copies, therefore dramatically reducing the latency between the active and the passive copies.

When copies of a Mailbox Database are initially created, the `Mailbox Database 0242942819.edb` file is copied from the first server to the servers that will hold the passive copies of the Mailbox Database; this process is called "seeding." However, when you have a 750 GB Mailbox Database, this seeding can take a considerable amount of time. So it is no surprise that it is recommended that you configure database copies as soon as a Mailbox Database is created. Unfortunately it can happen that a disk containing a passive copy of a Mailbox Database is lost. When the disk is replaced, you have to do a seeding again, and the complete Mailbox Database file is copied to the other Mailbox Server.

To reduce the strain on your network, though, it is possible to do an offline seeding. Using this method, you can copy the actual Mailbox Database file to other media, for example a USB disk, and then bring the Mailbox Database file to the other server.

Now, when the active copy of a Mailbox Database fails, or when the Exchange administrator initiates a Mailbox Database fail-over, a passive copy of a Mailbox Database will take over. Since the replication is asynchronous, there will always be a delay and the passive copy will miss a certain amount of data.

But do you remember the Hub Transport Server? All messages are always routed via the Hub Transport Server, and the Hub Transport Server has a Transport Dumpster where all messages are kept for some time. So, if a Mailbox Database switch-over takes place, the passive copy will contact the Hub Transport Server and request a retransmit of all missing messages. Therefore, you have very little chance of missing data after a Mailbox Database switch-over.

When building a highly available Mailbox Server environment by using a DAG, there's no need to build a fail-over cluster in advance, as additional Mailbox Servers can be added to the DAG on the fly. However, for the DAG to function properly, some fail-over clustering components are still used, but these are installed during a DAG's configuration (and removed when the server is removed from a DAG). All Management of the DAG and database copies is performed via the Exchange Management Console or the Exchange Management Shell; although available in the Administrative Tools under the Start menu, the Windows Fail-over Cluster Manager should no longer be used.

Note

The Database Availability Group with Database Copies is the only High Availability technology used in Exchange Server 2010. Older technologies like SCR, CCR, and SCR are no longer available. The traditional Single Copy Cluster (SCC) with shared storage is also no longer supported.

5.3.3.1 File Share Witness

Under the hood, a Database Availability Group is based on the principle of a Majority Node Set Cluster. A Majority Node Set Cluster wants to create a majority, in case of a split of the cluster, for example when you've a cluster spread across two datacenters. This means that a Majority Node Set Cluster, and therefore a Database Availability Group, will always consist of an odd number of nodes.

Imagine you have two datacenters with a Database Availability Group composed of four Mailbox Servers. The fifth member is the File Share Witness, and this File Share Witness is located in the second datacenter. If the connection between the two datacenters is lost, then the DAG in the first datacenter will consist of two members (both Mailbox Servers), but the DAG in the seconf datacenter will consist of three members (both Mailbox Servers *and* the File Share Witness), and therefore form a majority.

Chapter 5: High Availability in Exchange Server 2010 SP1

The DAG in the second datacenter will therefore continue to run, but the members of the DAG in the first datacenter will stop working until the connection is restored and the DAG is returned to its original state.

However, if the second datacenter becomes unavailable, for example due to a fire, the first datacenter cannot create a majority and will stop working, but since the second datacenter isn't available either, the entire DAG will be unavailable. In this situation, manual intervention is your only option; you have to create a new File Share Witness in the first datacenter to have the DAG create a majority again. Luckily, the DAG has the option to create an Alternate Witness Server for just such a scenario, as shown in Figure 5.8.

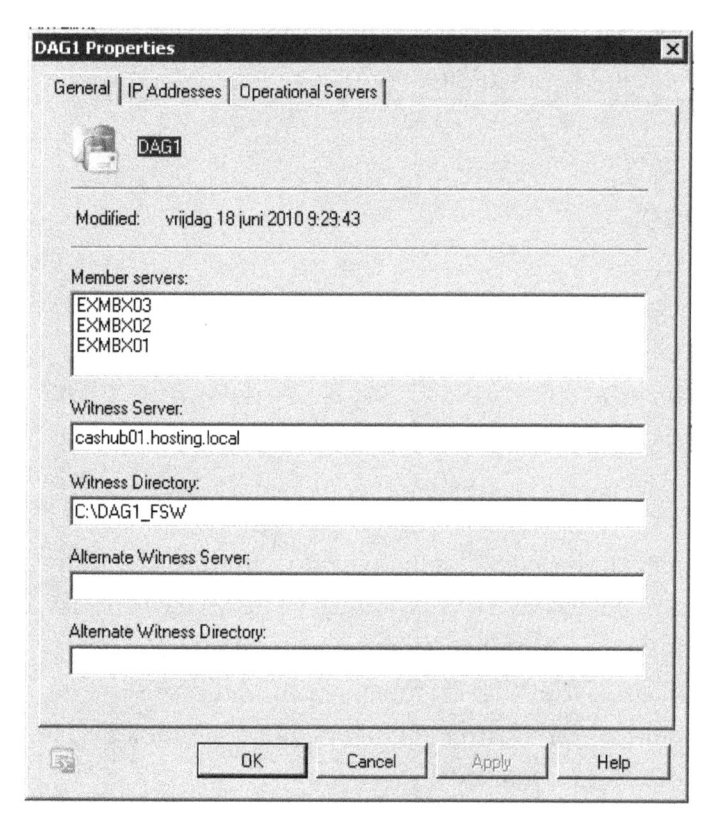

Figure 5.8: It is possible to create an Alternate Witness Server and Alternate Witness Directory on a DAG.

In Exchange Server 2010 RTM, the configuration of a Database Availability Group is no longer limited to a server holding just the Mailbox Server Role. It is possible to create a two-server situation with the Hub Transport, Client Access and Mailbox Server Role on both servers, and then create a Database Availability Group and configure database copies. However, it isn't a High Availability configuration for the Client Access or Hub Transport Servers unless you've put load balancers in front of them, since it's not possible to use the default Windows Network Load Balancing (NLB) in combination with the Windows fail-over clustering components. Regardless, this is a great improvement for smaller deployments of Exchange Server 2010 where high availability is still required. As a side note, you can use Round Robin for creating a highly available Hub Transport configuration, but this is not the case for the CA Server, though.

But wait, how about the situation where you lose a complete server with the Mailbox Server, the Hub Server and the CA Server Roles? Isn't there a chance that the passive copy of a Mailbox Database has to check the Transport Dumpster on the server we just lost? In theory, yes, but in such a scenario, under normal operations, the active copy of a Mailbox Database will route its messages through the other server, just to prevent both the Mailbox Database as well as the Transport Dumpster being lost at the same time.

5.3.3.2   Active Manager

In Exchange Server 2007, Cluster Continuous Replication uses the cluster resource management model to install and manage the High Availability solution. Initially, the Windows cluster is built and then Exchange setup is run in clustered mode, registering the `EXRES.DLL` in the fail-over cluster, and the Clustered Mailbox Server (CMS) is created. For a Highly Available Exchange Server 2007 environment it is *always* necessary to build a fail-over cluster in advance, even if it's just a one-node cluster!

The cluster components are now hidden in Exchange Server 2010, and a new component named the **Active Manager** has been introduced. The Active Manager replaces the resource model and fail-over management features offered in previous versions of Exchange Server.

Chapter 5: High Availability in Exchange Server 2010 SP1

The fail-over clustering components have not been completely removed, though, and some of them are actually still used. If you open the **Fail-over Cluster Manager** in **Administrative Tools** you'll find the DAG, cluster networks, etc. *Do not* try to manage the DAG using the Fail-over Cluster Manager, as this is not supported. The only way to manage the DAG is using the Exchange Management Console or the Exchange Management Shell.

The Active Manager runs on all Mailbox Servers that are members of a DAG, and there are two roles: the Primary Active Manager (PAM) and the Stand-by Active Manager (SAM). The PAM is running on the Mailbox Server that also holds the cluster quorum, and this is the server that decides which databases are active and which databases are passive in a DAG. The SAM is responsible for determining server or database failures (the PAM does this on its own server for its own local databases) and, if detected, communicates with the PAM to initiate a fail-over.

The replication service monitors the health of the mounted databases in a DAG, and monitors the ESE engine for any I/O issues or failures. If anything goes wrong here, the replication service immediately contacts the Active Manager. In the case of a fail-over, the Active Manager determines which database should become the active copy of the database (depending on the fail-over preference you've specified during configuration).

5.3.4 Configuring a Database Availability Group

To configure a highly available Database Availability Group, at least two Exchange Server 2010 Mailbox Servers are required. Imagine a four-server deployment, two combined Client Access / Hub Transport Servers and two Exchange Server 2010 Mailbox Servers (`EXMBX01` and `EXMBX02`). All four servers are located in the same Active Directory site, and this site is also the Internet-facing Active Directory site.

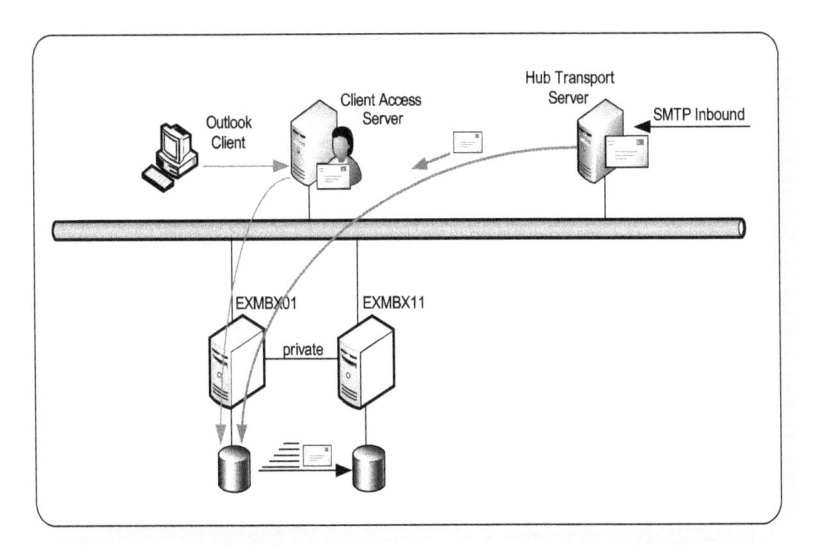

Figure 5.9: A four-server Exchange 2010 deployment.

Let's assume that all four servers are fully operational and working fine. To create a Database Availability Group for the two Mailbox Servers, an additional private network is recommended, which will be used for replication purposes. It is not needed to have a second network for replication, though, as a DAG with only one network is fully supported by Microsoft.

To create a Database Availability Group, follow these steps.

- Log on to an Exchange Server and open the **Exchange Management Console**.
- Expand the **Exchange On-Premises (SERVER)**, and then expand the **Organization** leaf. Click on the **Mailbox** and then click on the **Database Availability Group** tab. No items will currently be shown in the **Results** pane.
- In the **Actions** pane select **New Database Availability Group**.
- In the **New Database Availability Group** wizard, enter a name for the new DAG, for example "DAG1." If you want, you can manually select a **Witness Server** and a **Witness Directory** (which will be created on the Witness Server.

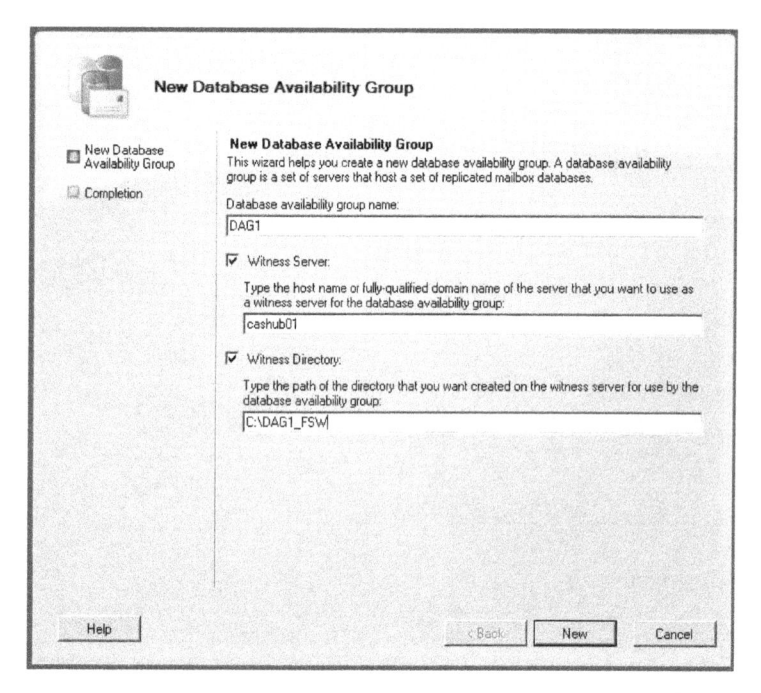

Figure 5.10: Creating a new DAG in the Exchange Management Console.

- Click **New** to create the new Database Availability Group. The DAG itself will initially get its IP address from a DHCP Server. If you want to assign a static IP address to the DAG, you have to open the DAG's properties and change it.

- Once created, you can open the **Database Availability Group** in the **Exchange Management Console** and check its properties. Right here you can add an **Alternate Witness Server** and an **Alternate Witness Directory**, or you can change the DAG's **IP address**.

Of course, it is also possible to create a Database Availability Group using the Exchange Management Shell. On the Mailbox Server, open the **Exchange Management Shell** and then enter the following command:

```
New-DatabaseAvailabilityGroup –Name DAG1
–DatabaseAvailabilityGroupIpAddresses 10.0.0.101
```

- A new Database Availability Group with the IP address of 10.0.0.101 will be created. Since the Database Availability Group is nothing more than a placeholder in Active Directory, it can be seen with `ADSIEdit`.

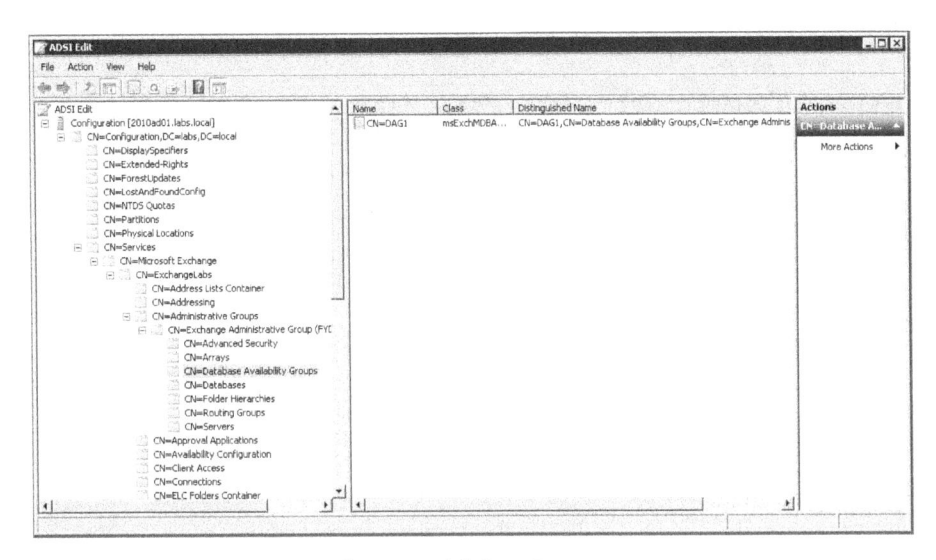

Figure 5.11: An empty Database Availability Group.

- To add the first Mailbox Server (`EXMBX01`) to the Database Availability Group, switch back to the **Exchange Management Console**, select the **Database Availability Group DAG1** and, in the **Actions** pane, select **Manage Database Availability Group.**

- In the **Manage Database Availability Group Membership** Wizard, click **Add** and select the first server, `EXMBX01`. Click **OK** to continue.

- In the Wizard, click **Manage** to continue.

Right now, under the hood, the actual Cluster is created as a building block of the Database Availability Group. The clustering binaries are installed (if not already present) and the Database Availability Group is created. After some time, usually between 60 and 90 seconds, the DAG is created and the Exchange Server is added to the DAG. The File Share Witness is not created at this point. Again, it is also possible to use the Exchange

Chapter 5: High Availability in Exchange Server 2010 SP1

Management Shell to add the Exchange Server to the DAG by entering the following command:

```
Add-DatabaseAvailabilityGroupServer –Identity DAG1 –MailboxServer EXMBX01
```

In the **Exchange Management Console**, you can now see the Database Availability Group (DAG1), as well as the EXMBX01 we just added.

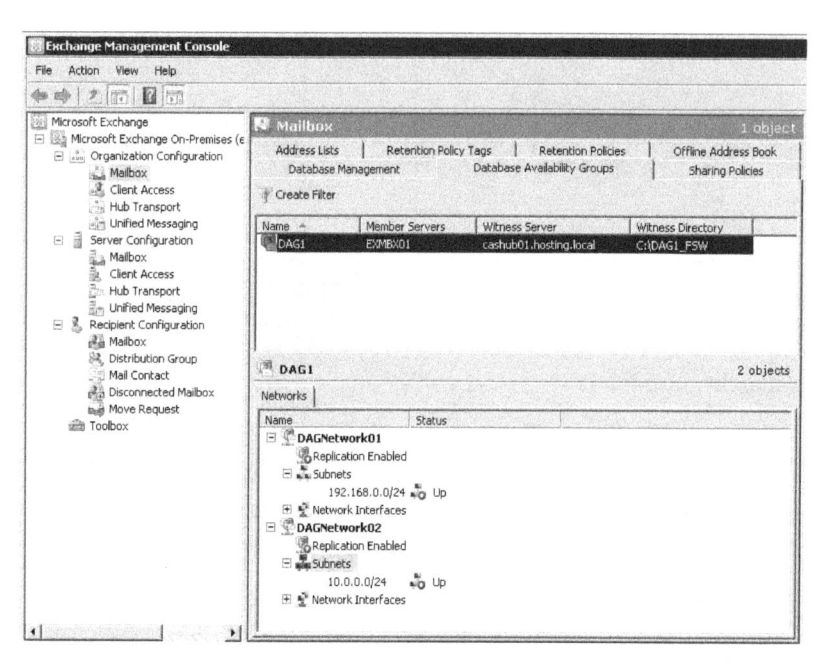

Figure 5.12: The newly created DAG with two Member Servers.

- Click the **Database Management** tab in the **Exchange Management Console**, and you'll see the initial databases on the first and second Mailbox Servers. Also notice that there's one database copy available on each server. No Mailbox Database copies have been created in the DAG at this point. When you select the **Public Folder Database** in the **Database Management** tab, the **Database Copies Results** pane is grayed-out. This is because Public Folder replication and database replication are not compatible with each other.

- To add the second Exchange Server 2010 Mailbox Server to the Database Availability Group, log on to the second server and open the **Exchange Management Shell**. Enter the following command:

```
Add-DatabaseAvailabilityGroupServer –Identity DAG1 –MailboxServer EXMBX02
```

- The second Mailbox Server will now be added to the Database Availability Group. As with adding the first Mailbox Server, this can take somewhere between 60 and 90 seconds to finish.

  Note

  If the Windows fail-over clustering components are not already installed on the Mailbox Server, they automatically will be. You can also manually install them in advance by opening a command prompt and executing the following command: `ServerManagerCmd.exe –i Failover-Clustering`.

Right, now we have created a Database Availability Group with two Mailbox Servers and we're ready to configure database copies. The Database Availability Group feature is very flexible. As I've explained, there's no need to configure a Windows fail-over cluster in advance; you can add a Mailbox Server to the DAG whenever needed – even a year later – without a problem. Just install a Mailbox Server, install the fail-over clustering bits, and add the server to the DAG. This is known as *Incremental Deployment*.

It is also possible to create site resilience on the database level using the Database Availability Group. Besides adding Mailbox Servers in the same Active Directory site (i.e. in the same datacenter), you can also add Mailbox Servers in another Active Directory site, such as in another datacenter. As long as the network connectivity is good enough to handle the replication in a timely manner, and as long as the Hub Transport and CA Servers have a reliable network connection to the other datacenter, you're ready to go. Database copies over multiple datacenters are supported as long as the network latency is less than 250 ms round trip.

Chapter 5: High Availability in Exchange Server 2010 SP1

If you want to add a Mailbox Server in another site to the DAG, a few configuration changes are needed. The IP Address of the DAG in the other site has to be added to the local DAG, which can be done using the Exchange Management Console (using the properties of the DAG), or using the following command in the Exchange Management Shell:

```
Set-DatabaseAvailabilityGroup –Identity DAG1
–DatabaseAvailabilityGroupIpAddresses 10.0.0.101,192.168.1.101
```

The first network in the DAG will be automatically created during the addition of the first Mailbox Server. Additional networks are not created automatically, so you have to add the subnet of the second site to the DAG manually:

```
New-DatabaseAvailabilityGroupNetwork -DatabaseAvailabilityGroup DAG1
-Name DAGNetwork02 -Description "Second Site" -Subnets 192.168.1.0/24
-ReplicationEnabled:$True
```

Note

If there are Domain Controllers in the site you just added, you must wait for the replication to finish, or else force the replication to start. Otherwise the Domain Controllers in the second site may not have enough knowledge about the changes you want to make.

At this stage you can add a Mailbox Server in the second site to the DAG using the Exchange Management Console or the Exchange Management Shell:

```
Add-DatabaseAvailabilityGroupServer –Identity DAG1 –MailboxServer EXMBX02
```

5.3.5 Managing database copies

A database copy is exactly what its name implies: a copy of a Mailbox Database, but on another Exchange Server, in the same Database Availability Group. When initially configured, a copy of the database file is copied via the network to the other server and, when finished, Exchange Server 2010 starts replication of the log files of this particular database over the network to the other server.

The relative location of the passive copy of the database is also identical to the location of the active copy. For example, an initial database on the Exchange Server 2010 Mailbox Server `EXMBX01` can be located in the directory `C:\Program Files\Microsoft\Exchange Server\V14\Mailbox\Mailbox Database 1539639680`. If a database copy is enabled for this server, the same directory is created on the second server. This makes sense of course, since it is the location of the Mailbox Database that's stored in Active Directory. As mentioned earlier the process of copying a database to an additional server is known as seeding.

It is best practice to use separate disks for Exchange databases, from both a performance perspective and a disaster recovery perspective. Although meant for earlier versions of Exchange Server, Microsoft Knowledge Base article 328794 (HTTP://SUPPORT.MICROSOFT.COM/KB/328794) explains more.

After configuring `Mailbox Database 1539639680` to use a separate disk, such as `F:\`, for storing its information, the database copy can be configured.

- On the target server (i.e. the server that will hold the database copy), make sure there's an identical volume to the one on the source server. The target server in this example needs a separate `F:\` disk as well.

- Open the **Exchange Management Console**, expand the **Microsoft Exchange On-Premises (EXMBX01)** node, then expand the **Organization Configuration** node, and click on the **Mailbox** node. Select the **Database Management** tab in the **Results** pane.

- Select **Mailbox Database 1539639680**. In the lower part of the **Results** pane there's one copy, the active copy, located on the first Exchange Server (**EXMBX01**). Right-click on **Mailbox Database 1539639680** and select **Add Mailbox Database Copy**.

- In the **Add Mailbox Database Copy** wizard, select **Browse** to select a Mailbox Server that will hold a copy of the database. The **Activation Preference Number** is the order in which Exchange will make a passive copy into an active copy when the preceding active copy fails. Of course, this number is only useful if multiple passive copies are configured (a complete rundown of the Activation Preference Number and what happens when a Database becomes active is on the Microsoft TechNet website at HTTP://TINYURL.COM/ACTIVEMANAGER). Click **Add** to continue.

- The database file `Mailbox Database 1539639680.edb` will now be copied to the target server and the replication will be set up. Depending of the size of the Database file, this can take some time.

- When the database is copied and the replication is activated, click **Finish**.

Once completed, log on to the target Exchange Server and you'll notice that on this server (on the `F:\` disk in the example in Figure 5.13) a `Mailbox Database 1539639680` directory has been created where the copy of the database is stored. You'll also see the log files that are replicated to this directory.

If a lot of databases are used on an Exchange Server, using mount points is a valid alternative. In a mount point scenario, all data disks are mounted to a directory on the server, for example, `F:\DB01`, `F:\DB02`, `F:\DB03` etc., using Server Manager.

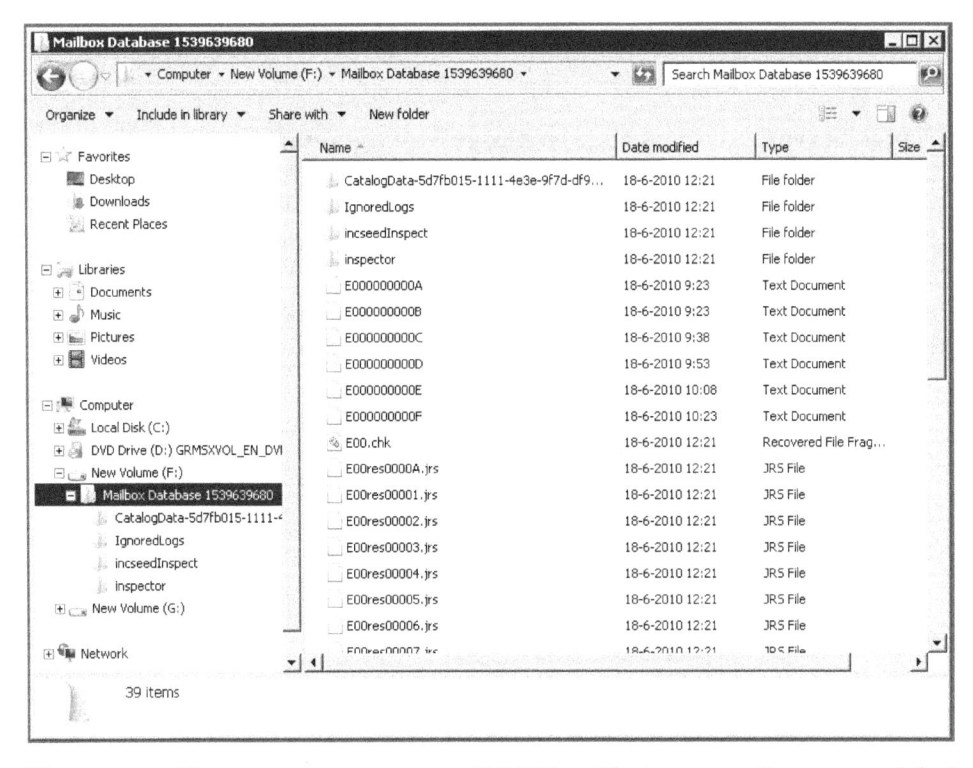

Chapter 5: High Availability in Exchange Server 2010 SP1

Figure 5.13: The passive copy on server EXMBX02. The inspector directory used during replication is clearly visible.

In an Exchange Server 2007 CCR environment, the active server also ships log files to the passive server, which also loads the log files into its copy of the database. However, the passive server is *really* passive, and the service responsible for the database and the log files (`store.exe`) is not running. The only service that is running is the replication service. During a fail-over, the passive node has to start all Exchange services, and all databases need to be mounted before that can happen. In Exchange Server 2010 the `store.exe` service is already running and the databases are already mounted on all computers in a Database Availability Group, meaning a database fail-over is much faster, and the result is a much shorter overall fail-over time.

For maintenance purposes it is possible to move an active database copy from one Exchange Mailbox Server to another.

- Log on to an Exchange Server and open the **Exchange Management Console**.
- Expand the **Exchange On-Premises (SERVER)**, and then expand the **Organization** leaf. Click on the **Mailbox** and then click on the **Database Management** tab.
- All of the databases in your Exchange Server 2010 environment show up in the upper half of the **Results** pane. Right-click the database you want to move (which is, of course, also a database that has multiple copies configured).
- Select **Move Active Mailbox Database** from the context menu.
- In the **Move Active Mailbox Database** wizard select **Browse** to select another server where you want the active copy to be moved to.
- Click the **Move** button to move the active copy of the database to the server just selected.

5.3.6 Lagged copies in a DAG

In Exchange Server 2007 SP1 there was a technology called **Stand-by Continuous Replication** or **SCR**, which was not a High Availability solution but a disaster recovery solution. One of the options available with SCR was to create a lag time in replaying the log files into the copy of the Mailbox Database. Using a lagged copy of a Mailbox Database, it is possible to return to a specific moment in time by choosing exactly which log files you want to replay.

SCR is no longer available, but the lagged copies are now available in the Database Availability Group. The idea is the same as a normal Mailbox Database Copy in a Database Availability Group, but instead of replaying the log file almost immediately, the log files are replayed after a configurable amount of time. This lag time can be configured to be up

Chapter 5: High Availability in Exchange Server 2010 SP1

to 14 days, at which point the Mailbox Database Server will keep the log files for up to 14 days before replaying them into a passive copy of the Mailbox Database.

Suppose we extend our example environment with a third Exchange Server 2010 Mailbox Server Role, `EXMBX03`, and we want to configure lagged copies of other Mailbox Databases on this Mailbox Server.

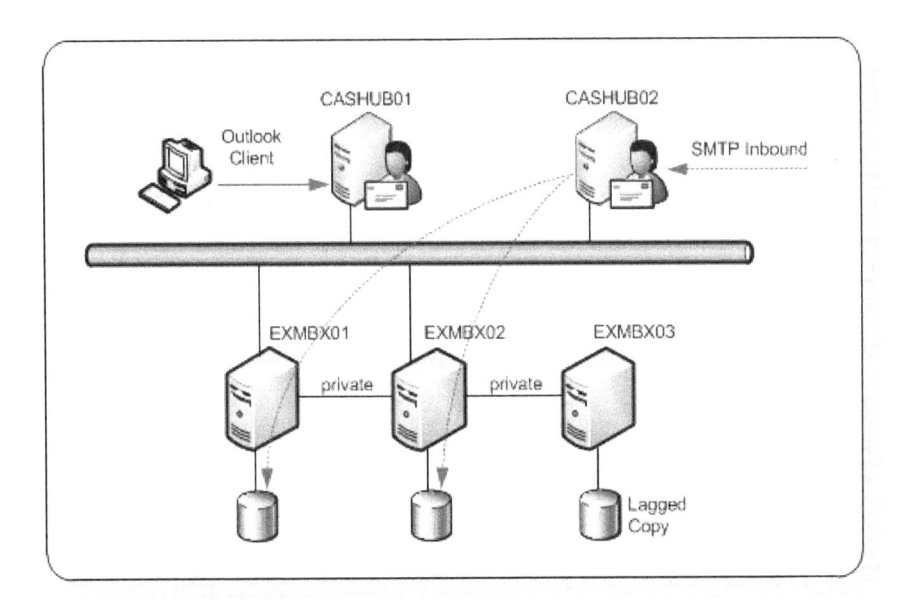

Figure 5.14: The DAG is extended with a third server for lagged copies.

Follow the steps below to set up a lagged copy of `Mailbox Database 1539639680`, with a lag of 1 day, on the `EXMBX03` Server.

- Use the procedure as outlined in Section 5.3.4 to add the Exchange Server 2010 Mailbox Server `EXMBX03` to the `Database Availability Group DAG1`.

Chapter 5: High Availability in Exchange Server 2010 SP1

- Once that's been done, use the procedure as outlined in Section 5.3.5 to create a third copy of the `Mailbox Database 1539639680`.

- When the seeding of the `Mailbox Database 1539639680` has finished, open an **Exchange Management Shell** and run the following command:

```
Set-MailboxDatabaseCopy -Identity "Mailbox Database 1539639680\EXMBX03"
-ReplayLagTime 1.0:0:0
```

- Using the Exchange Management Shell, it is also possible to create a Mailbox Database Copy and enter the lag time immediately:

```
Add-MailboxDatabaseCopy -Identity "Mailbox Database 0090905581" -MailboxServer
EXMBX03
-ReplayLagTime 1.00:00:00
```

You'll see a size difference between the Active Mailbox Database and the lagged copy of the Mailbox Database, but the number of log files on both servers should be almost identical. Remember that the log files are replicated to the other server almost immediately; it's the *replay* of the log files which is lagged.

This is also visible in the Exchange Management Console; during activity, the active copy of the database is growing and log files are waiting to be replayed on the lagged copy, which results in an increase in the **Replay Queue Length**.

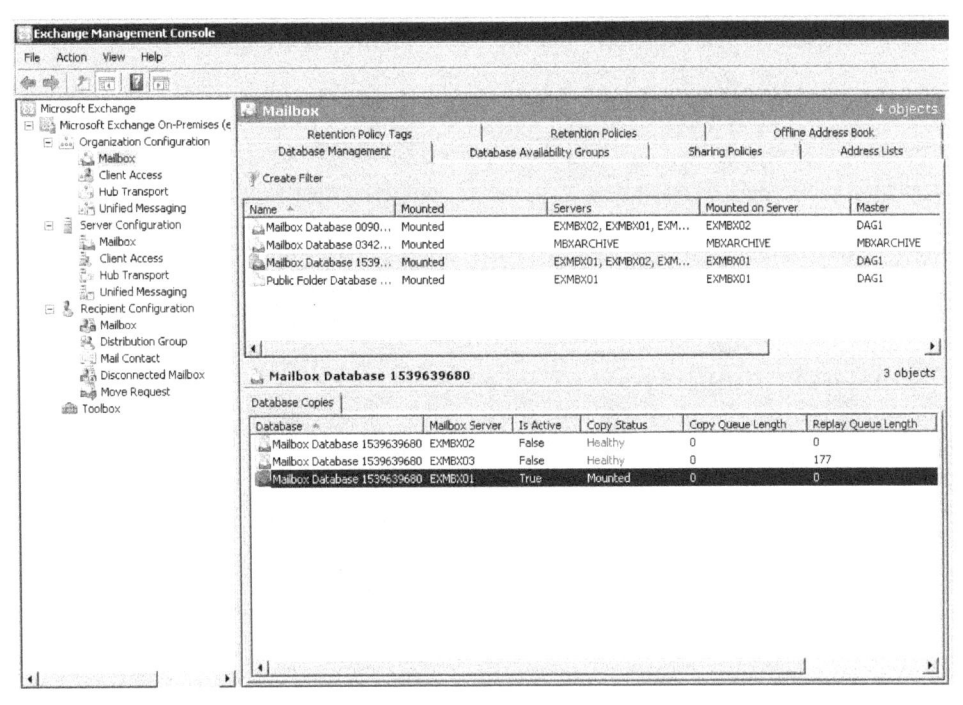

Figure 5.15: Log files are waiting to be replayed in the "Replay Queue Length" for the lagged copy.

Besides the Exchange Management Console, you can also use the Exchange Management Shell to retrieve replication information using the `Get-MailboxDatabaseCopyStatus` command as below.

```
[PS] C:\Windows\system32>Get-MailboxDatabaseCopyStatus | select Name,Status,CopyQue
ueLength,ReplayQueueLength

Name                              Status    CopyQueue   ReplayQueue
                                            Length      Length
----                              ------    ---------   -----------
Mailbox Database 1539639680...    Mounted   0           0
Mailbox Database 0090905581...    Healthy   0           0

[PS] C:\Windows\system32>
```

Chapter 5: High Availability in Exchange Server 2010 SP1

To retrieve a list of all database copies on all Mailbox Servers, you have to use the `Get-MailboxServer` output, piped into the `Get-MailboxDatabaseCopyStatus` cmdlet:

```
[PS] C:\Windows\system32>Get-MailboxServer | get-MailboxDatabaseCopyStatus | select
Name,Status,CopyQueueLength,ReplayQueueLength

Name                             Status     CopyQueue  ReplayQueue
                                            Length     Length
----                             ------     ---------  -----------
Mailbox Database 1539639680...   Mounted    0          0
Mailbox Database 0090905581...   Healthy    0          0
Mailbox Database 0090905581...   Mounted    0          0
Mailbox Database 1539639680...   Healthy    0          0
Mailbox Database 0342051937...   Mounted    0          0
Mailbox Database 1539639680...   Healthy    0          1444
Mailbox Database 0090905581...   Healthy    0          3

[PS] C:\Windows\system32>
```

The Replay Queue Length has a value of 1444, which means that 1444 log files are awaiting replaying. Normally this means there's an issue with the DAG, but in this example this is a lagged copy, as the log files are being copied to the server, but they haven't been replayed yet.

To retrieve information about the Mailbox Database, Mailbox Database Copies, replication, Lag Time, etc., you have to use the `Get-MailboxDatabase` cmdlet with the `Format-List (fl)` option as in the following example, which has been edited for readability.

Chapter 5: High Availability in Exchange Server 2010 SP1

```
[PS] C:\Windows\system32>Get-MailboxDatabase -Identity "Mailbox Database
1539639680" | fl

RunspaceId                : df2999c0-154d-4106-8feb-26f5ca426fd3
MailboxRetention          : 30.00:00:00
OfflineAddressBook        : \Default Offline Address Book
PublicFolderDatabase      : Public Folder Database 1177448183
ProhibitSendReceiveQuota: 2.3 GB (2,469,396,480 bytes)
ProhibitSendQuota         : 2 GB (2,147,483,648 bytes)
RecoverableItemsQuota     : 30 GB (32,212,254,720 bytes)
RecoverableItemsWarningQuota : 20 GB (21,474,836,480 bytes)
EdbFilePath               : F:\Mailbox Database
                            1539639680\Mailbox Database
                            1539639680.edb
ExchangeLegacyDN          : /o=E2010/ou=Exchange
                            Administrative Group
                            (FYDIBOHF23SPDLT)/
                            cn=Configuration /cn=Servers/
                            cn=webmail.inframan.nl/
                            cn=Microsoft Private MDB
DatabaseCopies            : {Mailbox Database 1539639680\
                            EXMBX01, Mailbox Database
                            1539639680\EXMBX02, Mailbox
                            Database 1539639680\EXMBX03}
Servers                   : {EXMBX01, EXMBX02, EXMBX03}
ActivationPreference      : {[EXMBX01, 1], [EXMBX02, 2],
                            [EXMBX03, 3]}
ReplayLagTimes            : {[EXMBX01, 00:00:00],
                            [EXMBX02, 00:00:00],
                            [EXMBX03, 02:00:00]}
TruncationLagTimes        : {[EXMBX01, 00:00:00],
                            [EXMBX02, 00:00:00],
                            [EXMBX03, 00:00:00]}
RpcClientAccessServer     : webmail.inframan.nl
DeletedItemRetention      : 14.00:00:00
Name                      : Mailbox Database 1539639680
LogFolderPath             : F:\Mailbox Database 1539639680
CircularLoggingEnabled    : False
LogFilePrefix             : E00
OriginatingServer         : HAD01.hosting.local
IsValid                   : True

[PS] C:\Windows\system32>
```

5.3.7 Online Move-Mailbox

The online Move-Mailbox feature is new in Exchange Server 2010. In older versions of Exchange Server, the mailbox is taken offline when it is being moved from one server to another server, to prevent users from accessing any of their data, and queuing up any incoming messages. There are situations when a huge (5 GB) mailbox has to be kept offline for more than an hour while the move takes place! None of these make for a particularly useable system.

With the new online Move-Mailbox functionality, now called `New-MoveRequest`, the time a mailbox is offline has been reduced to only seconds, and the end-user experience has been *greatly* improved.

This is what actually happens when an Exchange administrator initiates a `New-MoveRequest`, either from the Exchange Management Shell or the Exchange Management Console, when moving a mailbox from `EXMBX01` to `EXMBX11`, as seen in Figure 5.16.

1. The administrator initiates a Move Request like `New-MoveRequest –Identity J.Wesselius –TargetDatabase EXMBX11\MDB01`. Now a special message is placed inside the System Mailbox of the current Active Directory site, saying that the `Move Request` is initiated and that its status is `Queue`.

2. A service on the CA Servers periodically scans this System Mailbox for these messages. This service is the **Mailbox Replication Service**, or **MRS**, which will find the message and read that the `J.Wesselius` mailbox is `Queued`.

3. The Mailbox Replication Service will update the System Message to `In Progress`, and will start moving the Mailbox data from `EXMBX01` to `EXMBX11`, while keeping the old and the new mailboxes in sync. The user is still connected to `EXMBX01` via the CA Server, and arriving messages will be delivered via the Hub Transport Server to the Mailbox on `EXMBX01`.

4. At a certain point, when almost all data is moved from the old to the new Mailbox, the old Mailbox is locked, and the last pieces of data are moved from the old to the new Mailbox. Also, the Active Directory properties of the user are changed to point to the new Mailbox Database. At this point, the status of the Move Request (i.e. the message is the System Mailbox) is changed from In Progress to Completion in Progress.

5. The new Mailbox is activated, the old Mailbox is deleted and the user needs to restart his client (although there's a caveat to this, which I'll mention in just a moment).

6. Although the Mailbox has been moved from server EXMBX01 to EXMBX11, the Move Request itself is not deleted. This has to be performed by the administrator, either by using the Exchange Management Shell (Remove-MoveRequest) or by using the Exchange Management Console.

Regarding Step 5, when a Mailbox is moved from an Exchange Server 2010 SP1 Mailbox Server to another Exchange Server 2010 SP1 Mailbox Server, the user does *not* have to restart their client.

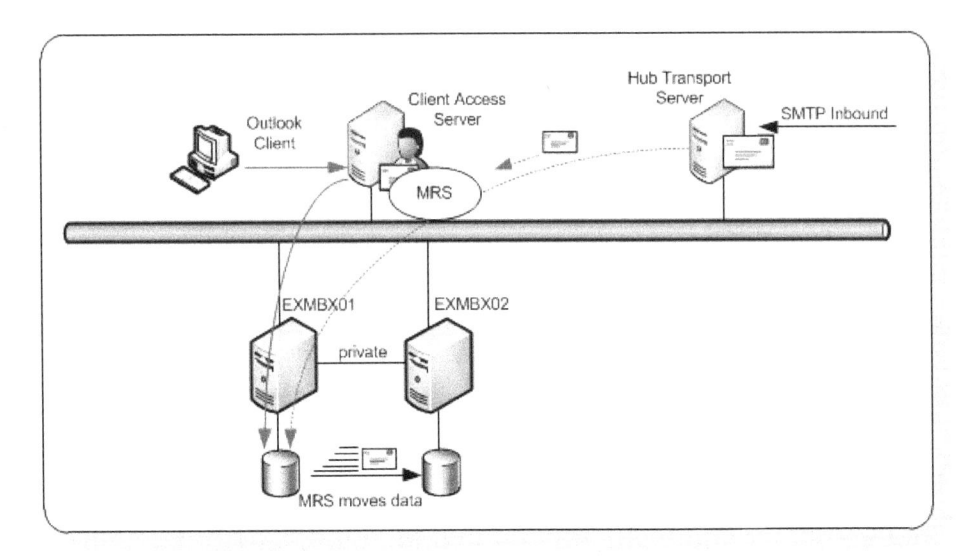

Figure 5.16: The Mailbox Replication Service (running on the CA Server) moves the mailbox from server EXMBX01 to server EXMBX11.

The Move Request can be working online when the Mailbox is moved from:

- Exchange Server 2010 to Exchange Server 2010, including SP1
- Exchange Server 2007 SP2 or SP3 to Exchange Server 2010, including SP1.

All other mailbox moves, for example from Exchange 2003 SP2 to Exchange Server 2010 SP1, or from Exchange Server 2010 SP1 back to Exchange Server 2007 SP2, are performed offline.

5.3.8 Import and export Mailbox

The option to import and export Mailbox data from, or into, a PST file has been available for a long time. In Exchange Server 2003, you can use the EXMERGE utility for this, but EXMERGE is no longer supported as of Exchange Server 2007. Exchange Server 2007 and Exchange Server 2010 have the Import-Mailbox and Export-Mailbox cmdlets available, but both cmdlets would only work when you had Outlook installed on the Exchange Server (or the Management Server). This dependency was always an issue, so Microsoft has completely re-engineered the process of importing and exporting Mailbox data.

The import and export Mailbox functionality is now built around the same technology as the Move Mailbox functionality, and it has resulted in two new cmdlets:

- **New-MailboxImportRequest** – to import Mailbox Data from a PST file into a mailbox
- **New-MailboxExportRequest** – to export Mailbox Data from a Mailbox into a PST file.

Both cmdlets have the option to work directly against a Personal Archive.

By default, nobody has the option to perform an import or export, and this permission has to be assigned manually. To grant this permission to a user named **ExAdmin**, enter the following Exchange Management Shell command (if you omit this step, the user cannot even start the cmdlets!).

```
New-ManagementRoleAssignment —Role "Mailbox Import Export" —User Exadmin
```

To import the contents of a PST file into a mailbox, enter the following Exchange Management Shell command:

```
New-MailboxImportRequest —Mailbox J.Wesselius —FilePath
\\Server\Share\J.Wesselius.pst
```

To view the status of the actual import, the `Get-MailboxImportRequest` can be combined with the `Get-MailboxImportRequestStatistics`:

```
[PS] C:\Windows\system32>New-MailboxImportRequest -Mailbox j.wesselius
-FilePath \\server01\pst$\j.wesselius.pst

Name              Mailbox                              Status
----              -------                              ------
MailboxImport     hosting.local/Accounts/J.Wesselius   Queued

[PS] C:\Windows\system32>




[PS] C:\Windows\system32>Get-MailboxImportRequest | Get-
MailboxImportRequestStatistics

Name              Status       TargetAlias     PercentComplete
----              ------       -----------     ---------------
MailboxImport     InProgress   J.Wesselius     92

[PS] C:\Windows\system32>
```

To import a PST file directly into the user's Personal Archive, you can just add the —IsArchive option, like this:

```
New-MailboxImportRequest —Mailbox J.Wesselius —FilePath
\\Server\Share\J.Wesselius-archive.pst -IsArchive
```

This part of the PST import process is now relatively pain-free (if you're happy to use the Exchange Management Shell), but finding PST files on your network still requires some PowerShell knowledge, manual work, help from your users, or one of the third-party tools on offer.

5.3.9 Backup and restore

Exchange Server 2010 only runs on Windows Server 2008 and Windows Server 2008 R2. This means that the (free) **NTBackup** utility in Windows Server 2003 cannot be used to back up Mailbox Databases on Exchange Server 2010. In any case, NTBackup was only capable of creating **streaming backups** of your Exchange data, not **Volume Shadow Copy Service** (VSS) backups of your Exchange database. Exchange Server 2010, including SP1 contains a plug-in for the Windows Server Backup (WSB) to make it possible to create VSS backups of your Exchange Server 2010 databases.

To protect your Exchange Server 2010 Mailbox Databases, there are several options:

- Windows Server Backup
- System Center Data Protection Manager
- Exchange Native Protection, also referred to as a "backup-less environment."

I'll go into more detail in the next sections.

5.3.9.1 VSS or snapshot backups

Before we continue with Windows Server Backup, and this is goes for other backup applications as well, we have to know a little bit more about a technology called Volume Shadow Copy Service, or VSS. With Exchange Server 2010, Microsoft has finally moved away from the traditional online streaming backup to VSS (or snapshot) backups. A snapshot is just an image of a database created at a particular point in time, which can be used to roll back the database in case of a disaster. The Volume Shadow Copy Service in Windows Server 2003 and later provides an infrastructure to create these point-in-time images, which are called Shadow Copies.

There are two kinds of Shadow Copies:

1. **Clone** (Full Copy or Split Mirror) – a complete mirror is maintained until an application or administrator breaks the mirror. From this point on, the original and clone are fully independent of each other, and the copy is effectively frozen in time.
2. **Copy on Write** (Differential Copy) – a shadow copy is created as a differential rather than a full copy of the original data. Using Copy on Write, a shadow copy of the original data is made before it is overwritten. Effectively, the backup consists of the data in the shadow copy combined with the data on the original location, and both need to be available to reconstruct the original data.

The Volume Shadow Copy infrastructure consists of the following components:

- **Requestor** – this is the software that invokes the VSS and creates, breaks or deletes the shadow copy. The requestor is typically the backup application.
- **Writer** – a software part that is provided by an application vendor. In our case this is provided with the Microsoft Exchange Server. A writer is responsible for providing a consistent point-in-time image by freezing or pausing the Exchange Server at the relevant moment. Please note that an Exchange writer is provided for Exchange Server 2003 and higher, right out of the box.

Chapter 5: High Availability in Exchange Server 2010 SP1

- **Provider** – a provider is the interface to the point-in-time image. This can either be on a storage array (hardware provider) or in the Operating System (software provider). Windows Server 2003 and above incorporate a software Provider with VSS functionality out of the box.

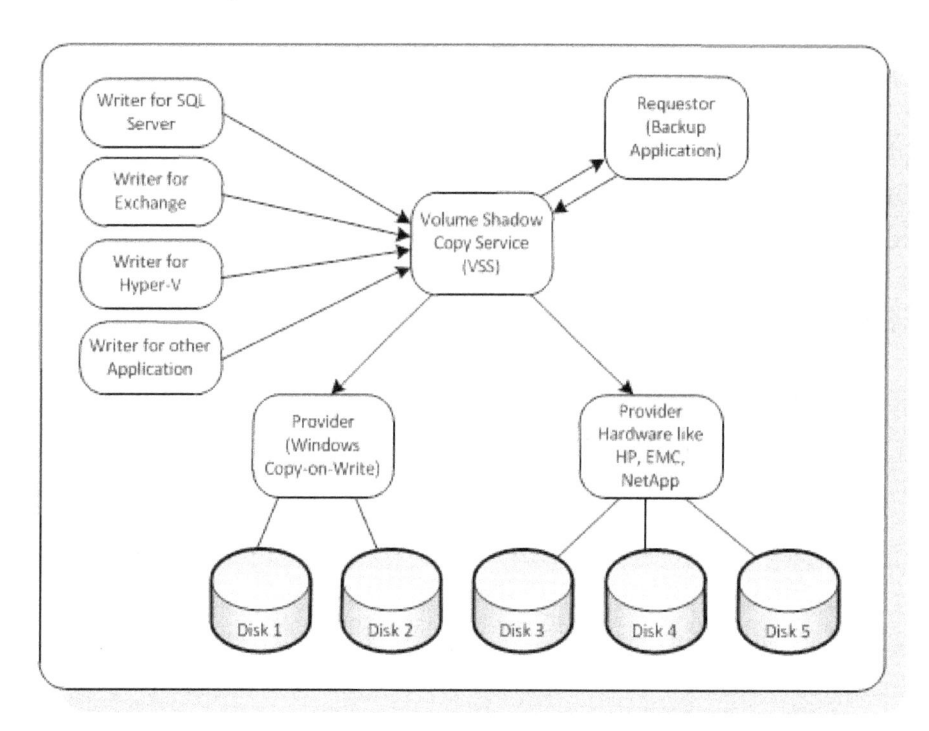

Figure 5.17: Volume Shadow Copy Server (VSS) infrastructure.

The following steps occur when a VSS backup is performed.

1. The requestor (i.e. the backup application) sends a command to the Volume Shadow Copy Service to create a shadow copy of the Storage Groups.

2. The VSS service sends a command to the Exchange writer to prepare for a snapshot backup.

3. The VSS service sends a command to the appropriate storage provider to create a shadow copy of the Exchange Storage Group. This storage provider can be a hardware storage provider or the default Windows storage provider.

4. The Exchange writer temporarily stops or quiesces the Storage Group and puts them in read-only mode. A log file roll-over is also performed to make sure that all data will be in the backup set. This will hold a couple of seconds for the snapshot to be created (in the next step). All write I/Os will be queued.

5. The shadow copy is now created.

6. The VSS service releases the Exchange Server to resume ordinary operations and all queued write I/Os are completed.

7. The VSS service queries the Exchange writer to confirm that the write I/Os were successfully held during the shadow copy creation. If the writes were not successfully held it could mean a potentially inconsistent shadow copy, so the shadow copy is deleted and the requestor is notified. The requestor can retry the shadow copy process or fail the operation.

8. If successful, the requestor creates either a differential or a clone snapshot, and then verifies the integrity of the backup set (the clone copy). If the clone copy integrity is good, the requestor informs the Exchange Server that the backup was successful and that the log files can be purged. The backup is now complete.

Note

It is the responsibility of the backup application to perform a consistency check of the shadow copy. The Exchange writer does not perform this check.

Steps 1 through 7 usually take about 10 seconds, as this is the time needed to create the actual snapshot. This is not the time to create a backup, though. A backup application still has to create the backup on another disk or to tape, which can still take hours to complete, depending on the size of the databases.

5.3.9.2 Backup with Windows Server Backup

Windows Server Backup is a feature in Windows 2008 (R2), and as such it can be installed using the Server Manager. Open the Server Manager, select **Features**, and then select the **Windows Server Backup** in the feature list to install it. When backing up your Exchange data using Windows Server Backup, at least one disk is needed to store the backups. This can be either a physical disk in the server or a disk on a storage device.

When starting Windows Server Backup there's no indication that it is Exchange Server 2010 aware; when the Exchange databases are located on separate drives, these drives have to be manually selected in Windows Server Backup. After selecting these disks, *another* disk needs to be selected to store the actual backup. This can be any disk, except the ones that are being backed up or the system disk (i.e. the C:\ drive). When the backup is running, you'll notice that Windows Server Backup checks the Exchange database for consistency (see Figure 5.18).

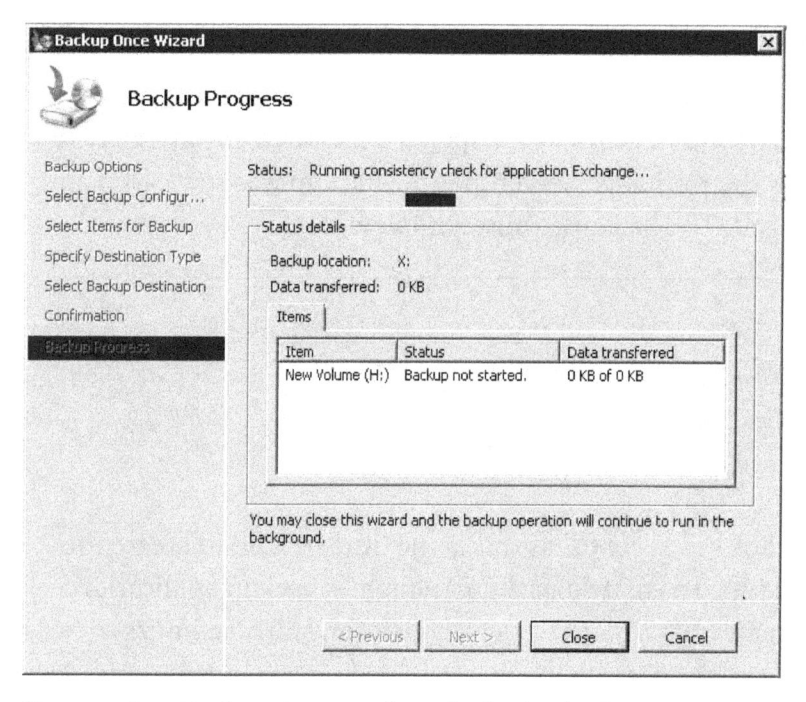

Figure 5.18: Windows Server Backup checks the database for consistency.

Chapter 5: High Availability in Exchange Server 2010 SP1

When Windows Server Backup has finished backing up the Exchange database, the header of the database is updated with relevant backup information. The status of the database can be examined using `ESEUTIL /MH`:

```
H:\Mailbox Database 8890905692>eseutil /mh "Mailbox Database 8890905692.edb"

Extensible Storage Engine Utilities for Microsoft(R) Exchange Server
Version 14.01
Copyright (C) Microsoft Corporation. All Rights Reserved.

Initiating FILE DUMP mode...
        Database: Mailbox Database 8890905692.edb


Previous Full Backup:
        Log Gen: 62-63 (0x3e-0x3f) - OSSnapshot
           Mark: (0x40,8,16)
           Mark: 06/18/2010 20:35:32

Previous Incremental Backup:
        Log Gen: 0-0 (0x0-0x0)
           Mark: (0x0,0,0)
           Mark: 00/00/1900 00:00:00

Operation completed successfully in 0.110 seconds.

H:\Mailbox Database 8890905692>
```

Edited for readability

Chapter 5: High Availability in Exchange Server 2010 SP1

Windows Server Backup also logs all activities in the Eventlog. When checking the Eventlog, you'll see the `ESE` and `MSExhangeIS` events, like:

```
Log Name:        Application
Source:          ESE
Date:            18-6-2010 20:35:32
Event ID:        2005
Task Category:   ShadowCopy
Level:           Information
Keywords:        Classic
User:            N/A
Computer:        EXMBX03.E2010.local
Description:
Information Store (2444) Shadow copy instance 1 starting. This will be a Full
shadow copy.

For more information, click http://www.microsoft.com/contentredirect.asp.
```

And

```
Log Name:        Application
Source:          MSExchangeIS
Date:            18-6-2010 20:35:32
Event ID:        9811
Task Category:   Exchange VSS Writer
Level:           Information
Keywords:        Classic
User:            N/A
Computer:        EXMBX03.E2010.local
Description:
Exchange VSS Writer (instance 1) has successfully prepared the database engine for
a full or copy backup of database 'Mailbox Database 8890905692'.
```

When the backup has successfully finished, the log files will be purged as well, depending on the type of backup which has just been executed; a full backup will purge the log files, a copy backup won't. Which log files are purged will depend on how busy the server is during backup (lots of new messages, moving mailbox, etc.) and the checkpoint depth. Purging the log files is logged in the Eventlog as well:

```
Log Name:       Application
Source:         ESE
Date:           8-8-2009 11:39:19
Event ID:       224
Task Category:  ShadowCopy
Level:          Information
Keywords:       Classic
User:           N/A
Computer:       EXMBX03.E2010.local
Description:
Information Store (2444) Mailbox Database 8890905692: Deleting log files H:\mailbox database Mailbox Database 8890905692\E0000000001.log to H:\mailbox database Mailbox Database 8890905692\E0000000043.log.
```

Note

Windows Server Backup is only capable of creating a full backup or a copy backup. Incremental or differential backups are not supported.

5.3.9.3 Windows Server Backup and database replication

Windows Server Backup can also create backups of databases that are in a Database Administration Group (DAG), although a limitation of WSB is that it can only create a backup of an active copy of the database. If you also have passive copies of a Mailbox Database on a server which you want to run Windows Server Backup on, the backup will fail and the error below is logged in the Eventlog.

Chapter 5: High Availability in Exchange Server 2010 SP1

```
Log Name:        Application
Source:          MSExchangeIS
Date:            18-6-2010 21:04:46
Event ID:        9782
Task Category:   Exchange VSS Writer
Level:           Error
Keywords:        Classic
User:            N/A
Computer:        EXMBX01.hosting.local
Description:
Exchange VSS Writer (instance e48f14f6-7136-474a-a6e6-d92f1dc3d256:1) has completed
the backup of database 'Mailbox Database 1539639680' with errors. The backup did
not complete successfully, and no log files were truncated for this database.
```

To create backups on this server, the Exchange Replication Service VSS Writer needs to be disabled, which can be achieved by adding a registry key.

- Log on to the Exchange Mailbox Server and start the **Registry Editor**.

- Go to `HKEY_LOCAL_MACHINE\Software\Microsoft\ExchangeServer\v14\Replay\Parameters`.

- Add a new `DWORD` value with the name `EnableVSSWriter` and set its value to zero.

- Restart the Microsoft Exchange Replication Service.

The next time you create a backup of a Mailbox Database on this server, it will be successful (or at least, it should be. Certainly, the VSS Writer will no longer be your problem if it isn't!).

The process of creating backups is identical as in earlier paragraphs, except for the truncation of log files. Log files are only truncated if all log files are replicated and relayed to other database copies. Only then will the log files on the active copy be truncated.

This can take some time, which is no reason for worry. It is also logged in the Eventlog:

```
Log Name:       Application
Source:         MSExchangeIS
Date:           18-6-2010 21:26:09
Event ID:       9827
Task Category:  Exchange VSS Writer
Level:          Information
Keywords:       Classic
User:           N/A
Computer:       EXMBX01.hosting.local
Description:
Exchange VSS Writer (instance 50884c76-30aa-4c5d-a5b7-c28044bc896a:3) has
successfully completed the full or incremental backup of replicated database
'Mailbox Database 1539639680'. The log files will be truncated after they have been
replayed.
```

Although you can create backups of Mailbox Databases using Windows Server Backup, its functionality is very, very limited. A better solution is to use a real backup solution like Microsoft System Center Data Protection Manager (DPM) 2010, which is also capable of backing up Exchange Server 2010 SP1 Mailbox Databases.

5.3.9.4 Exchange Native Data Protection

Microsoft has built a solution in Exchange Server 2010 called **Exchange Native Data Protection**, sometimes also referred to as a "Backup-less environment."

Exchange Native Data Protection is a solution built around the native High Availability options in Exchange Server 2010, i.e. a Database Availability Group with multiple copies, including one or more lagged copies.

To create a solid protection solution, the High Availability options should be used in conjunction with technologies like the Personal Archive, Legal Hold, Multi-Mailbox Search, and Single Item Recovery.

By combining these functionalities, you can create a solution that meets the following criteria:

- disaster recovery
- recovery of deleted items
- long-term storage
- point in time snapshots.

When implemented correctly, the Exchange Native Data Protection *can* be a viable alternative for a traditional backup solution. However, one of the functions of a traditional backup solution is that it purges the transaction log files after creating a full or incremental backup, and with an Exchange Native Data Protection solution there's no backup solution taking care of the transaction log file. To overcome this, circular logging (which has been around for quite a while) can be used.

With circular logging only a small number of log files are kept in the working directory. Exchange Server just deletes old log files and only keeps the most recent ones. The good thing about this is that you'll never run out of disk space due to too many log files, but the bad thing is you don't have a recovery option besides your last backup. Using circular logging, you cannot recover data processed after your last backup, since all data in log files newer than your backup is overwritten by new log files! So, enabling circular logging is generally speaking not a good idea, except maybe for lab environments.

A new type of circular logging was introduced in Exchange Server 2007, which is also available in Exchange Server 2010, called **Continuous Replication Circular Logging (CRCL)**. Whereas traditional circular logging is managed by the Information Store, Continuous Replication Circular Logging is managed by the Exchange Replication Service. The principle is the same, so older log files are not kept on the Mailbox Server, but they are only deleted when the log files are successfully replicated to other members in the DAG, and the log files are successfully replayed into the copies of the Mailbox Database.

But beware – if replication stalls, or log files cannot replay into the passive copy of the database, they can accumulate quickly, consuming a considerable amount of disk space (when you don't expect it).

Using CRCL, you no longer need older log files to recover information from, since you have a complete copy of the Mailbox Database for recovery purposes.

5.4 High Availability on Other Server Roles

For a completely highly available Exchange Server 2010 environment, not only do the Mailbox Servers need to be configured appropriately, but so also do the Hub Transport Servers, CA Servers and, if used, the Edge Transport Servers. Thankfully, the High Availability configurations for the Hub Transport and the Edge Transport Server are very similar to their Exchange Server 2007 configurations (which is why I'm not going to spend much time on them here). However, there are a few changes with respect to the CA Server Role when it comes to high availability, so I'll dwell on that topic a little more.

5.4.1 Hub Transport Servers

For redundancy of transport, at least two Hub Transport Servers are needed. When creating a Send Connector, you can define the source server that sends out the messages over this connector and, for redundancy, you can add a second Hub Transport Server as a source server.

- Log on to an Exchange Server and open the **Exchange Management Console**.
- Expand the **Exchange On-Premises (SERVER)**, and then expand the **Organization** leaf. Click the **Hub Transport** leaf and select the **Send Connectors** tab.
- Right-click the **Send Connector** that needs to be changed and select **Properties**.

- In the properties of the Send Connector, select the **Source Server** tab.
- Click the **Add** button to add a second **Hub Transport Server** to the Send Connector.
- After selecting the second server, click **OK** twice.

The Hub Transport Server will now have a redundant path, and will automatically load balance outbound messages over both source servers. A Round Robin mechanism is used for load balancing outbound SMTP traffic on both Hub Transport Servers.

For inbound messaging, a load-balancing solution needs to be manually implemented. This can be an ISA Server 2006 or any other hardware device that's capable of load balancing SMTP traffic. You can also use Windows Server 2008 Network Load Balancing, as this is an out-of-the-box Microsoft solution. Using NLB, a load-balancing solution can be built, running on Windows, which then keeps track of all the incoming connections and automatically load balances the requests between the Hub Transport Servers. This is a fully supported solution (since Exchange Server 2007 SP1). The last option is to use DNS Round Robin to load balance incoming traffic.

Note

NLB is only supported for inbound SMTP connections, not for outbound SMTP connections, and cannot be installed on any server hosting a DAG. A server hosting a DAG must have Windows fail-over clustering in operation, and NLB cannot coexist with WFC.

5.4.2 Client Access Servers

For redundancy on the CA Server layer, at least two servers need to be implemented and load balanced on the protocol layer, which you can implement on the CA Servers by using Network Load Balancing. Unfortunately, you cannot combine Network Load Balancing and fail-over clustering on the same servers, so if you want to implement a two-server High Availability with a DAG, combined with CAS and HUB on the same servers, you have to implement an alternative (hardware) load-balancing solution.

5.4.2.1. Client Access Server Array

When implementing a High Availability solution on the CA Server, you can use Network Load Balancing (NLB) on the CA Servers. The minimum number of CA Servers in an NLB Cluster is two (well, you *can* have a single-server cluster, but that would be pointless, clearly), and the maximum number of CA Servers in an NLB Cluster is 32, which is a limitation applied by NLB in Windows Server 2008 (R2). Microsoft recommends that you configure your NLB Clusters to have no more than 8 CA Servers because of internal efficiency. For more information regarding load balancing CA Servers, check the TechNet article, *Understanding Load Balancing in Exchange 2010* at http://tinyurl.com/UnderstandingLoadBalancing.

In our demo environment, we've set up two combined CAS/HUB Servers into an NLB Cluster, which is running in `UNICAST` mode (Whether you want to run in `UNICAST` or in `MULTICAST` depends on your own organization and environment).

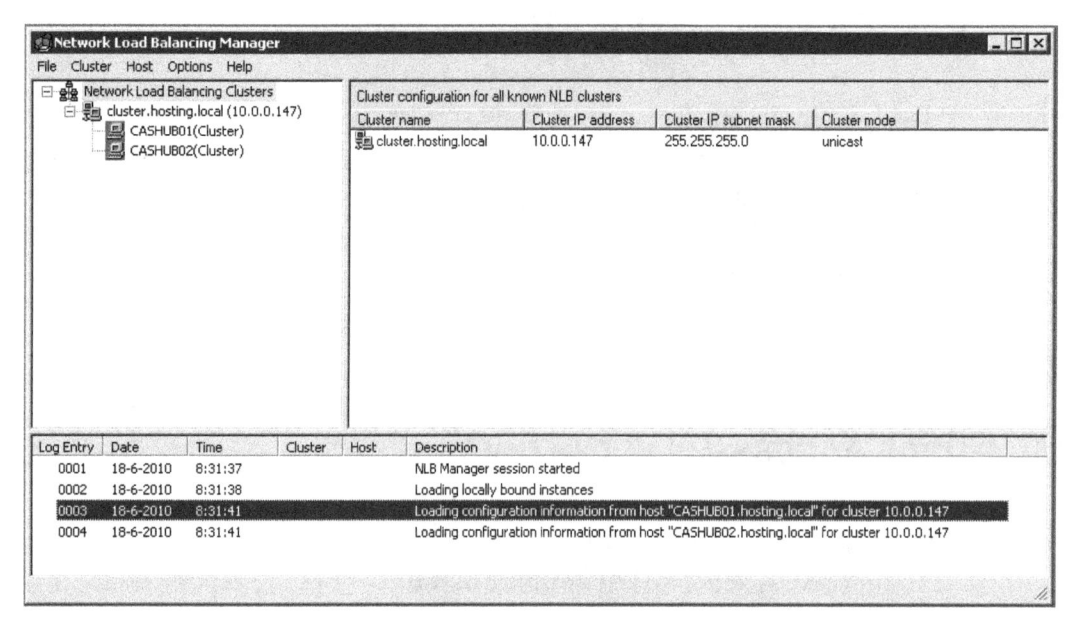

Chapter 5: High Availability in Exchange Server 2010 SP1

Figure 5.19: Two combined CAS/HUB Servers in an NLB Cluster.

The CA Servers automatically pick up the configuration of the NLB Cluster, so the various protocols are automatically load balanced across the NLB members.

You can create a **Client Access Server Array**, or **CAS Array**, to load balance the CA Servers for MAPI clients' end-point, and you can implement a single namespace for Outlook clients. However, bear in mind that the CAS Array is also used (instead of a single CA Server) as the "back link" on Mailbox Databases to the CA Server using the `-RPCClientAccessServer` property on the Mailbox Database. In other words, the Mailbox Database picks one of the CA Servers in the array as a load-balancing mechanism. If one of the servers fails, it is automatically excluded from the NLB Cluster and therefore it won't be used by the Mailbox Database.

The only way to create a new CAS Array is using the Exchange Management Shell:

```
[PS] C:\Windows\system32>New-ClientAccessArray -Name CASArray -FQDN "webmail.
inframan.nl" -Site "Default-First-Site-Name"

Name         Site              Fqdn                    Members
----         ----              ----                    -------
CASArray     Default-First-Si... webmail.inframan.nl   {CASHUB01,
                                                        CASHUB02}


[PS] C:\Windows\system32>
```

You can use the external URL on the FQDN of the CAS Array, but this is not a hard requirement. In fact, you can use any FQDN, and for example we've used `cluster.hosting.local` as our demo NLB Cluster, as can be seen in Figure 5.19. My personal opinion is not to make it more difficult than necessary, so use the external URL.

Now, with the CAS Array in place, when new Mailbox Databases are created, both on single servers as well as in a DAG, they will use the FQDN of the CAS Array for the RPC CA Server MAPI end-point. You can check this by requesting the properties of the Mailbox Database:

```
[PS] C:\Windows\system32>Get-MailboxDatabase -Identity "Mailbox Database
1539639680" | select Name,RPC*

<<nog ff aanpassen ;-)>>

RpcClientAccessServer      : webmail.inframan.nl
Name                       : Mailbox Database 1539639680

[PS] C:\Windows\system32>
5.4.3 Edge Transport Servers
```

When using an Edge Transport solution in the Demilitarized Zone (DMZ) of your network, at least two Edge Transport Servers need to be implemented. Bear in mind that all Edge Transport Servers have their own instance of the Active Directory Lightweight Directory Service (AD LDS, previously known as ADAM, Active Directory Application Mode), and all Edge Transport Servers have their own subscription to the Hub Transport Servers in the company network.

When multiple Edge Transport Servers are connected to the same site, they are all automatically added as source servers to the inbound Send Connector. Load balancing takes place across these Edge Transport Servers in the same way that load balancing takes place on the Hub Transport Servers.

5.5 Summary

With the new Database Availability Group functionality in Exchange Server 2010, you now have the ability to create High Availability solutions on the Mailbox Server level, and this functionality replaces the Continuous Cluster Replication (CCR) and Stand-by Continuous Cluster Replication (SCR) in Exchange 2007. To be honest, the Database Availability Group is what CCR/SCR should have been. It is flexible, powerful, and less complex than the CCR/SCR solution, and it combines the best of both worlds. I really recommend that everybody start looking at the Database Availability Group and, whenever possible, implement it. The Stand-by Continuous Replication in Exchange Server 2007 SP1 has evolved into the Lagged Copies of a Mailbox Database in a DAG. With a lagged copy, it is possible to implement a copy of your Mailbox Database that's a configurable amount of time "behind" the Active Database. Moreover, by implementing one or more lagged copies, combined with features like the Personal Archive, Legal Hold, and Single Item Recovery, you can implement an effective backup-less Exchange environment.

The High Availability Solutions on the Hub Transport Server Role and CA Server Role are implemented using protocol load balancing. This can be achieved using a hardware load balancer, Windows Network Load Balancing (NLB) or by using DNS Round Robin. The Hub Transport Server hasn't changed much though, compared to Exchange Server 2007, so I've only touched upon it lightly. The CA Servers are load balanced using a load-balancing solution like NLB, but also have an additional HA option – the CA Server Array. This is the link from the Mailbox Databases to the load-balanced CA Servers.

Having read this chapter you should now be able to ensure your Exchange Server Organization is always up and running when needed. Of course, as this is a just a practical guide to get you started, there's much more to learn to make your Exchange environment disaster-proof!

Chapter 6: Unified Messaging

One of the most compelling but, at the same time, least adopted features in Exchange Server 2007 and Exchange Server 2010 is the Unified Messaging (**UM**) Server Role, which is responsible for the integration of your phone system with your messaging platform. With a UM Server it is possible to configure a range of options.

- **Receive voicemail messages in your inbox** – when somebody calls and the phone is not answered, the UM Server will answer the call, play a welcome message, and record a voicemail message, which is stored in the user's Mailbox.

- **Have your email read to you** – you can call your own UM Server, log on using a PIN code and have the UM Server read your email to you. At the same time, you can create new messages using speech to text, and even change or cancel meetings. In fact, you can control all kinds of actions which you normally perform using a messaging client like Outlook.

- **Create your own telephony system** – when you're using an incoming line, you can configure what needs to happen with any incoming call. For example, does it have to be transferred directly into the UM Server Role? Does the call have to be routed to another phone, or a group of numbers? Or does it have to be transferred only after it has rung x times?

Before we start configuring the Exchange Server 2010 SP1 UM Role, we first have to explain the UM architecture as well as some telephone terminology, since this is quite different from what the typical SysAdmin is used to.

Compared to the rest of this book, this chapter on Unified Messaging may look a bit "light," in that it is just not as big as the other chapters. However, in this chapter I will only focus on the Unified Messaging technology and how to configure it with a simple ISDN telephone system. I don't focus on security, or High Availability, just on the basic functionality.

6.1 Unified Messaging Server Role Architecture

The heart of the Unified Messaging Platform is, of course, the Unified Messaging Server itself. The UM Server interacts with your phone system (**PBX, Private Branch eXchange**), and is responsible for recording the voicemail messages and for Outlook Voice Access. However, because the UM Server communicates with the PBX, it uses an IP Gateway. Of course, if you have a modern IP PBX then you probably don't need an IP Gateway, and you can connect the IP PBX directly to the UM Server. Either way, all phone calls, whether they are internal or external, are routed to your PBX system, and so you have to configure your PBX to forward unanswered calls to the IP Gateway. So, when an inbound call is placed and the call is not answered, the call is forwarded to the IP Gateway where it is converted into a VOIP (Voice over IP) protocol for incoming messages. The data is then delivered to the UM Server which, in turn, answers the call.

The UM Server recognizes the phone number of the intended recipient and plays an appropriate (and customizable) welcome message. After the message is played, the caller can leave a voicemail message, which is recorded by the UM Server and converted into an MP3 file which is then wrapped in an email message. When finished, the UM Server hands the message over to the Hub Transport Server, which delivers the message with its attached voicemail to the recipient's mailbox.

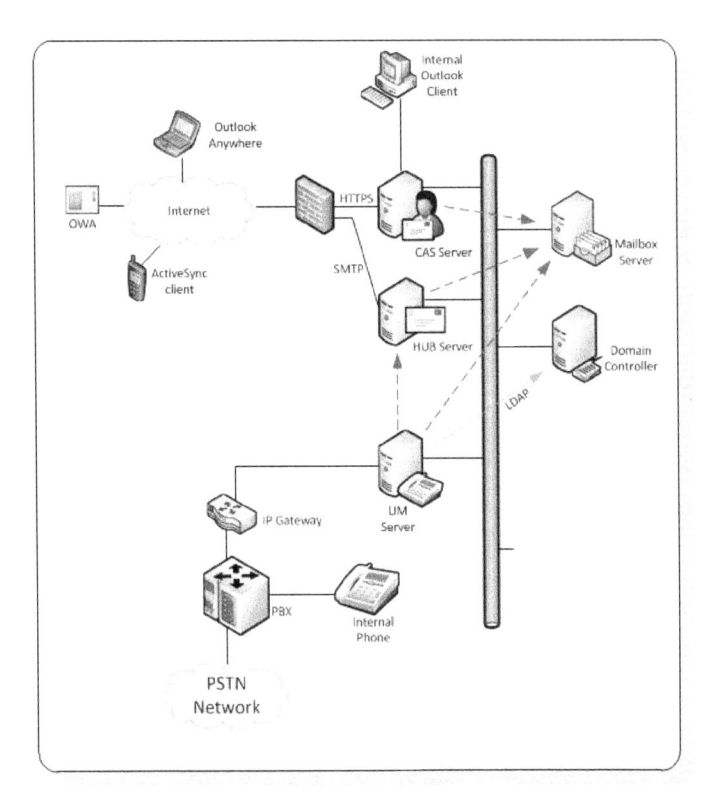

Figure 6.1: Exchange Server 2010 Unified Messaging Server Role architecture.

So, the voicemail message is delivered into the intended Mailbox as an MP3 file, and you can double-click on the MP3 file and listen to the voicemail, anywhere, anytime; isn't this a cool feature?

Chapter 6: Unified Messaging

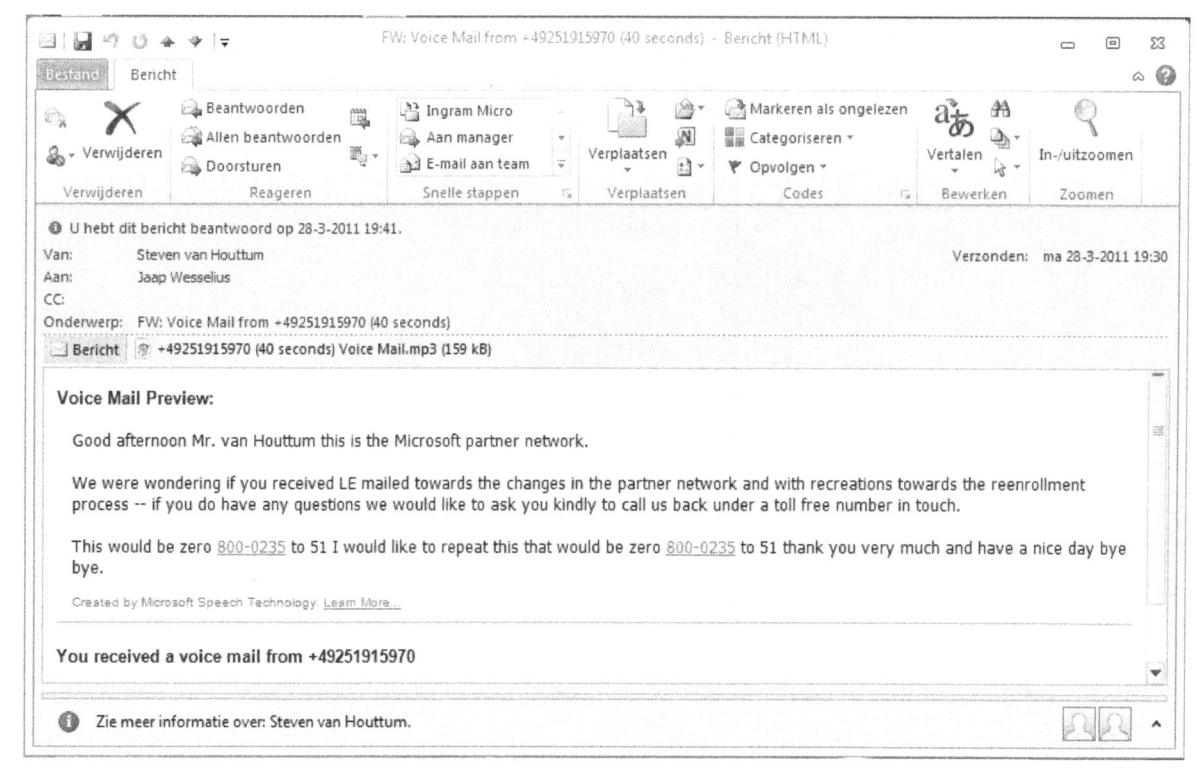

Figure 6.2: The voicemail as an attachment.

6.1.1 Voicemail preview

As you can see in Figure 6.2, a text voicemail preview is available in the email as well. This voicemail preview is generated by **Automatic Speech Recognition (ASR)** on the Unified Messaging Server, and is generated in real time during the actual recording of the voicemail message.

Now you can imagine that this ASR functionality is doing something extremely difficult. Imagine somebody leaving a voicemail message while calling from a mobile on a ship, or somebody not articulating very well, or somebody from Holland or Germany with this "hard" accent. These factors make it difficult for the UM Server to create an accurate preview, so the UM Server determines the accuracy of the voicemail transcription and stamps the message with a confidence level. This accuracy is based on:

- the language being used, including technical jargon
- how rapidly the user is speaking
- background noises or echoes.

You have to be wary of placing too much confidence in this feature at this stage, since it is in an ongoing development and improvement process, but if you're looking for a laugh then it can certainly give some funny results!

6.1.2 Play on Phone functionality

When the voicemail is delivered, you have this MP3 file in your inbox which you can then open and listen to. However, when you are in an Internet café, or in your office cubicle, this might not be an option. Therefore, Microsoft has created the **Play on Phone** functionality, which gives you the option to listen to the voicemail message on the phone in your own cubicle without everybody around you overhearing your voicemail messages.

The Play on Phone functionality is actually delivered through the Web Services on the CA Server, which are also used for recording a customized welcome message, and through which the user can interact with the UM Server. However, because of the necessity of these Web Services, the Play on Phone functionality is only available for Microsoft Outlook 2007 and higher, as well as Outlook Web App.

> **Note**
>
> *Since the Web Services are used for this functionality, you have to make sure that your certificates are OK in order for this feature to function correctly. Please check Chapters 2 and 3 (on Installation and Coexistence) for more information regarding the CA Server and the usage of Certificates, which allow the the data between the CA Server and the mail client to be encrypted. It does not encrypt the data between the CA Server and the Unified Messaging Server, though.*

6.1.3 Outlook Voice Access

Using the UM Server Role it is possible to implement **Subscriber Access**, also referred to as **Outlook Voice Access** (**OVA**). By using OVA, it is possible to call in to your UM Server and access Exchange functionality such as email and calendaring, using just your voice.

When users dial into the UM Server they have the following possibilities:

- change the welcome message, the spoken name, and PIN code
- listen to email and voicemail messages
- process messages through actions like forward, reply, and delete
- use calendar functionality, like moving meeting requests ("I'm running late")
- send a voice message to another mailbox.

To use the OVA functionality you need a dedicated phone number which has to be in your Dial Plan. When you dial this number, you have to enter your ID and PIN code, which will then give you access to the system, at which point you can then navigate through the menu and locate the options you need.

To accomplish this, the UM Server Role communicates with the Active Directory Domain Controller and the Mailbox Server Role. Specifically, it communicates with the Active

Directory to retrieve address book information, and it communicates with the Mailbox Server Role to retrieve, for example, calendaring information, or to have your messages read by the UM Server Role.

6.2 Unified Messaging Server Role Terminology

As I've mentioned, the Exchange Server 2010 SP1 Unified Messaging Server Role tightly integrates with your phone system, meaning that some telephone terminology is used to describe what it does, and this will almost certainly be new for the average SysAdmin. Below are some components and keywords you need to be aware of.

- **PBX** – a Private Branch eXchange; these systems are what all your internal telephones are connected to, and where all the incoming phone calls are delivered by your telephone company. The PBX is responsible for routing the phone calls between the different telephones and phone lines within your company.

- **Dial Plan** – a Dial Plan in your existing PBX is a number plan, consisting of each individual user's extension. A UM Dial Plan in Exchange Server 2010 represents the Dial Plan in your PBX, and requires that each user has their own extension number. Naturally, each extension number within a Dial Plan needs to be unique.

- **UM IP Gateway** – a UM IP Gateway is a physical hardware device that connects your UM environment with your phone system. This can be an IP PBX (typically a single box) or a combination of a traditional PBX and a separate IP Gateway (two boxes).

- **UM Hunt Group** – a UM Hunt Group is a set of extension numbers that are grouped together as a single unit. For example, the company's sales department has a group number. When somebody dials that number, all of the telephones in this Hunt Group will start ringing.

6.3 Installing the UM Server Role

Before installing the UM Server Role, you have to configure the PBX appropriately. The PBX has to know what to do when a call is not answered, and it has to know where to forward calls if necessary. In my test environment, the call is forwarded to an IP Gateway which, in turn, needs some additional software. The IP Gateway doesn't need Exchange-specific software, but it just needs some software that will translate the call into a VOIP data stream, which will be picked up by the UM Server. If your UM environment is not working as expected, the configuration and software are the first two items to troubleshoot.

Thankfully, installing the UM Server Role is fairly simple; it can be combined with other Server Roles on a single machine (except for the Edge Transport Server, of course), or it can be installed as a dedicated server. Personally I have seen both deployments and, as long as you don't have fifty concurrent inbound voicemail calls, there's no real need for a dedicated UM Server.

Note

Due to the real-time nature of voice data, the UM Server Role is not supported on a virtualized platform. That being said, it does work, and I've seen a number of customers successfully implement the UM Server on a virtualized platform.

The Exchange Server 2010 SP1 Unified Messaging Server Role is only supported on Windows Server 2008 SP2 (X64) and Windows Server 2008 R2, just like the other Exchange Server 2010 SP1 Server Roles. In the first table in Chapter 2, an overview is given of the Exchange Server 2010 SP1 prerequisite software, and that mostly covers the UM Server Role as well.

However, one additional feature that's needed on the Unified Messaging Role is the **Desktop Experience** feature. Using this feature, you'll be able to install some Windows 7 features on the Windows Server 2008 R2 Server, the most important of which is the **Sound Recorder**. The following components are part of this Desktop Experience feature:

- Windows Media Player
- Desktop themes
- Video for Windows (AVI support)
- Windows SideShow
- Windows Defender
- Disk Cleanup
- Sync Center
- Sound Recorder
- Character Map
- Snipping Tool.

Don't be afraid that your server might clog up with all kinds of unnecessary software; only the components that are needed are enabled by the setup application of Exchange Server.

Chapter 6: Unified Messaging

To install the Exchange Server 2010 SP1 Unified Messaging Server Role just follow the steps below.

- Log on to the server on which you want to install the Unified Messaging Server Role.

- There are two separate hot-fixes that need to be implemented on this machine before we can install the UM Server Role. This is new in Exchange Server 2010 SP1; these were not needed in the RTM version:

    - the **Unified Communications Managed API 2.0, Core Runtime (64-bit)**, HTTP://TINYURL.COM/UNICOMMSAPI. Be aware that installing this hot-fix is a two-step process. The first step only extracts the necessary files and stores them into a location that you have to specify during extraction. The second step is to start the actual installation of the hot-fix by navigating to this specified location and executing the installation from there.

    - **Speech Platform Runtime X64**, HTTP://TINYURL.COM/SPEECHRUNTIME.

- Before installing the Unified Messaging Server Role, there's also a special registry entry that has to be made, and Microsoft supplies a REG file (`UcmaCU6HF1.REG`) which contains this entry. Just double-click on the file to merge the information into the registry of the Unified Messaging Server.

- Navigate to the installation media (DVD, ISO, or network share) and start the `setup.exe` program, which will launch the setup splash screen shown in Figure 6.3.

- When you install the .NET Framework and Windows PowerShell as part of the prerequisite software installation you are able to directly choose the desired language as shown in Figure 6.3. Please note that this is the language of the Exchange Server and system messages, etc., but when you need additional languages for the UM-specific services, you'll have to download additional language packs, customized for the Unified Messaging Server Role. We'll cover that later in this chapter.

Chapter 6: Unified Messaging

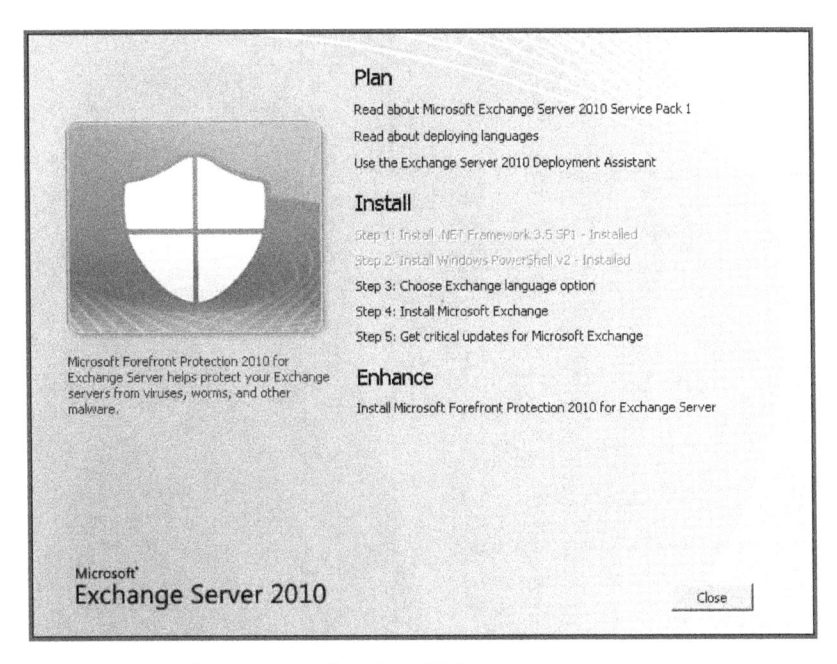

Figure 6.3: The setup application Welcome screen.

- Continue with the next step in the setup process, **Install Microsoft Exchange**, and follow the setup wizard.

- In the **Installation Type** window, you have to select a **Custom Exchange Server Installation**, since a typical installation, like we performed in Chapter 2, does not contain the Unified Messaging Server Role. After selecting the custom installation, click **Next** to continue.

- In the **Server Role Selection** window, select the **Server Roles** you want to install. As mentioned earlier, you can install the Unified Messaging Server Role with the Mailbox, Client Access and Hub Transport Server Role on the same server. Also check the **Automatically install Windows Server roles and features required for Exchange Server** check box. This will automatically install all prerequisite Windows roles and features for you, (but not the hot-fixes).

Chapter 6: Unified Messaging

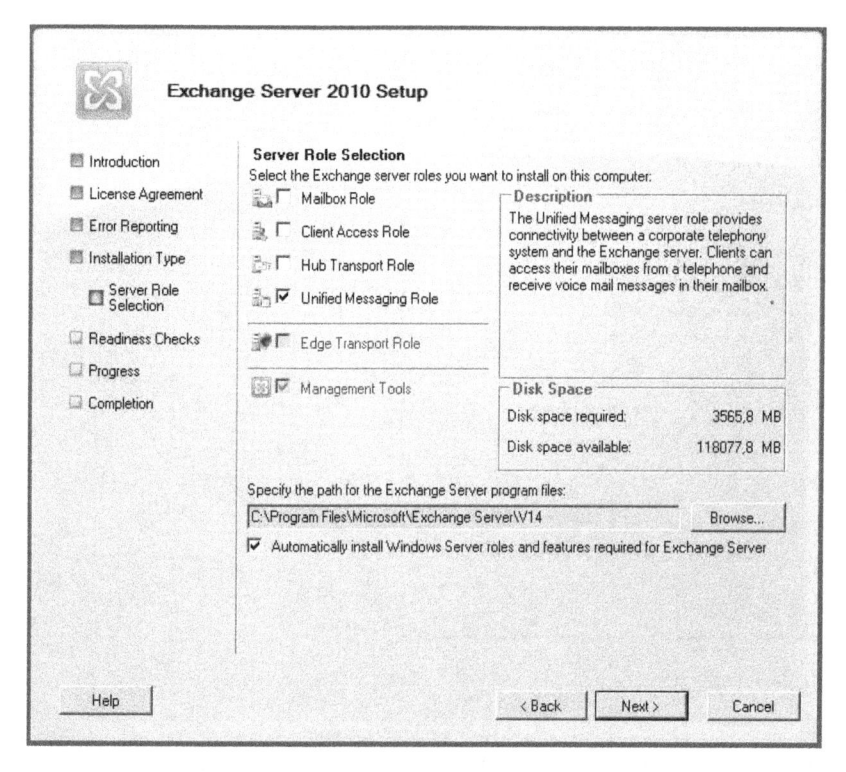

Figure 6.4: Select the UM Server Role (this will be a dedicated server). Do not forget the roles and features check box!

- The next step is the **Readiness Check** and, if all is well, then you can continue with installing the Exchange Server. The progress is shown, just like a typical setup.

- When the installation is finished, click the **Finished** button and, if requested, reboot the server. After rebooting, the server is ready to install additional language packs or to be configured straight away.

6.3.1 Installing additional language packs

To install additional language packs for the Unified Messaging Server, download them separately from the Microsoft website (HTTP://TINYURL.COM/UMLANGUAGEPACK) and, once downloaded, you have to install them individually. For example, to install the Dutch language packs, follow the steps below.

- Log on to the newly installed Unified Messaging Server and navigate to the downloaded language pack. In my scenario, that would be the file `UMLanguagePack.nl-NL.exe`. Double-click on the file to start the installation.
- Follow the **Installation** wizard, accept the license agreement, etc., select the **Unified Messaging Language Pack [Dutch (Netherlands)]**, and click **Next** to continue.
- A **Readiness Check** is performed and when it finishes successfully, click **Install** to start the actual installation of the language pack.
- After a minute or two, the installation is finished, and you can click **Finish** to end the setup application. Repeat these steps for any additional language packs when needed.

You can also install the language packs manually (i.e. without a GUI), if necessary. For example, to install the Dutch and German UM language packs on your UM Server, just open a command prompt (*not* an Exchange Management Shell), navigate to the Exchange Server 2010 SP1 installation media and enter the following command:

```
setup.com /AddUmLanguagePack:nl-NL,de-DE /s:d:\download\UMLanguagePacks
```

This will install the Dutch and German language packs that are located in the `D:\Download\UMLanguagePacks` directory.

6.4 Configuring the UM Server Role

Once the Exchange Server 2010 SP1 Unified Messaging Server is installed, it must be configured at two levels:

1. **organization level** – these settings are stored in Active Directory and available to all Unified Messaging Servers throughout the entire Exchange organization
2. **server level** – these settings are server-specific.

On an organization-wide level, we can (and should) configure the following options:

- UM Dial Plans
- UM IP Gateways
- UM Mailbox Policies
- UM Auto Attendants.

In the following sections, we'll take a closer look at these options and how to configure them.

6.4.1 UM Dial Plans

To configure a Dial Plan on your Exchange Server 2010 SP1 Unified Messaging Server, follow the steps below.

- Log on to the Unified Messaging Server as a domain administrator (with proper Exchange permissions, of course) and open the **Exchange Management Console**.
- Navigate to the **Organization Configuration** options and select the **Unified Messaging** option. In the **Actions** pane click **New UM Dial Plan...**, which will cause

the UM Dial Plan wizard to appear. Enter a **Dial Plan Name**, the number of digits in the extension numbers, the **URI Type** (Telephony Extension for a normal telephony environment, SIP URI for a combination with Office Communication Server (OCS) 2007 R2), and the **Country/Region code**.

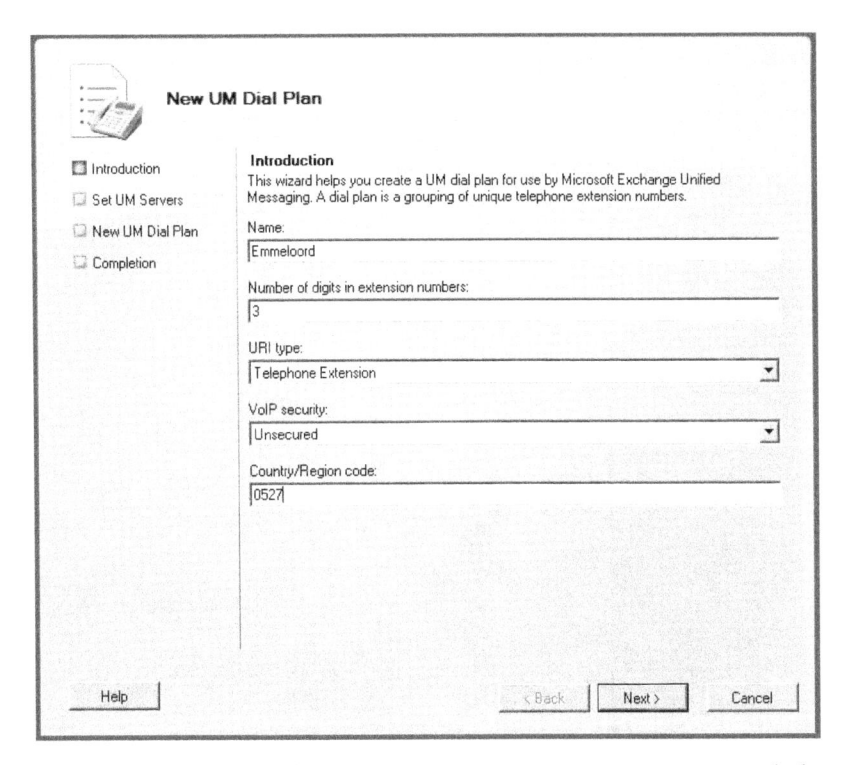

Figure 6.5: Enter the basic UM properties to create a new UM Dial Plan.

- In the next Window, you have to associate the new Dial Plan with a Unified Messaging Server which will be responsible for executing the new Dial Plan; click **Add**, select the **Unified Messaging Server** and then click **Next** to continue.

- Click **New** to actually create the new Dial Plan and, when this process is completed, click **Finish** to end the **Dial Plan** wizard.

- After creation, right-click on the new **Dial Plan** and select its **properties**.

Chapter 6: Unified Messaging

- Select the **Subscriber Access** tab. Under **Associated Subscriber Access Numbers** you can enter a **phone number** that users can dial to access the Outlook Voice Access (as this is also controlled by the Dial Plan). Enter an appropriate phone number, click **Add** and then click **OK**.

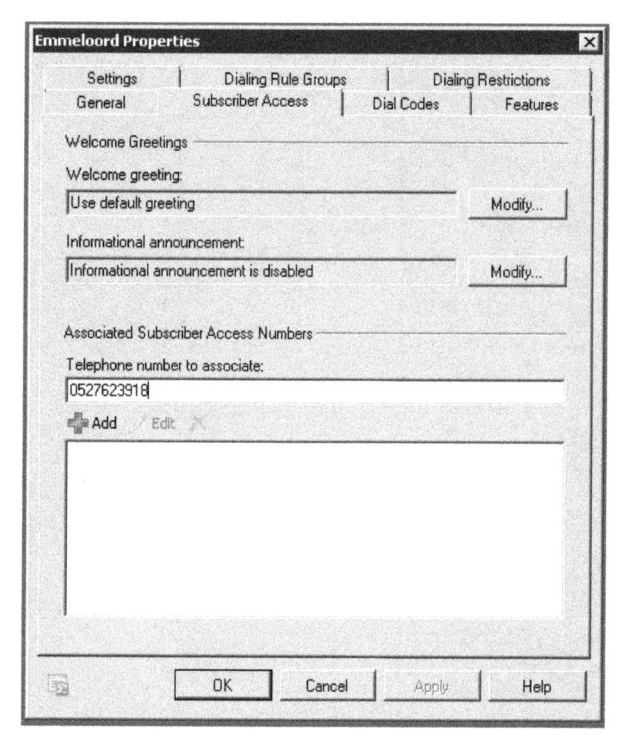

Figure 6.6: Add a number for OVA (Outlook Voice Access).

6.4.2   UM IP Gateway

After creating the UM Dial Plan and configuring the telephone number for the Outlook Voice Access, we can continue with configuring the IP Gateway on the Server. In my environment, I have an IP Gateway (Dialogic Diva BRI-2 PCIe v2 with additional Dialogic VOIP software) located in a separate server connected to the internal network.

- Continue in the Exchange Management Console from where we left in the previous process, and select the **UM IP Gateways** tab. In the **Actions pane**, click **New UM IP Gateway**.

- In the **New UM IP Gateway** wizard, enter a **name** for the new Gateway, the **IP address** that's needed for the UM Server to connect to the Gateway, and select a **Dial Plan** to associate with this Gateway. Bear in mind that, when you select a Dial Plan here, a new default **Hunt Group** is automatically created. Click **New** to create the IP Gateway in your Exchange environment, and once it's been created, click **Finish** to stop the wizard.

6.4.3 UM Mailbox Policy

When we were creating the UM Dial Plan, a default **UM Mailbox Policy** was created as well. You can find this in the third tab, **UM Mailbox Policies**.

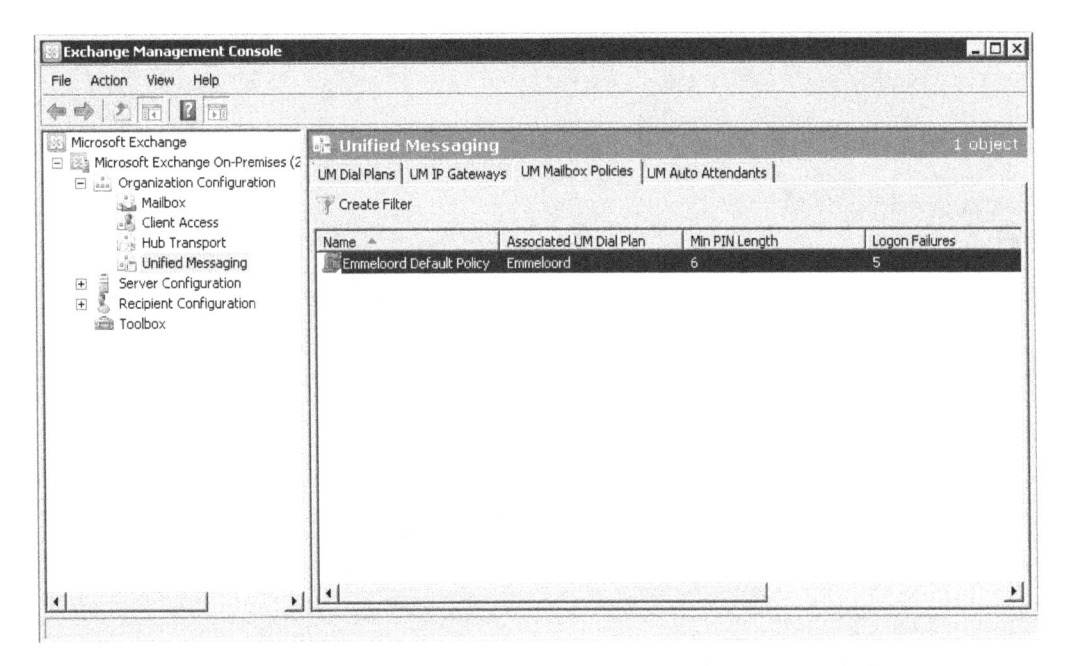

Figure 6.7: The default UM Mailbox Policy after creation of the UM Dial Plan.

The UM Mailbox Policy is used for defining UM-specific settings in your Exchange organization. You can use it to change settings for PIN length and lifetime, logon failures, and maximum greeting duration.

If you think this default UM Mailbox Policy is sufficient for your organization, then you can leave it as it is; otherwise you can change it as appropriate. For testing purposes, I would recommend leaving it in its default state.

6.4.4 UM Auto Attendant

It is also possible to create a personal UM Auto Attendant, which is a kind of electronic receptionist at the front desk of the UM system for external callers, and which makes it possible for users to transfer calls or create a custom menu. For example, you could configure the menu to be something like this:

- Choose 1 for the Sales department
- Choose 2 for the Accounts department
- Choose 3 for the Support department
- Choose 9 for Reception.

We'll leave the UM Auto Attendant set to its default configuration for now. For more detailed information regarding the its functionality, check the Microsoft TechNet website on HTTP://TINYURL.COM/UMAUTOATTENDANTS.

6.4.5 Configuring the actual UM Server

Now that we've configured the UM Settings on an organization level, it's time to configure the actual UM Server itself.

- In the Exchange Management Console, navigate to the **Server Configuration** option and select the **Unified Messaging** option. In the **Results Pane**, you'll see the server we installed earlier; right-click on this UM Server and select its **Properties**.

- In the **Properties** pop-up window select the **UM Settings** tab; you'll see the associated **UM Dial Plan** we created earlier, as well as the additional languages that we installed. In the **startup mode** menu you can select **TCP**, which is the default, or you can also select **TLS** if you want to set up a secure communication between the UM Server and the IP Gateway. If you change this setting, you have to restart the UM Server Service. For now we'll leave it with its default setting of TCP.

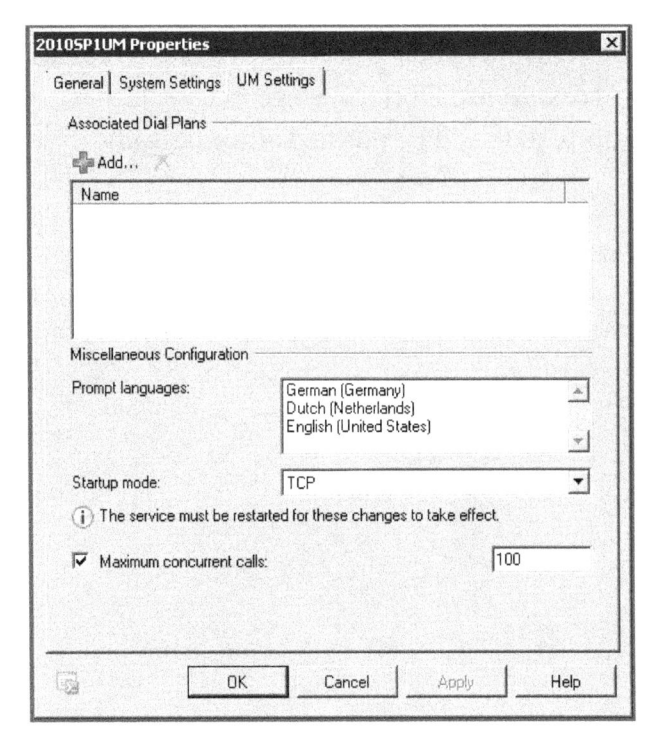

Figure 6.8: Properties of the UM Server before configuring.

The UM Server is now ready to use; if you configured the PBX and the IP Gateway correctly, and you dial the telephone number you configured for Subscriber Access, you'll hear the Exchange UM Server answer the call!

6.5 UM Enabling Mailboxes

Before users can actually use the UM functionality, their mailboxes have to be UM enabled. This can be achieved by using the Exchange Management Console.

- In the Exchange Management Console, navigate to the **Recipient Configuration** option and click on **Mailbox**. In the **Results** pane, select a Mailbox, right-click on it, and in the menu that appears, select **Enable Unified Messaging**.

- In the Introduction window that appears, use the **Browse** button to select a **Unified Messaging Mailbox Policy**. If you want, you can use the default generated PIN for the user, or you can manually enter a PIN code. This PIN code is used by the user to access their mailbox when using the Subscriber Access to use Outlook Voice Access. Either way, the PIN code is sent to the user's mailbox so they'll be notified automatically.

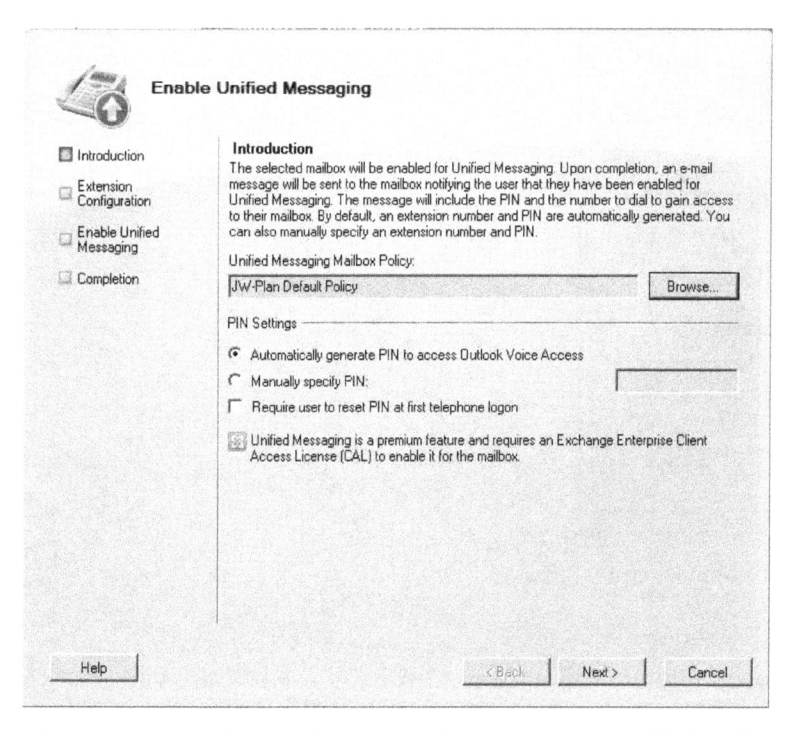

Figure 6.9: Configuring the settings for a user's UM-enabled mailbox.

- The next window is the **Extension Configuration** stage, where you need to enter the user's phone extension number, then click **Next** to continue.

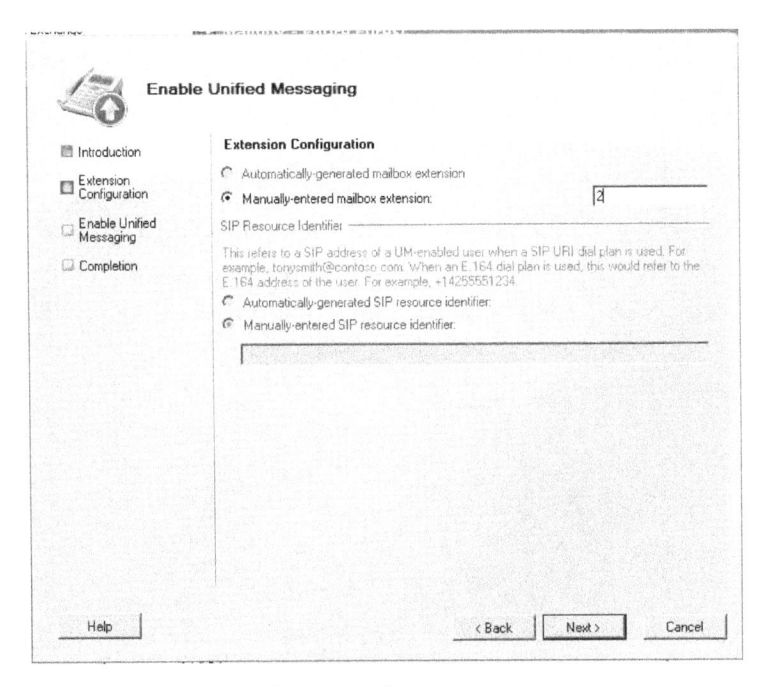

Figure 6.10: Setting the user's phone extension.

- Check the **Configuration Information** and, if you're happy with everything, click **Enable** to UM-enable this mailbox.

The mailbox is now ready to use the Unified Messaging environment. By using the Subscriber Access, the user can access their personal menu after entering their extension number and PIN code, and in this menu the user can change their welcome message, listen to voicemails, listen to email, and so on.

Now, when somebody tries to contact this particular user using the phone system, and the user is not available, the call will be automatically rerouted to the UM Server, which will answer the call, play the welcome message and, when needed, record the voicemail and deliver it to the user's Mailbox.

6.6 Summary

The Unified Messaging Server Role is one of the most compelling features in Exchange Server 2010 but, at the same time, it is one of the most misunderstood and therefore most difficult ones. Being SysAdmins, we typically do not have too much telephony experience, and this can make the UM Role hard to understand.

Besides the UM Server itself, you also need a PBX and something like an IP Gateway (complete with software) that will translate the phone call into an IP data stream that can be understood by the UM Server. Once you have this environment up and running, you'll be amazed by its features.

Chapter 7: Exchange Server 2010 Security

Being a trainer (as well as a consultant) I always complain that the "security" topic is always the last topic in a course. Now, when writing a book, I unfortunately find myself perpetuating the practice! That doesn't mean that security is less important than, say, High Availability; it simply means that it just happened to become the last chapter.

When looking at security, we can divide it into the subtopics below.

- **Server Security** – sometimes referred to as "Server Hardening" where the Exchange Server's security is configured more tightly.
- **Network Security** – usage of firewalls or a reverse proxy in your network infrastructure.
- **Message Security** – the implementation of Secure Messaging, not on the server in this case, but on the individual messages or message stream.
- **Anti-Spam** – the implementation of any one (or several) of the various options which are available in Exchange Server 2010 to effect a proper anti-spam solution.

I will go into more detail on each of these topics in the following sections.

7.1 Server Security

Server security is a topic that primarily has to do with the Windows Server instance on which Exchange Server 2010 is installed. For example, everybody is familiar with patching their servers, and most SysAdmins patch their servers regularly. However, when it comes to Server Hardening, the Baseline Security Analyzer or an Active Directory integrated PKI (Public Key Infrastructure), many SysAdmins start staring out of the window.

7.1.1 Server hardening

Server hardening is, as the name implies, the process of making it harder to compromise a server, and reducing the size of its attack surface. This can be achieved, for example, by disabling unnecessary services on your Exchange Server or by limiting the number of open ports on the Windows Firewall.

To make life easier, Microsoft has a tool available to help with hardening a server, called the **Security Configuration Wizard** (**SCW**). When the SCW application is started, you can select the various roles the server will be performing and, when you follow the wizard, SCW will generate a security policy which can be imported on the particular server. However, as helpful as that sounds, the server roles you can select in the SCW are very generic: File Server, Print Server, DNS Server, etc.

Chapter 7: Exchange Server 2010 Security

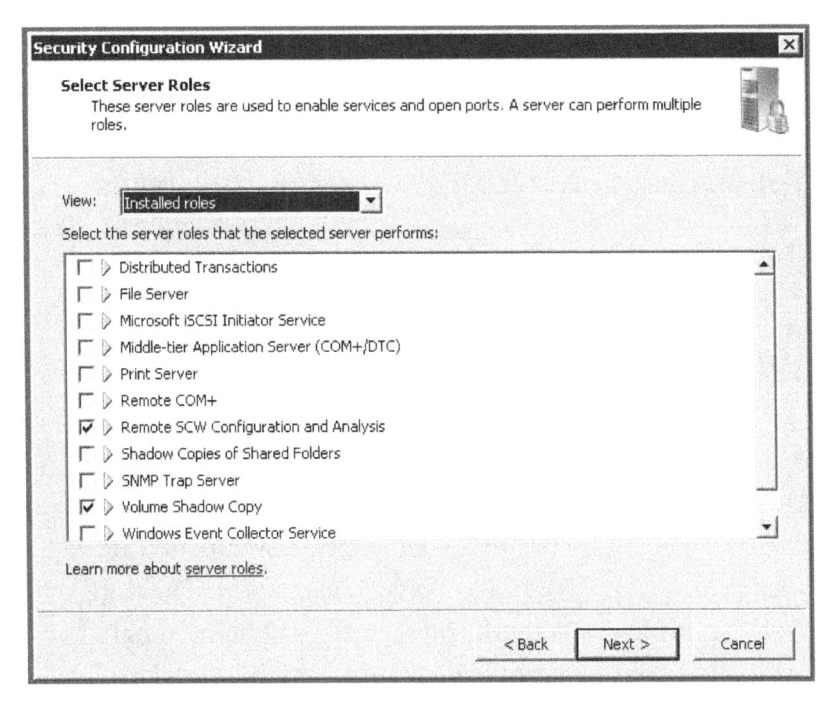

Figure 7.1: The Security Configuration Wizard on a regular (non-Exchange) server.

There is not an Exchange Server Role to be selected in the SCW, and apparently very little support in the tool for Exchange Server 2010 in general; I'll come back to that in a moment. Microsoft supplied template files for Exchange Server 2007, both for a regular Exchange Server 2007 and for an Exchange Server 2007 Edge Server. The templates had to be registered in the SCW, enabling it to create a security policy file that could be applied to the Exchange Server 2007 Server. The result was an Exchange Server with a minimal number of running services, an appropriate firewall configuration, and so on.

Although that sounds reasonably useful, Microsoft doesn't supply these template files for Exchange Server 2010 (including SP1). One of the design goals of the MS Exchange team was to implement a "secure by default" configuration, so there's no longer any need to use the Security Configuration Wizard to harden an Exchange 2010 Server (for more details, take a look at HTTP://TINYURL.COM/SCWIZARD).

So, when securing an Exchange Server 2010 server, are there any services that can be disabled because they are not in use? Absolutely, but it depends on the implementation of the particular Exchange Server 2010 server. For example, quite a lot of all implementations of Exchange Server 2010 do not use the POP3 and IMAP4 protocols and they are set to "manual" by default, so it's generally safe to disable these services on the server using the services MMC snap-in.

7.1.2 Baseline Security Analyzer

After installing Exchange Server 2010, and then afterwards on a regular basis, the **Microsoft Baseline Security Analyzer** (**MBSA**) can be used to check the server for possible security issues. The MBSA is an easy-to-use tool that can be downloaded from the Microsoft website by navigating to HTTP://TINYURL.COM/MBSANALYZER. This tool can help (small) organizations to determine the state of the security on their Exchange Servers. MBSA is a tool that's available in both a graphical version, which is ideal for looking after only one or two servers, as well as a command-line version more suited to larger organizations.

When the MBSA is started, there's the option to scan a computer based on its computer name or its IP address, and there are some additional options, some of which can be seen in Figure 7.2.

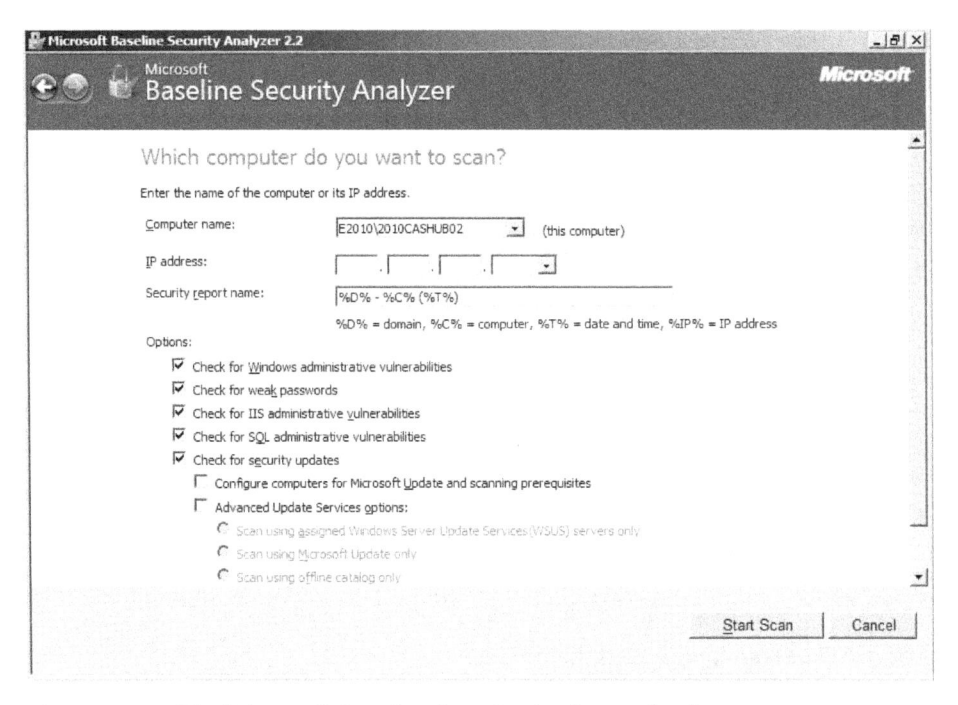

Figure 7.2: The Microsoft Baseline Security Analyzer selection screen.

MBSA automatically downloads the latest CAB file from Microsoft with the security information it needs, and checks the server against this CAB file. When all checks are performed, an overview containing the MBSA findings is presented on the screen, as seen in Figure 7.3.

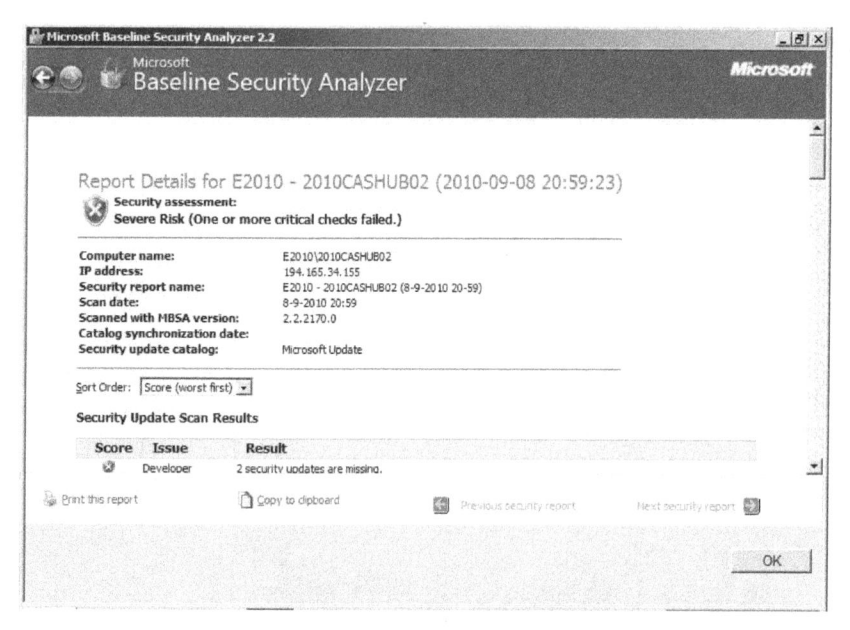

Figure 7.3: The results of an MBSA test. It is obvious that this server needs some maintenance.

Besides scanning the local host, MBSA also has an option to scan a remote host, targeted by name, and there's even the option to scan a range of targets based on IP addresses.

The command-line version of MBSA is called `MBSACLI.EXE` and can (also) be found in the directory `C:\Program Files\Microsoft Baseline Security Analyzer 2`. The command-line version accepts the same options as the graphical version but, to perform a default scan of your server and redirect the output to a text file instead of the console, you can use the command: `mbsacli.exe > c:\temp\mbsa-output.txt`.

Since the Microsoft Baseline Security Analyzer has so many options, there is also an extended help file available, which is installed on the local hard drive of the server at `C:\Program Files\Microsoft Baseline Security Analyzer 2\Help\mbsahelp.html`.

7.1.3 Patching your Exchange Servers

After running the Baseline Security Analyzer, you will probably find that you are missing one or more security updates or product updates. There are a number of ways to update your computer:

- Microsoft Update
- Windows Server Update Services (WSUS)
- System Center Configuration Manager 2007.

System Center Configuration Manager (**SCCM**) is a bit out of scope for this book, so I'll only discuss the first two options.

As you're hopefully aware, **Windows Update** is a free service from Microsoft that's available online, and which you can use to keep your computers and servers up to date. All Windows fixes are located on the Windows Update website. The Windows Update client is installed on your workstation or server by default, and checks the Microsoft Update site on a regular basis for new fixes, automatically downloading and installing the critical hot-fixes and patches (if you give it permission to do so).

> **Note**
>
> *You have to be careful, since there's a difference between Windows Update and Microsoft Update. Windows Update only takes care of updating Windows itself, while Microsoft Updates also supplies updates for other Microsoft applications. Windows Update and Microsoft Update are two different applications. You can change to Microsoft Update by selecting the* **Give me updates for Microsoft products...** *check box in the Windows Update tool.*

Chapter 7: Exchange Server 2010 Security

You can open the Windows Update client by navigating to the **Start** button, selecting **All Programs** and then **Windows Update**. When you select **Change Settings** in the navigation menu that then appears on the left, you can choose between the following options:

- Install updates automatically (recommended)
- Download updates but let me choose whether to install them
- Check for updates but let me choose whether to download and install them
- Never check for updates (not recommended).

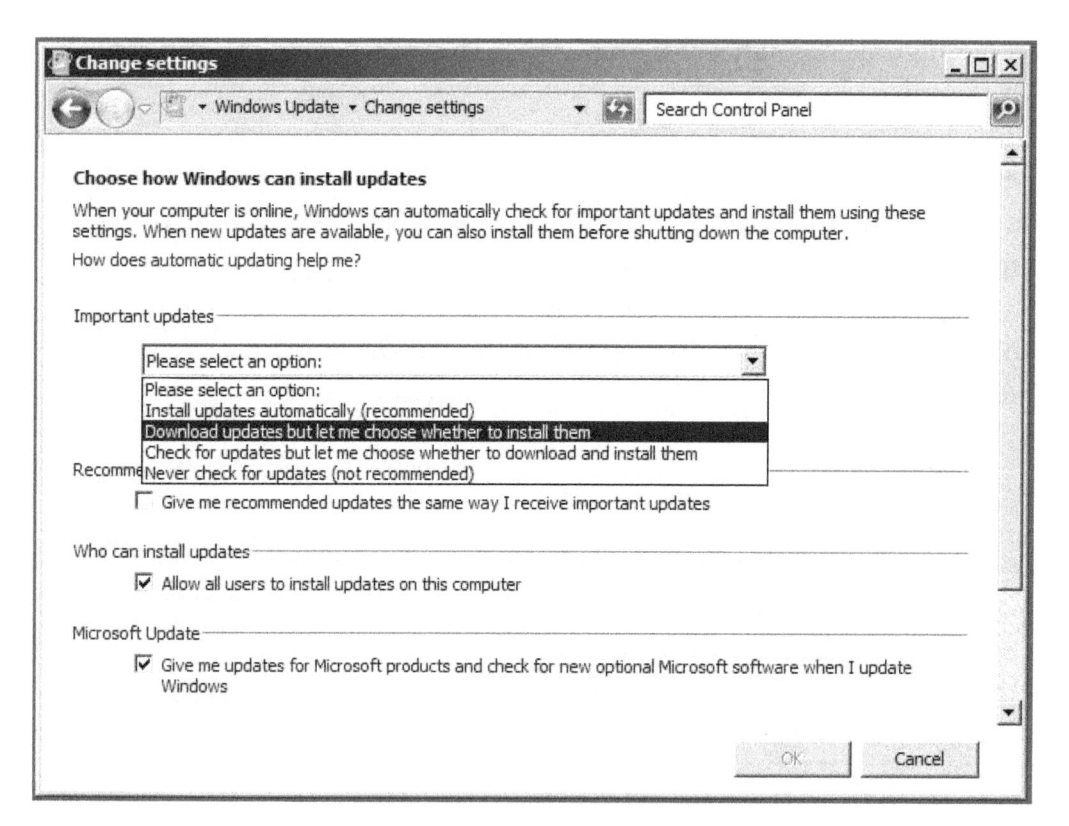

Figure 7.4: Select how to deal with Windows updates.

Personally, I select the **Download updates but let me choose whether to install them** option, which gives me the flexibility to install the updates at a convenient time. You can have Windows Update automatically install the updates for you, but I've seen it happen too often that the following reboot fails, resulting in an unavailable Exchange Server.

As I mentioned earlier, there is a distinction between Windows Update and Microsoft Update and, if you want to change from Windows Update to Microsoft Update, then you have to open the Windows Update applet. In the Results pane you'll see a message reading G**et updates for other Microsoft products. Find out more**. Click on the **Find out more** link, and you'll be redirected to the Microsoft Update website. Check the **I agree to the Terms of Use for Microsoft Update** check box and click **Next**. Select the option you want (**Use recommended settings** versus **Use current settings**) and click **Install** to install the Microsoft Update client software on your server.

The next time you select Windows Update in the Start menu, you'll find updates for other applications as well.

Another interesting option for keeping your systems up to date is **Windows Server Update Services** (**WSUS**). WSUS is a role in Windows Server 2008, so you can install it using Server Manager.

When using WSUS, updates from Microsoft Update are downloaded only once – to the WSUS Server, where they are then stored. This downloading, or synchronization as it's called in WSUS, is fully configurable; you can have WSUS check for updates and download them every night, for example. Once the updates are downloaded, you have to log on as an administrator on the WSUS Server and approve them for installation. Only after approval of the individual hot-fixes in the WSUS console has been given are the updates ready for distribution to the clients (workstations or servers).

Chapter 7: Exchange Server 2010 Security

It's worth knowing that the Windows Update client on a domain-joined computer can be managed using Group Policies. By creating and applying a WSUS-specific policy, you can control the client with a high degree of granularity. The Windows Update configuration can be found in a policy by navigating to **Computer Configuration > Administrative Templates > Windows Components**, and then selecting **Windows Update**.

Right here you can specify, for example, what functionality to enable or disable, the location of the WSUS Server, the automatic update frequency (of the client, not the WSUS Server), and whether or not you want to automatically install new updates.

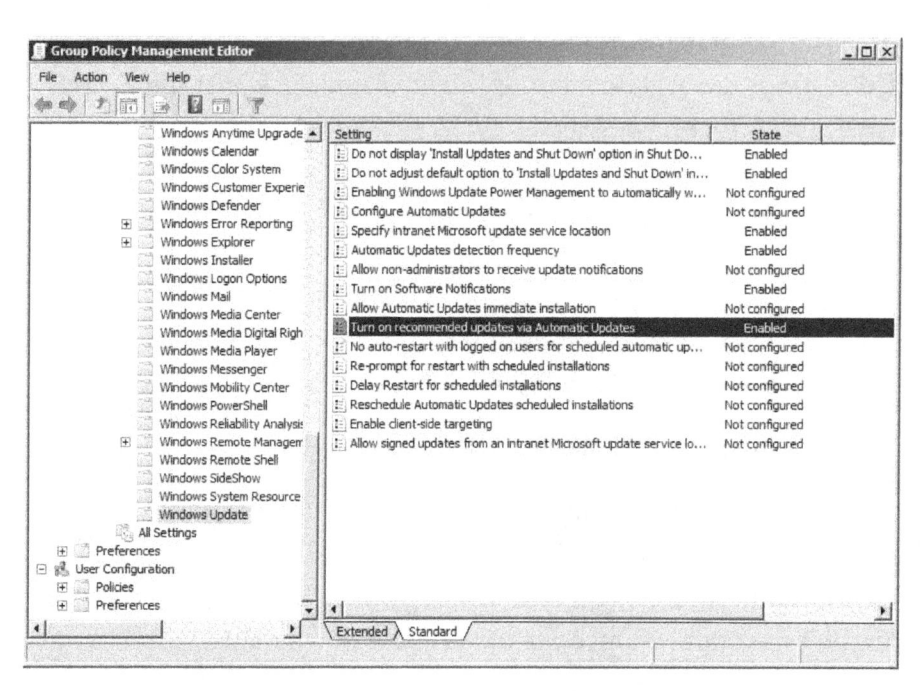

Figure 7.5: GPO (Group Policy Object) settings for configuration the Windows Update client on the servers.

The major advantage of WSUS is that updates are downloaded only once, from the Windows Update site to your WSUS Server, and are then distributed to your (Exchange) servers from there. This can save valuable bandwidth and it will also decrease the time needed to download and install the updates server by server.

7.1.4 Certificates or Public Key infrastructure

In *Chapters 2* and *3* (covering Installation and Coexistence) I explained the use of (third-party) certificates in an Exchange Server 2010 infrastructure. These certificates are used between a client and an Exchange Server 2010 CA Server to encrypt the traffic passing between them. This traffic encryption occurs, not only for the Outlook Web App, but also for Outlook Anywhere, ActiveSync, and between Hub Transport Servers.

When installing the Exchange Server 2010 CA Server, a self-signed certificate, containing just the server name, is generated and installed on the server, and can be used for testing purposes after installing the server. For testing purposes this self-signed certificate also contains the local FQDN in the **Subject Alternative Names** field for testing with Outlook Anywhere. It is naturally a best practice *not* to use this self-signed certificate in a production environment, but rather to use a third-party certificate on the CA Server. Microsoft has a list of supported third-party certificate vendors for Exchange Server solutions which can be found in Knowledge Base article 929395 at http://support.microsoft.com/kb/929395.

Does this mean that other third-party certificate vendors have lesser certificates? Absolutely not; the only difference is that, for whatever reason, their certificates are not tested by the Microsoft Exchange team. Personally, I know quite a few customers and consultants who use GoDaddy certificates, for example, on their Exchange Server 2010 installations without any problems.

An interesting alternative to third-party certificates is your own Public Key Infrastructure; in other words, the capacity to generate your own certificates. It is a bit out of scope of this book, but you would have to install Active Directory Certificate Services. I typically recommend using a dedicated server for this and not installing the role on a Domain Controller. For a testing environment, this is not an issue.

Active Directory Certificate Services can be installed using Server Manager; the base services have to be installed first and additional Role Services can be installed after that.

During installation, you have to decide whether you want to install an Enterprise CA (Certificate Authority) which is integrated with Active Directory, or a stand-alone CA. It depends on your own requirements, of course, but for a normal testing environment I typically use an Enterprise CA.

Once you've got your Public Key Infrastructure set up, the process for requesting an internal certificate is almost the same as when requesting a third-party certificate.

- Log on to the Exchange Server 2010 SP1 CA Server and open the **Exchange Management Console**.

- In the **Navigation** pane, expand **Microsoft Exchange On-Premises**.

- In the **Navigation** pane, click on **Server Configuration**.

- In the top half of the **Results** pane you'll see your Exchange Servers, and in the bottom half you'll see the corresponding certificate. This is the self-signed certificate that's created during the installation of your Exchange Server.

- In the **Actions** pane click on **New Exchange Certificate**, and the **New Exchange Certificate wizard** is displayed. Enter a friendly name, for example "Exchange 2010 SP1," and click **Next** to continue.

- With Exchange Server 2010 SP1 you have the option of enabling a wildcard certificate, and this is now fully supported by Exchange in the EMC GUI.

- The next page is the Exchange Configuration, where you can determine the usage of the certificate. Select the following services:

    - CA Server (Outlook Web App)

    - CA Server (Exchange ActiveSync)

    - CA Server (Web Services, Outlook Anywhere, and Autodiscover).

- In all three options, enter the external hostname for your organization. In the last option also select **Autodiscover used on the Internet** and select the proper URL. The default is the long URL, like autodiscover.inframan.com. Click **Next** to continue.

- You'll see an overview of the domain names that will be in the certificate, and the one with the bold typeface is the Common Name (CN) of the certificate. Click **Next** to continue.

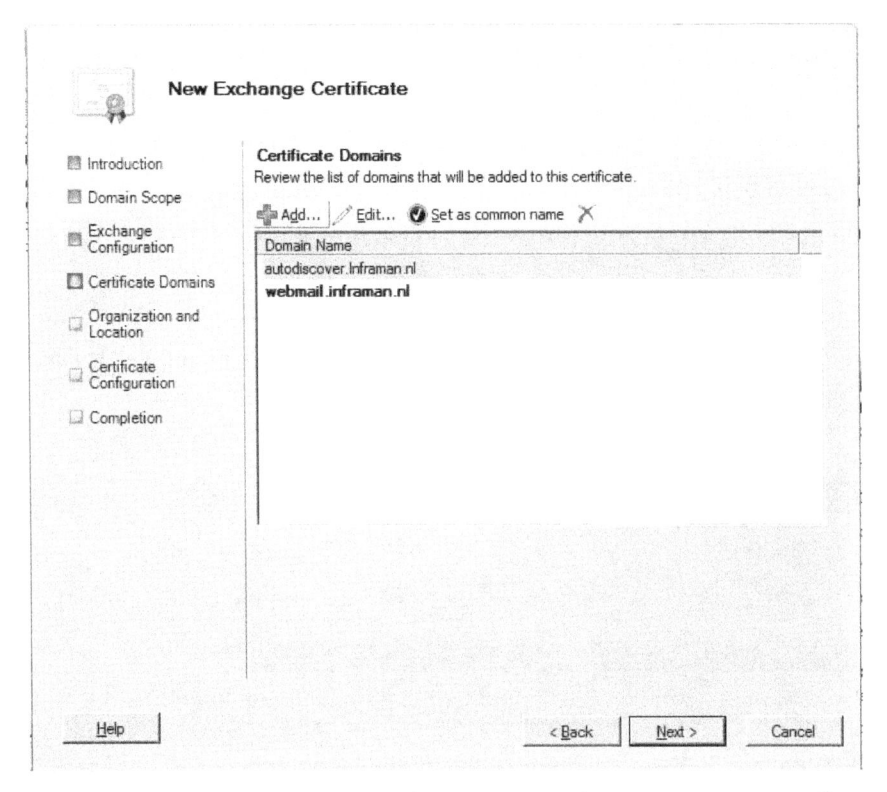

Figure 7.6: Overview of the certificate request. The Common Name will be webmail.inframan.nl.

- In the **Organization and Location** page, you have to enter your company-specific details, such as Organization, Organizational Unit, Country, etc. In the field for the **Certificate Request File Path**, click **Browse** to enter a location for the Certificate Request File. Enter a filename like C:\Temp\Exch-Cert.req and click **Save**. If you request a certificate with a third-party vendor, make sure that the information entered here is the same as the information registered in the WHOIS records. For an internal certificate this is not too important, but it has to make sense, of course. Click **Next** to continue.

Chapter 7: Exchange Server 2010 Security

- On the **Certificate Configuration** page, check your certificate request details and if all is OK, click **New** to generate the request file.

- On the **Completion** page, you'll see the PowerShell command that was used for generating this certificate request. If needed, you can use **CTRL+C** to copy the contents of this page to the server's clipboard. Click **Finish** to continue.

You can now find the file `C:\Temp\Exch-Cert.req` on your server. Normally, the next step would be to log on to the website of the vendor where you normally order your certificates, but now you have to log on to your own PKI Server's website to process the certificate request.

- On the CA Server where you generated the certificate request, open Internet Explorer and go to the Certificate Authority.

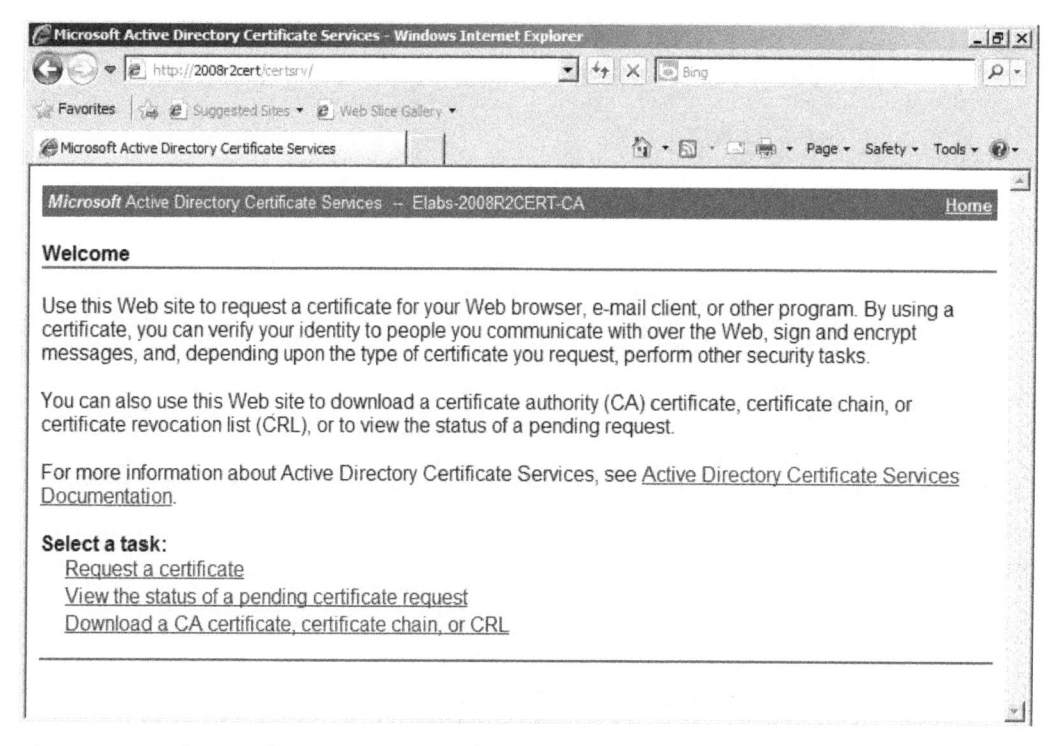

Figure 7.7: The Windows 2008 R2 Certificate Authority.

- Select **Request a Certificate**, select **Advanced Certificate Request** and select **Submit a certificate request by using a base-64 encoded CMC or PKCS #10 file**, or **Submit a renewal request by using a base 64-encoded PKCS#7 file**.

- In the **Submit a Certificate Request or Renewal Request** window, you have to enter the request file that was created earlier, the `exch-cert.req` file. Use Notepad to open this file, and then copy and paste the contents into the request field. In the Certificate Template field, select Web Server, and then click **Submit** to continue.

- The certificate request will be processed immediately by the Certificate Authority, and you have the option to download the certificate immediately. So, click **Download Certificate** and download the new certificate on the `C:\Temp` directory of the CA Server where the request file was generated.

- After saving the certificate, go back to the **Exchange Management Shell**. Right-click on the certificate that was requested earlier, and select **Complete Pending Request**.

- In the next window, use the **Browse** button to select the certificate we just generated (i.e. `C:\Temp\certnew.cer`). Click **Complete** to finish the certificate generation process and, when done, click **Finish** to close the wizard.

- The final step is to assign the Exchange services to the new certificate. In the **Exchange Management Console,** right-click on the new certificate and select **Assign services to certificate**. In the wizard that follows, select the appropriate CA Servers where you want to use the new certificate, and select the services you want to use, such as IIS (for OWA and Web Services), SMTP, POP3, or IMAP4.

- Click **Assign** to actually assign the certificate to these services.

- A warning message, as in Figure 7.8 might show up when other certificates will be overwritten.

Chapter 7: Exchange Server 2010 Security

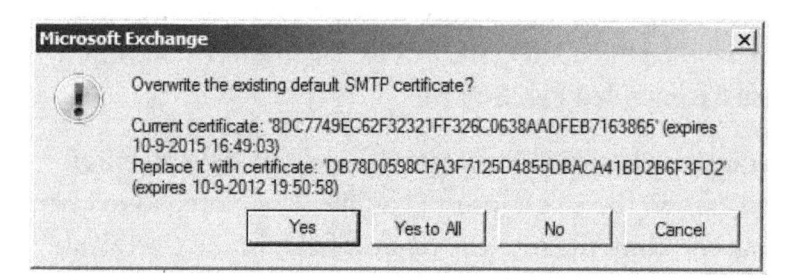

Figure 7.8: Warning message when the original certificate is overwritten.

- Click **Yes** to continue and, when the wizard is finished, click **Finish** to return to the Exchange Management Console. The CA Server is now secured by an internal Unified Communications Certificate.

When you open Outlook Web App using your browser, you can check the certificate and you'll see the server that has issued the certificate (your internal Certificate Authority), and you can check the Subject Alternative Name entries under the details tab of the certificate's properties.

Now, this will work fine for domain-joined clients, as these clients will automatically trust the Certificate Authority that generated the certificate, but non-domain-joined clients will not automatically trust this certificate, so the Root CA has to be imported on these clients.

- To accomplish this, log on to a domain-joined client or server, open Internet Explorer and navigate to the Certificate Server. After logging on to the Certificate Server, select **Download a CA certificate, certificate chain, or CRL**.

Chapter 7: Exchange Server 2010 Security

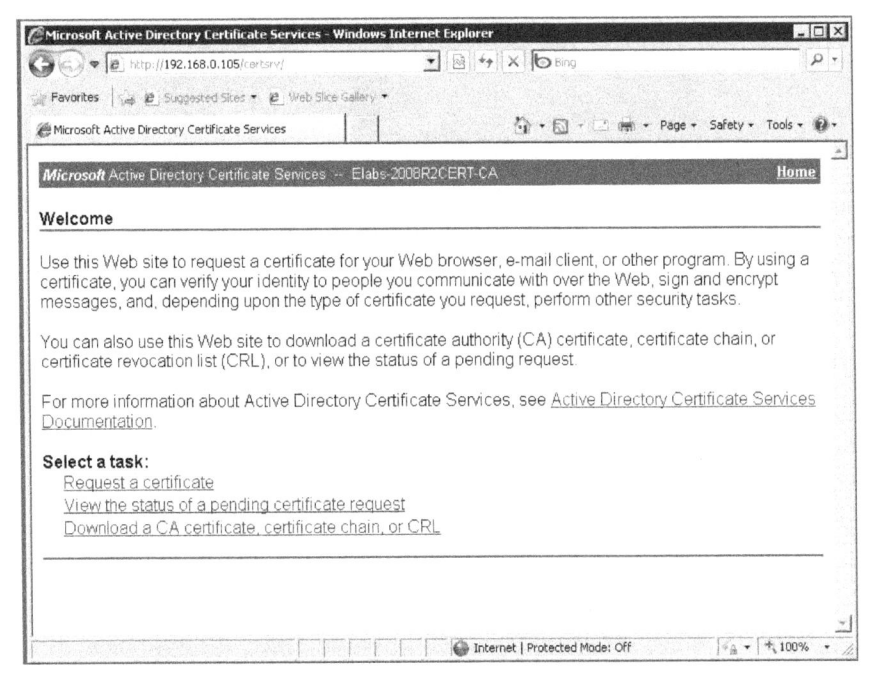

Figure 7.9: Choose **Download a CA certificate, certificate chain, or CRL**.

- Follow the wizard and save the certificate chain to the local hard disk, like C:\temp\certnew.p7b.

- Copy this file to the non-domain-joined client, where it will have to be imported into the local Certificate Store, for example, to C:\temp\certnew.p7b again.

- On the client, start a new **MMC console** (click the **Start** button, select **Run** and type **MMC**), and when an empty MMC console appears, select **Add/Remove snap-in** in the **File** Menu.

- In the **Add or Remove Snap-ins** window, select **Certificates** from the available snap-ins, then click **Add** and select **Computer Account**.

Chapter 7: Exchange Server 2010 Security

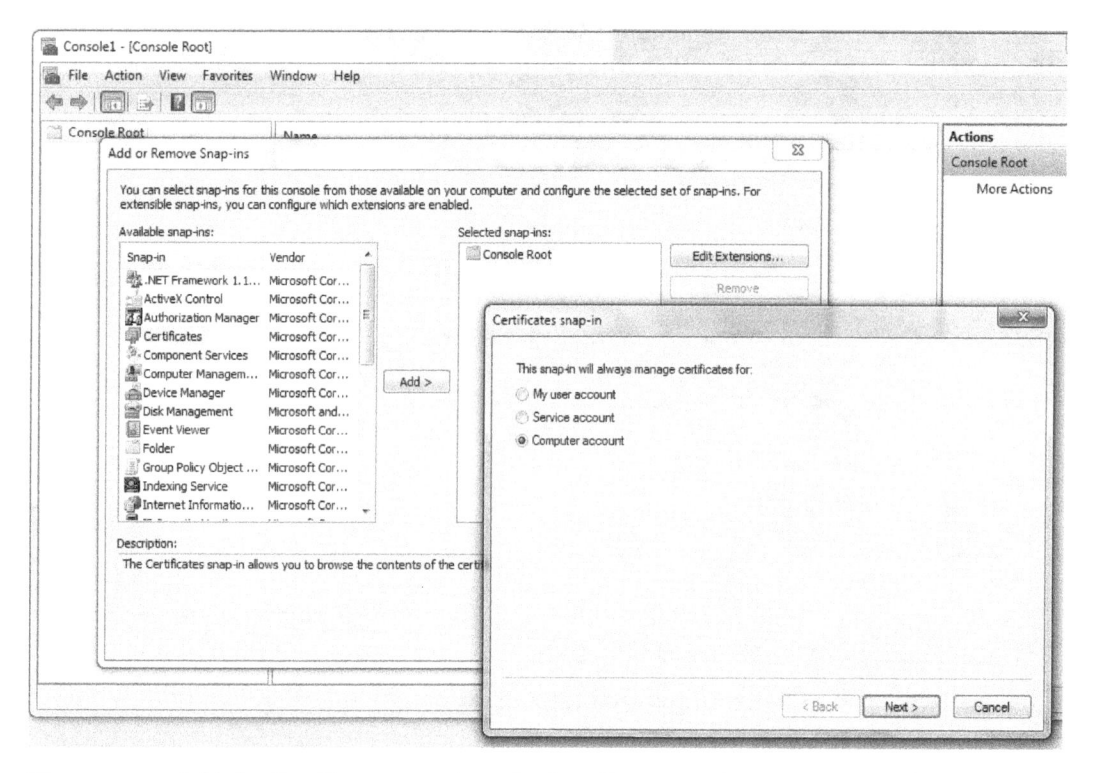

Figure 7.10: Add the Certificates snap-in and select **Computer Account**.

- Click **Next** to continue.

- In the **Select Computer** window, select **Local computer: (the computer this console is running on)** and click **Finish** to add the snap-in to the MMC console.

- Now you'll see the Certificate Store on the client. In the left-hand pane, right-click on the **Trusted Root Certification Authority**, select all tasks and then select **Import....**

Chapter 7: Exchange Server 2010 Security

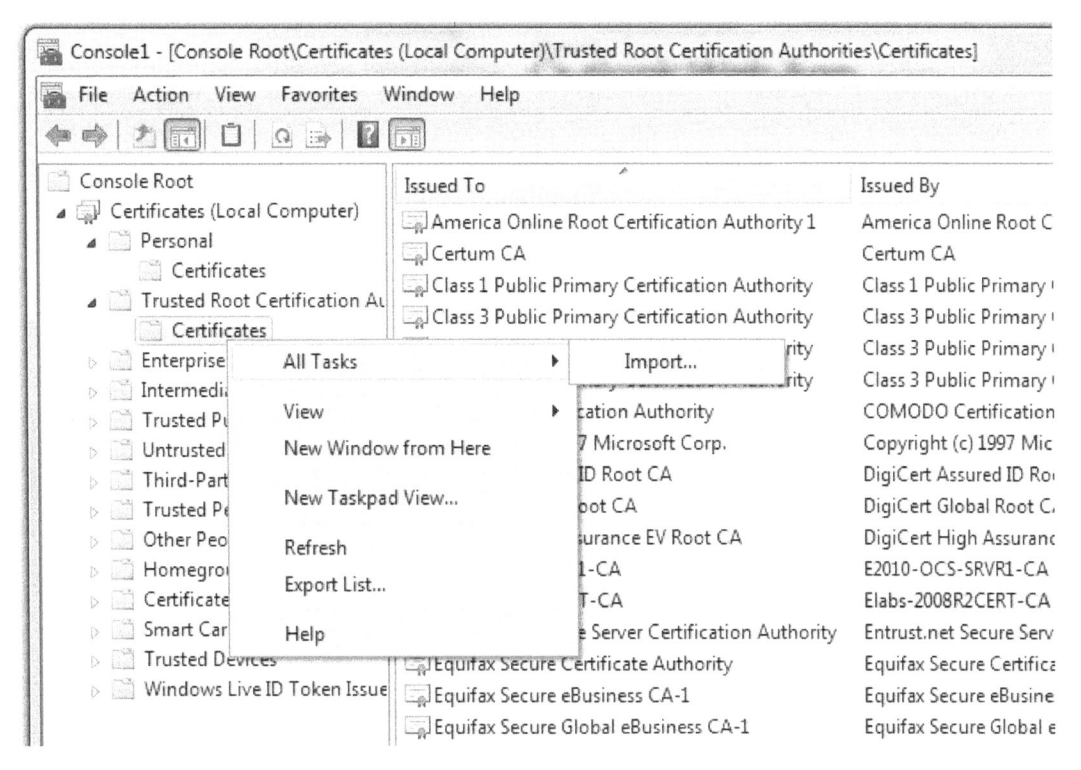

Figure 7.11: Import the Root CA into the local Certificate Store.

- Follow the wizard, browse to the Root CA (`C:\temp\certnew.p7b`) and, in the **Import** window, select **Place all certificates in the following store** and, if needed, use the **Browse** button to select the **Trusted Root Certification Authorities**.

Chapter 7: Exchange Server 2010 Security

Figure 7.12: Import the Root CA into the Trusted Root Certification Authorities.

- Click **Next** and then **Finish** to finish the wizard and add the Root CA to the local Certificate Store.

Now, when you open Internet Explorer on the non-domain-joined client and open Outlook Web App on the Exchange Server 2010 SP1 Client Access Server, the certificate on this server will be trusted, and the certificate error messages will not be shown.

Using this method, you can use an internal Windows Server 2008 R2 Public Key Infrastructure (PKI) for security on the CA Server without buying a third-party Unified Communications certificate.

Note

Communication between internal Hub Transport Servers, and between the Hub Transport Server and an Edge Transport Server is secured using SSL as well. It's worth bearing in mind that, by default, the self-signed certificate is used for securing this communication. You don't necessarily need to do anything about it, but it's worth knowing.

7.2 Network Security

Besides securing the Exchange Servers with certificates, it's also necessary to control access to the Exchange Servers 2010 SP1 servers in general, especially when connected to the Internet. The question which then arises is "What access is needed from the Internet to the Exchange Server 2010 SP1 Servers?" Let's take a look.

The Hub Transport Servers need to communicate on Port 25 for intra-server communications. If clients want to use the Hub Transport Server, Port 587 is used for authenticated access.

The CA Servers need open ports for Outlook Web App, Outlook Anywhere, Exchange Web Services, ActiveSync and, if needed, POP3 and IMAP4. These are, by default, Ports 443, 110, and 143 respectively. If Secure POP and Secure IMAP is used, then Ports 995 and 993 (respectively) are also used. While these are the default ports, each individual port can be changed, of course.

There are two ways to secure network traffic between the Internet and the CA Server:

- use a firewall between the Internet and the CA Server
- use a Microsoft Forefront Threat Management Gateway (TMG) between the Internet and the CA Server.

7.2.1 Firewall

The cheapest way of implementing a firewall on the CA Server is to use the Windows Firewall. That being said, I would not recommend this course, but would rather implement an enterprise-level firewall. For example, my own test servers are located in a datacenter in Amsterdam, and they are secured using a Juniper SSG350 firewall. Only

Ports 25, 80, and 443 are open from the Internet. RDP (Port 3389) is also open, but it is restricted on IP address, so RDP access is limited.

The downside of using a firewall is that there's no "deep level inspection" of HTTPS traffic, and an external IP address is needed for every CA Server or Hub Transport Server connecting to the Internet. On the other hand, this is an extremely fast solution in terms of HTTP traffic throughput.

7.2.2 Reverse Proxy by using TMG

It is also possible to implement a Microsoft Forefront Threat Management Gateway (TMG) Server in your environment, between the Internet and the CA Server and Hub Transport Server.

Note

Every now and then the question is raised about the difference between ISA Server and TMG Server. Although not entirely correct, I sometimes refer to TMG as "ISA Server 2010." It is effectively the successor to ISA Server 2006.

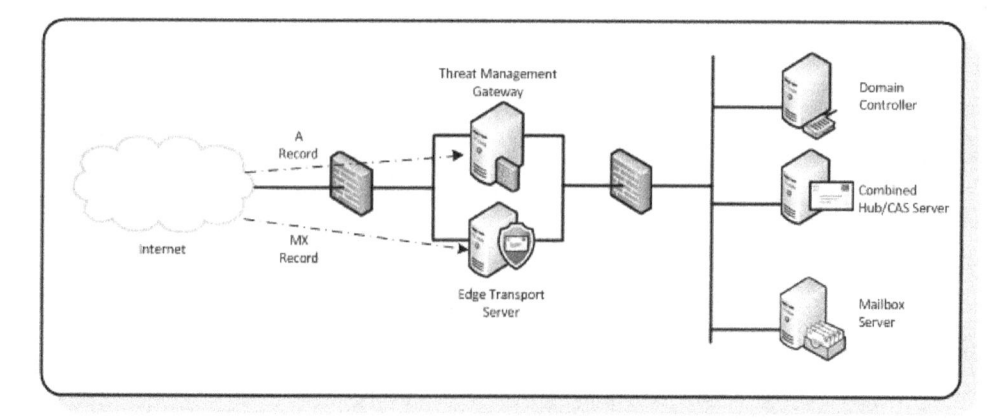

Figure 7.13: The TMG Server is located between the Internet and the CA Server.

The TMG Server publishes services offered by the CA Server to the Internet, like Outlook Web App, Outlook Anywhere, or ActiveSync. Clients from the Internet connect to the TMG Server, and the request is relayed from there to the CA Server.

Only one public IP address is used – the one on the public interface of the TMG Server, but the CA Server and the Hub Transport Server can use an internal IP address since they are not connected directly to the Internet. Also, the TMG Server can act as an additional layer of security by inspecting HTTP(S) traffic to and from the internal network.

So, to add a TMG Server between the Internet and the Exchange Server 2010 SP1 CA Server, the steps below need to be performed.

- A TMG Server has to be installed. One network interface is connected to the Internet and one network interface is connected to the internal network.
- The certificate of the CA Server needs to be imported in the TMG Server Certificate Store.
- The Root Certificate of the Windows Certificate Server needs to be imported into the TMG Certificate Store.
- A Web Listener needs to be configured on the TMG Server.
- A Web Publishing Rule needs to be configured on the TMG Server.

These steps (with the exception of the TMG Server installation) will be explained in the following paragraphs. Let's get started.

To export the certificate on the Exchange Server 2010 SP1 CA Server to the TMG Server, follow the steps below.

- Log on to the Exchange Server 2010 SP1 CA Server and open **the Exchange Management Console**.
- In the **Navigation** pane, expand **Microsoft Exchange On-Premises**.

- In the **Navigation** pane, click on **Server Configuration**.

- In the top half of the **Results** pane you'll see your Exchange Servers, and in the bottom half you'll see the certificates. Select the **Exchange Server 2010 SP1** certificate that was created in Section 7.1.4, and select **Export Exchange Certificate** in the Actions pane.

- In the **Export Exchange Certificate wizard**, enter a filename and enter a password, bearing in mind that the backup file will be protected with this password.

- Click **Export** to actually export the certificate and, when done, click **Finish** to end the wizard.

- Copy this export file to the TMG Server.

- Use the same procedure as outlined earlier (in Section 7.1.4 *Certificates or Public Key infrastructure*) to import this certificate into the Certificate Store of the TMG Server. Do not import the certificate into the **Trusted Root Certification Authorities**, but import it into the **Personal Certificate Store** of the TMG Server.

The Root Certificate of the Windows Certificate Authority needs to be imported into the **Trusted Root Certification Authorities** store on the TMG Server. Import the file C:\temp\certnew.p7b into the Certificate Store of the TMG Server, as explained earlier.

Once you've done that, you'll need to go through the following steps, which are to configure the Web Listener on the TMG Server. The Web Listener is the service on the TMG Server that intercepts the HTTPS traffic destined for OWA. To create a new Web Listener, follow the steps below.

- On the TMG Server, log on as an administrator and open the **Forefront TMG Management console** from the **Start menu**.

- When the Management console is shown, select **Firewall Policy** in the **Navigation** pane and in the **Actions** pane, click on the **Toolbox** tab and select **New Web Listener**.

- In the **New Web Listener wizard**, follow the steps below.

  - Enter a name for the Web Listener.

  - Select **Require SSL secured connections with clients**, since an encrypted connection between the client and the TMG Server is required.

  - Select the **External network** for incoming connections from the Internet.

  - Use the **Select Certificate** button to select the certificate that you just imported into the **Personal Certificate Store** of the TMG Server.

  - Select **HTML Form authentication**. If the TMG Server is a member of the same Active Directory domain as the Exchange Server 2010 SP1 CA Server, then you can select **Windows (Active Directory)**. If the TMG Server is a member server, then you can select **LDAP (Active Directory)**.

  - When needed, select **Enable SSO for web sites published with this web listener**.

  - Click **Finish** to end the wizard.

- In the main console, click the **Apply** button to save the new configuration.

The last step is to publish the Exchange CA Server services to the Internet. At this stage, the CA Server is "connected' to the Web Listener. So, to create the Web Publishing Rule on the TMG Server, follow the steps below.

- In the Actions pane of the main section of the TMG Management console, select the **Tasks** tab. In this tab, click on **Publish Exchange Web Client Access**.

- In the **New Exchange Publishing Rule wizard**, follow the steps below.

  - Enter a name for the new publishing rule.

  - Select the **Exchange** version; the default is Exchange 2007, so you'll need to change this to **Exchange 2010**. Also select the services that need to be published, for example, OWA.

- Depending on how many CA Servers there are, a selection needs to be made for a single website or a server farm.

- Select **Use SSL to connect to the Published Web Server or server farm**.

- In the **internal site name** text box, enter the name of the site, for example `webmail.inframan.nl`. Please note that TMG needs to be able to resolve this name to the internal IP address. If needed, add this name to the `HOSTS` file with the accompanying IP address.

- Enter the public name for which requests will be accepted, again, something like `webmail.inframan.nl`.

- Select the Web Listener that was created in the previous step.

- Keep the default method of **Basic Authentication**. The TMG Server will contact the CA Server, and the authentication method on the CA Server needs to be changed from **Forms Based Authentication** to **Integrated Windows** and **Basic Authentication**. If both the TMG Server and the CA Server are set to **Forms Based Authentication**, conflict will occur.

- Select the default of **All authenticated users** in the User Sets.

- Click **Finish** to end the wizard.

- In the main console, click the **Apply** button to save the new configuration.

When you open your browser and open the OWA page, you'll see the well-known OWA page, but now you'll see the text **Secured by Microsoft Forefront Threat Management Gateway**, as well.

Figure 7.14: OWA is now secured with the TMG Server.

If you want to configure ActiveSync or Outlook Anywhere, you'll have to create another Publishing Rule but, for now, let's look at the other services.

7.3 Anti-Spam Solutions

With Exchange Server 2007, Microsoft introduced a new Server Role, the Edge Transport Server Role. The primary purpose of this server is message hygiene and, as such, it offers anti-spam functionality. It can also offer antivirus functionality, but only after implementing Microsoft Forefront Protection for Exchange (FPE) or another third-party product.

Chapter 7: Exchange Server 2010 Security

As shown in Figure 7.13, the Edge Transport Server is typically located in the DMZ; the public MX records point to the Edge Transport Server, and messages from the Internet are delivered here. After the server's potential antivirus and anti-spam duties are performed, the remaining messages are delivered to the internal Hub Transport Server.

> *Note*
>
> *The actual installation of the Exchange Server 2010 SP1 Edge Transport Server, including setting up the Edge Synchronization, is covered in Chapter 2, Section 2.7.*

The Edge Transport Server has several different layers of protection, which are executed in the following order:

1. Connection filtering
2. Sender filtering
3. Recipient filtering
4. Sender ID filtering
5. Content filtering
6. Sender Reputation.

Connection filtering and Content filtering both have some additional configuration settings, which we'll look at now.

Chapter 7: Exchange Server 2010 Security

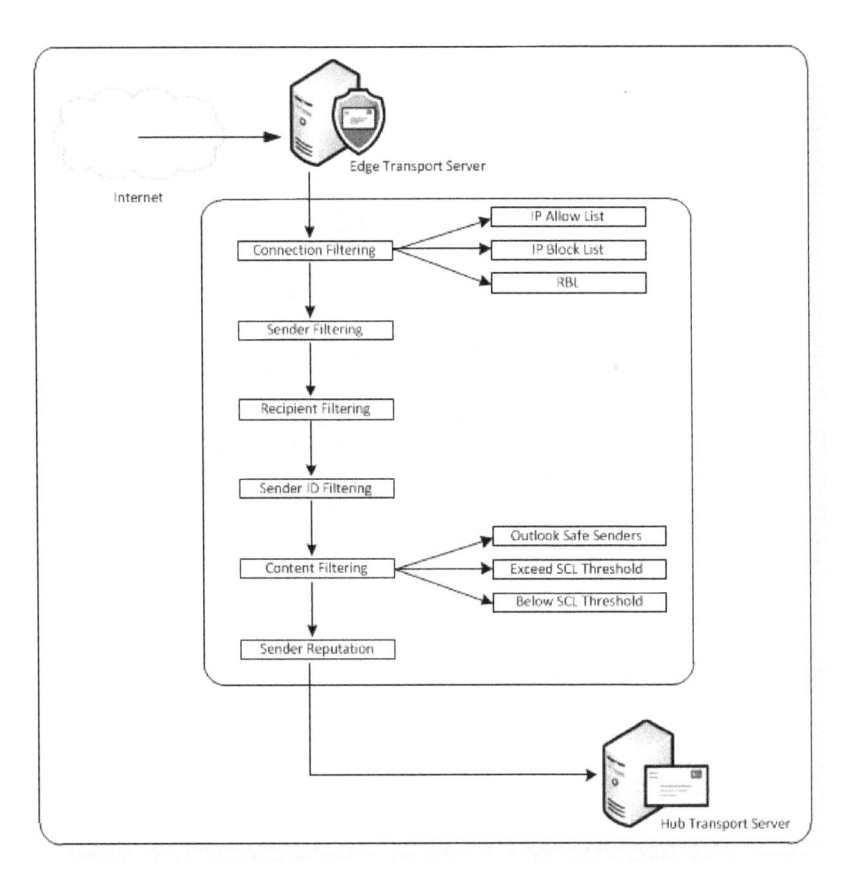

Figure 7.15: Various anti-spam functions in the Edge Transport Server.

To configure the anti-spam options on the Edge Transport Server you have to open the Exchange Management Console.

- Log on to the Exchange Server 2010 SP1 Edge Transport Server and open the **Exchange Management Console**.

- In the **Navigation** pane, select **Edge Transport** and, in the lower section of the **Results** pane, select the **Anti-spam** tab. You'll see that all anti-spam options are enabled by default (which will be used for all the filtering options we'll discuss here).

323

Chapter 7: Exchange Server 2010 Security

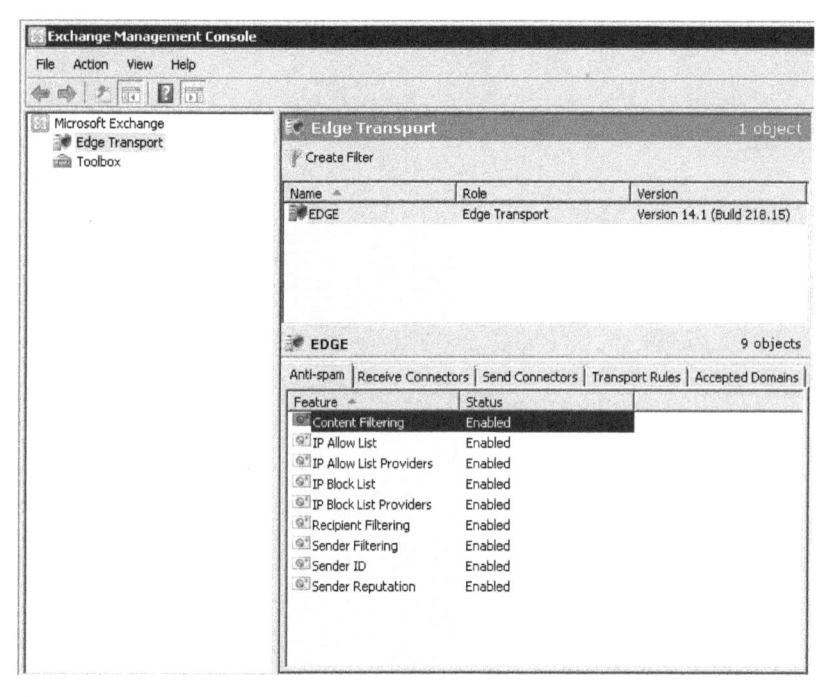

Figure 7.16: Configuring the anti-spam options in the Exchange Management Console.

From here, you can configure the individual anti-spam updates.

7.3.1 Connection filtering

Connection filtering is the first and most important step in anti-spam. When an external SMTP host sets up a connection to the Edge Transport Server, the server will check the sender's IP address and determine if this IP address is allowed to send SMTP messages or whether it is blocked. When you start monitoring this, you'll see that 97% of all inbound connections are blocked, so those messages never enter the Edge Transport Server, saving valuable resources.

A well-known block list (RBL) is **spamhaus.org** which offers a free service for small, non-commercial companies. You can find more information regarding their services on HTTP://WWW.SPAMHAUS.ORG. Spamhaus has multiple types of Block Lists, but a general one including all their services is ZEN. If you're an ISP, and therefore a heavy user of these services, they'll definitely contact you at some point, but let's not worry about that right now.

To configure the RBL follow the steps below.

- In the **Exchange Management Console**, select the **Anti-Spam** tab, right-click **IP Block List Providers**, select **Properties**, and then select the **Providers** tab.

- Enter a name for the provider and the Lookup Domain. In this scenario, enter `zen.spamhaus.org`. For the return status code, leave this with its default setting (**Match any return code**).

- Click **OK** to continue, and click **Apply** to save the settings.

- If you click the **Exceptions** tab, you can add particular mailboxes where messages will not be blocked, regardless of the return code from Spamhaus. This can be useful if you want to have all messages which are sent to (for example) SALES@YOURDOMAIN.COM delivered, regardless of the status. All messages for other mailboxes in your organization will still be blocked.

- Click **OK** to close the Properties window.

7.3.2 Sender filtering

Using Sender filtering on the Edge Transport Server, you can control whether there are any external users that cannot send email to your Exchange Servers. This can be set on a user level (i.e. SOMEUSER@DOMAIN.COM) or on a domain level.

Besides entering the individual email address or a complete domain, you can also define the action that needs to be taken if mail is received from those sources:

- reject message (this is the default setting)
- stamp message and continue processing.

7.3.3 Recipient filtering

Using Recipient filtering on the Edge Transport Server, you can set which users in your Exchange organization are allowed to accept email *from* the Internet. Again, there are two options available in Recipient Filtering.

1. **Block messages sent to recipients that do not exist in the directory** – when messages are sent to an email address like MAKEFREEMONEYNOW@YOURDOMAIN.COM (assuming this email address does not exist, of course!), the messages will be blocked.
2. **Block messages sent to the following recipient** – you can add specific email addresses in your organization here; you can add individual mailboxes or you can add distribution groups.

7.3.4 Sender ID filtering

Sender ID filtering is a DNS-based anti-spam solution. Sender ID filtering is based on checking a so-called SPF record in DNS. In the SPF record, you set which servers (IP addresses) are allowed to send SMTP messages on behalf of your domain.

When Sender ID filtering is enabled and a message arrives at the Edge Transport Server, the Edge Transport Server will check the external DNS for an SPF record. If found, the IP addresses in the SPF record are compared against the IP address in the message header. If they don't match, then there's a chance that the message is spoofed and therefore not a legitimate email message. Sender ID filtering was introduced in Exchange Server 2007 and was based on an open standard. However, since not everybody is using SPF records, there's a chance that the Edge Transport Server check will fail, even when the sending SMTP server is fully legitimate.

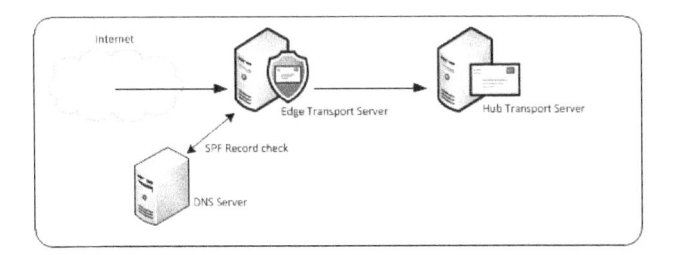

Figure 7.17: The SPF record is checked against a public DNS server.

The Sender ID filtering has three options for handling email messages when the check fails:

1. stamp the message and continue processing
2. reject the message (an error message is returned to the sending SMTP server)
3. delete the message (the sender will never know the message is deleted).

Looking at the adoption of Sender ID, it is my personal preference to use the first option, which is also the default setting on the Edge Transport Server. As mentioned, Sender ID filtering will stamp the header of the message and continue processing it.

However, you might be wondering what you should use for setting the SPF record? Microsoft has a wizard that you can use to determine its value, which you can find at HTTP://TINYURL.COM/WIZARDSPF. Since it is based on an open standard, you can also use the Open SPF website, which can be found on HTTP://WWW.OPENSPF.ORG. There are some differences, though, between SPF and SenderID, and more details regarding these differences can be found at HTTP://WWW.OPENSPF.ORG/SPF_VS_SENDER_ID.

If you're following the Microsoft wizard, enter your domain name; the wizard will check if SPF records already exist for that domain, and it will check the MX records for the domain. Also, you'll need to enter whether the inbound SMTP server (where the MX record points to) is also a valid outbound SMTP server.

When the wizard is finished, it will produce something like `v=spf1 a mx:mail.inframan.nl ~all`. Open the DNS application at your provider, create a new SPF record, and add the value returned from the wizard.

Now, when a message is sent from my domain and the receiving SMTP server does an SPF check, it will check the value `v=spf1 a mx:mail.inframan.nl ~all` and compare this with the IP data in the message header. Since there's a match, the SMTP server will continue processing my message (even if it's not set to just the first, most lenient option).

7.3.5 Content filtering

Content filtering is probably the most well-known option in anti-spam circles. In this kind of filtering you can use specific keywords, like "Viagra," "online casino" or "Back to school," to try and identify spam e-email messages. Of course, you can use keywords for blocking messages, but you can also use specific keywords for allowing certain messages. Of course, what keywords you want to use depends on your own organization and business.

If you configure the content filtering correctly, all messages with these specific keywords are filtered and rejected. Although this is useful, there are almost certainly situation where you don't want this to happen, such as with well-known email addresses like "postmaster," "abuse," "sales," or "info." You can control this by adding **Exceptions** to the content filtering.

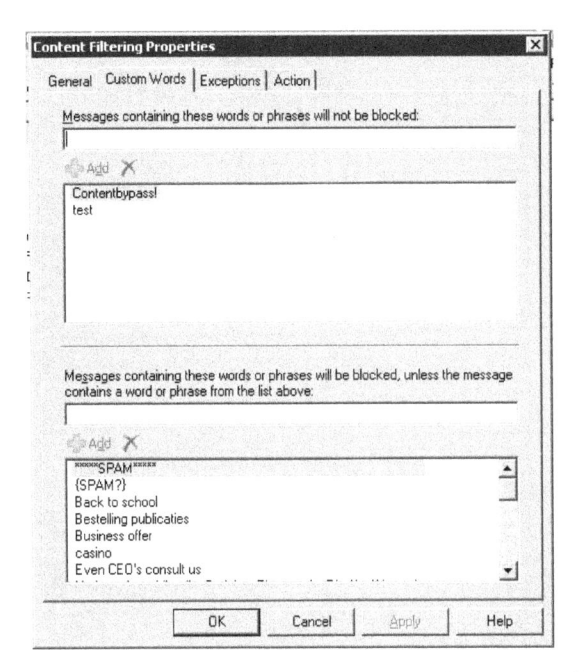

Figure 7.18: Enter specific keywords for content filtering.

If you select the **Exceptions** tab (as visible in Figure 7.18), you can enter specific email addresses that are excluded from content filtering. Examples for exclusion could be ABUSE@YOURDOMAIN.COM or POSTMASTER@YOURDOMAIN.COM.

Content filtering also rates messages, and this rating is known as the **Spam Confidence Level** or **SCL** rating, and ranges from 9 (most likely to be spam) to 1 (legitimate email). There's also a −1 rating, which is used between Exchange Servers in the same Exchange organization, and is also added to the message header before the Edge Transport Server continues processing the message.

Chapter 7: Exchange Server 2010 Security

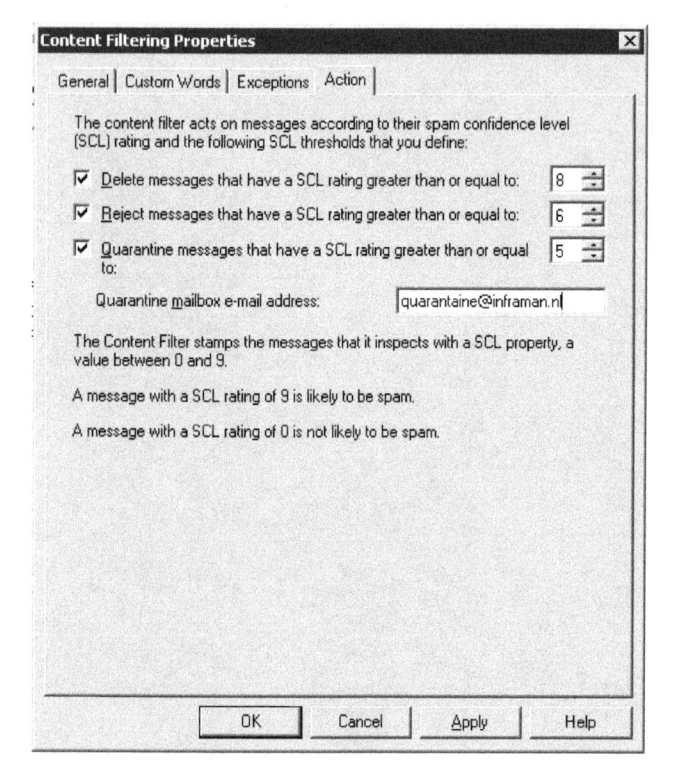

Figure 7.19: Make a selection of actions depending on the Spam Confidence Level.

As shown in Figure 7.19, there are multiple options for processing mail with content filtering, including those below.

- **Delete messages that have a SCL rating greater than or equal to:** you can enter an SCL threshold here, and messages with an SCL equal to or above this level will be deleted. The sender will never know the message has been deleted, but when this is real spam you really do not care. It is my personal experience that an SCL value of 8 never results in complaints.

- **Reject messages that have a SCL rating greater than or equal to:** you can enter an SCL threshold here, and messages with an SCL equal to or above this level will be rejected and an NDR (Non-Delivery Report) will be sent to the sender. In this instance, my personal experience is that an SCL value of 6 will give good results.

- **Quarantine messages that have a SCL rating greater than or equal to:** messages with this SCL rating and a rating smaller than the "reject option" will be sent to a special quarantine mailbox (please note that you have to create this quarantine mailbox manually). I typically find that entering an SCL value of 5 here will give good results and not send too many false positives to the quarantine mailbox.

It's worth bearing in mind that monitoring the quarantine mailbox is also a manual process. When false positives are found in the quarantine mailbox, you can open these messages and Outlook or OWA will show a **Resend** button.

7.3.6   Sender Reputation

Sender Reputation is exactly what its name implies. It is an anti-spam system that acts according to certain characteristics, or a reputation, that a particular sender has. To do this, the Edge Transport Server maintains a Sender Reputation Level (SRL). This SRL is calculated from several characteristics derived from message analysis and external tests. The tests below are conducted by the Edge Transport Server when the Sender Reputation is enabled.

- **HELO/EHLO Analysis** – Sender Reputation analyzes the HELO or EHLO command that the sending SMTP server provides. It does this to check if a particular IP address is used frequently or if a sending SMTP server uses various HELO/EHLO commands, which is also a characteristic of a spammer. It also compares the value of the provided HELO/EHLO command to the Connection Filtering database.
- **Reverse DNS Lookup** – Sender Reputation performs a reverse DNS lookup. It does that by submitting the originating IP address to DNS and checks the resulting domain name with the "From" address provided by the HELO/EHLO command. If the two don't match, then there's a risk that the sender might be a spammer, and as a result the SRL is increased (I'll explain the SRL scale right after I've explained these tests).

- **SCL rating of a message** – when a message is processed by the Content Filter, a Spam Confidence Level (SCL) rating is assigned to the message. Sender Reputation checks the ratio of all messages from a given sender that have a low SCL rating and all messages that have a high SCL rating. Sender Reputation also uses the number of messages that had a high SCL rating for calculating the SRL.

- **Open Proxy test** – Sender Reputation can perform an Open Proxy test to see if a sending SMTP host can relay messages on behalf of other users. This relay behavior can of course be a result of an (unattended) misconfiguration, but it could also be a result of a Trojan Horse running on the sending SMTP server. Sender Reputation will set up an SMTP connection to the sending SMTP server and try to relay a test message back to itself. If a connection is set up properly, then the sending SMTP server is considered to be an open relay server. As a result, the SRL level is increased. If needed, the Open Proxy test can be disabled on the Sender Reputation options.

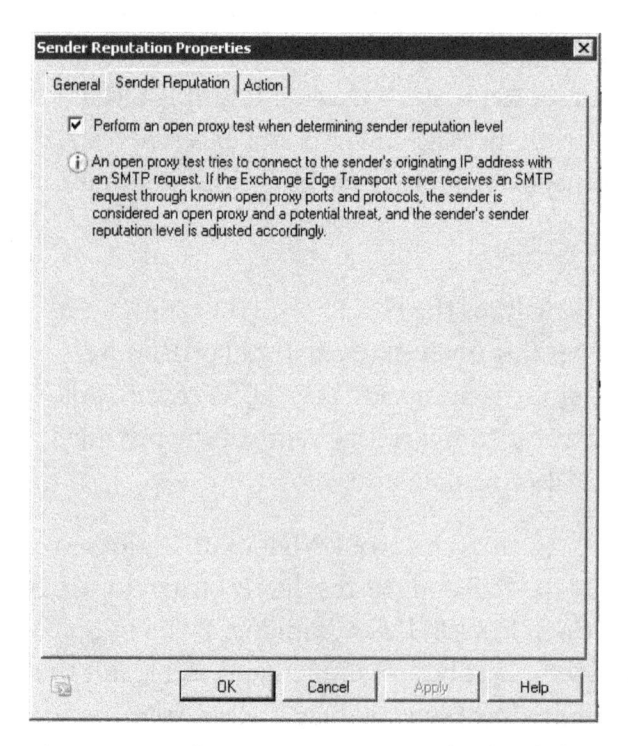

Figure 7.20: The Open Proxy test can be disabled by unchecking the "Perform an open proxy test" option.

Chapter 7: Exchange Server 2010 Security

All of these tests result in an SRL rating, which is a rating from 0 to 9. An SRL rating of 0 means that the sending SMTP server isn't likely to be a spammer, while an SRL rating of 9 means that it is most likely a spammer. The default threshold of Sender Reputation is 7, and all Senders that have an SRL rating exceeding the threshold are added to the Edge Transport Server's Sender block list for 24 hours. Both the threshold, as well as the length of time a sender is blocked for, are configurable.

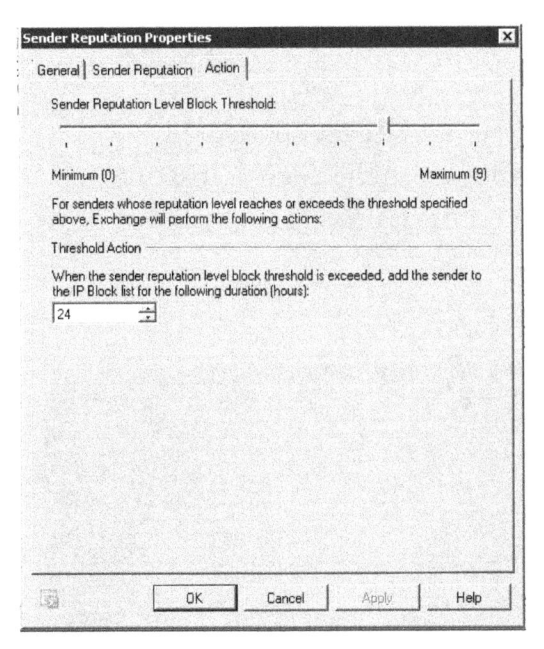

Figure 7.21: Set the SRL threshold and the time a sender should be blocked.

7.3.7 Attachment filtering

Attachment filtering in the Edge Transport Server is a bit more difficult to work with, since the option to manage it is not available in the Exchange Management Console. To configure Attachment filtering, you have to use the Exchange Management Shell. In my opinion this is a bit odd since attachment filtering is very important; quite a lot of malware is sent via attachments in messages.

333

You can filter attachments based on:

- **file name** or **file extension** – the exact filename can be used, or you can choose to filter specific extensions, for example *.exe
- **MIME type** – the MIME type indicates what kind of attachment is on a message: for instance, an executable, a JPEG image, an MP3 file, or a PowerPoint file; content types are expressed as filetype/subtype; a JPG image, for example, is indicated as an image/jpeg MIME type.

By default, a number of file extensions and MIME types are already configured on the Edge Transport Server. To view these entries, log on to the Edge Transport Server, open an Exchange Management Shell and enter the following command: `Get-AttachmentFilterEntry`.

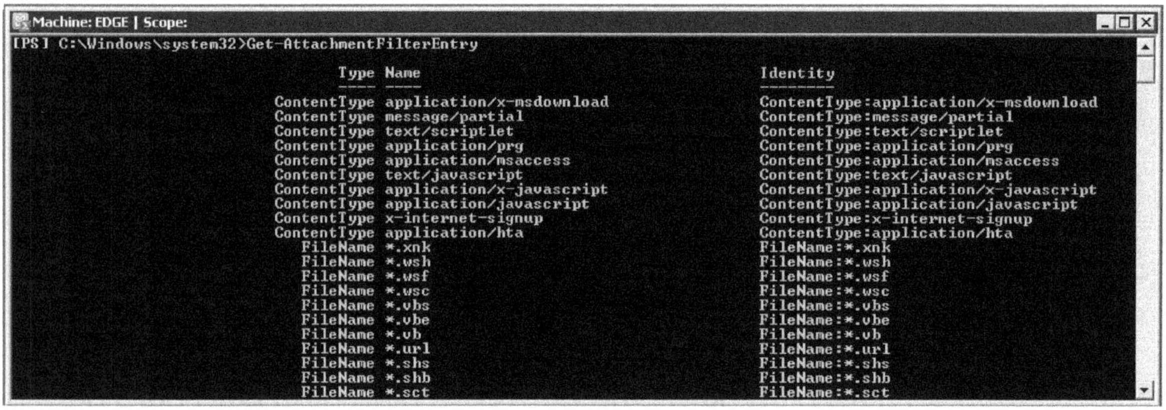

Figure 7.22: Preconfigured MIME Types and extensions in Attachment filtering.

Next to the file name, file name extension and MIME type, it is possible to configure what to do with messages containing attachments that are filtered.

- **Block whole message** – the complete message is blocked and a Non-Delivery Report (NDR) is returned to the sender.

- **Strip attachment** – the attachment is stripped from the email message and replaced with a small text file containing a "This attachment was removed" string.

- **Silently delete message** – the complete message is blocked and deleted from the Edge Transport Server, without sending an NDR to the original sender. The recipient will never know the message was sent, while the sender never knows the message was **not** received.

- **RejectResponse** – using the RejectResponse parameter, it is possible to customize the NDR message that is sent to the original sender when the message is blocked.

- **ConnectorException** – it is possible to use the ConnectorException parameter to exclude one or more connectors from attachment filtering.

If you want to configure, for example, JPEG attachment filtering, which is not configured by default, open the Exchange Management Shell and enter the following command:

```
Add-AttachmentFilterEntry -Name image/jpeg -Type ContentType
```

Alternatively, to filter on file extension, for example, on the PHP extension, enter the following command:

```
Add-AttachmentFilterEntry -Name *.PHP -Type FileName
```

To configure the NDR message that's sent to the sender, you can use the Set-Attachment-FilterListConfig in the Exchange Management Console:

```
Set-AttachmentFilterListConfig -Action Reject
-RejectResponse "The attachment in your e-mail message is not allowed and the
message cannot be delivered. Please remove the e-mail attachment and resend your
message."
```

If you made an error during configuration, or get complaints from users that certain attachments are being removed, it is naturally also possible to remove attachment filtering. For example, to remove the JPEG filtering we configured earlier, open the Exchange Management Shell and enter the following command:

```
Remove-AttachmentFilterEntry -Identity ContentType:image/jpeg
```

Note

The default Attachment Filter in Exchange 2010 looks at the extension, but also reacts when the extension is renamed, so `Yourapplication.ex_` *is also removed. Compressing an executable in a ZIP file isn't an option either, as this is still detected by the Attachment Filter.*

7.3.8 Anti-spam on the Hub Transport Server

By default, all anti-spam functionality that's available on the Edge Transport Server is also available on the Hub Transport Server, but it's not enabled by default. Microsoft does not really recommend doing anti-spam checking on the Hub Transport Server but, at the same time, they realize that smaller companies might not want to invest in an additional Edge Transport Server.

To enable the anti-spam functionality on the Hub Transport Server, open the Exchange Management Shell, navigate to the `C:\Program Files\Microsoft\Exchange Server\v14\scripts` directory and start the following script:

```
.\Install-AntispamAgents.ps1
```

> **Note**
>
> To navigate quickly to the scripts directory you can use the `cd $exscripts` command.

Restart the Microsoft Exchange Transport Service on the Hub Transport Server and, if needed, close and re-open the Exchange Management Console, and you'll see the anti-spam tab appear in the Exchange Management Console. For configuring the anti-spam functionality on the Hub Transport Server you can use the same guidelines as used for the Edge Transport Server.

7.4 Conclusion

Security is a very important aspect of an Exchange Server implementation, and in this chapter we've looked at a few important things.

A solid anti-spam solution will ensure that your Exchange environment doesn't suffer from receiving too many fake messages, and this is very important, if only for the provisioning of your resources. With that in mind, you should seriously consider implementing an Exchange Server 2010 SP1 Edge Transport Server and configuring it appropriately. If you have a small organization and cannot, or will not, invest in an Edge Transport Server, then you can also use the Hub Transport Server for anti-spam functionality.

Also, you should definitely implement a firewall or reverse proxy server for network security. This will safeguard your Exchange implementation against unwanted attempts to enter (read: hack) your servers.

And finally, after installing your Exchange Servers, take good care of checking your server, using tools like the Microsoft Baseline Security Analyzer, Windows Update, WSUS, or SCCM 2007, and keep your servers up to date with the latest (security) hot-fixes.

Summary

This book was intended as a *practical approach* to Exchange Server 2010, so I've tried to guide you through the new platform without writing a complete Resource Kit – I'll leave that to Microsoft. There's not a lot I can add at this stage but, in case you need some sound-bytes (maybe to convince your manager to let you upgrade), I'll give one last lightning-quick round-up of what's new in Exchange Server 2010.

- By far the most important change with respect to Exchange Server 2007 is the new Database Availability Group. This will allow you to create multiple copies of an Exchange Server database within your organization, and you are no longer bound to a specific site (like in Exchange Server 2007), but can now stretch across multiple sites. Microsoft has also successfully transformed Cluster Continuous Replication and Stand-by Continuous Replication into a new "Continuous Availability" technology.

- While on the topic of simplifying, a lot of SysAdmins were having difficulties with the Windows Server fail-over clustering, so Microsoft has simply "removed" this from the product. The components are still there, but they are now managed using the Exchange Management Console or Exchange Management Shell.

- With the new Personal Archive ability, a user can now have a secondary mailbox, acting as a personal archive – this really is a .PST killer! You now have the ability to import all the users' .PST files and store them in the personal archive, and using Retention Policies you can move data from the primary mailbox to the archive automatically, to keep the primary mailbox at an acceptable size, *without any hassle*.

To deal with ever-growing storage requirements, Microsoft also made considerable changes to the underlying database system. All you will need to store your database and log files with Exchange Server 2010 is a 2 TB SATA (or other Direct Attached Storage) disk. As long as you have multiple copies of the database, *you're safe*! And the maximum supported database size? That has improved from 200 GB (in an Exchange Server 2007 Cluster Continuous Replication environment) to 2 TB (in a multiple database copy Exchange Server 2010 environment).

Summary

If you haven't yet considered what your business case will look like when upgrading to Exchange Server 2010, bear in mind that this will truly save a *tremendous* amount of storage cost – and that's not marketing talk!

- Installing Exchange 2010 is not at all difficult, and configuring a Database Availability Group with multiple copies of the Mailbox Databases is just a click of the mouse (you only have to be a little careful when creating multi-site DAGs). Even installing Exchange Server 2010 into an existing Exchange Server 2003 or Exchange Server 2007 environment is not that hard! The only thing you have to be aware of is the additional namespace that shows up. Besides the standard namespaces like `webmail.contoso.com` and `Autodiscover.contoso.com`, a third namespace shows up in a coexistence environment: `legacy.contoso.com`. This is used when you have mailboxes still on the old (i.e. Exchange Server 2003 or Exchange Server 2007) platform in a mixed environment.

- Lastly, for a die-hard GUI administrator it might be painful to start managing an Exchange environment with the Exchange Management Shell. Basic management *can* be done with the graphical Exchange Management Console, but you really do have to use the Shell for the nitty-gritty configuration. The Shell is remarkably powerful, and it takes quite some getting used to, but with it you can do fine-grained management, and even create reports using features like **output to HTML** or **save to .CSV file**. Very neat!

I hope this book has guided you through the basic installation and configuration of Exchange Server 2010, and that the examples have given you some solid understanding of the processes involved, as well. I've certainly not provided everything. The Unified Messaging Role and integration with Office Communication Server (OCS) 2007 or Lync Server 2010, for example, would make for some interesting additional reading. By integrating Lync Server 2010 and Exchange Server 2010 you will not only get an interesting messaging environment, but also presence information, Instant Messaging (IM) functionality, and integration with your voice system.

If you have any comments or questions after reading this, don't hesitate to send me an email on MYBOOK@JAAPWESSELIUS.NL.

Index

A

Accepted Domains 84-86
Active copy 241
Active Directory 29-33
    Active Directory Certificate Services.
    See Certificates
    Active Directory Lightweight Directory Services
    (AD LDS) 79
    Active Directory Rights Management Service
    (AD RMS) 23
    management tools 53, 155
        domains and trusts MMC snap-in 155
        Sites and Services MMC snap-in 155
        Users and Computers MMC snap-in 155
    partitions 29
    sites 32
    upgrading 114-118, 141-144
Active Manager 233-254
    Primary Active Manager (PAM) 234
    Stand-by Active Manager (SAM) 234
Address rewriting 43
Administrative Groups 31, 105
Anti-spam. *See* Security
Archiving
    and compliancy 192-213
    solutions 192
Attachment filtering 333-336
Authoritative Domain 84
Auto Attendant 44
Autodiscover 89, 130, 145, 306
Automatic Speech Recognition 45
Availability Service 39

B

Best Practices Analyzer (ExBPA) 48
Bridgehead Server 88
Bulk user creation 161-163

C

Calendaring 15, 16, 61
Call Answering 44
Certificates 305-314
    Active Directory Certificate Services 305-314
    add to the Client Access Server Role 89
    certificate with multiple domain names 148
    installation 129-131, 147-149
    third-party certificate 129
Chapter summaries 13
Checkpoint 218
    depth 222
    file 221-222
Client Access Server (CAS) 38-40, 118, 145, 267-271
    CAS Role 34, 93-100
Client Settings window 61
Clone
    Full Copy or Split Mirror 255
Cluster Continuous Replication (CCR) 19, 225
Clustered Mailbox Server (CMS) 233
Coexistence 101-154
    with Exchange Server 2003 103-108
        64-bit support 104-105
        and Administrative Groups 105
        and Link State 107
        and Routing Groups 106

Index

installing into Exchange Server 2003 environment 109-137
    order of installation 111-112
    RUS vs. Email Address Policies 108
    SMTP infrastructure 134-136
with Exchange Server 2007 137-138
    64-bit support 138-140
    installing into existing Exchange Server 2007 environment 139-153
    order of installation 140
    SMTP infrastructure 152

Compliance 24
Configuration partition 30
Connection filtering 324-325
Content filtering 328-331
Core Store 27
Cross-premises message routing 23

D

Database
    managing database copies 241-244
    prefix 217
    replication 225-227
    technologies in Exchange Server 2010 216-223

Database Availability Group (DAG) 227-228
    configuring 234-240
    DAG architecture 228-234
    lagged copies in 244-249

Delegation of control 24, 30-31
Demilitarized Zone (DMZ) 35, 39, 42, 43, 76, 152, 270, 322
Deprecated features 16-17
Dial Plans 286-288

Direct Attached Storage (DAS) 225
Discovery search functionality 206-212
Domain partition 30
Dual Tone Multi-Frequency (DTMF) 45

E

EdgeSync. *See* **Edge Transport Server (Edge): synchronization**

Edge Transport Server (Edge) 42-44, 135
    Edge Role 34
    Edge Transport Rules 43
    installation 75-83, 79-81
    synchronization 81-83

Email Address Policies 86-87, 108
Emulator 95
Enhanced disclaimers 23
Enterprise CAL 16
Entourage 61-100
ESEUTIL 220, 259
Exchange ActiveSync 94
Exchange Best Practices Analyzer (ExBPA) 48
Exchange Control Panel (ECP) 22, 156, 180-184
Exchange Core Store 19
Exchange Management Console (EMC) 155, 174-180
    and Powershell 176-178
    evolution of 178-186

Exchange Management Shell (EMS) 156-174
    reporting with 167-176

Exchange Native Data Protection 263-265
Exchange Pre-Deployment Analyzer 48-49
Exchange Server 2000 102
Exchange Server 2010

Index

Client Access License (CAL) 16
database technologies 216-223
Discovery search functionality 206-212
Exchange Server 2010 SP1
    64-bit version 104
    and Active Directory 155
    managing 155-214
    what's new in SP1 25
new administration functionality 21
upgrading 97-99
versions 15
what's been removed 16
what's new? 17-25
Exchange Server coexistence 33-34. *See also* **Coexistence**
Exchange Web Services
    configuring 131-135, 149-154
ExecutionPolicy 164
Extensible Storage Engine (ESE) 216, 219
External domain 62, 131
External Relay Domain 85

F

Fiber channel 225
File Share Witness 231-233
Firewall 315
Forefront Protection 135. *See also* **Threat Management Gateway (TMG)**
Forest functionality level 47, 109, 139
Free/Busy information 131

G

Get-MailboxStatistics 169, 171, 172

Global Catalog Server 29, 39, 42, 46, 109, 139

H

HELO/EHLO Analysis 331
High Availability 19, 215-271
    in Exchange Server 223-265
    on other Server Roles 265-270
Hub Transport Server (HT) 118, 145, 265-266
    HT Role 34, 40-42

I

IMAP4 38, 39, 93, 298, 309, 315
Import and Export Mailbox 27
Incremental Deployment 239
Information Lifecycle Management 192
In-place upgrade of Exchange Server 2003 server to Exchange Server 2010 SP1 105
In-place upgrade to Exchange Server 2010 SP1 140
Installation 47-100
    checking 71-73
    into Exchange Server 2003 environment 109-137
    typical installation procedure 57-63
    unattended setup 64-71
Integration with SMS (text) messages 18, 25
Internal Relay Domain 84
Internet-facing Active Directory 139, 145, 234
Internet-facing server 120
Internet Information Server 49
Interop Routing Group Connector 106
IP Gateway 274
ISA Server 316
ISA Server 2006 266

343

Index

iSCSI 225
Itanium 16, 139

J

JBOD (Just a Bunch of Disks) 26
JET database 216
Journaling agents 41

L

Language packs for UM Server 285-286
Language support 25
Lazy writer mechanism 221
LDIFDE 64, 114
Legacy namespace 130
lGeneration 220
License key 84
Link State 107
Litigation Hold 213
Local Continuous Replication (LCR) 225
Log files 220-221

M

Mailboxes
    backup and restore 254-265
    import & export 252-254
    Mailbox Archive 25
    Mailbox Archive quota 195
    Mailbox Database 222-223
    moving to Exchange Server 2010 SP1 153
    online Move-Mailbox 250-252
    UM Enabling 292-293
Mailbox Policy 289-290
Mailbox Server (MB) 145-147
MB Role 34, 35-38, 124-126
Majority Node Set Cluster 231
Managed Folders 196
MAPI 38, 227, 268
Message hygiene 135
Message Tracking Tool 183
Messaging policy 24
Messaging Records Management (MRM) 196-205
Messaging Waiting Indicator 25
Microsoft Baseline Security Analyzer (MBSA) 298-300
Microsoft Cluster Service (MSCS) 19
Microsoft Exchange Security Groups 68, 117
Microsoft Exchange Speech Engine Service 45
Microsoft .NET Framework 3.5 SP1 49-100
Microsoft Online Services 20
Microsoft Update 301
Migrate 101, 196
Migration scenario 33
Mount point 242
MoveRequest 153, 159, 160, 250
MS Filter Pack 50-100

N

Namespace 130
Native mode 109, 139
NET.TCP port sharing 55
Network Load Balancing (NLB) 233, 266, 267
Network security 315-321
New-MoveRequest 153. *See also* **MoveRequest**
NTBackup 254

O

Offline Address Book 128
Online Move-Mailbox 250–252
Open Proxy test 332
Outlook
    Outlook Anywhere 96
    Outlook Voice Access (OVA) 278–284
    Outlook Web Access 18
    Outlook Web App (OWA) 18, 26, 94

P

Pages 217
Passive copy 241
Patching. *See* Security
PBX 279
Permissions 24
Personal archive 26
Personal archive mailbox 194
Physical Address Extensions (PAE) 104
Pipelining 159–160
Play on Phone functionality 277–278
POP3 38, 39, 93, 298, 309, 315
Post-setup configuration 83–96
PowerShell. *See* Windows PowerShell 2.0
PrepareAD 65
PrepareAllDomains 68, 118, 144
PrepareDomain 67
PrepareLegacyExchangePermissions 114
PrepareSchema 64
Prerequisites 47, 110
    installing 49–57
Primary Active Manager (PAM) 234

Provider 256
PST files 192
Public Folder replication 126–129
Public Key infrastructure 305. *See also* Security: certificates

Q

Quarantine mailbox 331
Quick Reference Guide 159

R

Readiness Check 62, 113, 125, 126, 284
Recipient filtering 326
Recipient Update Service (RUS) 108
Remote PowerShell 163–166
Remote signed scripts 164
Reporting 167–176
Requestor 255
Retention
    policies 28, 196–205
    tags 197
        default policy tags 198
        personal tags 198
        retention policy tags 198
Reverse DNS Lookup 331
Reverse proxy 295, 316–324
Role Based Access Control (RBAC) 105, 184–191
    architecture of 187–192
Role Groups 185
Roll-over 220
Round Robin 266
Routing Group 106
Routing Table 107

345

Index

S

Schema Master 29, 47
Schema partition 30
SCL rating 332
Secure Messaging 295
Security
    anti-spam 295, 321–337
        attachment filtering 333–336
        connection filtering 324–325
        content filtering 328–331
        on the Hub Transport Server 336–337
        recipient filtering 326
        sender filtering 325–326
        sender ID filtering 326–328
        sender reputation 331–333
    certificates 305–314
    firewall 315–316
    groups 65, 116, 186. *See also* Microsoft Exchange Security Groups
    message security 295
    Microsoft Baseline Security Analyzer (MBSA) 298–300
    network security 295, 315–321
    patching Exchange Servers 301–304
        Windows Server Update Services (WSUS) 301
        Windows Update 301
    Security Configuration Wizard (SCW) 296
    server hardening 295–296
    server security 295, 296–314
    Threat Management Gateway (TMG) 315, 316–324

Seeding 241
Send Connector
    configuration 88–89
Sender
    filtering 325–326
    ID filtering 326–328
    Reputation 331–333
Server hardening. *See* Security
ServerManagerCmd.exe 54
Server Roles 34. *See also* **Entries for individual Roles**
    install dedicated Server Roles 74–75
    install Server Roles 69
Shadow copy
    Copy on Write (Differential Copy) 255
    Split Mirror 255
Shadow Redundancy 23
Shared storage 223
Single Copy Cluster (SCC) 231
Single Instance Storage (SIS) 20
SMS 18, 25
SMTP 309
SMTP connector 88
Snapshot backup 255
Standard CAL 16
Stand-by Active Manager (SAM) 234
Stand-by Continuous Replication (SCR) 19, 225, 244
Storage Groups 17, 21, 37, 256
Subject Alternative Names (SAN) 129
    property 148
Subnet 32, 227, 240
Subscriber Access 44

Index

System Center Configuration Manager (SCCM) 301
System Manager 108, 117, 122, 126, 136

T

Telephony system 273
Text to Speech 45
Third-party certificate. *See* Certificates
Threat Management Gateway (TMG) 315
Transition scenario 33
Transport and routing 23
Transport Dumpster 226
Transport Rule agents 41
Typical server installation 35

U

Unified Messaging (UM) 25, 273-294
    additional language packs 285-286
    configuring UM Server 290-294
    UM Auto Attendants 286, 290
    UM Hunt Group 279
    UM IP Gateway 279, 288-289
    UM Server Role 34, 44-46
        architecture 274-279
        configuring 286-291
        installing 280-285
        terminology 279
    voicemail preview. *See* Voicemail: preview
Upgrading the Active Directory 114-118, 141-144

V

Voicemail
    messages in your inbox 273
    preview 276-277
Voice over IP (VOIP) 274
Volume Shadow Copy Service (VSS) 254, 255-257

W

Web-based distribution 133
What's new? 17-25
Windows clustering 223
Windows Mobile 6.5 emulator 95
Windows PowerShell 2.0 49
    and the Exchange Management Console 176-178
Windows Remote Management (WinRM) 49, 164
Windows Server Backup (WSB) 254, 258-261
    and database replication 261-263
Windows Server Update Services (WSUS) 301, 303
Windows Update 301-304
Windows Vista SP2 52
Windows Vista x64 49, 52
Writer 255

.NET and SQL Server Tools
from Red Gate Software

Pricing and information about Red Gate tools are correct at the time of going to print. For the latest information and pricing on all Red Gate's tools, visit www.red-gate.com

redgate®
ingeniously simple tools

ANTS Memory Profiler $495
Find memory leaks and optimize memory usage

- Find memory leaks within minutes
- Jump straight to the heart of the problem with intelligent summary information, filtering options and visualizations
- Optimize the memory usage of your C# and VB.NET code

"Freaking sweet! We have a known memory leak that took me about four hours to find using our current tool, so I fired up ANTS Memory Profiler and went at it like I didn't know the leak existed. Not only did I come to the conclusion much faster, but I found another one!"
Aaron Smith IT Manager, R.C. Systems Inc.

ANTS Performance Profiler from $395
Profile your .NET code and boost the performance of your application

- Identify performance bottlenecks within minutes
- Drill down to slow lines of code thanks to line-level code timings
- Boost the performance of your .NET code
- Get the most complete picture of your application's performance with integrated SQL and File I/O profiling

"ANTS Performance Profiler took us straight to the specific areas of our code which were the cause of our performance issues."
Terry Phillips Sr Developer, Harley-Davidson Dealer Systems

"Thanks to ANTS Performance Profiler, we were able to discover a performance hit in our serialization of XML that was fixed for a 10x performance increase."
Garret Spargo Product Manager, AFHCAN

Visit **www.red-gate.com** for a 14-day, free trial

.NET Reflector ® From $35
Browse, compile, analyze and decompile .NET code

- View, navigate and search through the class hierarchies of .NET assemblies, even if you don't have access to the source code for them
- Decompile and analyze .NET assemblies in C#, Visual Basic and IL
- Step into decompiled assemblies whilst debugging in Visual Studio, with all the debugging techniques you would use on your own code

> "One of the most useful, practical debugging tools that I have ever worked with in .NET! It provides complete browsing and debugging features for .NET assemblies, and has clean integration with Visual Studio."
> **Tom Baker** Consultant Software Engineer, EMC Corporation

SmartAssembly ® from $795
.NET obfuscator and automated error reporting

- Obfuscate your .NET code and protect your IP
- Let your end-users report errors in your software with one click
- Receive a comprehensive report containing a stack trace and values of all the local variables
- Identify the most recurrent bugs and prioritize fixing those first
- Gather feature usage data to understand how your software is being used and make better product development decisions

> "I've deployed Automated Error Reporting now for one release and I'm already seeing the benefits. I can fix bugs which might never have got my attention before. I really like it a lot!"
> **Stefal Koell** MVP

Visit **www.red-gate.com** for a 14-day, free trial

SQL Compare® Pro $595
Compare and synchronize SQL Server database schemas

- ↗ Eliminate mistakes migrating database changes from dev, to test, to production
- ↗ Speed up the deployment of new databse schema updates
- ↗ Find and fix errors caused by differences between databases
- ↗ Compare and synchronize within SSMS

> "Just purchased SQL Compare. With the productivity I'll get out of this tool, it's like buying time."
> **Robert Sondles** Blueberry Island Media Ltd

SQL Data Compare Pro $595
Compares and synchronizes SQL Server database contents

- ↗ Save time by automatically comparing and synchronizing your data
- ↗ Copy lookup data from development databases to staging or production
- ↗ Quickly fix problems by restoring damaged or missing data to a single row
- ↗ Compare and synchronize data within SSMS

> "We use SQL Data Compare daily and it has become an indispensable part of delivering our service to our customers. It has also streamlined our daily update process and cut back literally a good solid hour per day."
> **George Pantela** GPAnalysis.com

Visit **www.red-gate.com** for a 14-day, free trial

SQL Prompt Pro $295

Write, edit, and explore SQL effortlessly

- ↗ Write SQL smoothly, with code-completion and SQL snippets
- ↗ Reformat SQL to a preferred style
- ↗ Keep databases tidy by finding invalid objects automatically
- ↗ Save time and effort with script summaries, smart object renaming and more

> "SQL Prompt is hands-down one of the coolest applications I've used. Makes querying/developing so much easier and faster."
> **Jorge Segarra** University Community Hospital

SQL Source Control $295

Connect your existing source control system to SQL Server

- ↗ Bring all the benefits of source control to your database
- ↗ Source control schemas and data within SSMS, not with offline scripts
- ↗ Connect your databases to TFS, SVN, SourceGear Vault, Vault Pro, Mercurial, Perforce, Git, Bazaar, and any source control system with a capable command line
- ↗ Work with shared development databases, or individual copies
- ↗ Track changes to follow who changed what, when, and why
- ↗ Keep teams in sync with easy access to the latest database version
- ↗ View database development history for easy retrieval of specific versions

> "After using SQL Source Control for several months, I wondered how I got by before. Highly recommended, it has paid for itself several times over"
> **Ben Ashley** Fast Floor

Visit **www.red-gate.com** for a 28-day, free trial

SQL Backup Pro $795

Compress, encrypt, and strengthen SQL Server backups

- ↗ Compress SQL Server database backups by up to 95% for faster, smaller backups
- ↗ Protect your data with up to 256-bit AES encryption
- ↗ Strengthen your backups with network resilience to enable a fault-tolerant transfer of backups across flaky networks
- ↗ Control your backup activities through an intuitive interface, with powerful job management and an interactive timeline

> "SQL Backup is an amazing tool that lets us manage and monitor our backups in real time. Red Gate's SQL tools have saved us so much time and work that I am afraid my director will decide that we don't need a DBA anymore!"
>
> **Mike Poole** Database Administrator, Human Kinetics

Visit **www.red-gate.com** for a 14-day, free trial

SQL Monitor

SQL Server performance monitoring and alerting

- ↗ Intuitive overviews at global, cluster, machine, SQL Server, and database levels for up-to-the-minute performance data
- ↗ Use SQL Monitor's web UI to keep an eye on server performance in real time on desktop machines and mobile devices
- ↗ Intelligent SQL Server alerts via email and an alert inbox in the UI, so you know about problems first
- ↗ Comprehensive historical data, so you can go back in time to identify the source of a problem
- ↗ Generate reports via the UI or with Red Gate's free SSRS Reporting Pack
- ↗ View the top 10 expensive queries for an instance or database based on CPU usage, duration and reads and writes
- ↗ PagerDuty integration for phone and SMS alerting
- ↗ Fast, simple installation and administration

> "Being web based, SQL Monitor is readily available to you, wherever you may be on your network. You can check on your servers from almost any location, via most mobile devices that support a web browser."
>
> **Jonathan Allen** Senior DBA, Careers South West Ltd

Visit **www.red-gate.com** for a 14-day, free trial

SQL Virtual Restore $495

Rapidly mount live, fully functional databases direct from backups

- ↗ Virtually restoring a backup requires significantly less time and space than a regular physical restore
- ↗ Databases mounted with SQL Virtual Restore are fully functional and support both read/write operations
- ↗ SQL Virtual Restore is ACID compliant and gives you access to full, transactionally consistent data, with all objects visible and available
- ↗ Use SQL Virtual Restore to recover objects, verify your backups with DBCC CHECKDB, create a storage-efficient copy of your production database, and more.

> "We find occasions where someone has deleted data accidentally or dropped an index etc., and with SQL Virtual Restore we can mount last night's backup quickly and easily to get access to the data or the original schema. It even works with all our backups being encrypted. This takes any extra load off our production server. SQL Virtual Restore is a great product."
>
> **Brent McCraken** Senior Database Administrator/Architect, Kiwibank Limited

SQL Storage Compress $1,595

Silent data compression to optimize SQL Server storage

- ↗ Reduce the storage footprint of live SQL Server databases by up to 90% to save on space and hardware costs
- ↗ Databases compressed with SQL Storage Compress are fully functional
- ↗ Prevent unauthorized access to your live databases with 256-bit AES encryption
- ↗ Integrates seamlessly with SQL Server and does not require any configuration changes

Visit **www.red-gate.com** for a 14-day, free trial

SQL Toolbelt $1,995

The essential SQL Server tools for database professionals

You can buy our acclaimed SQL Server tools individually or bundled. Our most popular deal is the SQL Toolbelt: fourteen of our SQL Server tools in a single installer, with **a combined value of $5,930 but an actual price of $1,995**, a saving of 66%.

Fully compatible with SQL Server 2000, 2005, and 2008.

SQL Toolbelt contains:

- **SQL Compare Pro**
- **SQL Data Compare Pro**
- **SQL Source Control**
- **SQL Backup Pro**
- **SQL Monitor**
- **SQL Prompt Pro**
- **SQL Data Generator**

- **SQL Doc**
- **SQL Dependency Tracker**
- **SQL Packager**
- **SQL Multi Script Unlimited**
- **SQL Search**
- **SQL Comparison SDK**
- **SQL Object Level Recovery Native**

"The SQL Toolbelt provides tools that database developers, as well as DBAs, should not live without."
William Van Orden Senior Database Developer, Lockheed Martin

Visit **www.red-gate.com** for a 14-day, free trial

Performance Tuning with SQL Server Dynamic Management Views

Louis Davidson and Tim Ford

This is the book that will de-mystify the process of using Dynamic Management Views to collect the information you need to troubleshoot SQL Server problems. It will highlight the core techniques and "patterns" that you need to master, and will provide a core set of scripts that you can use and adapt for your own requirements.

ISBN: 978-1-906434-47-2
Published: October 2010

Defensive Database Programming

Alex Kuznetsov

Inside this book, you will find dozens of practical, defensive programming techniques that will improve the quality of your T-SQL code and increase its resilience and robustness.

ISBN: 978-1-906434-49-6
Published: June 2010

Brad's Sure Guide to SQL Server Maintenance Plans
Brad McGehee

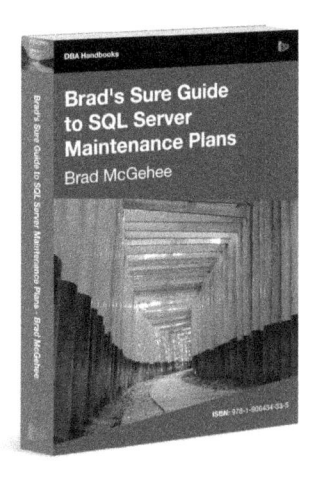

Brad's Sure Guide to Maintenance Plans shows you how to use the Maintenance Plan Wizard and Designer to configure and schedule eleven core database maintenance tasks, ranging from integrity checks, to database backups, to index reorganizations and rebuilds.

ISBN: 78-1-906434-34-2
Published: December 2009

The Red Gate Guide to SQL Server Team-based Development
Phil Factor, Grant Fritchey, Alex Kuznetsov, and Mladen Prajdić

This book shows how to use of mixture of home-grown scripts, native SQL Server tools, and tools from the Red Gate SQL Toolbelt, to successfully develop database applications in a team environment, and make database development as similar as possible to "normal" development.

ISBN: 978-1-906434-59-5
Published: November 2010

CPSIA information can be obtained
at www.ICGtesting.com
Printed in the USA
LVHW102257150720
660817LV00007B/266

9 781906 434663